The Global Sport Economy

This book examines the global sports ecosystem through three of its central pillars: Sport marketing, sports equipment manufacture and sales, and sport governance and organization. By focusing on these three themes, the book presents a nuanced and multi-faceted view of how the global sports economy works and what its main strategic challenges and opportunities are.

Offering a balance between theory and practice, and adopting an international perspective with case studies and examples from the Americas, Europe and Asia, the book addresses key issues such as corporate social responsibility, the impact of culture on international sport business, innovation and entrepreneurship, and consumer behaviour.

The Global Sport Economy is fascinating reading for students, researchers and practitioners with an interest in sport business and management, sport marketing, the sporting goods industry and distribution and sport governance.

Michel Desbordes is Professor in Sports Marketing at the University of Paris-Saclay, France. As a Media Consultant, he is regularly consulted by *BFM*, *France Télévisions*, *Europe 1*, *Le Monde* and *L'Équipe* to discuss matters of sports business. He is also the Chief Editor of the *International Journal of Sports Marketing and Sponsorship*.

Pascal Aymar is Managing Director of his own consultancy company, Twins Coaching and Consulting, providing strategic advice to companies in the sporting goods industry at an international level. He is also Development Director for INSEEC, a French Management School, Vice-President of the Outdoor Sports Valley, and a non-executive Board Member of several sports companies in Europe.

Christopher Hautbois is Associate Professor at Université Paris-Saclay, France, where he oversees a master program in sport management. He is a specialist in sport and city branding as well as sports federations.

I0894893

Routledge Research in Sport Business and Management

Managing Drugs in Sport
Jason Mazanov

Elite Youth Sport Policy and Management
A comparative analysis
Edited by Elsa Kristiansen, Milena M. Parent and Barrie Houlihan

Women in Sport Leadership
Research and practice for change
Edited by Laura J. Burton and Sarah Leberman

International Sports Betting
Integrity, Deviance, Governance and Policy
Edited by Jean-Patrick Villeneuve and Martial Pasquier

Emerging Technologies in Sport
Implications for Sport Management
Edited by Cheryl Mallen

Global Sport Leadership
Stephen Frawley, Laura Misener, Daniel Lock and Nico Schulenkorf

International Sport Marketing
Issues and Practice
Edited by Michel Desbordes and André Richelieu

The Global Sport Economy
Contemporary Issues
Edited by Michel Desbordes, Pascal Aymar and Christopher Hautbois

For more information about this series, please visit www.routledge.com/Routledge-Research-in-Sport-Business-and-Management/book-series/RRSBM

The Global Sport Economy

Contemporary Issues

Edited by
Michel Desbordes, Pascal Aymar
and Christopher Hautbois

Routledge
Taylor & Francis Group
LONDON AND NEW YORK

First published 2019
by Routledge
2 Park Square, Milton Park, Abingdon, Oxon OX14 4RN

and by Routledge
605 Third Avenue, New York, NY 10017

First issued in paperback 2020

Routledge is an imprint of the Taylor & Francis Group, an informa business

British Library Cataloguing-in-Publication Data
A catalogue record for this book is available from the British Library

Library of Congress Cataloging-in-Publication Data
A catalog record for this book has been requested

ISBN 13: 978-0-367-72900-4 (pbk)
ISBN 13: 978-1-138-39371-4 (hbk)

Typeset in Goudy
by Apex CoVantage, LLC

Contents

List of contributors vii

Introduction: the current situation and outlook for sports markets 1

PART I
Sports marketing **7**

1 **Sports marketing, from humble beginnings to maturity** 9
MICHEL DESBORDES

2 **Watching a game or experiencing it: theoretical foundations and practical cases of the fan experience** 71
BORIS HELLEU

3 **CSR and sports-event organizers: state of play, controversies and perspectives** 89
AURÉLIEN FRANÇOIS, EMMANUEL BAYLE AND OLIVIER MUTTER

PART II
The sporting goods industry and distribution **117**

4 **Growth, growth drivers and the energy sources** 119
PASCAL AYMAR

5 **A short history of the sporting goods industry** 160
EUGENIO DI MARIA

6 **New behaviour trends among consumers of sporting goods** 191
ANTOINE HAINCOURT

7 **Innovation in the sports industry** 209
ANNA GERKE

PART III
Sport governance **225**

8 **From monopoly to competition: the new strategic challenges facing public sports organizations** 227
CHRISTOPHER HAUTBOIS

9 **The governance of sports federations: current challenges in an international context** 274
THIERRY ZINTZ, MATHIEU WINAND AND SIMON GÉRARD

10 **Sports tourism: contemporary issues and new trends on a global market** 295
PATRICK BOUCHET AND CLAUDE SOBRY

Conclusion 318

Index 321

Contributors

Emmanuel Bayle is Professor in Sports Management at the Institute of Sport Sciences of the University of Lausanne (ISSUL). He is a specialist of governance, management and performance for sport olympic organizations and sport national systems and has several experiences in executive education in this area.

Patrick Bouchet is Professor of Sport Management and Marketing within the Sport Sciences Faculty at the University of Burgundy, France. He is Director of the Doctoral School in Human and Social Science and President of the Scholarly Society of Sport Management (S2MS) in France. He is also a member of the Culture, Sport, Santé, Société (C3S) research group and is widely interested in actors' behaviours (consumers, groups and organizations) linked to the sport and active leisure consumption (tourism, event and retailing).

Eugenio Di Maria is Editor and Publisher of four international business newsletters for decision-makers, including the European edition of *Sporting Goods Intelligence and The Outdoor Industry Compass*. He and his team have put out reports on the sporting goods market in all the European countries and the four BRICs.

Aurélien François is Lecturer at the University of Rouen, France. He was previously a member of the Research Center of Sport in Canadian Society at the University of Ottawa, Canada. His research topics are focused on CSR in sport, public management specifically for sports infrastructures and arenas as well as the professional sports leagues regulations.

Simon Gérard is Lecturer in Sport Management in the Faculty of Business and Law at Coventry University, UK, and Research Associate in the Olympic Chair Henri de Baillet Latour & Jacques Rogge in Sport Management at the Université Catholique de Louvain, Belgium. His research focuses on organizational change and the governance of sport organizations, with a special interest for the Paralympic Movement.

Anna Gerke is Associate Professor at Audencia Business School, France, where she teaches Sport Management and Marketing. She is also Head of the specialized Master of Management of sport organizations. Her research focuses on organizational theory, strategy, innovation and economic geography, notably in the context of sport organizations.

Antoine Haincourt is Associate Head of MSc SIM at EM Lyon Business School, France. Antoine's focus is to bridge the world of education together with the sport's industry to have an impact on students' employability. His area of focus includes consumer behaviour, branding strategy and sports industry culture. Antoine is also a Consultant in Branding Strategy aiming to help ambitious leaders and corporations define their reason why, their sense of meaning and how to achieve it.

Boris Helleu is Lecturer in Sport Management at the University of Caen Normandy, France. He has headed the Sport Management programme since 2010. His work looks at the relationship between social media and the fan experience. He shares his international sports marketing and economy press review on his Twitter account (@bhelleu). He also runs a blog dedicated to sports marketing (Hell of a Sport).

Olivier Mutter is PhD Candidate and Lecturer in Sport Management at the University of Lausanne, Switzerland. He was the Director of the Sport Department at the State of Geneva, Switzerland, for several years and he contributed to the organization of many international and local sport events. He is now a member of the Lausanne 2020 Youth Olympic Games Organizing Committee and he also works as a Consultant for public authorities in the sport policy sector.

Claude Sobry is Professor at the University of Lille, France. He created a sport management Master's degree in Lille and led a research laboratory for 10 years. He collaborated with the European Commission to develop the sport tourism side of the economy of sport.

Mathieu Winand is Professor of Sport Management and Head of Department of International Sport Management at LUNEX International University of Health, Exercise and Sports in Luxembourg. His research interests are in the area of sport governance and innovation in sport and he has conducted research on key determinants leading to high performing sport organizations. Mathieu is Deputy Editor of *Sport, Business and Management: An International Journal* and is Past Chair of the Strategic Interest Group "Managing Sport" at the European Academy of Management (EURAM).

Thierry Zintz is Professor of Sports Organisations Management at the Faculty of Sports Sciences of the Université Catholique de Louvain, Belgium. He is in charge of the Olympic Chair Henri de Baillet Latour – Jacques Rogge in Management of Sport Organizations, specializing in governance, change management and social responsibility of national and international sports organizations. He is President of the European Observatory of Sport and Employment (EOSE) and Director of the Executive Master in Management of Sport organizations, organized by the International Olympic Committee and 12 universities in the world (MEMOS).

Introduction

The current situation and outlook for sports markets

With an overall growth rate of nearly 5% per year for more than 20 years, the sports market, or should we say markets, are looking very healthy, attracting attention from the financial sector and offering numerous job opportunities. Students, universities, management schools, companies, sponsors, local authorities, manufacturers, distributors, agencies, event organizers, etc. are just some of the very diverse actors interested in sport, though sometimes with very different strategies and objectives.

Today, numerous economic models exist to try and calculate how much sport is worth. According to a study carried out in 2011 by management consulting firm A.T. Kearney, the global sports industry is worth an estimated €450 billion.[1]

In France, a sports ministry study published in 2016 calculated that the sector, excluding charity work, represented 1.8% of the GDP, or €38.1 billion in 2013.[2]

According to A.T. Kearney, if we aggregate sports events (ticketing, sponsorship, broadcast rights and licenced products) structural equipment, textiles and accessories, global spending in the sector totalled $600 billion in 2014.[3]

Sport economists have been arguing for decades that the numbers are generally underestimated, because in every country, the statistics only take the narrowest definition of the sports sector into account. Advertising connected with sports events, sales of sports-related newspapers, TV rights, spending on sports-related food or pharmaceuticals, transport costs for sports activities, spending on sports medicine, etc., are all excluded. By taking a broader and more realistic view of this expenditure, we estimate that, depending on the country's level of development, we would be closer to 5–10% of the GDP.

On the other hand, what is interesting and indisputable is that these sports markets are growing faster than average national GDP across all geographical areas.

In order to better analyze the sports economy, we can break it down into three major universes, some of which are broken down into several sub-universes.

1 Sports marketing

Sports marketing is the most visible universe because of media coverage and its popular quality.

It can be divided into two major sub-universes:

- Events, covering all global, national and local sporting events. From the football World Cup to the local half-marathon, this activity follows very strict rules and requires trained and responsible personnel.
- Sponsoring (or partnerships), which covers investments made by companies of all types, whatever their sector of activity (manufactured products, services, local and even State government). They aim to become better known by working with athletes or sports competitions and to boost their image through association with specific sports.

The values represented by sport are particularly sought after by brands, and strategic plans for association with individuals, clubs or events can be complex.

In economic terms, this "Sports Marketing" universe is currently estimated at $140 billion worldwide and is particularly dynamic.

The average annual growth rate for the period 2011–2015 is +3.7% globally and +4.7% for recurring events.

The value of events alone is estimated at $80 billion and continues to grow faster than average GDP.[4]

'Sports market growth has been constant for more than 10 years, and the market has doubled from 2005 to 2017'.

"The growth reached +6% from 2005 to 2009, +7% from 2009 to 2013 and +5% from 2013 to 2017".[5]

The Europe-Middle East-Africa (EMEA) zone represents 43% of the events market, with football accounting for a large majority of that, while North America represents 38%, essentially from the American professional sports leagues (MLB, NFL, NHL, NBA, MLS), the Asia-Pacific zone has 13% and Latin America 6%. Football is the No. 1 sport in Europe, where it accounts for the bulk of revenue.[6]

2 The sporting goods industry

With some large leading players, although it is still extremely fragmented, the sports goods market quite naturally divides into two sub-universes:

- Those who design and produce, that is, the manufacturers
- Those who sell to consumers, that is, the retailers

Above all, the industry designs and produces, or has produced, goods intended mostly for sport.

Three main categories of sports products are marketed by manufacturers:

- Sports equipment (snowshoes, balls, bikes, cycles, GPS, etc.) which represents 40% (in value terms) of the total market
- Sports shoes, for anything from running to mountain running to flip-flops, which account for 25% of world supply

- And textiles and accessories, from specialist clothing through to sportswear and backpacks, estimated at 35% of the market

Sporting goods retailers market products to consumers both through physical stores and e-commerce sites.

This field has undergone significant changes over the last 30 years, first with the appearance of sports superstore chains (Décathlon, GO Sport, DICK'S Sporting Goods, Xebio, etc.) which has generated a significant phenomenon of loyalty to strongly marketed brands (Intersport, Sport 2000, etc.), then with the explosion of monobrand stores and Internet commerce.

Competition is fierce in this market and the changes offer many opportunities to those who have the sales skills and want to be part of the new retail environment.

Today, both groups are increasingly blurring the boundaries between manufacturing and retailing. Salomon, Nike and Adidas have become retailers, operating their own stores, while at the same time, Décathlon is producing sporting goods through its many own brands such as Tribord, Wedze, Artengo, Geonaute, Quechua, etc. This integration, upstream for some, downstream for others, has muddied the waters somewhat and complicated the notion of competition in sports markets.

And parallel to that, all the players, whether traditionally manufacturers or physical retailers, are today present and competing with each other on the e-commerce market.

> *This "sporting goods" market was worth an estimated €390 billion in 2016, according to market research company NPD, almost triple the volume of business generated by sports marketing.*[7]

3 Sports organization

This is undoubtedly the most diverse and complex area of this industry and therefore, of course, the most difficult to put a value on. It covers all the different actors who organize and govern sport, from the small village managing its own sports facilities to the governance of motor sport by the FIA, via the winter sports resorts and all the associations offering leisure sports to a wider audience.

The regulatory and legal frameworks are countless and constantly evolving and the challenges facing sports organizations have given rise to many jobs in the fields of law, economics, management, political science and coaching of athletes and sporting events.

It is difficult to categorize all the sub-universes in this area but we can make a distinction between

- National, European and international federations
- Amateur leagues, clubs and unions
- Public authorities (government administration and local authorities) and European institutions

- Leisure sports operators
- Sports-tourism operators

The governance of institutions and the establishment of international rules for sports competitions are the most visible and widely publicized tip of the iceberg, the part where everyone would like to work, but there is also a part hidden below the waterline in the public sector and associations that is not always taken into account in any analysis of sales opportunities for the sports industry in general.

> *It is very difficult to quantify the economic importance of "Sports Organization" as it is composed of both international "blockbusters" and national and local micro-structures.*
>
> *Specialists nevertheless estimate that it is worth at least as much as Sporting Goods, i.e. €400 billion.*[8]

These three universes and their sub-universes, while naturally linked and interdependent, are nevertheless subject to their own trends which currently offer exciting employment opportunities, often international in nature and reflecting the evolution of society as a whole.

The aforementioned studies estimate the sports job market at around 200,000 in France (compared with 730,000 for the car industry), 1.6 million in Europe and 5 million worldwide.

Here are some facts about the job market and the way it is represented in education:

- Both internationally and in France, sports marketing predominates in the programmes offered by universities specializing in sports sciences, law and management schools
- This is why 80% of young people end up with training in sports marketing, a sector where opportunities are scarce and career prospects are weak
- This is linked to the exaggerated importance of the media in sport which distorts market reality
- Sporting goods and sports organization, both of which offer rich employment potential, are given relatively short shrift by both students and educators

Finally, few programmes have an international focus, while the market is increasingly global

In conclusion, from an academic point of view, there are opportunities to create diversified programmes that better respond to the labour market in what can be described as the "global sports economy". This book published by Routledge takes a totally fresh approach, aiming to investigate the three universes to the best of their ability. This represents a different take after 20 years in which the majority of books have focused on a single area, most often related to the media aspect of sports marketing to the detriment of others.

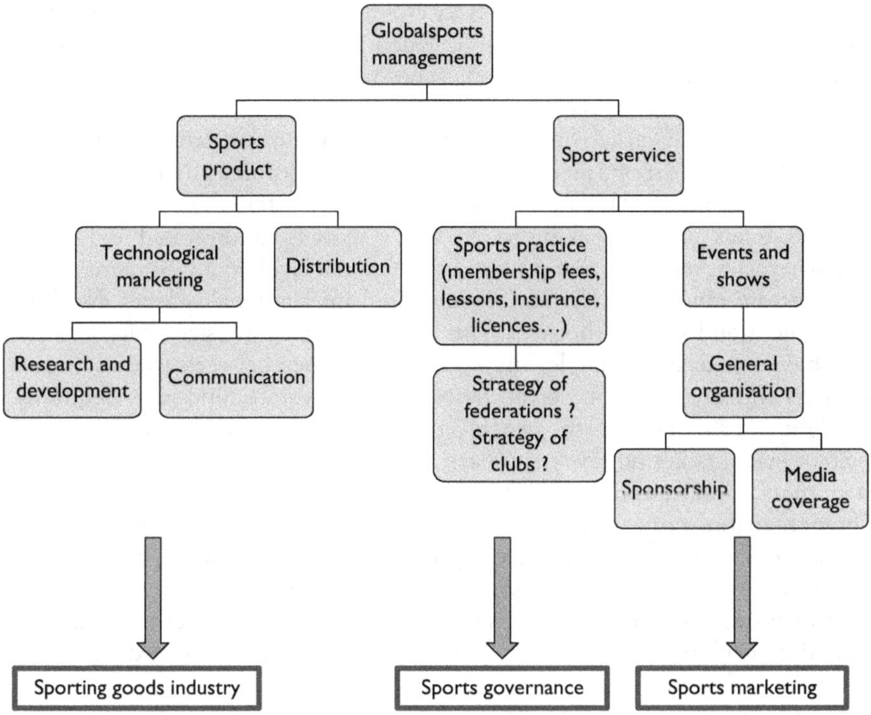

Figure 0.1 Global sports economy

So, to sum up, here are the three areas that will be covered in the rest of the book.

Part I deals with **sports marketing**. It shows how sports management has had to deal with a constantly changing environment including, for example, the creation of many jobs that simply did not exist a few years ago. It also highlights how sports management has become a highly international field. It stresses the growing role of technology in the way sport is consumed, with spectators becoming true "ConsumActors". Finally, this first part reminds us that, alongside the increasingly high commercial stakes sports marketers face, there are growing questions over the role these organizations play in our society, with the whole question of social responsibility raised in Chapter 3.

Part II deals with **the manufacture and distribution of sporting goods** and is perhaps the most original as this subject is only rarely dealt with in sports management studies. It highlights the profound upheavals that have marked this intrinsically global business for half a century. It deals in turn with issues of innovation, the sociological evolution of customers and thus demand, and notes increasingly blurred borders between sporting goods manufacturers and retailers.

Finally, for forecasting purposes, this second part raises the main issues the sector faces for the future: The fruitful but risky closer ties with the fashion world, new ways to tap the youth market (some of which is turning away from sports), the impact a particular sport's image (sometimes tarnished by doping or corruption scandals) can have on sales etc.

Finally, Part III, focusing on **sports governance and organization,** looks at the least visible facet of sports management, which alone accounts for half the global market, or around €400 billion. Sports governance, a catch-all term if ever there was one, refers simply speaking to the way a sport is administered and organized, whether at national, European or international level. Many different parties are therefore involved, including national and international federations, State government and local authorities. This last part details the significant changes they have faced. For example, the search for balance between the traditional missions entrusted to public organizations (which require hindsight, neutrality, foresight and should be in the general interest) and the need to adopt the strategic or even marketing-savvy approach of private organizations for its development plans. Finally, it highlights the upheaval seen in the field of sports tourism. These three innovative studies are part of an approach that has never really been undertaken before, that of global sports management. Each field is covered by a recognized specialist: Michel Desbordes for sports marketing, Pascal Aymar for sporting goods and Christopher Hautbois for governance. Each of them has also invited contributions from professional or academic experts to shed light on a particular or essential aspect.

They form a trilogy that allows us to get to the heart of each of the major areas of the sports economy and, ultimately, better understand the way they interact.

Notes

1 Study available at: www.atkearney.com/paper/-/asset_publisher/dVxv4Hz2h8bS/content/the-sports-market/10192 (last accessed 27 March 2018).
2 Source: www.sports.gouv.fr/IMG/pdf/le_poids_economique_du_sports_en_2013-2.pdf (last accessed 27 March 2018).
3 Source: www.lesechos.fr/16/07/2014/LesEchos/21729-119-ECH_le-sport-business---un-marche-d-opportunites.htm (last accessed 27 March 2018).
4 Source: PWC. www.pwc.fr/le-sponsoring-premiere-source-de-revenus-et-de-croissance-sur-le-marche-francais-du-sport-a-horizon-2015.html (last accessed March 27, 2018).
5 Source: www.atkearney.com/communications-media-technology/winning-in-the-business-of-sports/full-report (last accessed March 27, 2018).
6 Source: www.atkearney.com/documents/10192/5258876/FG-Winning-in-the-Business-of-Sports-3.png/c8e05d3f-2723-4aab-b9b6-b979fc60c474?t=1414620657857 (last accessed March 27, 2018).
7 Source: PWC. www.pwc.fr/le-sponsoring-premiere-source-de-revenus-et-de-croissance-sur-le-marche-francais-du-sport-a-horizon-2015.html (last accessed March 27, 2018).
8 Source: PWC. www.pwc.fr/le-sponsoring-premiere-source-de-revenus-et-de-croissance-sur-le-marche-francais-du-sport-a-horizon-2015.html (last accessed March 27, 2018).

Part I

Sports marketing

Foreword: presentation of the three chapters of Part I

Sports marketing is one of the most fertile areas of sports management research. As highlighted in the general introduction to our book, it is the most visible part, thanks to the media, though not necessarily the most important in terms of economic activity and employment. The three chapters of this first section highlight the major trends in the field, including the most recent research and developments in the business world.

Chapter 1, written by Michel Desbordes, paints a picture of a thriving industry that has now reached maturity. Although we consider that sports marketing only really emerged in Europe at the end of the 1990s, it has a longer history in North America. With its strong links to the "real" world of sports business, research in this field has developed over time, with academics working hand-in-hand with their professional counterparts. Indeed, major sporting events serve as a laboratory and fertile testing ground. Sports management professions have gradually emerged, but the speed with which certain tools have developed has forced organizations to adapt almost continuously. Stadium manager, sports TV rights buyer, sports statistics analyst, community manager, sponsorship officer, sports lawyer, federation development officer, etc. are all jobs that did not exist 15 years ago. That trend will continue; indeed, it has become something of a cliché to say that "80% of the jobs that we'll see 10 years from now don't exist yet". The younger generation needs to adapt to a constantly changing, international, global, multidisciplinary environment, and education must, therefore, also adapt, with new subjects, new professions, new organizations, new challenges, sometimes even new sports . . . the challenges are considerable. The analysis of these major trends forms the backbone of this first chapter, focusing on the future.

Chapter 2, by Boris Helleu, looks at how the consumer experience is changing for spectators at sporting events. The simple "transactional" approach of buying a ticket is no longer enough, it is now all about having a literally "extraordinary" experience. The use of digital technology and engagement techniques has played a big role in the way spectators perceive their time in the stadium or arena. Helleu gives his chapter an international angle by using the example of the major American professional sport leagues (NFL: American football, NHL: ice hockey, NBA: basketball, MLB: baseball, MLS: football). His comments include references to the theories of "emotion curve" and "customer path", "fan experience" and "fan relationship management", given the importance of optimizing the consumer experience before, during and after sports events. American franchises obtain the best results by providing customer services to their fans. But this is a global and globalized marketing practice, and Helleu shows that even if the Americans were the pioneers in this domain, the French LFP (Professional Football League) is also very attentive to these notions of entertainment and customer satisfaction in its stadiums. The stadium is a key variable since it is the delivery point for the sports-event service. Finally, he concludes with the "money can't buy" operations that have set sponsors looking to make the biggest possible impact buzzing over the last few years.

But sports marketing has evolved in recent years under the influence of fans, consumers, spectators and users of social media who want the sector, which creates a lot of money, to be more in phase with society's values and lead by example. The techniques used have often been grouped under the heading of CSR (Corporate Social Responsibility) in English-speaking countries and are the subject of Chapter 3, written by Aurélien François, Emmanuel Bayle and Olivier Mutter.

After outlining the fundamentals of CSR, the authors turn to its emergence in the sports sector over the last 10 years or so. From a functional perspective, they outline the potential for development by sports-event organizers while emphasizing, from a critical perspective, its limits. By sports events, they imply "*events organized, on a national scale, by professional sports leagues and clubs whose meetings can have some influence at this level and, on a global scale, via international sports institutions (IOC, UEFA, FIFA)*". The proposed dual integrative and critical analysis shows strategic opportunities for the integration of CSR in key functions of sporting events, but also the long fight ahead to counter the criticism the concept usually attracts.

Chapter 1

Sports marketing, from humble beginnings to maturity

Michel Desbordes

Introduction

This chapter is divided into three parts.

The first takes a trip back in time to the birth of sports marketing in the United States and its gradual expansion to Europe.

The second concerns the Europeans' somewhat tentative approach to the emerging field of sports management. This hesitation can be explained by a very different institutional landscape, which was not dominated by commercial professional sport as in North America. It was, therefore, necessary to integrate non-commercial elements to take into account government thinking, ethics, the associative world and see how marketing tools from the business sector could be adapted to this less homogeneous context.

Finally, the last part provides a much more open and international perspective, showing how globalization affects the marketing strategies of sports organizations such as federations, private companies, leagues, event organizers, sponsors and even cities and countries. We will illustrate this using the examples of China and Qatar.

1 The birth of sports marketing in North America and its development in Europe

1.1 America leads the way from the 1950s onwards

- Professional sport developed earlier in the United States than in Europe. The main reason for this lies in the country's overall level of economic development, as it has been proven that the richer a country is, the more important sport becomes, both as entertainment and as an activity. Sport could thus be seen as a category 3, 4 or 5 in Maslow's hierarchy of needs, or a "superior good" in economist-speak. It is not a basic necessity, nor an essential service for most people. There is, therefore, a strong correlation between sports consumption and standard of living (GDP per capita), as shown by sociological studies.

- By the 1950s, professional sports championships were already well established in the United States: Historically, baseball had always been middle America's favourite sport, but three other major sports were starting to emerge (basketball, American football and ice hockey). Later on, American football would undeniably take the No. 1 spot from a business point of view, while basketball would become the most successful internationally. MLS (Major League Soccer – the American name for "classic" football), created in 1993, became the fifth major league in 1996. Since 2007, it has included 20 teams from the United States and Canada (Browlee and Lorgnier, 2015).
- From the 1950s and 1960s, the sports business sector needed to come up with some theoretical solutions to a number of problems and provide answers to the questions the clubs were asking themselves (Rottenberg, 1956; Neale, 1964).
- As the financial stakes rose, it was only logical that the clubs should ask more and more questions. Television rights were steadily increasing, while ticket sales, for example, were falling. Our first reaction might be to conclude that television is the enemy of the box office and that broadcasting a sporting event somehow discourages spectators from travelling to the game, preferring to watch in comfort at home. We now know that this is not the case, and that, on the contrary, being broadcast on television is a sign of a club's quality and popularity.[1]
- At the same time, the New York Yankees' uninterrupted run of success from 1947 to 1953 in the baseball league (MLB) was a real cause for concern (Surdam, 2008) and the first issues of market domination/regulation began to emerge. How to guarantee the league's success and market it if it was overwhelmingly dominated by a single team? That was the reasoning behind the regulations introduced in the United States, putting paid to the idea that the American professional sport is a free market system with little outside intervention.
- Research by sports economists starts from the widely accepted premise that the excessive domination of a sport by any individual or team reduces spectator interest, because the result becomes predictable and uncertainty is reduced.

Neale (1964), for example, supports what he calls "the Louis-Schmeling paradox". Joe Louis was a boxer undefeated during his first 27 fights, including 23 knockouts. He had only three defeats in his career. The first took place on June 6, 1936, against the German Max Schmeling who knocked him out in the 12th round. This defeat is interesting from a financial point of view, as the American boxer's income was falling because he had become too strong for his opponents. Thanks to this defeat, his revenue increased and that is what we call "the Louis-Schmeling paradox". The rematch between Louis and Schmeling took place on June 22, 1938, and Louis completely dominated the icon of the Nazi regime (who later became his friend). In front of 80,000 spectators at Yankee Stadium, Louis knocked Schmeling to the floor in two minutes and four seconds. He opened the way for black athletes in a similar way to Jesse Owens, who accomplished an incredible feat, winning four Olympic titles in the hostile context of the Berlin Olympics where Hitler refused to shake his hand. For this single match, Louis earned more money than for the first 28 fights of his career. The uncertainty over the outcome and the huge excitement surrounding the fight made this possible. Today, all boxing matches are based on the same model: Well-organized storytelling, with rivalry built up by the media, effective "pay per view" and the sale of rights to private channels, clever promoters, a good choice of date, an emblematic location, a perfectly honed merchandising policy, etc. These all make it possible to organize a so-called "Fight of the Century every year"! Foreman-Ali on October 30, 1974, Pacquiao-Mayweather on May 2, 2015 and Joshua-Klitschko on April 29, 2017 are all legendary and very well-marketed fights which fit into this framework.

This need to regulate professional sport to make it both fairer and more uncertain is part of what is known as "competitive balance": The clubs (known as franchises because the model is similar to the rights granted to operate a label or brand along the lines used by McDonalds or Starbucks) must, if possible, have financial resources that are sufficiently similar to make competition meaningful. It was, therefore, necessary for the big closed leagues in the United States to come up with a system of market regulation (intervention), a system that has become increasingly dirigiste. Overall, regulatory policy has been based for several decades now on three main principles:

- Equal sharing of television rights: In order to stop any team that stands out from the others from a sporting point of view and that is, therefore, overall a good performer and popular, from attracting more money from television channels, national television rights are distributed equally between all the clubs in the league.
- Salary cap: In order to prevent large teams from attracting the best players by offering them salaries that are considerably higher than the others, it was decided to introduce an overall wage cap. Therefore, a player does not necessarily have any incentive to change clubs for financial reasons, he usually does so for sporting reasons (e.g., winning a title). This has the effect of stabilizing team membership, limiting transfers (unlike the European football transfer market which disrupts the whole sector twice a year), but also of protecting the finances of the clubs, who are less likely to rush headlong into granting crazy increases to players.
- Finally, the draft system is used to allocate young players (called "sporting talents") once a year. The system is complex, based on different odds and the drawing of lots, but the general idea is that the teams who have performed the worst over the past season are more likely to be able to choose the best

players, generally selected from American universities (under the NCAA training system, four years of schooling between the ages of 18 and 22), or coming from Europe, Africa, or South America.

These three principles have been implemented differently by the major leagues, sometimes with subtle differences, but overall the NBA is the league that has gone the farthest in their implementation. While it is difficult to judge the results precisely, we can say that a league like the NHL is very unpredictable, at least regarding the final winner of the championship (the Stanley Cup), which has had a very varied list of winners over the last 15 years. On the other hand, the Spanish football league is much more predictable, with two big clubs (FC Barcelona and Real Madrid) traditionally dominating the league, outsiders being rare. This duopoly, which has dominated Spanish football for decades, is firmly rooted in different financial resources.

Over 16 seasons (given that the 2005 championship was cancelled, owing to the lockout), we can see here that there were 10 different Stanley Cup winners.

At the same time, only three teams have won the Spanish Liga over the last 13 seasons, Atletico having won once, with the other 12 seasons split between Real and Barça.

Germany's Bundesliga, with Bayern Munich winning five times in a row from 2013 to 2017 and Italy's Serie A, where Juventus Turin won six consecutive championships from 2012 to 2017, are hardly unpredictable either.

It is easy to find a financial explanation for this lack of a level playing field and we will return to this in the next section of this chapter.

Table 1.1 NHL hockey championship winners 2001–2017

Year	*Winner*	*Finalist*	*Score*
2001	Colorado Avalanche	New Jersey Devils	4-3
2002	Detroit Red Wings	Carolina Hurricanes	4-1
2003	New Jersey Devils	Mighty Ducks of Anaheim	4-3
2004	Tampa Bay Lightning	Calgary Flames	4-3
2005	Season and series cancelled	because of lockout	
2006	Carolina Hurricanes	Edmonton Oilers	4-3
2007	Anaheim Ducks	Ottawa Senators	4-1
2008	Detroit Red Wings	Pittsburgh Penguins	4-2
2009	Pittsburgh Penguins	Detroit Red Wings	4-3
2010	Chicago Blackhawks	Philadelphia Flyers	4-2
2011	Boston Bruins	Vancouver Canucks	4-3
2012	Los Angeles Kings	New Jersey Devils	4-2
2013	Chicago Blackhawks	Boston Bruins	4-2
2014	Los Angeles Kings	New York Rangers	4-1
2015	Chicago Blackhawks	Tampa Bay Lightning	4-2
2016	Pittsburgh Penguins	San José Sharks	4-2
2017	Pittsburgh Penguins	Nashville Predators	4-2

Source: https://fr.wikipedia.org/wiki/Coupe_Stanley (last accessed Dec. 10, 2017)

Table 1.2 Spanish La Liga football championship 2005–2017

Year	*Winner (pts, trainer)*	*Second Place (pts)*	*Third Place (pts)*
2017	Real Madrid (93 pts, Zinedine Zidane)	FC Barcelona (90 pts)	Atlético Madrid (78 pts)
2016	FC Barcelona (91 pts, Luis Enrique)	Real Madrid (90 pts)	Atlético Madrid (88 pts)
2015	FC Barcelona (94 pts, Luis Enrique)	Real Madrid (92 pts)	Atlético Madrid (78 pts)
2014	Atlético Madrid (90 pts, Diego Simeone)	FC Barcelona (87 pts)	Real Madrid (87 pts)
2013	FC Barcelona (100 pts, Tito Vilanova)	Real Madrid (85 pts)	Atlético Madrid (76 pts)
2012	Real Madrid (100 pts, José Mourinho)	FC Barcelona (91 pts)	Valencia CF (61 pts)
2011	FC Barcelona (96 pts, Josep Guardiola)	Real Madrid (92 pts)	Valencia CF (71 pts)
2010	FC Barcelona (99 pts, Josep Guardiola)	Real Madrid (96 pts)	Valencia CF (71 pts)
2009	FC Barcelona (87 pts, Josep Guardiola)	Real Madrid (78 pts)	FC Seville (70 pts)
2008	Real Madrid (85 pts, Bernd Schuster)	Villarreal (77 pts)	FC Barcelona (67 pts)
2007	Real Madrid (76 pts, Fabio Capello)	FC Barcelona (76 pts)	FC Seville (71 pts)
2006	FC Barcelona (82 pts, Frank Rijkaard)	Real Madrid (70 pts)	Valencia CF (69 pts)
2005	FC Barcelona (84 pts, Frank Rijkaard)	Real Madrid (80 pts)	Villarreal CF (65 pts)

Source: www.maxifoot.fr/palmares-liga.htm (last accessed June 1, 2017)

1.2 The situation in France and Europe

1.2.1 Amateur sport and the public sector

Historically, sport in France, and more generally in Europe, developed in and around the public sector.

"Sport in schools", sport within federations and "sport in the city" are all concepts that are characteristic of this, the legacy of several decades of government policy putting sport at the heart of the French education system.

- In 1936, France's Popular Front literally created the concept of "the weekend" by reducing the working week to 40 hours (five eight-hour days). At the same time, by granting two weeks of paid leave for the first time in the country's history, it also introduced the notion of "leisure time". It was necessary to fill this leisure time as healthily as possible, and cycling, swimming and walking, all free or almost free, quickly established themselves as ways to to do this. The emergence of company sports clubs throughout Europe, for example in Sochaux (Peugeot), Clermont-Ferrand (Michelin), Turin (Fiat), Eindhoven (Philips) and Leverkusen (Bayer), also helped drive the workers' sports movement forward.

Box 1.1 The birth of Sochaux FC

Sochaux FC was created in 1928. Less than a year later, Jean-Pierre Peugeot's club hired its first "star players" without troubling to hide the fact that it was paying them, given that "fake amateurism" was the norm then. The aim was to fly the Peugeot flag throughout France and provide quality entertainment for the carmaker's employees.

The Peugeot Cup, forerunner of the French championship

In 1930, the club merged with AS Montbéliard to form FC Sochaux-Montbéliard and launched a competition, the Peugeot Cup, bringing together the top French clubs. This early professional French championship was won by FCSM on May 17, 1931.

This followed on from another victory in January, when the FFFA (French association football federation) voted in favour of paying players. The "commission for the implementation of professionalism", set up at that time, included Sam Wyler, Jean-Pierre Peugeot's right-hand man, as vice-chairman.

Professional football became a reality on January 17, 1932. It was deemed necessary for the organization of a French championship, basically because the amount of travelling involved prevented players from having another job.

The first French championship, based on the Peugeot Cup, got underway a few months later. The FCSM was one of the favourites for the first match, scheduled for September 11, 1932.

Source: www.fcsochaux.fr/fr/index.php/component/content/article/40-club/4409- (last accessed Dec. 1, 2017)

In the 1960s, General de Gaulle continued to pursue this public sports policy, focusing also on the highest level of performance, national sports institute INSEP, the federations, and the development of sports studies, youth and leisure centres, guided by André Malraux. This policy was no accident, arising from the bitter failure of the French delegation at the Rome Olympics, with a humiliating zero gold medals for a nation seeking to make its mark internationally in the context of the Cold War between the United States and the USSR.

Box 1.2 For the French State, the Olympic Games are also political

In 1960, French athletes returned from the Olympics having failed to win any gold medals. General De Gaulle was angry, and this sparked the start of a major programme to bring sport to the people, the effects of which are still being felt today.

In France, the longest lasting memory, paradoxically, remains one of bitter failure. In 1960, France returned empty-handed from Rome, with only five medals and no gold. Total humiliation. Especially as it was the army who had trained the French athletes, putting them up in a military sports centre during their long preparation. The day after this crushing defeat, member of parliament Hervé Laudrin (UNR) declared to the National Assembly: "The Olympic Games in Rome saw our youth humiliated in front of the whole world".

The humiliation of 1960 marks the starting point of French sport

The French government's reaction was to decide to get more involved in sport. General De Gaulle started the turnaround when he declared: "If France is admired abroad for its thinkers, its scientists and its artists, it must also be admired for its sportsmen. A country's greatness is demonstrated by the quality of its youth, a youth that cannot exist without a sporting ideal".

From then on, the government launched a massive programme to provide greater access to sport. Under Maurice Herzog, Secretary of State for Sport from 1958 to 1965, sports facilities sprang up all over the country.

In addition to this came the creation of INSEP, via the 1975 merger of the P.E. teacher-training college ENSEP and the national sports institute (INS), creating a gigantic sports centre set in more than 30 hectares in the Vincennes public park in eastern Paris.

In the 1980s, France finally comes into its own

The final stage of this very political creation of a French sporting identity was decentralization. In the 1980s, local and regional government gained greater powers, and local authorities took over the subsidies for the building of sports facilities from central government.

France was now firmly established in the Top 10 of Olympic nations. From 1988 to 2008, it ranked at worst 10th (Beijing, 2008) and at best 5th (Atlanta, 1996).

In exchange for this investment, the politicians expect to see medals, so much so that now before each Olympic Games, it has become traditional for the country's highest officials to set a target.

Source: www.lexpress.fr/actualite/politique/pour-l-etat-francais-les-jeux-olympiques-sont-aussi-politiques_1143141.html (last accessed December 1, 2017)

- **Changes in school hours and the role of the town hall in sports policy**

The change in school hours, a subject of great controversy from 2013 onwards, was part of a wider plan initially designed to encourage student development through extracurricular activities. This reform was intended, among other things, as a move towards the "German model" where pupils finish work early, making it possible for them to play more sport in the afternoon. Although there are some advantages to this system, it also comes with some fundamental problems, such as the way it could penalize women's access to the job market, owing to the difficulty of reconciling work and family life with this kind of schedule.

Box 1.3 School hours change could be good news for French sport (article from 2013)

The date: The president, along with the three ministers responsible for education and youth matters (Vincent Peillon, Valérie Fourneyron and George Pau-Langevin) is making it the main issue for the start of the 2013 school year: the introduction of new school hours in 4,000 towns and villages, affecting 20% of nursery and primary school pupils, to be extended nationwide in a year's time. This reform, praised by child-behaviour specialists but questioned by parents and teachers, will face intense scrutiny. Because the towns and villages who have chosen not to wait until September 2014 to adopt the changes do not have the financial resources of Paris, where 7,700 "extracurricular" workshops will be offered on Tuesday and Friday afternoons in 662 schools (in order to compensate for the three hours of lessons moved to Wednesday mornings).

Denain, the town chosen for the president's visit: This reform is an opportunity, particularly for the poorest areas, where access to culture and sport is becoming more and more difficult.

At a time when Germany has backed away (notably because of a demographic decline, which is not the case in France) from its much-vaunted model of "school in the morning, sport in the afternoon", but where 80% of schools still work closely with clubs and associations, French sport cannot afford to miss the boat. This new situation could get the increasingly parallel worlds of "sport in school" and "sport outside school" talking to each other again. If the school hours reform manages to correct this anomaly, it would be a nice achievement in its own right.

Source: www.huffingtonpost.fr/claude-droussent/rythmes-scolaires-sports_b_3855299.html (last accessed December 1, 2017)

- The role of subsidies in French sports federation budgets

The role of the sports federations, set up as associations, is to organize and manage one or more sports from simple leisure activity through to the highest level.

They can be divided into several categories:

- The 92 single-sport federations, which are subsequently split into Olympic (31) and non-Olympic federations (61)
- Multisport federations, 25 in number, within which several subsets can be distinguished: Affinity groups (18), sport and disability federations (2) and school and university sports federations (5)

Even if legally speaking they are private bodies, historically they have had a lot of support from public authorities, particularly the Sports Ministry. Subsidies, therefore, make up a large part of their budgets. The figures for 2011 are shown in Table 1.3.

Table 1.3 Subsidies to French sports federations

Olympic and sports federations	*2011 SUBSIDIES (€)*	*RATE OF SUPPORT 2010 (%)*
Athletics	3,979,995	26.82
Rowing	3,484,501	51.41
Badminton	1,148,396	14.52
Basketball	2,572,830	11.50
Boxing	1,425,257	36.57
Canoeing-kayaking	3,362,005	51.14
Cycling	3,564,092	22.68
Horse riding	1,808,012	4.08
Fencing	3,184,116	52.16
Football	2,855,190	1.48
Golf	666,955	2.50

(*Continued*)

Table 1.3 (Continued)

Olympic and sports federations	*2011 SUBSIDIES (€)*	*RATE OF SUPPORT 2010 (%)*
Gymnastics	3,361,649	26.63
Weightlifting	852,576	31.97
Handball	3,883,537	22.98
Hockey	1,037,790	40.32
Ice hockey	1,111,369	28.26
Judo-Jujitsu	3,524,001	13.13
Wrestling	1,645,216	55.93
Swimming	3,745,228	29.10
Modern pentathlon	825,000	83.40
Rugby	1,270,781	1.38
Skiing	4,498,311	27.52
Ice sports	1,802,006	36.12
Taekwondo	1,212,592	31.14
Tennis	1,285,000	0.74
Table tennis	1,573,747	30.37
Shooting	2,014,457	26.04
Archery	973,447	25.12
Triathlon	757,295	18.85
Sailing	3,707,103	30.77
Volleyball	1,675,406	21.81
Baseball and softball	497,405	44.64
Orienteering	370,268	33.95
Cycling tourism	150,147	2.37
Dance	93,847	6.77
Chess	74,000	6.38
Underwater sports and studies	308,167	5.44
American football	415,084	33.89
Karate	858,396	9.54
Mountaineering and climbing	569,702	13.75
Motorcycling	1,301,904	9.29
Speedboat	17,000	4.02
Parachuting	869,427	30.24
Petanque	170,770	8.21
Hiking	509,838	5.17
Roller skating	1,264,238	38.72
Rugby League	547,397	20.85
French kickboxing	499,184	25.52
Waterskiing	724,945	53.96
Potholing	260,847	20.69
Motorsport	1,134,917	5.94
Squash	412,679	34.94
Surf	321,976	28.62
Gliding	625,437	25.12
Hang gliding	479,003	15.00

Source: CROS Provence Alpes (last accessed December 1, 2017)

Table 1.4 Federation dependency on the State[2]

Federation	*2001*	*2008*
FFF (football)	4%	4%
FFR (rugby)	8%	6%
FFA (athletics)	53%	48%
FFBB (basketball)	28%	30%
FFHB (handball)	34%	45%

Source: French Sports Ministry

Of course, the more amateur a federation is, with little television coverage and no lucrative sporting events, the more dependent it is on subsidies. Wrestling, fencing and rowing are prime examples of Olympic federations that only get a little media coverage every four years. On the other hand, football and rugby are professional sports with significant commercial revenue (sponsorship, merchandising, VIP tickets), extensive television coverage and, therefore, expensive TV rights. They are, therefore, much less dependent on the State (see Table 1.4).

1.2.2 Professional sport

In Europe, professional sport gradually developed after World War II, either officially (notably the case with football), or behind a facade of "fake amateurism" which concealed a professional or semi-professional reality (for example, rugby union only became officially professional in 1995, skier Jean-Claude Killy was supposed to be an amateur when he won three gold medals at the 1968 Winter Olympics, hurdler Guy Drut was an amateur when he won Olympic gold in 1976, etc.).

Box 1.4 The development of professional football in England from the 1880s

Professional football was authorized in 1885 and the first championship was held in 1888–1889. The English Football Association played a major role in its development, imposing a single set of rules via the creation of the FA Cup, before the clubs took over. The creation of the League was not the work of the FA, however, but an initiative on the part of the clubs, seeking to establish a stable and sensible fixture list. The existence of a rail network also made this change, initiated by Aston Villa president William McGregor, possible. This first league was professional and no clubs from the south of the country took part.

England was, therefore, split in two, with the north fully accepting professionalism and the south rejecting it.

There was a sociological explanation for this difference. The south of England was dominated by the traditional idea that sports clubs were reserved for a social elite. In the industry-led north, however, professional football was run by the big bosses who didn't hesitate to pay their players to produce a stronger team, just as they recruited better engineers to make their companies stronger. For five seasons, the championship was limited to northern clubs. London club Arsenal turned professional in 1891. The London league then excluded the Gunners from its competitions and the team joined the main League in 1893. The Southern League was created in reaction to this (1894). This competition gradually opened up to professional teams but couldn't avoid the defection of many clubs to the League. The best remaining clubs in the Southern League were incorporated into the main League in 1920.

Source: https://fr.wikipedia.org/wiki/Histoire_du_football#Apparition_du_professionnalisme (last accessed December 1, 2017)

Thus, professional football in England can trace its origins back to the relationship between the clubs and industrial companies. Football was a way to entertain the workers, to make them forget their often deplorable working conditions and at the same time reinforce the standing of the sponsor or, in some cases, owner. Studies carried out in Italy in the 1970s showed that the number of strike days in FIAT factories was minimal in the years when Juventus Turin was riding high at the top of the European football league and championship.

In France, as we note in Box 1.5, professional football developed later, in the 1930s, but in a very confused way, since it was a question of operating within a club structure based on the 1901 definition of associations. Changes in club governance only came much later in the 1990s with the development of the SASP (*Société Anonyme Sportive Professionelle* or Professional Sports Limited Company).

Box 1.5 The beginnings of professional football in France

French football held out against professionalism until 1932, its founding fathers being Georges Bayrou, Emmanuel Gambardella and Gabriel Hanot.

The inevitable march towards professionalism led to a smaller number of top teams, as many clubs were no longer able to keep up financially. Before 1932, players were either paid discreetly or given "courtesy jobs". Even as professional sport was gaining official recognition, these practices were still rife at amateur clubs. Rugby Union, which only became professional much later, was still facing this kind of problem at the end of the 20th century. Indeed, several players recently declared they were earning more as amateurs than as pros! French football underwent this "professional transition" during the 1930s in the middle of an economic crisis. As a result, some players used pseudonyms to keep their jobs, for example French international Mercier, whose real name was Furois, or judge Adolphe Touffait who played at the Rennes Stadium under the name Delourme from 1933 to 1936.

The advent of professional football in January 1932 did not, however, change the clubs' legal structure and status. The only difference between them and the thousands of amateur clubs was their status as "1901-type associations", that is still amateur, but authorized by the French Football Federation to field paid players as "official clubs".

Professional football, which favoured a smaller elite group of teams, coincided with the creation of a national championship. The rise of this professional championship meant a loss of prestige for the regional leagues as the best clubs left their Division of Honour (D.H.) competitions. The reticence of some league leaders, such as Jooris in Lille, was therefore understandable.

Source: https://fr.wikipedia.org/wiki/Histoire_du_football_en_France#Le_football_fran.C3.A7ais_d.C3.A9couvre_le_professionnalisme_.281932-1939.29

Rugby, on the other hand, became professional even later, in 1995, even though the Rugby World Cup was created in 1987. It seems rather paradoxical that players like All Black Jonah Lomu or Frenchman Abdelatif Benazzi were amateurs at the peak of their careers, but that was the case. The reality of the situation was, however, very different. There was money in rugby, but it was passed around "under the table", so to speak. A town in southwestern France might hire a player as an employee though, in fact, he would almost never come to work. Captains of industry financed rugby, either with their own money, or via their company (for example, Pierre Fabre in Castres, Serge Kampf in Biarritz or Grenoble and Pierre Martinet in Bourgoin).

Box 1.6 The beginnings of professional rugby in 1995

In August 1995, the International Rugby Board (IRB) did away with the compulsory amateur status and transformed the sport into a profession. "A *change of culture and, quite simply, a change of life*", according to Bernard Lapasset, the current president of the IRB, now World Rugby. The French clubs took their first steps into the professional era, if a little more reluctantly than the southern hemisphere countries (South Africa, New Zealand and Australia), which in June had accepted Australian tycoon Rupert Murdoch's $550 million offer to acquire the exclusive rights to broadcast their matches for a decade.

"*Before 1995, we made a little money from rugby, but it wasn't our main activity, it was a bonus. We simply shook hands on it with our chairmen, there was nothing contractual, nothing formal, it worked more like a system of match bonuses*", recalls Emile Ntamack, a former member of the French XV and national champion that year with Stade Toulousain.

In France, the changeover to professional rugby gained momentum in the summer of 1998 with the creation of the National Rugby League (LNR in French), which ran the professional Top 14 and Pro D2 championships. "*It's more rigorous now. I remember when red wine was served at pre-match meals. That wouldn't be possible today*", says Scotland coach Vern Cotter, who played in France in the 1990s and, as trainer, led Clermont to league victory in 2010.

Once he turned professional, Emile Ntamack had to give up his studies to become a sports teacher: "*We started to feel the difference when the pace of training increased. We went from two training sessions a week to almost two sessions a day. And today, if a trainer schedules an extra session, everyone has to do it, no one will try and get out of it by saying they have a dentist appointment or something*".

Source: www.lemonde.fr/rugby/article/2014/12/31/les-vingt-ans-qui-ont-metamorphose-l-ovalie_4548178_1616937.html (last accessed December 1, 2017)

Turning professional did not mean the end of club subsidies, though. This is one of the great paradoxes of French sport. The importance of the government, and especially local government, for some large sports clubs, should not be underestimated. At the same time, it is completely reasonable from a communication or "city branding" point of view. What would Auxerre or Sochaux be without football? Orthez, Bourges or Gravelines without basketball? Oyonnax or Brives without rugby? Gap or Briançon without ice hockey?

Other cities have introduced marketing/communication strategies linked to specific events such as the Tour de France (Alpe d'Huez) or the Vendée Globe (Les Sables d'Olonne). It is, therefore, clear that sports marketing, and marketing in general, ended up having an impact on all sectors of the economy in the 1990s, including non-commercial activity.

Table 1.5 The role of public finance in French professional sport

Sport	*Amount in euros*	*% of revenue*
Football (Ligue 1)	€32 million	4%
Football (Ligue 2)	€28 million	17%
Basketball (Pro A)	€16 million	36%
Handball (Division 1)	€14 million	58%
Rugby (Top 14)	€13 million	11%
Rugby (Pro D2)	€10 million	30%
Volleyball (Division 1)	€8 million	54%
Basketball (Women's league)	€6 million	40%

Source: Jean-François Bourg, from a public report by state auditor Cour des comptes "Local authorities and professional sports clubs", December 9, 2009.

Table 1.6 Estimated subsidies and services for the 2013/2014 season

Sport	*Football*		*Rugby*		*Basketball*		*Handball*	*Volleyball*		
Division	Ligue 1	Ligue 2	Top 14	Pro D2	Pro A	Pro B	D1	LAM	LAF	LBM
Subsidy as a % of revenue	1%	1%	3%	6%	26%	40%	29%	60%	62%	78%

Source: www.sports.gouv.fr/IMG/pdf/confsportpro_2016_rapport_hd4.pdf (last accessed December 1, 2017)

But, as with all other sectors, the government has gradually backed away from subsidizing sport, and clubs are being forced to seek private financing. Nevertheless, the share of subsidies remains very high for professional basketball, volleyball and handball (see Tables 1.5 and 1.6).

Box 1.7 The importance of subsidies for French professional sports clubs

Data supplied by state auditor Cour des comptes show total subsidies of €157 million for the 2011–2012 season, with grants ranging from 2% of club budgets for League 1 football to 79% for League B men's volleyball, with 12% for Pro D2, 30% for Pro A basketball and 52% for the women's handball league. In rugby, public subsidies represent 3% of the Top 14 budget and 5% of the Pro D2 budget.

Subsidies account for only 2–5% of revenue for football or rugby clubs, against 70–80% for volleyball or handball teams, whose competitions are less professional.

> In fact, local authorities support the development of professional teams in different ways; some sports would be unable to survive without public subsidies, while others enjoy almost complete financial autonomy.
>
> Source: www.senat.fr/rap/r13-484-1/r13-484-12.html (last accessed December 1, 2017)

Various laws were introduced prohibiting subsidies for professional sport, which therefore had to turn to "hidden" payments (ticket purchases, training centre funding, stadium renovation, etc.) for support. If professional sport remained subsidized in this way, it did not change the fact that there had been very little regulation by public authorities since the 1950s, and then only to try and ensure fair competition.

Unlike the United States, where we have seen that professional sport was strictly regulated, even controlled, by the all-powerful leagues, European sport developed in much more of a "free market" fashion. This was in total contradiction to the "real" economy (that is, outside sport) where it was rather the United States which championed the free market and France which was based more on a State-controlled system. Generally speaking, a competitive approach without outside intervention, often described as "pure and perfect competition", can work and even be favourable overall for both parties (that is, consumers and producers) if certain conditions are met.

There are five conditions: Three to ensure pure competition and two to guarantee perfect competition.

The conditions for pure competition are these:

- Atomicity: The players are small and cannot influence prices. They are said to be price-takers
- Homogeneity: For the consumer, all goods are identical, homogeneous and substitutable
- Free market entry and exit: No barriers (such as qualifications, authorization, high costs, etc.) preventing entry or exit

The conditions for perfect competition are these:

- Free movement of production resources: They are perfectly mobile and can move from one industry to another
- Transparency: All market participants have access to all available information

If we try to apply this model to European football, we can immediately see a major problem. Atomicity does not exist, some clubs have become much larger than others, more important from both a financial and a sporting point of view and, therefore, much more influential. Within UEFA, the existence of the big clubs' lobby group (formerly known as "the G-14") has been known for years. Florentino Perez (president of Real Madrid), Karl-Heinz Rummenigge (chairman of Bayern Munich) or Nasser El-Khelaifi (chairman and CEO of Paris Saint-Germain) are all big names who are likely to influence the organization of the lucrative Champions League, the way it is governed and, above all, the sharing out of the wealth it generates.

Free entry to the market is not a feature of European football either: Rules (essentially national championship rankings and European results) determine whether you are in or out.

Finally, free movement of production resources is also not straightforward here. The players, who represent the bulk of these resources, are "goods" that are exchanged, bought and resold, with the help of agents often on large commissions, after tough negotiations. But we all know that when a great player is up for transfer at around €100 million, only three or four clubs can afford to buy him.

In conclusion, we can say that European professional football is more like an oligopoly than a competitive system where everyone stands an equal chance. This oligopoly groups together the biggest European clubs, with only big cities with more than 1 million inhabitants standing a chance in the Champions League. Since the 1990s, the Deloitte Group has published the Deloitte Football Money League which provides information on the clubs' financial ranking every year. Back then, Manchester United was often called the "cash machine" of football, becoming the first club to pass the €100 million revenue mark.

A club's income can be divided into three categories[3]:

- "Match Day": The box office
- "Broadcasting": Media rights, still mainly TV rights (Internet rights are still marginal but could become more important in the future through pay per view)
- "Commercial": Commercial revenue, including sponsoring, VIP areas, and merchandising (products such as team shirts)

According to the 2017 Deloitte report, Europe's biggest clubs all have revenue far in excess of €300 million, with Manchester United back at the top of the financial rankings with turnover of almost €700 million, overtaking Real Madrid, which has held the number one slot for the last 11 years.

This top 20 ranking calls for a number of comments:

- The top of the list is very concentrated and turnover declines very sharply as we move down the list: Revenue at Juventus, in 10th position, is half that at Manchester United, and Leicester City, ranked 20th, has less than a quarter of the leader's income.

Table 1.7 Revenue at the 20 biggest European clubs for 2015–2016, according to the Deloitte Football Money League 2017 report

1	Manchester United – €689M
2	FC Barcelona – €620.2M
3	Real Madrid – €620.1M
4	Bayern Munich – €592M
5	Manchester City – €524.9M
6	Paris Saint-Germain – €520.9M
7	Arsenal – €468.5M
8	Chelsea FC – €447.4M
9	Liverpool – €403.8M
10	Juventus – €341.1M
11	Borussia Dortmund – €283.9M
12	Tottenham Hotspurs – €279.7M
13	Atlético de Madrid – €228.6M
14	Schalke 04 – €224.5M
15	AS Roma – €218.2M
16	AC Milan – €214.7M
17	FC Zenit Saint Petersburg – €196.5M
18	West Ham United – €192.3M
19	Inter Milan – €179.2M
20	Leicester City – €172.1M

Source: www.sportbuzzbusiness.fr/classement-clubs-generent-plus-argent-deloitte-football-money-league-2017.html (last accessed December 1, 2017)

- Few countries are represented in this top 20: There is one Russian team, one French one, four Italian, three German, three Spanish, and eight English teams. That's a total of six countries, while UEFA has 55 member countries.
- Countries that were once great footballing nations, and that still produce talented players, have disappeared from view at the club level. The Netherlands, Portugal, Belgium, Croatia, Serbia, etc. all have populations that are too small and, therefore, are too limited in media and marketing potential for their clubs to have competitive budgets. They have become "exporters", feeding players to the major clubs, especially since the 1995 Bosman ruling which said a team could have an unlimited number of foreign European players.
- The correlation between a team's performance and its financial ranking is also indisputable. Over a 15-year period, Deloitte data shows that "*the richer you are, the more likely you are to perform well in sporting terms*". In some ways, this is reassuring as it means that the money is being used wisely to improve club management, and that there is, therefore, some kind of logic behind it. But at the same time, it is worrying because it means that football is losing a lot of its appeal as it becomes less uncertain and much more predictable. It also makes it much more complicated to attract spectators from "smaller" countries that are no longer represented in European competitions, which thus lose much of their universal reach.

Table 1.8 shows little notable movement from one year to the next, with the Top 6 remaining relatively little changed. Any variations can usually be explained by a remarkable performance in the Champions League or, on the contrary, failure to qualify for this lucrative competition.[4]

Having a limited range of clubs and countries in the TOP 20 is one thing, but the same is also true of the championship ranking. Real Madrid has won three of the last four Champions League competitions, with only four countries represented

Table 1.8 Changes in revenue at Europe's 20 largest football clubs in 2015–2016 compared with 2014–2015, according to the DFML (Deloitte Football Money League) 2017 report

2015/16 Revenue (€m)

DFML position	Change on previous year	Number of positions changed	Club	Revenue
1	↑	2	Manchester United	689
2	↔	0	FC Bancelona	620.2
3	↓	(2)	Real Madrid	620.1
4	↑	1	Bayenn Munich	592
5	↑	1	Manchester Oty	524.9
6	↓	(2)	Paris Saint-Genmain	520.9
7	↔	0	Arsenal	468.5
8	↔	0	Chelsea	447.4
9	↔	0	Liverpool	403.8
10	↔	0	Juverntus	341.1
11	↔	0	Bonussia Dortmund	283.9
12	↔	0	Tottenham Hotspur	279.7
13	↑	3	Atletico de Madrid	228.6
14	↓	(1)	Schalke 04	224.5
15	↔	0	AS Roma	218.2
16	↓	(2)	AC Milan	214.7
17	↑	1	FC Zenit Saint Petersburg	196.5
18	n/a	new	West Ham United	192.3
19	↑	1	Intennazionale	179.2
20	n/a	new	Leicester City	172.1

2014/15 Revenue (€m)

DFML position	Change on previous year	Number of positions changed	Club	Revenue
1	↔	0	Real Madrid	577
2	↑	2	FC Bancelona	560.8
3	↓	(1)	Manchester United	519.5
4	↑	1	Paris Saint-Genmain	480.8
5	↓	(2)	Bayern Munich	474
6	↔	0	Manchester City	463.5
7	↑	1	Arsenal	435.5
8	↓	(1)	Chelsea	420
9	↔	0	Liverpool	391.8
10	↔	0	Juverntus	323.9
11	↔	0	Bonussia Dortmund	280.6
12	↑	1	Tottenham Hotspur	257.5
13	↑	1	Schalke 04	219.7
14	↓	(2)	AC Milan	199.1
15	n/a	new	AS Roma	179.1
16	↓	(1)	Atletico de Madrid	176.6
17	↑	2	Newcastie United	169.3
18	n/a	new	FC Zenit Saint Petersburg	167.8
19	↑	1	Everton	165.1
20	↓	(3)	Internnazionale	164.8

■ DFML position ■ Change on previous year ■ Number of positions changed

Source: www.sportbuzzbusiness.fr/classement-clubs-generent-plus-argent-deloitte-football-money-league-2017.html (last accessed December 1, 2017)

Table 1.9 Champions League rankings from 2006 to 2017

	Vainqueur	*Score*	*Finaliste*
2017	Real Madrid	4–1	Juventus Turin
2016	Real Madrid	1–1 (5–3 tab)	Atlético Madrid
2015	FC Barcelona	3–1	Juventus Turin
2014	Real Madrid	4–1 ap	Atlético Madrid
2013	Bayern Munich	2–1	Borussia Dortmund
2012	Chelsea FC	1–1 (4–3 tab)	Bayern Munich
2011	FC Barcelone	3–1	Manchester United
2010	Inter Milan	2–0	Bayern Munich
2009	FC Barcelone	2–0	Manchester United
2008	Manchester United	1–1 (6–5 tab)	Chelsea FC
2007	Milan AC	2–1	Liverpool FC
2006	FC Barcelone	2–1	Arsenal FC

Source: https://fr.wikipedia.org/wiki/Ligue_des_champions_de_l%27UEFA (last accessed December 1, 2017)

in the final over 12 years (out of a possible 24), seven Spanish victories in 12 years, four wins for FC Barcelona in nine years, etc., all facts that do nothing to boost the general public's optimism about the random nature of the competition.

Tables 1.10 and 1.11 show this concentration of teams in the competition as a whole since its inception in 1956, with few countries and clubs sharing the winner's crown.

So, in conclusion, as regards the development of European professional sport, and football in particular, we can see a real trend towards concentration. This situation is becoming problematic and counterproductive. Over the years, average ratings per match have been falling in Europe, and UEFA has had to come up with a string of excuses to implement new rules, sometimes designed to give a more important role to the "small countries", but above all aimed at broadcasting the games as widely as possible in an attempt to increase the total audience.

At the same time, high levels of investment and spending are needed to achieve significant sporting results, and many clubs are heavily indebted, particularly the best performing ones. The level of players' salaries and their progression no longer seems viable in the long term. In 2010, English clubs were €3.5 billion in debt (including €800 million each for Manchester United and Chelsea), Spanish clubs were in for €4 billion (€570 million for Valencia, €337 million for Real Madrid and €311 million for FC Barcelona), Italy €2.3 billion, Germany €770 million and France €109 million (*source: http://lefootballetsonfinancement.e-monsite.com/pages/les-depenses-et-les-actifs.html, last accessed December 1, 2017*).

Bayern Munich and Arsenal have been the traditional "model students" in European football over the past 10 years. But it is interesting to note that the latter is regularly accused of "winning nothing and hanging on to its money instead of buying star players". As if there were some contradiction between making money and playing well.

Table 1.10 Champions League ranking by country since its creation

Ranking	*Country*	*Wins*	*Finals Lost*
1	Spain	17	11
2	Italy	12	16
3	England	12	7
4	Germany	7	10
5	The Netherlands	6	2
6	Portugal	4	5
7	France	1	5
	Scotland	1	1
8	Romania	1	1
	Serbia	1	1
	Greece	0	1
11	Belgium	0	1
	Sweden	0	1

Source: https://fr.wikipedia.org/wiki/Ligue_des_champions_de_l%27UEFA (last accessed December 1, 2017)

Table 1.11 Champions League rankings by club

Ranking	*Club*	*Wins*	*Finals Lost*
1	Real Madrid	12 (1956, 1957, 1958, 1959, 1960, 1966, 1998, 2000, 2002, 2014, 2016, 2017)	3
2	AC Milan	7 (1963, 1969, 1989, 1990, 1994, 2003, 2007)	4
3	Bayern Munich	5 (1974, 1975, 1976, 2001, 2013)	5
4	FC Barcelona	5 (1992, 2006, 2009, 2011, 2015)	3
5	Liverpool FC	5 (1977, 1978, 1981, 1984, 2005)	2
6	Ajax Amsterdam	4 (1971, 1972, 1973, 1995)	2
7	Manchester United	3 (1968, 1999, 2008)	2
	Inter Milan	3 (1964, 1965, 2010)	2
9	Juventus FC	2 (1985, 1996)	7

Source: https://fr.wikipedia.org/wiki/Ligue_des_champions_de_l%27UEFA (last accessed Dec. 1, 2017)

Nevertheless, it appears that the system has reached the point of no return. Roman Abramovitch at Chelsea, Mansour bin Zayed al-Nahyan at Manchester City and Qatar Sport Investment at PSG have already been caught out by UEFA's Financial Fair Play regulations, introduced to try and control club spending and create a more level playing field (basically, do not spend more over the year than you have earned in revenue).

"Full" American-style regulation does not seem viable, because the draft system could not be implemented in Europe, where the training centres produce the talent. An NHL-style "revenue sharing" operation (where profitable clubs give a part of their earnings to those in deficit) does not look possible either.

On the other hand, regulation through salary caps and fairer distribution of television rights seems more feasible. A salary cap at the European level would prevent the big Spanish and English clubs from being the only ones likely to attract the top players. It will become all the more necessary as the explosion of TV rights in the UK is likely to further widen the gap with the rest of the European clubs.

The signing of a new UK TV rights contract from 2016 raises real concerns because it widens the gap with other countries, resulting in a situation where the top French team is getting less than the club at the bottom of the Premier League. This concentration of resources via television, marketing, ticketing, merchandising etc. will make the English clubs richer, boosting their leading position in the Deloitte Football Money League TOP 20. In 2005, 8 out of the 20 clubs were English, as in 2016, but all the clubs in slots 20 to 30 will be English in coming years. Eventually, the best players will inevitably go to play in England, and even Spain will not be able to keep them.

2 The beginnings of sports marketing in Europe in the 1980s

2.1 Marketing sports events

In the 1980s, the marketing of sports events was influenced by two factors: The boom in television rights and an increase in marketing rights, mostly through sponsorship.

This change was particularly important for the two biggest events in world sport: The Olympic Games and the football World Cup.

- TV rights

Table 1.12 The increase in Summer Olympics television rights since 1960 ($ million)

Year	*Host City*	*US rights*	*Europe rights*	*World rights*
1960	Rome	0.5	0.67	1.2
1964	Tokyo	1	0.38	1.5
1968	Mexico City	4.5	1	9.75
1972	Munich	7.5	1.70	11.8
1976	Montreal	25	4.50	34.8
1980	Moscow	85	5.95	101
1984	Los Angeles	225	19.8	287
1988	Seoul	300	28	407
1992	Barcelona	401	90	636
1996	Atlanta	456	250	907
2000	Sydney	715	350	1,350
2004	Athens	793	400	1,700
2008	Beijing	894	460	2,000

Source: J-F. Bourg and J-J. Gouguet (1998), *Analyse économique du sport*, page 233, PUF.

Table 1.13 Air time devoted to sport on French television in 2016

	SPORT	*TOTAL*	*TF1*	*FRANCE2*	*FRANCE3*	*CANAL+*	*M6*	*C8*	*W9*	*TMC*	*FRANCE4*	*CSTAR*	*FRANCEÔ*	*LEQUIPE*	*N-23*	*RMCD*
1	FOOTBALL	847h57	64h49	14h16	25h40	340h17	21h56	30h09	28h55	01h49	105h38	34h11	09h15	166h16	04h39	
2	RUGBY	530h34		60h39	04h25	331h58					90h37			42h53		
3	CYCLISME	336h16		62h59	86h58	10h57							12h49	162h31		
4	PETANQUE	274h46			07h31									267h15		
5	VOLLEY BALL	196h25		05h26	12h50	14h27							45h05	118h34		
6	BASKET	191h29		04h54	10h29	43h38							85h40	41h17	05h29	
7	HOCKEY SUR GLACE	154h41				112h52								41h49		
8	TENNIS	152h54		65h21	10h15	06h05			04h27		49h47		05h49	09h30	01h38	
9	RALLYE AUTO	145h49					00h38							145h11		
10	BOXE	138h07		05h34	06h41	22h19					00h43			102h49		
11	ATHLETISME	137h21		25h43	33h16	64h24							12h36	01h20		
12	MOT0 GP	113h15			01h32									111h43		
13	HANDBALL	111h51		06h33	09h20	15h59					01h42		73h35	04h40		
14	BIATHLON	102h35												102h35		
15	GOLF	96h25		01h43	01 h58	92h44										
16	KICK BOXING	77h17												77h17		
17	NATATION	71h43		20hl5	17h23	22h18							11 h46			
18	F1	57h56		03h02	02h30	52h07		00h16								

(*Continued*)

Table 11.3 (Continued)

	SPORT	*TOTAL*	*TF1*	*FRANCE2*	*FRANCE3*	*CANAL+*	*M6*	*C8*	*W9*	*TMC*	*FRANCE4*	*CSTAR*	*FRANCEÔ*	*LEQUIPE*	*N-23*	*RMC D.*
49	HOCKEY SUR GAZON	Q2h54		01h25	00h29	00h59										
50	RODEO	02h52				02h52										
51	LUTTE	02h32		00h35	00h36	01h20										
52	TIR	02h26		01h11		01h15										
53	PATINAGE DE VITESSE	02h00												02h00		
54	HALTEROPHILIE	01h27		00h55	00h11	00h19										
	TOTAL	4246h53	64h49	337h14	272h07	1245h29	22h35	30h25	37h56	01h49	257h05	34h11	269h14	1659h26	11h47	02h38

Source: www.sportannualreport.com (last accessed December 1, 2017)

Table 1.14 The increase in World Cup TV rights[5]

Year	*TV rights*	*Aggregate global audience*
1990	95 million Swiss francs	26.7 billion tv viewers
1994	110 million Swiss francs	32.1 billion tv viewers
1998	135 million Swiss francs	33.4 billion tv viewers
2002	1.3 billion Swiss francs	28.8 billion tv viewers
2006	1.5 billion Swiss francs	

Source: *https://fr.wikipedia.org/wiki/Football_et_télévision#Montant_des_droits_t.C3.A9l.C3.A9vis.C3.A9s* (last accessed December 1, 2017)

In 2010, the Vancouver Winter Olympics generated $1.279 billion in TV rights, while those for the London Summer Games in 2012 amounted to $2.569 billion. In 2014 and 2016, these amounts were higher still, even if the rights for the Winter Olympics remain well below those of the Summer games, for easily understandable reasons related to popularity and audience.

Overall, the rights increase can be explained by several factors:

1 The overall increase in the number of hours broadcast, which automatically increases the audience and, therefore, advertising revenue. From a few hours a day in the 1970s and 1980s, we have switched to almost complete 24-hour television coverage.
2 An impressive increase in the number of broadcasters competing for rights in all countries has led to higher prices, as the Olympics remains a unique product. In France, at least 10 groups are likely to bid for the rights (France Télévisions, TF1, M6, Canal Plus, Eurosport, SFR Sports, BeIn Sports, etc.), compared with just two in the 1980s. The market is becoming a monopoly, or at least an oligopoly.
3 The audiences achieved by sporting events, generally the highest in each country in the year-end balance sheets, mean that channels are anxious to acquire the rights and rights sellers are eager to promote their event.
4 Channels have also become aware that sport can be a way for them to communicate on their own behalf. If it has now been proven that direct investment in TV rights does not pay for itself through advertising, being the "Tour de France and Roland-Garros channel" (France Télévisions), "the 1998 World Cup channel" (TF1), "the Premier League channel" (SFR Sports), "the NBA channel" (BeIn Sports), is both rewarding for the broadcaster and its brand positioning.

This air time is largely dedicated to football, rugby and cycling. It also does not take into account pay-tv channels such as Eurosport, BeIn Sports and SFR Sports, which, because they cover sports 24 hours a day, would inflate the figures by several thousand additional hours.

Even without taking into account the even-numbered years which are traditionally more exposed to sport, owing to the Summer and Winter Olympics, the football World Cup or the European championship, sports broadcasting has steadily increased over the last 10 years.

The results for the Summer Olympics can be explained by three factors:

- They are broadcast at a time of year when people watch less television
- They are regularly organized in cities located in time zones that are not very conducive to attracting large audiences (Atlanta 1996, Sydney 2000, Beijing 2008)
- The majority of the events take place in daytime slots that do not guarantee the widest possible TV audience.

The deterioration observed during the second half of the 2000s is all the more striking since the 2006 and 2010 competitions took place in Europe and South Africa, respectively, and thus made it possible to broadcast a large number of matches at favourable audience hours, rather than in the morning or early afternoon as was the case in 2002.

2.2 *The trigger: France 1998 and beyond*

Interest in sports marketing has been fuelled by what has been happening in sports business. In 1998, France became world football champion, bringing "sport and its markets" into the spotlight. Companies were suddenly interested and wanted to understand how to operate in this field, at first out of curiosity ("you have to be there"), and then later motivated by profit.[6]

Marketing agencies and sports-event companies, helped by more up-to-date theoretical knowledge, initially provided answers to these questions: 1998 can therefore be considered as the end of the "dinosaur age" of sports marketing in France. As others did with the Internet and new technologies, companies (including sponsors and equipment manufacturers) discovered that you could make money, improve your competitive position, boost your brand or change your image through sport. Later on, success in other sports (handball, rugby, volleyball) confirmed that sport can be a good investment for companies wishing to do the following:

- Increase their notoriety
- Improve their image
- Stimulate internal communication
- And, last but not least, increase sales[7]

What has sports news got to do with sports marketing? Quite simply, sports marketing is being developed by specialist agencies (Havas Sports, Carat Sport, IMG, Octagon, Sportfive, Keneo, so many great names who have emerged since the

Figure 1.1 The London Nike Town store

Source: author's photo, 2006.

1980s), broadcasters (TF1, Canal +; France Télévisions, Eurosport, M6, BeIn sports, SFR Sport, l'Equipe 21), equipment manufacturers (Adidas, Nike, Reebok, Salomon, Rossignol), leagues (France's professional football league and national rugby league) and, with more difficulty, by the federations (FFF, FFR, FFT with the Roland-Garros tournament).

It has been the same story for "real sport", that is, the sort "people play as opposed to watching".[8] Equipment manufacturers and retailers no longer think of sport as they did 20 years ago. Everything has changed. The sports consumer is more and more demanding, retailing has become global, new ideas are needed to speed up the pace of repeat purchases, retailers have fallen out with equipment manufacturers after the latter started developing "concept stores" (i.e., stores specific to their brand). The "idyllic" world of the 1990s has become "a battlefield" in 2018, especially given the market's tendency to stagnate.

Sports business, on the other hand, has largely evolved as a result of accelerated commercialization following 1995's Bosman ruling, reinforced by the Malaja ruling,[9] on the freedom of movement for professional players in Europe, which led to a concentration of the best football talent in England, and of rugby talent in France, for fairly obvious salary reasons. In France, 2002 brought a temporary halt to all this sports marketing euphoria after the French team, odds-on favourite to win the 2002 World Cup, was knocked out in the first round. This has been followed by many other failures, in football and other sports, starting with the infamous "Knysna strike".[10] As a result, many of the texts published over the past decade have focused on "risk management applied to sponsorship" (Arthur and Chadwick, 2007; Beech and Chadwick, 2007; Friends and Cornwell, 2005).

2.3 The beginnings of sport management from a managerial and academic point of view

In parallel with the growth seen on the business side, driven by an ever-increasing demand for televised sport and sports shows, the academic world has had to adapt to the professional reality of the sector.

The years 1990–2000, therefore, saw the emergence of real scientific studies on sports marketing. The publication of the book *Marketing du sport* (Desbordes, Ohl and Tribou, 1999) helped to lay the foundations for this area of study in the French-speaking world. While it was considered essential reading at the time, naturally the book's approach now looks outdated and numerous successors have provided a much more complete picture of how sponsorship, retailing, events or strategic marketing can be applied to sport. The field has matured, becoming much richer with the integration of neo-marketing elements and thus constitutes a fertile ground for marketing overall.

Education

The development of the business side and the resulting need for specialist skills in public or private organizations have led to the creation of new higher education courses. The same type of institutions operate in the academic field across the globe.

- Universities (generally public, and often free or almost free): It was the sports sciences faculties that started courses, firstly in "social sciences" (sociology or history of sport) in the 1970s, then gradually in sports management, then sports marketing. In the United States and the rest of the English-speaking world, these are called "faculties of sport sciences" or "kinesiology" and are made up of people from the sports world who are moving to management (whereas the opposite is true in the next category).
- Business schools: Conversely, these are private and fee-paying institutions which have moved from management to sport. Strangely, very few public business schools have turned to sport.[11]
- Some universities specializing in sports law (in France: Limoges, historically the leader; Marseille; or Paris 1 Panthéon Sorbonne).
- Finally, there are management schools entirely dedicated to sport. These are small bodies and few in number, as they are totally out of step with the trend to merge and the creation, seen at the international level, of large institutions, under pressure from the Shanghai ranking.

Is is hard to establish a full list of programs worldwide, but some organizations tried to.

> "*There are over 200 schools offering some sort of master's degree in Sports Management or a related field*" (Source: www.sports-management-degrees.com/best-masters/).
>
> "*437 programs have a degree at Bachelor's, Master's or Doctoral level in the US, 17 in Canada, 32 in Europe (largely underestimated), 13 in Australia, 4 in New Zealand, 19 in Asia (largely underestimated)*" (www.nassm.org/Programs/AcademicPrograms).

Sports management has not escaped the current fashion for evaluations, classifications and rankings. These can help to build or destroy reputations, though sometimes the assessments are not always objective.

At the international level, and among the wealth of information available online, we can rely on this ranking: http://degreesinsports.com/default.asp (last accessed Oct. 24, 2017) or that of Sport Business Journal www.sportbusiness.com/system/files/sportbusiness_postgraduate_course_rankings_2017_pdf_3.pdf (last accessed December 1, 2017).

In France, this review of Masters programmes in sports management is widely respected: www.meilleurs-masters.com/master-management-du-sport.html (last accessed Dec. 1, 2017).

Generally speaking, this shows a fairly sharp increase in competition, education having become a marketplace like any other. However, the subject matter does not always reflect developments in the job market.

As mentioned earlier, and this is the main theme of this book, three universes constitute the global field of sport management: "sports marketing", "sporting goods" and "sports governance". But the observation made by almost all professionals is rather problematic:

- Internationally, as in France, "sports marketing" predominates
- Observation: 80% of students emerge with training in "sports marketing", an area where job opportunities are rare and career prospects poor
- The "sporting goods" and "sports governance" fields, although rich in employment potential, attract little interest not only from students but also from teaching staff
- Few programs are international, while the market is increasingly global
- In conclusion, there is an opportunity and even a need to create diversified and international programs that respond to job market demand

3 Sports marketing today

When it was published in 1999, *Marketing du sport* was the first French book on the subject of sports marketing. Awarded first prize by the country's Académie des Sciences Commerciales (Academy of Business Studies) in 2000, it remained the only French-language work in its field for some time.

In the English-speaking world, *Sport Marketing*, by Mullin, Hardy and Sutton, also had a monopoly for a while when it was published in 1993. Reprinted for the fourth time in 2014, today it faces a lot more competition from the many North American works on the subject, as well as publications in English by European academics and their Asian colleagues (China, Hong Kong, Japan, Korea).

3.1 A proliferation of publications

3.1.1 Published works

As of 2017, there was a wealth of books on offer from English-language publishers on the subject of sports management.

French-language publications, though fewer in number, have also seen exponential growth in terms of the number of references.

Table 1.15 Number of references in books from English-language publishers in 2017 (updated June 1, 2017)

	Source	*Sport*	*Sports management*	*Sports marketing*
Routledge	www.routledge.com	872	64	22
Elsevier	www.elsevier.com	1,130	497	192
FIT	www.fitpublishing.com	95	54	30
Human Kinetics	www.humankinetics.com	700	172	145
Sage	http://journals.sagepub.com	24 journals and 132,792 articles	1 journal and 6,141 articles	32,613 articles
Taylor & Francis	http://taylorandfrancis.com	79 journals and 244,593 articles	18 journals and 118,180 articles	2 journals and 73,920 articles

Source: author

Table 1.16 Number of references in books from French-language publishers in 2017 (updated June 1, 2017)

	Source	*Sport*	*Comments*
Economica	www.economica.fr/index.cfm	11	
PUF	www.puf.com	92	
Dunod	www.dunod.com	399	
De Boeck		327	Nine works in the "Sports Management" collection
Editions d'Organisation		108	Compilation of works from Economica, PUF, Dunod, EO and Studyrama.

Source: Author, publishers' websites (last accessed December 1, 2017)

3.1.2 Scientific journals

The number of specialist journals in the field is also constantly growing. Since the creation of the *Journal of Sport Management* (JSM) in 1987, we can consider that the leading scientific articles are distributed in the ten or so publications listed in Table 1.17. Of course, you can also find some very high-quality articles

Table 1.17 English-language academic journals on sports management

Title	*Website*	*Comments*	*Impact factor as of Oct. 24, 2017*
Europeand Sport Management Quarterly	www.tandfonline.com/toc/resm20/current	Journal of the EASM (European Association for Sport Management), created in 1994.	1.966
Journal of Sport Management	http://journals.humankinetics.com/journal/jsm	Journal of the NASSM (North American Society for Sport Management), created in 1987	2.169
International Journal of Sports Marketing and Sponsorship	http://emeraldgrouppublishing.com/products/journals/author_guidelines.htm?id=ijsms	Journal created in 1999	0.622
International Journal of Sports Marketing and Management	www.inderscience.com/jhome.php?jcode=IJSMM	Journal created in 2005	None
Sport Management Review	www.journals.elsevier.com/sport-management-review	Journal of the SMAANZ (Sport Management Association of Australia and New Zealand), created in 1998	3.516
Sport Marketing Quarterly	http://fitpublishing.com/journals/smq	Affiliated with the SMA (Sport Marketing Association), first published in 1997	None
Sport, Business and Management	www.emeraldinsight.com/journal/sbm?expanded=undefined	Journal created in 2011.	None
Journal of Sponsorship	www.sponsormap.com/journal-of-sponsorship/	Journal created in 2008	None

in more generalist publications such as the *Journal of Consumer Research*, *Journal of Marketing*, *Academy of Management Journal*, etc.

We can see a very significant increase in the number of academic journals and articles published, but also an improvement in their "quality", as shown by their impact factor.[12]

3.2 The shift towards Asia and the Middle East, and away from Europe and the United States

History shows us that sport in the 19th century was primarily a European affair.

Companies gradually developed their sporting interests, creating clubs, some of whom would become legendary: FIAT's Juventus in Turin, Philips' PSV Eindhoven, Bayer's Bayer Leverkusen and Michelin's rugby team AS Montferrand. If the primary goal was to entertain the workers and improve their health through fitness, there was also, of course, a desire on the part of employers to "control" or even subjugate the workforce, with sport becoming the "opium of the people" so dear to Karl Marx. England, the birthplace of the industrial revolution, became the main source of these clubs, sometimes called "circles" in the case of organizations with more bourgeois connotations. Indeed, sport was also developing in the higher echelons of society, with riding (recalling the nobility, knights of old and the cavalry) promoting leadership values, or athletics and middle-distance running the idea of testing one's limits.

But the US economy started to take off at the beginning of the 20th century, with growth surpassing even that of Europe.

All the writing on sports sociology – including works in French by Pociello, Defrance, Duret and Ohl – shows that sporting activity automatically increases with higher income, qualifications, social class and urbanization. It was, therefore, logical that sport should develop in the United States, but with governance based on the private system (development of franchises and private leagues for professional sport) and school or university (high school, then university where the NCAA – National Collegiate Athletic Association – gradually became very powerful in sport and the development of semi-professional sports entertainment).

Gradually, the major world sporting competitions boiled down to a confrontation between the United States and Europe: The America's Cup in sailing, the Grand Slam tournaments in tennis, and the Olympic Games. The only exception was the football World Cup, where Europe was more in competition with South America.

It should be noted that before the 1956 Melbourne Olympics, this event had always been held in Europe or the United States and the medal tallies reflected this bias.

Television was also an important source of financial support for major sports events. From the first televised Olympics in Rome in 1960 to the 1990s, American networks and European channels accounted for around 90% of television rights.

This dominant position was also acknowledged by pioneering and far-sighted equipment maker Adidas. Company founder Adolf Dassler believed that the advent of television would benefit the most visible brands, and that it was necessary to seize this advantage before anyone else. That is why very early on he began sponsoring football teams for the World Cup, as well as dozens of sports federations around the world for the Olympics. The brand thus acquired a virtual monopoly (see Tables 1.18 and 1.19). But the arrival of Nike (in 1972) and the emergence of other brands in the 1990s led to the erosion of the brand's ranking.

The decline in market share is explained by the emergence of Nike, the revival of the Puma brand and, of course, increased competition across all sports: Reebok, ASICS, Mizuno, New Balance, Li-Ning, Hummel, Macron and Peak are just some of the many new players in the sports equipment sector.

NB: The emergence of the whole communist bloc after 1945 in the sports world and, in particular, the Olympics, should also be noted, replacing the traditional two-way split with a three-way division. But while this new power quickly made its presence felt on the playing field (with the USSR, Romania, Poland, Czechoslovakia, etc. taking a very large share of Olympic medals), that did not translate into sports business (TV rights, sponsorship, equipment manufacturers, event organization) for obvious political reasons. The Moscow Olympics, boycotted by the United States under the pretext of the Soviet invasion of Afghanistan, was really the only major sporting event organized by these countries.

Table 1.18 Adidas at the Olympics

1928	First appearance at the Olympics
1932	1st Olympic medal
1936	Jesse Owens wins four gold medals
1956	33 world records for Adidas
1960	75% of the competitors wear Adidas
1964	80% of the competitors wear Adidas
1968	85% of the competitors wear Adidas
1972	78% of medal winners wear Adidas footwear
1976	83% of the competitors wear Adidas
1980	63 medal winners at the Winter Olympics, and 85% of competitors at the Summer Olympics wear Adidas
1984	40 medal winners at the Winter Olympics, 259 at the Summer Olympics wear Adidas
1988	365 medal winners at the Summer Olympics wear Adidas
2002	55% of competitors at the Winter Olympics wear Adidas

Source: Adidas sales presentation, Olivier Lorans, 2003

Table 1.19 Adidas at the World Cup

1958	The majority of the players wear Adidas
1962	All 32 teams wear Adidas
1966	75% of the players wear Adidas
1970	85% of the players wear Adidas
1974, 1990, 1998	The winning teams wear Adidas

Source: Adidas sales presentation, Olivier Lorans, 2003

From the 1980s onwards, the rise of Asia in the global economy was reflected in a shift in sports business.

3.2.1 Organization of major sports events

The 1988 Summer Olympics in Seoul, the Sydney games in 2000, Beijing 2008, Tokyo 2020, Nagano in 1998, PyeongChang in 2018, Beijing in 2022, the football World Cup in South Africa in 2010 and the Rugby World Cup in Japan in 2021 are all major events which illustrate world sport's shift towards emerging countries and, in particular, Asia.

The world championships for athletics, the king of Olympic sports, were held in Osaka, Japan in 2007, Daegu, South Korea in 2011, Moscow in 2013 and Beijing in 2015, and are scheduled to take place in Doha in 2019.

The 2018 World Cup was held in Russia and is scheduled to take place in Qatar in 2022. China, led by President Xi Jinping, has made football a "national priority". China's aim is now to qualify for the competition, organize it (perhaps in 2030?) and, ideally, win it. If the first two stages of this plan seem relatively easy to achieve, the third could be tricky. Indeed, although China managed to climb to first or second place in the 2008 Olympic rankings (depending on how you count the medals won) with the United States, it is much easier to shine in individual sports (through naturalizations, the hiring of foreign coaches, application of proven training techniques, early scouting in the Chinese population, etc.) than to be competitive at a global level in the world's most popular and fiercely competitive sport.

Formula 1 is a good example of a closed organization that got to grips very early on with the ins and outs of sports marketing. A small group of people took charge of things from the very beginning, creating a monopoly which they transformed into a huge global business. National federations such as the FFSA (the French motorsport federation) found themselves excluded from this lucrative market, managing only the non-market-related (and therefore cost-generating, rather than money-making) aspects of the sport, such as the training of young drivers. The FFSA finds itself in a similar position to that of the French boxing and cycling federations in that it manages everything at the amateur level but finds itself shut out of the professional sport.

Box 1.8 Formula 1 organization and governance since the 1950s

Three bodies are responsible for organizing Formula 1 competitions:

- the Fédération Internationale de l'Automobile (FIA), chaired by Jean Todt, who is responsible for technical and sports management and sets the rules

- Formula One Administration (FOA, formerly FOCA), chaired by Bernie Ecclestone until January 2017, which holds the exclusive rights to the audio and video content of FIA competitions under the terms of the Concorde Agreements
- Formula One Management (FOM), which manages FOA's television and other rights

In the early 1970s, Ecclestone (who bought the Brabham team at the end of the 1971 season) decided to bring most of the Formula 1 teams together to form an association and so the Formula One Constructors Association (FOCA) quickly emerged with two main aims.

The revenue generated by the races, as well as team spending, increased considerably as public interest in the sport grew.

Organizing the sports side of the world championship had always been the exclusive responsibility of the International Sporting Commission.

Frenchman Jean-Marie Balestre tried to block the rise of Bernie Ecclestone's influential association from the moment he became president of the ISC (the sports arm of the FIA) which later became FISA, and so the FISA-FOCA war began. In 1981, the two adversaries decided to bury the hatchet, giving rise to the first version of the Concorde Agreements (named after the Place de la Concorde in Paris, where FIA/FISA has its headquarters), which outlines the division of power between FISA (which retains all authority in sporting and regulatory matters) and FOCA, with whom the FIA agreed to share the profits, leaving it in charge of the commercial side of the races.

When the first Concorde Agreements ended in 1987, Ecclestone decided to stop being a team owner and create FOPA (Formula One Promotions and Administration), a new body in charge of handling television rights for teams (FOPA later became Formula One Management). FOPA received 23% of TV rights revenue, with 47% going to the teams and 30% to FIA. However, FOPA also received rights payments from the Grand Prix organizers. Premiums were paid to the teams according to their performance.

In January 2017, the American group Liberty Media finalized a full purchase of Formula 1. Bernie Ecclestone was pushed aside after being in charge for 40 years in favour of a management trio composed of Chase Carey (president), Sean Bratches (sales director) and Ross Brawn (technical and sports director).

Source: *https://fr.wikipedia.org/wiki/Formule_1#Organisation* (last accessed December 1, 2017)

Table 1.20 Grand Prix host countries, past and present

Formula 1 Grand Prix – 2016	*From*	*Past Formula 1 Grand Prix*	*Years held*
British Grand Prix	1950	Indianapolis 500	1950–1960
Monaco Grand Prix	1950	Swiss Grand Prix	1950–1954/1982
Belgian Grand Prix	1950	French Grand Prix	1950–2008
Italian Grand Prix	1950	Netherlands Grand Prix	1952–1953/1955/1958–1971/1973–1985
German Grand Prix	1951	Argentine Grand Prix	1953–1958/1960/1972–1975/1977–1981/1995–1998
Spanish Grand Prix	1951	Pescara Grand Prix	1957
U.S. Grand Prix	1959	Portuguese Grand Prix	1958–1960/1984–1996
Mexican Grand Prix	1963	Moroccan Grand Prix	1958
Austrian Grand Prix	1964	South African Grand Prix	1962–1963/1965/1967–1980/1982–1985/1992–1993
Canadian Grand Prix	1967	Swedish Grand Prix	1973–1978
Brazilian Grand Prix	1973	U.S. Grand Prix (West)	1976–1983
Japanese Grand Prix	1976	U.S. Grand Prix (East)	1976–1980/1982–1983
European Grand Prix	1983	San Marino Grand Prix	1981–2006
Australian Grand Prix	1985	Las Vegas Grand Prix	1981–1982
Hungarian Grand Prix	1986	Detroit Grand Prix	1984–1988
Malaysian Grand Prix	1999	Dallas Grand Prix	1984
Bahrain Grand Prix	2004	Pacific Grand Prix	1994–1995
Chinese Grand Prix	2004	Luxembourg Grand Prix	1997–1998
Singapore Grand Prix	2008	Turkish Grand Prix	2005–2011
Abu Dhabi Grand Prix	2009	South Korean Grand Prix	2010–2013
Russian Grand Prix	2014	Indian Grand Prix	2011–2013

Source: https://fr.wikipedia.org/wiki/Grand_Prix_de_Formule_1

Formula One Management, set up as a "cash machine", has gradually built up a monopoly. Notably, it has the power to choose the racing circuits and, therefore, the countries, in which the F1 Grand Prix is held. It has taken advantage of this

Table 1.21 List of Grand Prix host nations for 2017 and 2018

	2017	*2018*
1	Australia	Australia
2	China	China
3	Bahrain	Bahrain
4	Russia	Azerbaijan
5	Spain	Spain
6	Monaco	Monaco
7	Canada	Canada
8	Azerbaijan	France
9	Austria	Austria
10	Great Britain	Great Britain
11	Hungary	Germany
12	Belgium	Hungary
13	Italy	Belgium
14	Singapore	Italy
15	Malaysia	Singapore
16	Japan	Russia
17	United States	Japan
18	Mexico	United States
19	Brazil	Mexico
20	Abu Dhabi	Brazil
21		Abu Dhabi

Source: *https://fr.wikipedia.org/wiki/Grand_Prix_de_Formule_1*

position to "up the ante", playing one country off against another, to get the best terms. Some countries have "got down on their knees and begged" to host part of "The Greatest Show on Earth".

The two previous tables show that the focus of Formula 1 has shifted towards Asia and the Middle East for several reasons:

- Increasingly strict legislation in Europe and North America on advertising by cigarette and alcohol manufacturers (e.g., France's 1991 Evin law) has led the organizers to turn to more "open" markets
- Emerging countries' desire to make a name for themselves on the world stage through sport
- Rising environmental concerns have made some European countries "car-phobic", with Formula 1 clearly no longer "socially acceptable" in the light of sustainable development concerns
- A higher standard of living in emerging countries has boosted demand for sports shows and, therefore, interest from television stations and sponsors there
- At the same time, the emergence of a new middle class in China, India, Malaysia, Russia and the Middle East is transforming these countries into new "natural" markets for car manufacturers.

Box 1.9 China remains the world's leading automotive market

At the Shanghai Auto Show in 2017, PwC Autofacts experts shared their analysis of the Chinese automotive market at the beginning of the year, that is, that the country will remain the world's leading automotive market.

In 2016, as in the previous year, the Chinese automotive market saw strong sales growth, up 13.3%, compared with 8.2% in 2015. According to PwC Autofacts, China should maintain its world leadership in 2017, with 28.2 million vehicles sold (+6.5% annual growth).

"*The majority of Chinese households now own a car. Particularly in rural areas in the centre and west of the country, they should continue to equip themselves with a first or second vehicle in the coming years, despite the slowdown in the country's economic growth*", commented François Jaumain, partner in charge of the Automotive sector at PwC.

- Slow but sustainable growth

Due to slower GDP growth in China in recent years (+6.7% in 2016, compared with +7.7% in 2012 and +9.6% in 2008), PwC Autofacts anticipates slower but continued automotive sector growth (in terms of production) over the next six years: +3.7% per year on average through to 2023. In addition, plant utilization, which has been declining since 2010, is expected to gradually increase to 78% by 2023.

- Strong growth in electric and hybrid vehicles

Public policies aimed at limiting carbon dioxide emissions have contributed to the development of electric and hybrid vehicles, known as NEVs (New Energy Vehicles). With production growth of 13.3% in this segment in 2016, NEV market share reached 2.6% of total assembled vehicles in China in 2016, rising to an estimated 4% in 2017.

PwC Autofacts analysts estimate that by 2023 electric and hybrid vehicles will account for 7.5% of the market, or 2.6 million vehicles, 1 million of which will be 100% electric. This growth should benefit domestic carmakers, who will produce more than half of the NEVs in circulation in 2023.

Source: http://auto-infos.fr/La-Chine-reste-le-premier-marche,9712 (last accessed December 1, 2017)

Cycling has recently attempted to go down a similar path to Formula 1 but, for historical reasons, has not been able to centralize revenue to the same extent.

The "Grand Tours" (France, Italy, Spain) and the prestigious "Classics" (Paris-Roubaix, the Tour of Flanders, Liège-Bastogne-Liège, Paris-Nice, etc.) are run by various organizations, such as the ASO (Amaury Sport Organisation) in France. These independent entities, which are sometimes very powerful financially and politically speaking, had complete control over their races until 2000, particularly over which teams were allowed to compete. The UCI (Union Cycliste Internationale) carried little weight when it came to governance in world cycling. A desire to take back control led this organization to launch the ProTour in 2004. By moving the seat of power to UCI headquarters, they have succeeded in making teams compete in more races, creating a system of "divisions with promotion and relegation", forcing teams to make long-term commitments and thereby drastically increase their annual operating budgets. The idea was also to take cycling international, making it an all-year-round global activity (with races in China, Australia, Africa, the Middle East, South America, Russia, Poland, the United States and Canada). From that point of view, the model is similar to that of the NBA and Formula 1, though with less control over the profits.

Box 1.10 The UCI World Tour

The UCI World Tour, known as the UCI ProTour until 2010, is a cycling competition bringing together teams and races that hold a World Tour licence. It was created in 2004 by the Union Cycliste Internationale, with its first season taking place in 2005. A maximum of 18 professional teams hold a UCI World Tour licence and are called World Teams. This status guarantees their participation in the circuit events. Riders are awarded points according to their ranking and the race category, making it possible to establish annual individual, team and nation World Tour classifications. These replace both the former UCI and the World Cup rankings.

Teams that do not have WorldTeam status may take part in these races but do not score points. The teams that do may participate in other events but score no points for these races (continental circuit rankings), which are, in any case, based on a different rating system.

In 2016, a UCI world ranking was created alongside the World Tour1 ranking. This classification was not limited to the status of teams and riders and took into account the entire international racing calendar, as it had over the period 1984 to 2004. Since 2017, the two rankings (World Tour and World) have used the same ratings system.

Source: https://fr.wikipedia.org/wiki/UCI_World_Tour (last accessed December 1, 2017)

Table 1.22 2017 World Tour teams by nationality

UCI WorldTeams		
Team name	*Country*	*Code*
AG2R La Mondiale	France	ALM
Astana	Kazakhstan	AST
Bahrain-Merida	Bahrain	TBM
BMC Racing	United States	BMC
Bora-Hansgrohe	Germany	BOH
Cannondale-Drapac	United States	CDT
Dimension Data	South Africa	DDD
FDJ	France	FDJ
Katusha-Alpecin	Switzerland	KAT
Lotto NL-Jumbo	Netherlands	TLJ
Lotto-Soudal	Belgium	LTS
Movistar	Spain	MOV
Orica-Scott	Australia	ORS
Quick-Step Floors	Belgium	QST
Sky	United Kingdom	SKY
Sunweb	Germany	SUN
Trek-Segafredo	United States	TFS
UAE Abu Dhabi	UAE	UAD

Source: *https://fr.wikipedia.org/wiki/UCI_World_Tour* (last accessed December 1, 2017)

As part of this trend, cycling has also become more international in terms of riders and teams (see Table 1.22), helping to make it a truly global sport.

Here too, the change can be explained by a geographical shift in the focus on cycling: Sponsors and television channels in emerging markets have invested massively in the sport, undermining Europe's traditionally dominant position.

3.2.2 Making leagues more international

The business side of any sport cannot develop if it gets stuck at a national or regional level, and this is still a major problem for rugby. Despite all the efforts of the IRB (International Rugby Board) whose 2021 World Cup will take place in Japan, the sport remains dominated by five or six countries at the international level: The three nations of the southern hemisphere, plus some European countries and Argentina. In these conditions, and despite the massive investment made by Rupert Murdoch's television channels in the *Tri Nations* (now the Four Nations) tournament, rugby's impact remains too limited. None of the major economic nations (United States, China, Russia, Germany, Italy, Spain, Brazil, South Korea) play rugby. That was the idea behind seven-a-side rugby, which became an Olympic sport at the Rio games in 2014, namely to boost rugby's development and international profile by making it easier to play, more accessible and simpler to organize. It already looks as if this strategy could pay off relatively quickly as there are a lot more countries taking part in seven-a-side than there are playing Rugby Union.

In France, rugby is also in a weak position because of the difficulty the TOP14 championship has had in shaking off its "regional" tag: It is hard to take things to the next level when the sport is too deeply rooted in the south and hardly present at all in the north, apart from two clubs in Paris. Given this situation, any hope of trying to make the LNR (*Ligue Nationale de Rugby* or National Rugby League) more international remains a pipe dream.

Unfortunately for the LNR, the geographical spread at the Pro D2 level is no better, which means rapid change would be difficult (see later).

Only a change in the way French rugby is run, with a powerful league able to set up teams from scratch in commercially attractive areas (basically the big cities in northern France) could alter things. But that would require a closed league model, with set-ups and relocations depending on financial projects backed by powerful investors in partnership with proactive local authorities.

The NHL has also had to face this "regional" problem, which was a major handicap to its development throughout North America. From when it started until 1967, the NHL was made up of six teams, all in the northeast of the region (Chicago, Detroit, New York and Boston in the United States, Montreal and Toronto in Canada). This meant that the league had little impact, with virtually no interest from either the public or the media, given that 90% of North America did not feel any connection with the sport.

It took a very proactive expansion policy on the part of the league and, in particular, very strict financial regulation (e.g., revenue sharing, where the historically profitable clubs in the northeast were forced to share their gains with the generally unprofitable teams in the west and the south) for the NHL to succeed in establishing a presence across the whole of North America (see Box 1.11).

Of course, the commercial activity of the NHL has become much more important, with merchandising, ticketing and TV rights increasing dramatically over time.

Box 1.11 NHL television rights in Canada and the United States

Canadian broadcasting rights have traditionally included Hockey Night in Canada (HNIC), a long-standing tradition dating back to 1952 on television, and even earlier to the 1920s on radio. Other Canadian broadcasters include CTV, Global, TSN and Sportsnet, with French-language programming on SRC and RDS.

Rogers Communications is the current holder of the tv and digital rights, under a 12-year agreement valued at C$5.2 billion that began in 2014–2015 and replaced CBC and Bell Media, respectively, as national rights holders.

In the United States, the NHL has traditionally never fared as well as the other American professional leagues. The league's US broadcast partners have been in constant flux for decades, and have included networks such as CBS, SportsChannel America, USA Network, Fox, ABC and ESPN.

The US national television rights are currently held by NBC Sports. The current 10-year $2 billion contract, which began in the 2011–2012 season, extended and unified rights agreements established for the 2005–2006 season, when Comcast (via OLN, later Versus) acquired cable rights to replace ESPN, and NBC acquired broadcast tv rights under a revenue-sharing agreement to replace ABC.

Source: *https://en.wikipedia.org/wiki/National_Hockey_League_on_television*

The financial clout of a North American team is directly correlated with the catchment area in which it operates. There are many geomarketing studies[13] that show the number of professional sports teams increases depending on the size of the urban area under consideration.

The process of taking the North American leagues international began in the 1990s, following the path established in the 1960s in product life cycle theory. A product typically goes through four stages (introduction, growth, maturity and decline) over time, and when revenue declines, there are several solutions:

- Innovate, and thus replace the product with another, as in the Schumpeterian "creative destruction" process
- Export the product to other markets to find new customers

The major American leagues chose to go down the second route (to varying degrees).

At the MLB (Major League Baseball), the process never really got underway. With 162 regular team matches per season (and a total of 2,430 matches per year!), average attendance of over 30,000 and more than 73 million tickets sold per year, the MLB has a domestic market that is sufficient for its needs. While it has begun a branding policy in the Spanish-speaking countries that are traditionally passionate about baseball, it is not really necessary for the MLB to go international.

Similarly, global expansion was not really an end in itself for the NFL (National Football League): With an average 68,000 spectators over the season, the phenomenal impact of the Super Bowl and especially the exorbitant TV rights in the United States, there is no real need to export American football. There are a few exceptions, with matches relocated to London (Wembley stadium since 2007, Twickenham since 2016) and Mexico City since 2016, but it is not a major part of the NFL's strategy, even though it developed a championship called NFL Europe in the 1990s.

NB: American football and baseball's desire to avoid becoming too international also results from the fact that both sports are very difficult for the uninitiated to understand and there is a very strong cultural barrier. They are typically seen as the "most American" sports, not only in people's minds but also for the purpose of building national unity through sport, American football being more of an urban and university-based sport, and baseball more of a rural and midwestern game.

The NBA, however, had to start its international push much earlier. With fewer games than in baseball, much less TV revenue than American football and smaller venues (and thus, fewer ticket sales), the NBA needed an international strategy to increase revenue.

This was achieved in several ways:

- The recruitment of more foreign players, boosting the impact the NBA has in their home countries. In 2016, there were 113 foreign players representing 41 different countries (including 10 from France, the next largest group after Canada).[14] China's Yao Ming, France's Tony Parker, Germany's Dirk Nowitzki, Spain's Pau Gasol, Argentina's Manu Ginobili are all legendary players who have helped establish new markets for the NBA.
- NBA match tours in Europe, such as the NBA Europe Live Tour (pre-season matches organized since 2006) or regular season matches at the O2 Arena in London (16th edition in January 2018) help to grow and engage with the "remote" fan community, according to the well-known theory that showing people the product helps them to like it.
- Following these two moves, the logical progression was an increase in export TV rights,[15] thereby increasing both match broadcasts and audiences, resulting ultimately in higher merchandising revenue.

European football has more or less followed the same path as the NBA over the last 10 years. Relatively "cramped" on the European market, where the population is both ageing and stagnating, it cannot count on a potential increase in income there in the near future:

- TV rights have increased considerably but will not continue rising forever in Europe, so only selling these rights on other markets will make further increases possible
- Sponsorship deals (in particular, contracts with equipment manufacturers) have also grown exponentially and are set to plateau[16]
- Almost all the major European clubs have a fill rate close to 100% at their home grounds, which means there is little hope of increasing ticket sales

It is the international TV rights that have driven the English Premier League's income to such high levels, not without raising some fairness and balance issues

Tables 1.23a and 1.23b Average and total attendance for the major professional sports leagues worldwide

Top 10 leagues in total attendance[17]

League	*Sport*	*Country*	*Season*	*Games*	*Average attendance*	*Total attendance*
Major League Baseball	Baseball	United States/ Canada	2015	2,430	30.517	73,760,020
Nippon Professional Baseball	Baseball	Japan	2015	848	28,248	24,236,920
National Basketball Association	Basketball	United States/ Canada	2015–2016	1,230	17,864	21,972,129
National Hockey League	Ice hockey	United States/ Canada	2015–2016	1,230	17,481	21,501,156
National Football League	American football	United States	2015	256	68,400	17,510,312
Premier League	Association football	England/Wales	2015–2016	380	36,451	13,851,698
Bundesliga	Association football	Germany	2015–2016	306	42,421	12,980,815
La Liga	Association football	Spain	2015–2016	380	27,739	10,541,068
Football League Championship	Association football	England/Wales	2015–2016	552	17,577	9,703,004
Ligue 1	Association football	France	2015–2016	380	20,894	7,939,636

Top 10 Stadiums in total attendance in a calendar year[18]

Stadium	*Sport(s)*	*Country*	*Season*	*Games*	*Average attendance*	*Total attendance*
Dodger Stadium	Baseball	United States	2015	81	46,479	3,764,815
Yankee Stadium	Baseball/ Association Football	United States	2015 2015	97	38,011	3,687,062
Busch Stadium	Baseball	United States	2015	81	43,467	3,520,889
AT&T Park	Baseball	United States	2015	81	41,677	3,375,882
Melbourne Cricket Ground	Cricket/ Australian Rules Football/ Association Football	Australia/ International	2015 2015 2015	60	51,859	3,111,593
Angel Stadium of Anaheim	Baseball	United States	2015	81	37,194	3,012,765
Tokyo Dome	Baseball	Japan	2015	71	42,270	3,001,187
Wrigley Field	Baseball	United States	2015	81	36,540	2,959,812
Fenway Park	Baseball	United States	2015	81	35,564	2,880,694
Koshien Stadium	Baseball	Japan	2015	71	39,977	2,878,352

Source: *https://en.wikipedia.org/wiki/List_of_sports_attendance_figures* (last accessed December 1, 2017)

at the European level, since the team at the bottom of the English league earns more than the national champions in the other "Big 5" countries (Germany, Italy, Spain, France).

Table 1.24 shows that the Latin countries are lagging when it comes to fill rates. While this can partly be explained by the economic crisis, it can also be blamed on the condition of the stadiums, particularly in Italy. France took advantage of the renovation or construction of stadiums for Euro 2016 to improve capacity and/or comfort at its grounds (Marseille, Bordeaux, Lyon, Nice and Lille).

At the individual club level, Arsenal, Manchester United, Chelsea, Bayern Munich, Dortmund and Juventus are the fill-rate champions.

In Europe, higher income is only possible through an increase in all forms of commercial revenue, including VIP seats and boxes ("hospitality programmes"), catering and drinks and merchandising (sales of tie-in products, especially team shirts). Merchandising is a key factor on the Asian market.

For years, the famous Asian tours have helped spread the fame of European football teams and their stars. While necessary to ensure the clubs' notoriety and image in these countries (i.e., "showing the product"), they are nevertheless very difficult to organize in longer seasons where downtime for the players is minimal, particularly in World Cup or Euro years. Indeed, in the economics of professional sport, the production of a service is carried out using limited, unique and non-duplicable resources (the players): It is not possible to build a new production unit, such as a second factory, when demand increases. That is what makes it so special: There is only one Ronaldo and he is the one the fans in China, Japan, Indonesia or India want to see! The tours will often be combined with the

Table 1.24 Fill rates for European league stadiums (2015–2016 data)

COUNTRY	*COMPETITION*	*LEAGUE*	*AVERAGE UTILIZATION*
ENG-PL	Premier League	Premier League	94.95%
GER-DFL	Bundesliga	Deutsche Fussball Liga GmbH	91.27%
NED-ED	Eredivisie	Eredivisie CV	88.23%
FRA-LFP	Ligue 1 Conforama	Ligue de Football Professionnel	70.67%
ESP-LL	Liga Santander	LaLiga | Liga De Fútbol Profesional	67.50%
NOR-TF	Eliteserien	Norsk Toppfotball	63.33%
SCO-PFL	Ladbrokes Premiership	Scottish Professional Football League	61.89%
BEL-PL	Jupiler Pro League	Belgium Pro League	58.22%
ITA-A	Serie A Tim	Lega Serie A	57.11%

Source: *https://europeanleagues.com/wp-content/uploads/FINAL-EPFL_FA_18-VERSION-2018.01.12.pdf* (last accessed October 31, 2018)

opening of a "football academy" to spot new talent. Every club dreams of discovering "the next Chinese Messi" who would be the best ambassador imaginable, as Yao Ming was for the NBA and basketball in China when he was drafted by the Houston Rockets in 2002 (he spent his entire career with them until he retired from the game in 2011). David Beckham, who joined PSG in February 2013, only played until June of the same year, but then became the club's ambassador, allowing it to benefit from his image as a global icon.[19]

Sometimes clubs also sign so-called regional sponsorship deals, which are a new take on the usual process. Traditionally, clubs look for sponsors who are looking to improve their notoriety or image in order to boost sales, in exchange for a sum of money paid to the club. In "regional" sponsorship, this process is reversed. The club seeks out sponsors in countries where it may be in its interest to increase its influence and develop its relationship with the fans. The club's motivation, therefore, is not the revenue gain, but the potential market that may open up.

Box 1.12 2016 brings an Indonesian partner for PSG

PSG announced on Monday the signing of its first "global" partnership with an Indonesian tyre brand, and as a result, the Multistrada group is now linked to the Paris-based club until 2019.

PSG chose to sign the three-year agreement with Multistrada in one of the French automobile industry's top venues, the Automobile Club de France. The Indonesian tyre group is better known to car fans through its main Achilles brand. This "global" accord is being presented as a first, because until now PSG only had this kind of partnership with Qatari companies. Both PSG and the Indonesian company declined to say how much Multistrada will invest in the club.

What is a "global" partnership?

At PSG, there is a sponsorship pyramid. At the very top are the shirt sponsors and just below them are the "global" international partnerships, a select group of six to eight companies featured on the LED panels around the field on match nights at the Parc des Princes.

Why sign with an Indonesian group?

Indonesia has 255 million inhabitants, making it the world's fourth most populous country. It is a market that PSG has been eyeing for more than three years, in fact in 2013 the club launched a version of its website in Bahasa, the country's first language. A move that paid off, because a year and a half ago, PSG and Multistrada began initial talks. "*Indonesia is clearly a very connected country web-wise, and its young people are football mad. Thanks to this, we're going to develop our presence there alongside a young company (Multistrada was set up in 1988) that has big international ambitions*", said Frédéric Longuépée, deputy director of PSG.

Is an Indonesian trip on the cards for PSG?

Over the past three years, the Parisian team has got into the habit of going on summer tours abroad. This season, PSG is going to the United States (west coast July 21–30), but Asia could be on the itinerary very soon, according to Frédéric Longuépée. "*We haven't yet decided on our destination for 2017, but after two years in the USA, it seems likely that we'll go to Asia and, why not, Indonesia*".

Source: www.francebleu.fr/sports/football/economie-un-sponsor-indonesien-pour-le-psg-1464014812 (last accessed December 1, 2017)

This strategy of going international has also been made possible by the Internet and social media which have helped make both players and teams better known (see next section).

3.2.3 The role of the Internet in building a loyal customer- and fan-base

The Internet, connected stadiums, social media, fan relationship management, social landmarks, etc. are all issues that have set the sports marketing community buzzing in recent years. As mentioned previously, clubs are developing and putting in place sometimes costly social media strategies to get a return on investment (ROI), or at the very least a return on objectives. If this communication via social media by all sports brands (including equipment makers, sponsors, event organizers, federations, venues, stadiums and arenas, athletes) seems obvious, necessary, useful and profitable, given the importance of emotional connection and the concept of customer experience, that is not the case for B2B, utilitarian or less emotionally charged brands. What exactly is the link between a customer and a producer of taps, or flour, or silicon rubber seals, fertilizers and electric fences?

Sports brands these days design their advertising strategy by and for social media. As with product innovation, Nike is ahead of the curve and now spends 50% of its $2.4 billion advertising budget on the web and digital resources (see Box 1.13).

Box 1.13 Nike's social media strategy

From being first off the starting blocks, Nike now has millions of fans on Facebook, Instagram and Twitter. Its applications have also allowed it to create sports communities, particularly for runners. All formidable weapons in the battle for customer loyalty.

Every Wednesday at 7 pm, the same scene plays out close to the Sorbonne in Paris, as hundreds of runners congregate in front of the nearby Nike store. They don't necessarily know each other but they're all here for the same thing; a 10km run along the Seine with the Nike+ Run Club (NRC). At the front of the line, dressed from head to toe in Nike, are the "pacers" like Mathieu, a sports teacher by day, who is here to make a little extra cash: "*We come here to go running with our mates and to make new ones*", he sums up, while using his megaphone to gee up the 70% female crowd.

Four of these sessions, on average, take place every week in Paris. Participants do not have to wear Nike shoes, but everything possible is done to encourage it: The coaches' tips, the Nike Running France Facebook page which you have to sign up to (246,429 members) and the use of the Nike+ Running app, which lets you analyze your performance.

Created 10 years ago in New York, NRC is now the world's biggest runners' community, with six million fans sharing their experiences, posting photos and taking part in races.

Even if all sports brands have now made the switch to digital, Nike is still leading the pack. Consistently since 2010, its social media presence has been unrivalled in the sector: 130 million followers on Facebook, 50 million more than Adidas. It is the same story on Twitter where Nike has 17 million subscribers, twice as many as Adidas. And on the photo- and video-sharing platform Instagram, it is even more impressive. With 43 million fans, Nike is one of the world's Top 3 most-followed brands, alongside National Geographic and lingerie group Victoria's Secret.

Half of the $2.4 billion Nike spends every year on marketing now goes on the Web and digital resources, and the other half on traditional media, according to consultants NDP. And it works: in 2014, the year of the Brazilian World Cup, two of its ads were among the 10 most watched on YouTube, with a huge audience of over 100 million views.

Source: www.capital.fr/entreprises-marches/nike-cartonne-sur-les-reseaux-sociaux-avec-ses-applis-running-1143785 (last accessed December 1, 2017)

If the digital connection with fans is important in the product and leisure sports fields, it is even more so in the case of spectator sport events. Brand strategy is often conceived by and for digital resources. Virality is what determines the success of ads longer than five minutes in a format deliberately designed for social media (the length and cost, for example, would be completely prohibitive for TV or cinema broadcasts).

Digital is by far the most effective way to get a message across internationally. Access to the Chinese market is via WeChat, not Facebook, and Nike has already been working on that for several years (see Box 1.14).

Box 1.14 Digital ad campaigns during major sporting events: the Nike example

- **The success of Nike's marketing campaigns on WeChat**

What makes a marketing campaign successful? Nike can show us a couple of examples with its "Find your greatness" campaign launched in 2012 at the London Olympics, and with 2015's "Better for it" campaign. Let's take a look back at these campaigns and, in particular, how Nike managed to make an impact in China, via WeChat.

- **"Find your greatness"**

This was based on the idea that, unlike in traditional campaigns highlighting athletes and prestigious achievements (i.e., "You're only important if you win gold"), personal glory and greatness belong to those who decide to put their trainers on, get out there and play sport, even if it isn't at the highest level.

- **Nike first adapts to Chinese cumture, then changes it**

The Chinese are raised to seek excellence, with lots of activities and little tolerance for failure. This can quickly become an obstacle to playing sports as a hobby.

"Chinese kids don't play sports because they're afraid of failure".

- **The Golden Age of social media: WeChat**

We know that China has the largest number of Internet users in the world, and that 90% of them use mobile phones to connect to the Web via social media.

Using WeChat, Nike planned to work from 2012 on the brand's commitment to its customers, saying it wanted to change strategy by building its CRM system on the WeChat platform,

- **WeChat**

Launched in 2011, the mobile platform quickly became a benchmark for Chinese social media and is now the most popular platform.

Nike used the social network to implement a "storytelling" marketing strategy, both on- and offline. The brand put QR codes in public places, taxis and on posters and flyers, allowing people to subscribe to Nike's official WeChat account just by scanning the QR code.

- **Campaign success**

Nike was not the official sponsor for the London Olympics, that was Adidas, despite expectations to the contrary during the campaign.

- **Who runs the world?**

When Tencent launched the WeChat mobile app in 2011, Nike saw the potential of the mobile messaging platform and immediately took advantage of it, starting with its first global marketing campaign at the 2012 London Olympic Games. Now it's turning to women.

- **"Better For It" marketing campaign (2015)**

Following the success of its previous campaign, Nike has continued in the same vein but this time targeting women.

Source: www.marketing-chine.com/analyse-marketing/nike-le-succes-de-ses-campagnes-marketing-sur-wechat (last accessed December 1, 2017)

The race to win fans and followers internationally is something of an obsession for European football clubs. If the strength of a brand is measured primarily by its results on the pitch, with a Champions League win (something neither Manchester City nor PSG had managed by 2017) seen as the ultimate achievement, competition is also rife on the digital playing field. Indeed, what were once called "long-distance supporters" (fans of a team who do not live in the same town, or even in the same country) have practically become the norm, what with the teams becoming more international following the Bosman ruling in 1995, the boom in smartphones and tablets that make it possible for fans to watch videos whenever and wherever they want, and the spread of Wi-Fi and digital resources that allow teams to stay in touch with fans by showing scenes from the changing room and other "exclusive" content.

Living in Paris and liking Bayern Munich, supporting Arsenal in Marseille or being a Liverpool fan in Strasbourg, all of these situations are becoming increasingly commonplace, which is why FRM, or Fan Relationship Management, is gradually replacing CRM. The aim is to grow the fan base and then monetize it, which means selling them tie-in products (starting with team shirts), increasing the value of sponsorship deals and even looking at new ways of broadcasting.

"Pay per view" for single matches is a real driver of revenue growth from these consumers; if there is no real financial incentive for Chinese channel CCTV to show a Dortmund match during prime time, the game could still interest several thousand German expats who might pay €10 via Facebook or some other social network to watch it. Apply that thinking to a large number of other countries worldwide and revenue could quickly grow exponentially, particularly when a club plays about 60 matches a year.

Football clubs have also positioned themselves strongly in digital resources because there could be significant change in the way championship matches are shown. The financial resources of GAFA (Google, Amazon, Facebook, Apple) and their desire to create social links, consumer experiences, brand capital, and thus business, is pushing them more and more towards acquiring television rights to the world's biggest sports events. This is one of the key issues for the French Ligue 1 in its call for bids for 2020 rights, given that Amazon has already bought some of the rights to Germany's Bundesliga, that Facebook shows NBA games and Twitter NHL matches in the United States and that Amazon acquired the right to broadcast 10 NFL games for $50 million in April 2017.[20]

This strategy focusing on digital resources was introduced several years ago by PSG, which made sure it had a presence on all platforms and media (see Box 1.15). Indeed, given all the targets and the cultural, legal or institutional differences in the various countries, a single global digital strategy is unworkable. Some like photos, some videos and others "stories". If Facebook is the market leader in the west, it is banned or "filtered" in China, where it has been replaced by WeChat, while Telegram is dominant in Russia or Iran. All the more reason to diversify your digital tool box.

Table 1.25 The 25 football clubs with the strongest global digital presence (as of July 2017)

Club	*Digital community*
FC Barcelona	206 Million
Réal Madrid	205 Million
Manchester United	111 Million
Chelsea	76 Million
Arsenal	63 Million
Bayern Münich	61 Million
Liverpool	48 Million
Juventus	45 Million
PSG	45 Million
Manchester City	43 Million

Source: www.sportune.fr/wp-content/gallery/clubs-plus-influents-digital/Clubs-influents-digital-foot.jpg (last accessed December 1, 2017)

Box 1.15 PSG's quest to become a digital champion

Since its acquisition by Qatar's QSI in 2011, the Parisian football club has climbed its way into the top 10 most famous sports clubs in the world. Frédéric Longuépée, PSG's deputy managing director, looks back at the digital strategy used to transform the fans into Paris Saint-Germain brand customers.

Mid-season, Paris Saint-Germain football club currently ranks third in France's Ligue 1, with results that fall short of last year's victory. However, if there is one area in which the club, created in 1970, excels, it is digital resources. Social media, mobile apps, a connected stadium, the Parc des Princes team is building its presence in all areas in order to become an iconic brand. "*Beyond our performance and the visibility it gives the brand, becoming a major international sports brand is difficult, if not impossible, without a powerful digital strategy*", says Frédéric Longuépée, PSG's deputy managing director.

• Optimizing the customer experience for fans

"*We've yet to find a better way of promoting a product than word of mouth*", Frédéric Longuépée points out. Quality of experience is therefore of paramount importance. An experience that begins as soon as the ticket is purchased (at the ground, via PSG's online ticket office or on its own integrated Ticketplace exchange/resale platform launched last August), unfolds during the match and continues into everyday life.

For matches at the Parc des Princes, the Parisian team's home ground, the focus is very much on the customer experience, as the former deputy director of the French tennis federation explains: "*If supporters choose to come to the stadium, we need to make sure that the experience is at least as pleasant as if they were watching the match in their own sitting room*".

• Promoting the brand digitally

In order to increase its customer knowledge, the club focuses on content platforms. Facebook (more than 26 million fans on the main page), Twitter (4 million followers for the French account), Instagram (7 million followers), Snapchat, YouTube, etc. PSG was ranked as the 15th most influential sports team worldwide in a Forbes list published last June. Its deputy managing director nevertheless maintains that a numbers race "*makes no sense if we're not able to identify and communicate with the fans*".

Source: www.e-marketing.fr/Thematique/media-1093/Breves/Comment-PSG-veut-devenir-champion-digital-312438.htm#A2bdZcIEfWBUjsOj.97 (last accessed December 1, 2017)

Finally, the entire brand strategy has been overhauled, with digital just one means of reaching the goal, rather than an end in itself. And the cost is not negligible, contrary to what people thought at the outset. Getting started on Facebook may be free, but doing effective business there is costly.

Without an international branding approach, conceived and developed to increase awareness and popularity, social media would not be effective. That was the reasoning behind the repositioning of the PSG brand starting in 2013.

Box 1.16 A new logo and visual identity for PSG

The date the club was founded no longer appears on the PSG logo, and so QSI can use it for all divisions of its multisport brand. To put it another way, it is no longer exclusively the logo of PSG football club, but rather that of the multisport brand. The change of logo in 2013 was an important step in the process of building the PSG brand and taking it global. In this way, the club has adopted a visual identity that showcases its values, its home town and its history. An identity that reflects its strategy and is part of a drive to raise the Parisian club to the status of a major global sports brand, to bring it into the circle of the world's best-known commercial franchises. There is a dream element to this visual identity, the dream that Paris embodies the world over. The city of Paris, at the heart of the club's identity, is supposed to infuse it with its own strength and aspirations, both ethical (freedom, the quest for perfection, rigour etc.) and aesthetic (beauty, elegance etc.). If the new logo is a sign of PSG's global ambitions, the club does not want to break away from its roots completely. So the new logo contains a few modifications.

The cradle, representing the birth of Louis XIV at Saint Germain-en-Laye, no longer seemed very meaningful and so, reasonably enough, it was replaced by the fleur de lys, a symbol of French royalty. The date of the club's creation, 1970, was also removed as it didn't really bear comparison with rival clubs such as Manchester United (1878), Juventus (1897), Bayern Munich (1900) or Real Madrid (1902). Paris' iconic Eiffel Tower has been made smaller, but it has also been moved to the centre of the logo. "Paris", a global icon in itself, is now more imposing, taking up the upper half of the logo. "Saint-Germain" has been disconnected from Paris and moved to the lower half of the logo to make it easier to read. Elsewhere, red and blue, the club's traditional colours, are still there, though the blue has been made a little more intense to bring it closer to the famous Paris blue, and the red is brighter to provide better contrast. A touch of gold, symbolizing excellence, has also been added. The logo appears on anything and everything that seeks to convey the brand's strategic vision. More than ever, PSG wants to link its brand image with that of Paris. Frédéric Longuépée explained the reasons for this change: "*The idea is to stake a claim on Paris, to bind ourselves to this city's extraordinary values, its high standards, respect and elegance. We wanted to place Paris at the heart of this redesigned logo*".

Source: Chapter 13 of "Marketing et Football", Chanavat, N., Desbordes, M. (2015), Editions Economica, 623 pages, November.

3.2.4 "Country branding" and legitimization through sport: What strategies should Qatar and China adopt, and to what ends?

The aim here is not to compare these two countries' relationship with sport. However, both have invested massively in the sector, although not at the same time nor with the same aims

- **Case study 1: Qatar, or "soft power" politics through sport**[21]

In 2011, Qatar bought PSG and aimed to use it to win its first Champions League. However, if Qatar's sports policy is often summed up in France as this one achievement, the takeover was actually part of a much more global sports policy.

Qatar is a small country, 11,586 square km (the size of the Ile-de-France region around Paris), with a population of 2.6 million (only 300,000 of whom are Qataris). It is also the richest country in the world with GDP per capita of $128,000.

It suffers from a bad image, accused of financing extremism and Islamist terrorism. At the same time, it fears falling victim to "Kuwait syndrome", named after the small, very rich country with a weak military which was invaded by Saddam Hussein's Iraq in 1990. It therefore needs military support in order to ensure its protection.

So Qatar embarked on a strategic shift that was both unique and impressive in geopolitics to quickly and sustainably change its image through sport. In addition to football, the most visible part of the iceberg, thanks to PSG and its controversial selection as host country for the 2022 World Cup, Qatar hosted dozens of world and Asian championships, while sponsoring numerous events and teams (FC Barcelona, Grand Prix de l'Arc de Triomphe).

The strategy was exactly that of a private company looking to make sponsorship deals: be known, be liked, and ultimately, be bought. In Qatar's case, "being bought" means doing business in Europe, for example by acquiring stakes in large French CAC 40 companies, or making prestigious real-estate investments in Paris. If PSG had not been so well known to politicians, the media and the public, these investments would probably not have been possible. Mohamed Al-Fayed, an Egyptian billionaire, had done a similar thing: Before buying Harrod's, the famous London department store that supplies HM the Queen, he had taken care to invest massively in Fulham football club "with no ulterior motive".

Similarly, Roman Abramovitch ensured his international notoriety and helped his image with the purchase of Chelsea FC which put him centre stage, enabling him to do all kinds of business linked to football (in England, but also in Russia in real estate, among other things).

So, even if it is difficult, if not impossible, to make money in football, the change of image it can bring makes it possible to do a lot of other business. In this sense, football is more like cinema or other parts of the entertainment industry, rather than just an activity like any other.

Box 1.17 Select webography for Qatar's sports policy

www.lesechos.fr/week-end/business-story/enquetes/030784621435-le-qatar-si-riche-et-si-mal-aime-2125720.php
www.cairn.info/load_pdf.php?ID_ARTICLE=GEOEC_062_0067
www.cairn.info/article.php?ID_ARTICLE=COME_084_0117
www.lejournalinternational.fr/Le-Qatar-nouvel-acteur-du-sport-a-l-international_a2744.html
www.rfi.fr/sports/20170606-crise-qatar-consequences-monde-sport-psg-mondial-foot-2022-bein
www.lepoint.fr/sport/le-qatar-royaume-de-la-diplomatie-sportive-06-06-2017-2133217_26.php
www.huffpostmaghreb.com/2017/06/14/crise-qatar-sport-coupe-monde_n_17094186.html

(last accessed December 1, 2017)

• Case study 2: Football in China, or how to establish oneself as a world power through sport?

Football, and indeed sport more generally in China, is a completely different affair from what we have seen in Qatar.

China is a huge country in terms of its surface area (9,596,961 square km) and population (1.4 billion inhabitants in 2017). Communist since 1949, it gradually opened itself up to capitalism after Deng Xiaoping came to power in 1978 and the reforms of the 1980s. In doing so, the country has opened up at all levels: Political, economic and sporting. Gradually, it has returned to centre stage and understood all the benefits sport can bring internationally when it comes to establishing a country's power and visibility. This policy's major achievement occurred at the Beijing Olympics where China succeeded in becoming the leading (or second, depending on the medal-counting method used) sporting power on the planet, neck and neck with the United States. These 2008 Olympic Games were also an opportunity to demonstrate the country's power with facilities of an originality and quality never seen before, flawless organization, an unprecedented respect for deadlines, and, or course, sporting success. Thus, these Olympic Games confirmed China's pre-eminence, way ahead of Japan, Russia, Germany or France, economically speaking.

This trend has continued ever since and, after starting with rather "easy" sports (i.e., where there was little competition), China has decided to conquer the world's biggest: Football. Beforehand though, the country won the right to host the 2022 Winter Olympics, Beijing becoming the first city in history to organize both the Summer and Winter games.

Taking on football will be trickier: It is the world's leading sport, totally global, extremely competitive, and one where Europe and South America have been present for over 100 years. President Xi Jinping was one of the architects of this massive commitment to football and he has set specific objectives for the country over the past few years:

- Qualify for the World Cup
- Host the World Cup
- Win the World Cup

The first target was missed in 2018, when China failed to qualify, despite a rather easy group. The country will have to wait until 2022 to up its game.

The second should be easier to pull off. The financial firepower and enthusiasm of the public, the quality of facilities now that professional football has really taken off in China, the attractiveness of the plan for local investors and the event organizing skills already mentioned would all enable China to offer a top-class event. People are already talking about 2030 being the year they show their strength.

However, the third target will be difficult to meet as the national team remains weak by international standards.

Even if President Xi Jinping's impact on football is indisputable, this movement should not be dismissed as "the whim of an autocratic head of state". The whole country is now football mad. That is why China has invested massively in football in recent years, in several different ways:

- The purchase of European players was the trigger. At first, they were South American or European players whose careers were coming to an end (Anelka or Drogba), then came players and/or coaches of a higher standard (Tevez, Oscar)
- Then the country got Chinese businessmen involved as sponsors or shareholders in its biggest clubs (Jack Ma of Alibaba, Pony Ma of Tencent, Baidu's Robin Li)
- Chinese companies have increased their stakes in European clubs[22]:

The policy towards young footballers has changed and scouting now starts very early in schools. Giant academies have also been set up, sometimes financed by major European clubs.

If the arrival of professional football has been marred by numerous scandals, corruption, rigged matches and/or betting, the situation seems to be improving and we are moving towards a real business model in the financial sense. But the construction of a global sector that is both economically viable and capable of great sporting success will necessarily take time.

Box 1.18 Select webography for football in China

www.francetvinfo.fr/monde/chine/le-plan-de-la-chine-pour-devenir-une-superpuissance-du-football_1307000.html

www.lexpress.fr/actualite/sport/football/quand-la-chine-s-eveillera-au-foot_1798718.html

http://sport24.lefigaro.fr/le-scan-sport/2017/01/12/27001-20170112 ARTFIG00210-l-academie-de-foot-chinoise-de-la-demesure-a-canton.php
www.gavroche-thailande.com/actualites/sport/107-academie-jean-marc-guillou-les-futures-stars-du-foot-thailandais
www.lesechos.fr/23/09/2015/lesechos.fr/021347586271_pekin-cree-plus-de-8-600-ecoles-specialisees-dans-le-football.htm
www.letemps.ch/sport/2016/09/12/guangzhou-evergrande-roi-football-chinois

(Last accessed December 1, 2017)

Conclusion: On to new topics and areas of investigation

At the end of this chapter, it is clear how much the sports marketing ecosystem has changed over the past 20 years. From this point of view, sport has been able to skip a few steps, compared with more traditional business sectors.

Thus, in the automotive world, the Ford T made its appearance in 1908, but did not need marketing. With little competition and strong demand, the only aim was cost reduction, not product differentiation. Marketing came in the 1930s when the General Motors group started to differentiate its brands according to customers' needs, their habits, financial means and the importance of the image given to the product (the Cadillac was high-end, Oldsmobile and Buick mid-range, with Chevrolet and Pontiac at entry-level). Then gradually, in the 1950s, the automobile industry began to adopt traditional marketing, making the "marketing mix" (the famous "4Ps": Product, price, place, promotion) the cornerstone of their strategy. Finally, changes in consumption patterns, economic crises and the emergence of new competitors led manufacturers to rethink their marketing approach, making it less "transactional" and more "experiential". Some manufacturers such as Audi or BMW have transformed their points of sale, which are now similar to luxury boutiques or Nespresso stores, making the customer a "permanent VIP".

This journey towards merchandising and "marketization" has been much more rapid in sports business. As we have seen, some major sports were still amateur just 20 years ago. Recent upheaval and the speed of change brought about by new technologies have created an even more fluid environment. These days, it is unthinkable to devise a communications strategy that is not "viral" or "digital", to build a stadium that is not "connected" and "multifunctional", to come up with a marketing strategy that is not "anti-ambush", to implement ticketing tools without thinking about yield management and CRM, and all this while respecting the environmental, economic and social standards that characterize sustainable development.

These challenges will make sports marketing even more exciting in the years to come for organizations that are able to adapt to this hyper-connected constantly changing environment.

Notes

1 Since 1984 and the first live broadcasts of League 1 matches on television, French football clubs want to be Canal +, BeIn Sports or SFR Sports' "first choice". The clubs know that the more their games are shown, the more famous their players will be, and the popularity of the club will increase.

Back in 1978, TF1 created Telefoot, and the league offered rival channel Antenne 2 money to produce a programme on the French 1st division. Antenne 2 refused, not seeing any interest in such a programme. Today, the situation has, of course, been completely reversed and it is the channels that are competing for sport, and football in particular, in some cases for hundreds of millions of euros.

2 The dependency rate represents public funds (subsidies from the state and the CTS) in a federation budget.

3 Here Deloitte's approach prevails; there are only three types of income listed for a football club, whereas traditionally statistics separate sponsorship from commercial activities (merchandising), leading to an analysis of the budget using four types of income.

4 In 2016, Real Madrid collected €80 million of the total €1.35 billion distributed. Manchester United did not qualify, so they did not get anything. Cf. https://fr.uefa.com.

5 China not included. With China, the 1998 World Cup reached an audience of 40 billion and, in 2002, 42.6 billion. The aggregate audience is the total number of viewers for all World Cup finals matches. The average audience for a 2002 World Cup match was around 659 million viewers.

6 This profitability rationale came into force in the mid-2000s, and intensified during the financial crisis after 2008. Companies have moved from being "patrons" to "sponsors", which implies that they are accountable both internally to their managers and externally to their shareholders.

7 This process is classically presented as taking place in this order by all sponsoring specialists. And it is true that a product that is not liked cannot be bought, while a product that is not known cannot be liked.

8 We are referring here to a famous expression coined by Alain Loret, former professor of Sports Management at the University of Rouen.

9 The Bosman judgment is a decision of the European Court of Justice (ECJ) on December 15, 1995, abolishing nationality quotas for players from the 1996–1997 season onwards. The result is that a club's financial power ensures that it can recruit the best players. In 2000, the Malaja ruling extended this measure to players from Eastern European and African countries. Bosman was a footballer while Malaja was a basketball player.

10 During the 2010 FIFA World Cup, the French team players "went on strike" to protest against the dismissal of their team-mate Nicolas Anelka, accused of having insulted coach Raymond Domenech. The incident caused a public outcry, and came just eight months after Thierry Henry's famous "handball" led to the team qualifying, without glory, against Ireland. Since 2010, and in order to show its commitment, ethics and transparency, the FFF grants a "discount" to its partners if regular checks against various benchmarks show that its image has deteriorated.

11 With the exception of the University of Limoges, which created the CDES (sports law and business centre) in 1978, the University of Paris Dauphine, which had a master's degree in "sports management" science and techniques for some 15 years (diploma now no longer available) or a few university management schools which have agreements with sports science faculties (STAPS).

12 The impact factor, sometimes abbreviated to IF, is an indicator that estimates the visibility of a scientific journal. The IF of a journal is the average number of citations of each article published in that journal. Impact factors, which indeed measure a certain visibility, are considered by some research managers and researchers as relevant criteria: A journal with a high IF would thus be considered more important (because more visible, i.e., more widely read and cited) than one with a low IF. Impact factors have a definite influence in the scientific publications field. They are also used by proponents of quantitative research evaluation (a controversial subject). IFs are indexed in the Thomson Reuters Journal Citation Reports and published annually.

13 Geomarketing is a branch of marketing that analyzes the behaviour of individual economic actors, taking notions of space into account.

Geomarketing has various applications, such as studies of catchment areas (e.g., for a sales outlet), commercial location studies, potential studies, sectorization, optimization of direct marketing resources (direct mail, phoning etc.), network optimisation, etc. It frequently uses geographic information systems (GIS) to process data using computer tools.

English speakers use the term "Business Intelligence Leasing", which is more appropriate when the approach concerns marketing, but the discipline also applies to spatial planning in the context of socio-economic studies.

14 www.eurosport.fr/basketball/nba/2016-2017/113-joueurs-etrangers-en-nba-cette-saison-c-est-un-record-la-france-2e-pays-le-plus-represente_sto5925974/story.shtml (last accessed December 1, 2017).

15 It is the international rights that largely explain the increase in the new contract, worth €19 billion over nine years, signed in 2014.

16 It is important not to be misled by the way the media or the clubs announce a "fantastic" new contract. When Nike or Adidas sign this type of deal, it is to the detriment of individual contracts or other sports that receive less media coverage. The overall amount of sponsorship remains unchanged, as in the theory of "interconnectivity".

17 https://en.wikipedia.org/wiki/List_of_sports_attendance_figures (last accessed December 1, 2017).

18 https://en.wikipedia.org/wiki/List_of_sports_attendance_figures (last accessed December 1, 2017).

19 There is a downside, however. PSG is sponsored by Nike, while Beckham has been signed to Adidas for many years, and this has sometimes been problematic for prominent marketing campaigns.

20 www.lequipe.fr/Football/Article/Dans-l-oeil-des-gafa/841603 (last accessed December 1, 2017)

21 www.lesechos.fr/week-end/business-story/enquetes/030784621435-le-qatar-si-riche-et-si-mal-aime-2125720.php (last accessed December 1, 2017)

22 In 2014, the Dutch ADO Den Haag team became the first professional club in Europe to be owned by a Chinese company when it was acquired by United Vansen International Sports. Two seasons later, 12 clubs were either partly or wholly Chinese owned – including some of the most prestigious European clubs such as AC Milan, Inter Milan, Atletico Madrid and City Football Group, the company that runs Manchester City.

References

Arthur, D., Chadwick, S. (2007). *International cases in the business of sport*. Routledge, London, UK. 484 p.

Beech, J., Chadwick, S. (2007). Business of sport management. *Prentice Hall Financial Times*, Harlow, London, UK. 526 p.

Browlee, E., Lorgnier, N. (2015). Marketing des clubs de football professionnels: le cas de la Major League Soccer, in N. Chanavat, M. Desbordes (Eds), *Marketing du football*. Economica. Paris, France.

Desbordes, M., Ohl, F., Tribou, G. (1999). *Marketing du sport* (1st ed.). Economica, Paris. Awarded 1st prize by the Académie des Sciences Commerciales in 2000. Paris, France.

Lorans, O. (2003). *Adidas sales presentation*. Course given at the University Paris Sud, France, Masters Degree Program, unpublished.

Neale, W.C. (1964). The peculiar economics of professional sports: a contribution to the theory of the firm in sporting competition and in market competition. *The Quarterly Journal of Economics*, 78(1), 1–14.

Rottenberg, S. (1956). The baseball players' labor market. *Journal of Political Economy*, 64, 242.

Surdam, D.G. (2008). *The postwar Yankees: baseball's golden age revisited*. University of Nebraska Press. Lincoln, NE, USA.

Chapter 2

Watching a game or experiencing it

Theoretical foundations and practical cases of the fan experience

Boris Helleu

Introduction

Considered to be the temple of basketball, Madison Square Garden became a place for experimentation during the game opposing the New York Knicks and the Golden State Warriors on March 5, 2017. During the first half of the game, the video board displayed the following message "*the first half of today's game will be presented without music, video, or in-game entertainment so you can experience the game in its purest form. Enjoy the sounds of the game*". The players came out on to the field without any sound or visual effect, no animation had been planned to fill up the time-outs and the audience was not encouraged to make any noise to support their team. The sound atmosphere was only made up of the sound of the players' shoes on the ground, of the sound of their voices and of the chatters of the audience. The experience met mixed reactions. Steve Kerr, the Warriors' coach, found the atmosphere somewhat peculiar, stating that "*You sort of take it for granted because every NBA game, you got all this stuff going on, music in the background. You don't even think about it until it's not there*". The player Draymond Green reacted harshly to the experiment, considering it to be regressive and affecting the atmosphere in the stands and the pace of the game: "*To me, I think it was completely disrespectful to everyone from [NBA senior VP of entertainment and player marketing] Michael Levine to [Warriors president and COO] Rick Welts and all these people who've done these things to change the game from an entertainment perspective*".[1]

Without any gimmicks, the show, which was nothing more than just a game to watch, seemed to lack a little something. This is where the experience of the audience lays. The notions of *match-day experience* and *fan experience* have recently aroused the keen interest of the actors of the sporting industry (clubs, professional leagues, event organizers, sports equipment operators). Indeed, the added value of a good experience that would no longer be based solely on what is happening on the playing ground but rather in the stands, around the stadium and even at home, would help increase the loyalty of the public and attract a new audience that is less receptive to the game product.

However, the audience's experience does not only exist in the marketing and commercial strategies of sports performance professionals. It is also a concept that is widely discussed in the academic literature of Sports Management. This chapter is therefore divided into two parts. The first one refers to the concept of experience while the second one is there to illustrate it.

1 Sports entertainment is an experiential activity

This first part reviews the theoretical foundations of experiential marketing. Even though it is particularly adapted to the performing arts, it has also been the subject of numerous academic studies. In an article published in 2017, Masayuki Yoshida reviews the literature dedicated to the quality of the consumer's experience in sports and identifies almost 60 contributions published in major academic journals in this field, which highlights the increasing rate of publications: 6 articles published in the 1990s, 16 in the 2000s, and 36 since 2010. The first point considers the particular case of sporting shows, which favours an experiential approach. The second point focuses on the match day in stadia experience. The last one illustrates the topic via the presentation of data from satisfaction surveys conducted on professional football audiences.

1.1 The consumption experience: before, during, after

In a founding article published in 1982, Holbrook and Hirschman note that the consumer only operates purchasing actions in rational and calculating homo œconomicus. While the classic cognition-affect-behaviour model remains operational where the consumer is looking for a functional product that solves a problem, Holbrook and Hirschman introduce the triad fantasies-emotions-pleasure that is more adapted to certain areas promoting hedonistic consumption. Based on the model of experience-seeking in theatres, Bourgeon and Filser (1995, p. 7) note that "*the public will appreciate the work of art or cultural manifestation through the emotions it inspires*". Everything seems to be going the same way in the case of sporting shows, whose primary function is to generate emotions. Thus, Puhl, Bourgeon-Renault and Bouchet (2005) considered that performing arts can be divided into cultural and sports performances, noting that both involve a meeting between performers, an audience and a work integrating aesthetic and event items in their production process. According to the authors, there are profiles of consumer experiences (opportunistic, aesthetic, sympathetic, interactive) that require adapted marketing strategies.

In an article published in 2003, Bourgeon-Renault, Filser and Pulh highlight the singularity of marketing strategies when applied to cultural activities. Dance, music, opera or theatre are products characterized by the production/consumption simultaneity. In this respect, they add, the performing arts are closer to a sports competition and embody the enhancement of the consumer experience characterized, among other things, by the importance of the stimulation research process. Should we then consider that the marketing techniques used in live performance adapt to the sporting spectacle or that the latter can bring out a singularity? In sport marketing, Mullin, Hardy and Sutton (2014) identify among other aspects the following distinctions of sporting events marketing:

- The intangible nature of the product: Impalpable and not reducible to physical characteristics, the sporting event highlights a customer's benefit of any type other than a traditional product: Excitement, socialization, escape etc.
- Simultaneity of production and consumption: The game is co-produced by the opponent teams while the audience/consumers produce the atmosphere in the stadium.
- The changeable nature of the product: The sports show is a show of uncertainty that does not prejudge the quality of the product. Unlike cultural activities, sports competition does not follow any scenario, script, score or choreography.
- The lack of control over the core business: considering it a game, the marketing manager of a club has no leverage over transfers, the composition of the team or the tactics adopted.
- The importance of extensions: Related to the earlier points, the marketing manager must promote the stadium experience more than the game itself by promoting various activities and being attentive to the "related sides".

We could say that a sports show is essentially and necessarily an experiential product. If it is part of its nature, this is because the dramaturgy of a show between rivals having a more or less equivalent level makes the outcome uncertain, causes unexpected emotions (joy of victory, pain of defeat, the disillusion linked to a potential relegation, the hope for a levelled score, the excitement caused by a sudden turn of events etc.). If it is by necessity, this is because the organizer of the sporting event cannot merely afford to feed customer satisfaction with a game whose outcome is uncertain.

In other words, the unpredictability of sports shows is both a considerable strength since the fan is led to experience strong emotions and exceptional moments, as well as a weakness since the tickets price does not guarantee the quality of the show. The organizer of the sporting event cannot therefore consider victory as the only marketing technique to attract people to the stadium. This would mean relying attendance on sporting scores only and entrusting the function of marketing manager to the coach of the team. The organizer is therefore seeking to optimize the quality of peripheral services in order to truly establish audience loyalty, even in the event of defeat.

Mark Cuban, owner of the Dallas Mavericks, defines his mission as follows:

> *We in the sports business don't sell the game, we sell unique, emotional experiences. We are not in the business of selling basketball. We are in the business of selling fun. We are in the business offering a time-out. We are in the business of giving you a chance to create shared experiences.*[2]

It then remains to identify the various types of consumer experience that developed during a sports show, knowing that it spreads beyond the duration of the game.

In an article entitled "Consumer Experiences and Experiential Marketing", Caru and Cova (2006) explain how the new experiential perspective of marketing constitutes an epistemological rupture. While it was traditionally a matter of buying simple services and products that would meet a need, experiential consumption rehabilitates the pleasure and even the subjectivity of each individual. In short, pleasure replaces need, function gives way to emotion, usefulness disappears in favour of playfulness, the extraordinary is there to replace the routine and the product is now not only a product to be consumed but a product to be co-produced. While detailing the process of generating experiential consumption, the authors identify four phases:

- The experience of anticipation that prepares the experience
- The buying experience
- The experience itself
- The experience of recollection

Here are the moments that punctuate the fan's experience in the minds of sports professionals: Before – During – After. This is what Jean-Claude Blanc, Deputy Chief Executive Officer of Paris Saint-Germain, said in March 2012: "*The spectator's experience begins before arriving at the stadium, when he purchases his ticket. He needs to be treated better. The spectator's experience is to see a quality show, experience a positive pre-game, and walking back to his car or have easy access to public*[3] *transport*".

Taking this line of thought further, we could mention the following elements

- Before: Ticket purchase, game anticipation, stadium accessibility, access to exclusive game-related content
- During: Watch and experience the game, access/generate content on a terminal, quality services, entertainment, comfort and security
- After: Access content that embodies memory and materializes the fan's pride ("I was there!")

Considering that the fan's experience is not only limited to his presence in the stadium, even if it is the highest point of the experience, professionals consider it as a flow of events drawing a curve of emotions. As an illustration, the Stade de France holds it first and foremost as a place made to share experiences. He considers his relationship to the visitor/spectator according to these three stages. Before the show, it is necessary to inform and sell, making the site easily accessible, greet the audience. During the show, it is necessary to create the stadium atmosphere. After the show, it is necessary to keep in touch. In association with the French mobile phone industry Orange, the Stade de France is working on the concept of a customer journey with the ambition of "*maximising moments of emotion*" by creating "*an interactive and participative stadium with expanded secure access control, and making mobile phones a vector of emotion*"[4].

1.2 The fan experience in the stadium

Anyone who attends sporting events understands the notion of fan experience. Behind this apparent simplicity, all attempts have been made to establish a definition that was quite difficult to find, and therefore sometimes led to confusion or reduction. The fan experience is not simply based on the environment, the atmosphere or the quality of the entertainments. The field of experience is so broad that its definition also has to be broadened. Thus, for Yoshida (2017, p. 429): "*a sport consumer experience is defined as sport consumers' cognitive, affective, social, and physical reactions to direct (e.g., purchase and consumption) and indirect (e.g., media and social network) encounters with a sport organization, its products, and other consumers*".

In the following excerpt, Lionel Maltese sketches the conception of the fans' experience. We can draw three lessons from this:

1. The fan experience comes from the United States. The concern to optimize fan satisfaction no longer only through the game itself can be attributed to two main factors. Firstly, there is a culture of hospitality in the United States that supports greeting the audience in excellent conditions of comfort and safety. In many stadia and arenas, visitors are invited to complete satisfaction surveys intended to improve the conditions in which they are treated on site. Secondly, the duration of the show forces the organizer to develop peripheral services and animations to fill in gaps or retain fans in the event of a weak show. We should keep in mind that a baseball (MLB) or football (NFL) game lasts an average of about 3 hours. A basketball (NBA) or hockey (NHL) game lasts about 2 hours and 15 minutes.
2. Fan experience cannot be decided. This is the result of a proactive strategy to improve the quality of the items disconnected from the game.
3. The willingness to improve the experience of the fans requires investing in equipment.

Box 2.1 The need for fan relationship management

Sports fans' stadium experience is one of the trademarks of North American franchises, but they benefit from a very different environment, both in terms of sports culture and marketing. Like the PSG, for example, though it is not the only one for which the concepts of "servicing", customer journey, game scripting, branding or entertainment are integrated into the missions and activities of the club's marketing and game production teams. But what is the economic or rather the marketing utility of such an investment that aims to improve the experience, in other words the well-being of the fans in a stadium?

First, how can we define the fan experience? It is the result of a set of services dedicated to the fans' journey in a stadium and aiming at optimising their well-being, and the pleasure they take in a stadium. Sports entertainment is one of the few services that provide consumers with unique individual and collective emotions. Sports performance is obviously the main emotional factor that feeds the pleasure experienced by the fan, but the stadium must become a peripheral support for the sports experience. In practical terms, its accessibility, the optimisation of waiting times, catering, comfort and visibility, digital, mobile, video and technological content, the musical atmosphere, the role of the official speaker, the songs and tifos of supporters or even the possible shows integrated into the pre-game, half-time or post-game are the main factors in building the experience and atmosphere of a game. (. . .)

If clubs have a real brand strategy and especially if this asset is controlled by the club, the fan experience is essential. It is also a privileged means of communication to better get to know the fans in terms of behaviour and consumption habits in order to better serve them by customising commercial offers. It is therefore logical that CRM (Customer Relationship Management) managers become FRM (Fan Relationship Management) managers. It should be recalled that the economic leverage of the clubs, in addition to TV rights, particularly concern incomes from partner companies, which obviously see it as an opportunity to promote and activate their own brand.

Excerpt from "*Choyer ses fans, mais pour quoi faire?*" by Lionel Maltese – Eco review published on March 25, 2015 on francefootball.fr: www.francefootball.fr/news/Choyer-ses-fans-mais-pour-quoi-faire/545819

While Lionel Maltese insists on "*a set of services dedicated to the fans' journey in a stadium in order to optimize their well-being*", we must now try to understand the dimensions of this service experience. When Otto and Ritchie (1995) set out to characterize the notion of quality as a service experience, they identified six dimensions that perfectly fit into the sports experience.

1 Hedonism: Pleasure, excitement, emotions felt during a sports show.
2 Interactivity: Exchanges with other members of the audience, generate the atmosphere, animate the stands.

3 Novelty: Dream of evasion.
4 Comfort: Visibility, physical comfort.
5 Safety: Safety in and around the stadium.
6 Stimulation: Quality of animations.

Some or all of these criteria can be found in recent research. In 2007, Kao, Huang and Yang tried to evaluate the importance of the experience on the level of fan's satisfaction. While working on games of the Taiwan Professional League, the authors divide the fan's experience into three elements:

- The surprise: The authors consider that an exciting, extraordinary and unique experience will leave an even greater impression on a fan.
- Participation: The authors seek to understand the levers of interaction between fans and the sports show. In short, how the public is an actor in its own consumer experience.
- Immersion: The authors define immersion as the degree of involvement of the fan in the sports show to the point that he or she is detached from his or her environment. For example, when a game is so exciting that the audience forgets about time.

They successfully test the importance of the link between an emotional experience of surprise, participation and immersion, which determines the fan's behaviour and satisfaction and influences loyalty and recommendation.

In an article published in 2011, Clemes, Brush and Collins consider that the fans' experience is crucial since sports-event organizers operate in an increasingly competitive world and the game, by its very nature, is uncertain and this could be a source of disappointment. Thus, they state that a positive consumption experience cannot be based solely on the outcome. They build a conceptual model of the consumer's experience in which fan satisfaction depends on the quality of the service, which is itself declined in three dimensions:

- The quality of interactions: With security guards, snack bar staff and also players
- The quality of the environment: Sound and light, accessibility, space and cleanliness of the stadium
- The quality of the game outcome: The atmosphere, the quality of the game, the quality of the entertainment

The authors build a system made of 16 hypotheses to test the positive link between the above criteria, perceived quality of service, satisfaction and fan loyalty/recommendation. The model was tested on 390 spectators from a Super 14 Rugby Union game. According to their results, only animations do not appear as a determining criterion. All the other variables, over which marketers have control, make it possible to design a quality experience. Hence, the fan's satisfaction is not only based on the victory of his team.

1.3 Illustration: the audiences of the French Professional Football League

These academic approaches also have their practical counterparts. Since the end of the 2000s, the French professional football league has conducted studies to better understand the characteristics, expectations and grounds for satisfaction of its audiences. In 2008, a survey conducted by IPSOS showed that three quarters of the people that are actually interested in football in France do not travel to a stadium. Safety in and around the stadium, the atmosphere and the cleanliness of the sanitary facilities were at the time important criteria to the audience. In 2013, one another survey for the Union of Professional Football Clubs revealed that the public could possibly be waiting for more entertainment. In 2014, the professional football league commissioned a study from Ipsos and Repucom on L1 and L2 audiences at club level. The reasons for not coming to the stadium for both L1 and L2 audiences were insecurity, accessibility to the stadium, comfort and lack of animation.

In July 2017, the LFP (professional football league) released the results of a recent survey conducted by the Nielsen Sports Institute. It was conducted in November and December 2016 among 36,000 people (subscribers and spectators of Ligue 1 Conforama and Domino's Ligue 2, online survey). Since the first survey in 2008, catering in the stadium has been criticized: The offer is limited, the products are expensive, the waiting time is long, the service is of questionable quality. Even though the respondents say they have the money they need to buy something to eat when they come to the stadium, they prefer eating outside, in a place where they can order a beer. The survey also shows a significant increase in satisfaction with the technological aspects (stadium sound system, giant screens, telephone network) while having access to an Internet connection. Finally, the study shows public facilities have become better and better. The LFP has also contributed to the training of hospitality staff and promotes this criterion in its licence. It also rewards good initiatives by awarding LFP Experience Stadiums Awards to "*recognize the best ticketing initiatives aimed at priority targets such as families, students and women, in order to improve their audience experience*".[5]

Box 2.2 Motivations and satisfaction of French football audiences

Key features of the 2008 survey (LFP)

- Three quarters of the people interested in football do not go to the stadium
- 43% of the spectators arrive to the stadium more than half an hour before the kick-off

- The time spent on the outing to the stadium is 4 hours
- One in two consumers feels that they have difficulties accessing the refreshment bar
- People who are not used to consuming are now ready to spend 9 euros on a food budget

Key feature of the 2013 survey (UCPF)

- 43% of respondents follow the L1 in the club's overlapping catchment areas
- The following keep "L1 customers" away from the stadium: Price, other leisure activities, weather conditions
- What supposedly attracts "stadium customers": The price, tickets by invitations, a better game level
- 80% of the respondents would like to see more animations on the giant screens
- 73% would fancy seeing an animation during the warm-up phase of the game

Key feature of the 2014 survey (LFP)

- 16% of individuals aged 16 to 75 living in club catchment areas claim to be interested in football but have not attended any football games in a stadium in the last 12 months
- Reasons for not coming to the stadium in L1: Reasons related to the stadium, lack of interest, schedules incompatibility
- The main actions to get people to the stadium (L1): Prevent the violent behaviour of some of the supporters, better protection against the cold/weather, easier access to the stadium by car, better atmosphere in the stadium, greater safety around the stadium
- The motivations to come to the stadium: Support your team (88% for the L1, 90% for the L2), experience the event on site (70% for the L1, 72% for the L2), the atmosphere (67% for the L1, 60% for the L2)
- Arriving at the stadium: On average 39 minutes before kick-off in L1, on average 30 minutes in L2
- Total duration of the stadium experiment: 4 hours 24 minutes for the L1 and 3 hours 34 minutes for the L2
- Two out of three spectators buy food and are willing to spend an average of 8 euros
- For 30% of L1 spectators and 34% of L2 spectators, it is necessary to improve the quality of service

2 The match-day experience: Good practices

Since it provides emotions, sport is in fact an experiential product. However, the experience does not only lie in the stimuli caused by the game but also in the satisfaction provided by the services and the entertainment. This requires an appropriate tool. The first point aims to show that stadiums and arenas are no longer just places where people go to see a game but also a place where they can experience it. If the experience creates value (Pine and Gilmore, 1998), it also creates value for advertisers. They are increasingly inclined to use it as a support for partnership activation. This is the purpose of the second point. Finally, the last point shows how sports show organizers involve fans in designing their own experience.

2.1 The stadium, a key factor in fan satisfaction

The emergence of new platforms and the development of new terminals have generated uses and consumption patterns of sport that were still unknown 10 years ago. According to a study carried out by Hootsuite and We Are Social, 40% of the world's population is reported to be active on social media. Facebook has more than 2 billion active users, Instagram more than 700 million, Twitter more than 300 million and Snapchat more than 255 million. In France, the same report estimates that people spend an average of 2 hours and 46 minutes in front of the television but also just half of it (1 hour 23 minutes) consulting their social media. By providing access to content or by generating and maintaining a conversation within a peer community, social media has changed the way sport is consumed. According to the "Know The Fan" study published in 2014, 96% of French sports fans watch sports on TV, 37% travel to a stadium but still 30% access sports content on their smartphone while 21% view sports content on social media (compared to 12% in 2011). In addition, 40% of French fans watch sports on TV holding a second screen in their hand to follow live comments (53%), watch video clips (24%) or read reviews. In fact, sports shows are no longer just experienced in the stadiums, seen on TV, read in the newspapers or listened to on the radio, they are now the subjects of new practices.

According to Twitter, for instance, more than 2/3 of French users use this microblogging platform for football related activities, 39% follow a football club and nine out of ten were actively involved with 2014 World Cup-related content. Indeed, this competition generated more than 672 million tweets, of which 36.5 million were posted during the semi-final between Brazil and Germany. In France, the Euro 2016 competition generated more than 106 million tweets, making it the fourth most commented event in the world in 2016 after the Rio Olympic Games (187 million tweets), the American elections and the Pokemon Go phenomenon. In 2012, Facebook released a computer graphics of the most connected places based on the platform's geolocation tool. In the top 25 are seven stadiums and arenas. In the same year, the San Francisco Giants and Los Angeles Dodgers baseball stadiums and the Staples Center, which hosts NBA and NHL franchises, were among the top ten most photographed locations on this platform.

Thus, the fan's digital activity is not limited to commenting on a game from home. Within the stadium, sports fans meet the tourists, who are keen to expand their horizons, and share a common interest with them: the "I was there!". The "I was there!" (and his fellows "I am there" and "I will be there") enable you to tell about the show and to show off. In other words, it is about talking about one's own experience and setting it up by posting a selfie on Instagram, posting photos of players on Facebook, feeding a snapchat story etc. The stadium thus becomes the tool of a digital experience. It is no longer a receptacle designed to fill as many seats as possible. It is a generator of experience that has to satisfy both the most ardent supporters and the neophyte public. The North American model shows that the latest equipment (AT&T stadium in Dallas, Metlife Stadium in New York, Mercedes-Benz Stadium in Atlanta, Levi's Stadium in Santa Clara) is designed to provide a fan experience that begins well before the game and continues long after it is ended: Entertainment for children and adults, living and dining areas, museum and connectivity. During the 51st edition of the Super Bowl held at NRG Stadium in Houston in February 2017, at least 37.6 TB of data were consumed as follows:

- 11.68 TB on Wi-Fi
- 11 TB on the Verizon network
- 9.8 TB on the AT&T network

1.7 TB were consumed on social media and 49% of spectators connected to the stadium's Wi-Fi network. If the fan's satisfaction no longer lies as much in the outcome of the game as in the variables that make a good experience, then it is might be the entry point for thinking about the stakes of the connected stadium. The vocabulary diversity associated with this tool (connected stadium, smart stadium, stage 2.0, M Stadium) reflects its various uses (Abdourazakou, 2016; Bal and Badier, 2016). The connected stadium has a "social" function since it allows content and services to be generated on terminals, but it also has a technological aspect (Wi-Fi spots, DAS antennas, beacons, screens). While the connected stadium provides fans with a unique experience, it also facilitates the operators' work (automation of certain tasks) and opens up new marketing and sales opportunities (recovery, processing and exploitation of fan data from a Big Data perspective).

Thus, many new services associated with smartphones aim to improve the fan experience, who, in some stadiums, can now reach his or her seat with a dematerialized ticket, view exclusive content on an application, order food from his or her seat and have it delivered, use contactless payment, see his or her shared content on social media also broadcast on giant screens. All the clubs start using these tools. A few months before the inauguration of the new Olympique Lyonnais stadium, Jean-Michel Aulas, the club's president, talked about the connectivity of his new stadium:

> *Fans will have access to all of the game's statistics, they will be able to review the most relevant actions, they will be able to order their sandwich, order their scarf, order*

their meal without having to pull out a credit card. It's all integrated and thanks to the NFC technique all transactions are controlled and secure and quickly taken into account. More than 25,000 people will be able to use wifi at the same time.[6]

However, it should not be construed that the improvement of the fan experience in the stadium is only a question of new media or new technologies. More prosaically, the politeness of the reception staff, the cleanliness of the toilets, the waiting time at the bar, the diversity and quality of the products on offer or the comfort of the seat are all elements that generate (or not) public satisfaction. Since 2010, the Stadium Business Awards have been rewarding good practices and innovations in the design and operation of stadiums and arenas. There is a Fan Experience category that rewards "*the stadium, arena or major sports venue that has delivered consistently outstanding levels of service and fan experience at every stage of the customer journey*".[7] The recent list of winners shows that even though the experience might sometimes be digital, it has many other aspects.

- 2017: Setting up of self-standing stands (secure standing stands) at Celtic Park
- 2016: Voetbalkijken 2.0 at the Amsterdam ArenA: Launch of a match-day application for Ajax in Stadia fans
- 2015: The World Cup Living Room by the FC Union Berlin: Games from the 2014 World Cup were broadcast on a giant screen in the stadium. The Berliners were invited to come with their own sofa
- 2014: The Leicester Tigers' Family Friendly scheme. The English rugby club has developed a programme of activities taking place throughout the year for children and families (competitions to play mascot or be the speaker of the game, a family festival to open the season, free membership for children under 10, a Christmas market etc.)
- 2013: Amway Center, Orlando Magic Hall (NBA). Since the opening of the hall in 2010, the club has launched a specialized training program on consumer service. The programme, conducted in collaboration with the Disney Institute, trains more than 2,000 employees each year

2.2 "Money can't buy" operations

In a report entitled "commercial trends in sports 2016", Repucom identified major trends that it believes are affecting the sport business market. Among other trends, we can read the following:

- That partnerships have become more and more immersive and rewarding
- That new technologies radically change the fan's experience at home and in the stadium
- How important it is to build a strong relationship with the fans

These points reflect a significant evolution in sponsorship strategies. While previously looking for display, visibility and notoriety, the sponsor of a club, event, league or federation is now looking to become a partner in the fans' experience. The brands set up activations that involve and satisfy fans, thus making them spokespeople for the brands. The most common schemes consist in social media contests to win "money can't buy it" experiences. The partner brand gains benefits in terms of image from awarding prizes that allow the winners to experience the sporting spectacle in exclusive conditions.

Some operations focus on the way you see the game. In 2016, on the occasion of the BNP Paribas Masters, Accor Hotels Arena launched the "Tweet your seat" operation. Spectators in the room were invited to tweet their seat number with the hashtag #tweetyourseat. A groom came to take the winners to a four-seat terrace on the edge of the court lines. Many clubs allow partner brands to welcome fans to spaces located on the edge of the pitch. Others imagine devices that accentuate sensations. For the final of the French Football Cup between Paris and Marseille in 2016, the French betting company PMU replaced its VIP sofa usually located on the edge of the pitch by a nacelle hung under the roof of the Stade de France at a height of 45 metres. The Money Can't Buy bonus is not only a matter of quality of the location within the stadium. On the occasion of the 2013 edition of Roland Garros, and to celebrate its 40th partnership anniversary with the tournament, the BNP Paribas bank invited tennis fans to share their stories and make their dreams come true. Here, the memory experience made it possible to gather 300 spectators' anecdotes about the tournament. In addition, BNP Paribas offers fans an exceptional experience: Be in charge of tournament lottery, become an official photographer, become a ball boy, exchange tennis balls with WTA players, make the final toss and bring the trophy etc.

This type of device takes as a value the emotion and gratification it generates, to such an extent that some people try to market it (see Box 2.3). We must then wonder if the oxymoron "sold money-can't-buy-experience" is meaningful. Isn't it so that by seeking to monetize a unique experience, we kind of take away its exclusive, exceptional and rewarding character?

Box 2.3 Marketing of exclusive experiences

(. . .) Provided by a small company, the Sport Inbox concept, launched with the help of two football players, the former Auxerrois Jean-Pascal Mignot and the Clermontese Ludovic Genest, actually aims at marketing exclusive support experiences (attending a training session behind closed doors, kicking off, sitting on the bench during a game, etc.).

On the surface, the Club Box looks like all boxes already sold by some clubs. But its content and philosophy differ. Until now, these gift boxes contained fairly classic products (game tickets with a few additional by-products). But this box now contains luxurious collectible cards from the players of a team with access to an online game prediction platform and lottery tickets to win less common prizes. "The objective is to make people live unique moments", explains Jean-Pascal Mignot, who retired last season. It's part of a new mindset in which clubs wish to generate a better image and bring players and supporters closer together".

(. . .) A search for proximity that is not entirely coincidental. Marketers call this the "fan engagement", i.e., how to make the consumer-supporter feel involved in the club and the products they sell. Sport Inbox will thus provide clubs with an annual marketing study analysing the behaviour of their fans, in addition to the royalties paid for each box they sell. "We have to find new ways of consuming, of reaching the millennials (created between the early 1980s and early 2000s), people who are highly involved in the digital culture", says Christophe Rousseau, founder of Troisième Ligne, which manages the distribution of products derived from many football clubs (Nantes, Lille, . . .) and the National Rugby League. He goes on: "The Club Box is a different product category that allows you to tell a story, consume differently and also make the club brand present in all outlets".

The Club Box, of which 20,000 copies should initially be sold, is intended to be sold in both club shops and supermarkets.

Source: "How to hit on fans in the clubs" by François-Guillaume Lemouton in L'Equipe – Tuesday, November 15, 2016

2.3 Co-production of the experience

The quality of the match-day experience and its resulting satisfaction are based on a multitude of levers that can be activated by the show organizer. In doing so, he or she becomes the producer of a potential experience that he or she delivers to his or her audience. How can they get involved in designing their own game experience? For the Hand Star Game 2015, the National Handball League relies on its fans, who are given the opportunity to vote to determine the shirt that will be worn by players, team captains or even the dressing of goal areas. As an ideal experiential entertainment (dramatization and sets, plot and staging – see Helleu, 2011), World Wrestling Entertainment (WWE) involves its fans in the very design of the show. In 2018, it launched a new program called WWE Mixed Match Challenge, which puts teams composed of a male and a female wrestler into competition. The programme is designed as participatory and interactive. Since it is broadcast live on Facebook Watch, fans can interact with the participants but can also choose the stipulations of the fights or the composition of the teams. The fan is no longer a passive spectator of a show over which he or she has no control. His or her commitment gives him or her the status of consum'author and consum'actor since he or she can influence the progress of his or her favourite event.

The scope of co-production is not limited to the game attributes. As the AS Roma club wanted to launch a new website, they turned to their expert fans to design it. This fan-sourcing strategy took the form of a message posted by the club on the Reddit platform inviting them to share their experience and expertise. Other clubs have gone even further by organizing hackathons (Portmanteau word for Hack and Marathon), a short-term competition where teams work on a project submitted by a sponsor. In April 2015, the Vinci group organized a hackathon at the Allianz Riviera dedicated to the customer experience of both travellers and spectators, inviting participants to "*imagine and design new digital services that optimise the experience of users enjoying these infrastructures throughout their journey, to enable them to fully enjoy the services provided, and bring them ever more serenity, comfort and satisfaction*".[8] More recently, the Malherbe Stadium in Caen has been the first professional football club to organize a hackathon in partnership with the Normandy French Tech. About 50 supporters, developers, engineers, graphic designers, communicators, artists and students were invited to come to the stadium and spend 24 hours there to discuss ways to improve the quality of the services provided on the day of the game. The NBA, the Bayern Munich, the Manchester City, the Denver Broncos, the MLB or the Seattle Sounders (MLS) organized hackathons with a view to better integrate new technologies into the fan experience.

Conclusion: Head up, VR Headset on or eyes down?

In a review article entitled "Introducing a Sport Experience Design (SX) framework for sport consumer behaviour research", Daniel C. Funk, a marketing professor specializing in the study of the behaviour of sports show consumers, reminds us:

> *The sport user experience includes a multitude of interactions that occur between the sport consumer and the experienced environment produced by the sport organization. Consider the potential number of touchpoints and interactions a sport consumer has attending a live sporting event from start to end. These interactions could range from searching for information about a game, purchasing tickets online, traveling to the game, enjoying pre-game activities, listening to music and announcements, watching the game and digital content on the jumbotron, doing the wave, using a mobile device to tweet or Instagram pictures from the game, interacting with other spectators, purchasing concessions and merchandise, using restrooms, participating in rituals, and finally leaving the venue.*

He therefore considers that the fan's experience is getting richer. Due to the great diversity of interactions between the actors of the experience, in the stadium as well as outside, during the game as well as at any other point of the week, online as well as offline, the sports entertainment is getting more complex. Everything happens as if there existed a shift in the perimeter of the show that preserves its initial attributes (seeing a sports competition to feel emotions) but also undercovers new ones (qualities of service and entertainment). In short, the sporting show seems to be influenced by two forces:

- A movement coming from the centre and spreading to the periphery (from the field to the outside of the stadium): The experience is no longer limited to looking at the field but increasingly resides in the stands (comfort, security) as well as in the infrastructures of the stadium (refreshments, hospitality areas) and outside its walls (following a game on social media).
- An increase in the consumption experience that only seems possible if you hold a computer terminal in hand. Sports show organizers, ever since they have had to face competition of television or secondary screens, started integrating these elements into the stadium design, which now contains giant screens and Wi-Fi network.

At the interface between these two trends, the virtual reality helmet makes it possible to experience the sports show both on site and from home, as if you were sitting by the field without being alone. Thus, the NBA is expanding its game broadcast to include virtual reality with the aim of making it a social experience. Jeff Marsilio, NBA's VP of Global Media Distribution, explains:

> *I think probably the biggest complaint or concern that we hear is, "It's great, it's immersive, but it's also very isolating. You're in your living room. You're transported somewhere else. If you don't know someone when you walk in the room, you can't communicate with your friend". Those are kind of software problems really, and those will be resolved actually pretty quickly.*[9]

The ways of accessing the sports show as well as the reasons for fans' satisfaction requirements have changed considerably. It's no longer just about watching a game, it's about living it. It is no longer just a question of "going to see the game" but "going to see the game in the stadium". It is no longer just a question of saying "I was there" but of proving it and capturing the moment through shared content on social media. Everything happens as if the peripheral elements were distractions dedicated to limit the attention paid to the game. Mark Cuban explains how he wants to produce an NBA team game:

> *I want it to be very participatory. I want it to be very social. I want it to be very inclusive. I want it to be memorable. I want it to be so much fun people talk about it to their friends and can't wait to go back. I want every parent to get tears in their eyes when they see their kids jumping up and down whether the score is 2 to 0. or 120 to 84. (. . .) I know I can't control what happens on the court every game, but I can do my very best to make sure that no matter what the score is, we have done*

everything we could to make the fan experience feel like a huge wedding. IMHO, that means eliminating as many of the "look down" moments in the game as I possibly can. Once you sit in your seat, the only time I want you to look down is to pick up the soda or beer you set down under your seat and maybe to check your phone to see if you got a text from the sitter or your buddy about where to meet after the game. I want you to keep looking up.[10]

As if, finally, it were necessary to remind us that the etymology of the word "spectacle" comes from the Latin word *spectare* meaning to look. Hence, maybe the New York Knicks were pioneers in rehabilitating the pure experience of watching unvarnished games.

Notes

1 Published on 6 March 2017 on espn.com: www.espn.com/nba/story/_/id/18832748/draymond-green-golden-state-warriors-calls-new-york-knicks-decision-go-game-music-pathetic
2 "The Fan Experience at Sporting Events – We dont need no stinking smartphones!.", Blog Maverick. The Mark Cuban Weblog: http://blogmaverick.com/2011/12/24/the-fan-experience-at-sporting-events-we-dont-need-no-stinking-smartphones//
3 "J.C. Blanc advocates the spectator's experience" published on March 22, 2012 on eurosport.fr: www.eurosport.fr/football/ligue-1/2011-2012/les-stades-selon-jc.-blanc_sto3205796/story.shtml
4 Orange Business Services, white paper "Customer journey: the nécessité of a seamless multi-channel strategy"
5 "Stands, lawns, entertainers, spectator experience; it's time for prizes" article published on the Ligue de Football Professionnel website on June 13, 2016: www.lfp.fr/corporate/article/tribunes-pelouses-animateurs-experience-spectateurs-c-est-l-heure-des-prix.htm
6 Presentation of the Grand Stadium Connected 2.0. Video uploaded on April 8, 2015 on the youtube channel of the entrepreneurs' spring. To consult on: www.youtube.com/watch?v=V7Dbxqy_2qQ
7 "Who should win the Fan Experience Award 2018?" article published on January 5, 2018 on stadiumbusinessawards.com: www.stadiumbusinessawards.com/win-fan-experience-award-2018/
8 "Hackathon VINCI – Nice Côte d'Azur 2015", published on April 10, 2015 on the website allianz-riviera.fr: www.allianz-riviera.fr/fr/actus/hackathon-vinci-nice-cote-dazur-2015
9 "Three Reasons NextVR Is Excited About Future Of VR NBA Broadcasts" published on sporttechie.com on 6 July 2017: www.sporttechie.com/three-reasons-nextvr-excited-future-vr-nba-broadcasts/
10 "The Fan Experience at Sporting Events – We dont need no stinking smartphones!" by Mark Cuban, published on his blog on December 24, 2011: http://blogmaverick.com/2011/12/24/the-fan-experience-at-sporting-events-we-dont-need-no-stinking-smartphones/

References

Abdourazakou, Y. (2016). Connected stadiums in the United States: state of play, challenges and perspectives. *European Review of Sport Management*, 48, 27–50

Bal, C., Badier, M. (2016). Les stades connectés : pilier du développement marketing des clubs de football?, in N. Chanavat, Mr Desbordes (Eds.), *Football marketing*. Economica. Paris, France.

Bourgeon, D., Filser, M. (1995). Les apports du modèle de recherches d'expériences à l'analyse du comportement dans le domaine culturel: Une application conceptuelle et méthodologique. *Recherche et Application en Marketing*, 10(4), 5–25.

Bourgeon-Renault, D., Filser, M. Pulh, M. (2003). Le marketing du spectacle vivant. *Revue française de gestion*, 142, 113–127.

Carù, A., Cova, B. (2006). Expériences de consommation et marketing expérientiel. *Revue française de gestion*, 162, 99–113.

Clemes, M.D., Brush, G.J., Collins, M.J. (2011). Analysing the professional sport experience: a hierarchical approach. *Sport Management Review*, 14(4), 370–388.

Funk, D.C. (2017). Introducing a Sport Experience Design (SX) framework for sport consumer behaviour research. *Sport Management Review*, 20(2), 145–158.

Helleu, B. (2011). "Be ready to be excited" – WWE's marketing strategy and business model, in M. Desbordes, A. Richelieu (Eds.), *Neo-marketing of sport, crossed views between Europe and North America*, from boeck. De Boeck publisher, Brussels, Belgium.

Holbrook, M.B., Hirschman, E.C. (1982). The experiential aspects of consumption: consumer fantasy, feelings and fun. *Journal of Consumer Research*, 9(2), 132–140.

Kao, Y-F., Huang, L.S., Yang, M-H. (2007). Effects of experiential elements on experiential satisfaction and loyalty intentions: a case study of the super basketball league in Taiwan. *International Journal of Revenue Management*, 1(1), 79–96.

Mullin, B.J., Hardy, S., Sutton, W.A. (2014). *Sport marketing* (4th ed.). Human Kinetics.

Otto, J.E., Ritchie, J.R.B. (1995). Exploring the quality of the service experience: a theoretical and empirical analysis, in T. Swartz, D. Bowen, S. Brown (Eds.), *Advances in services marketing and management: research and practice*. JAI Press. Greenwich, CT, USA.

Pine, B.J. II, Gilmore, J.H. (1998). Welcome to the experience economy. *Harvard Business Review*, 76(4), 97–105.

Pulh, M., Bourgeon-Renault, D., Bouchet, P. (2005). Spectacles vivants, logiques de consommation et construction d'expériences: le paradoxe d'une offre à la fois unique et plurielle. *Décisions Marketing*, 37, pp. 57–66.

Yoshida, M. (2017). Consumer experience quality: a review and extension of the sport management literature. *Sport Management Review*, 20(5), 427–442.

Chapter 3

CSR and sports-event organizers

State of play, controversies and perspectives

Aurélien François, Emmanuel Bayle and Olivier Mutter

Introduction

This chapter examines the concept of corporate social responsibility (CSR) in relation to sports-event organizers (SEOs), focusing on two categories of sports event: National competitions run by professional leagues and sports clubs, and global and continental events organized under the auspices of international governing bodies such as the International Olympic Committee (IOC), Fédération Internationale de Football Associations (FIFA) and Union of European Football Associations (UEFA). On the national level, we compare approaches to CSR by professional leagues in two European countries – France and England – and in the two most popular spectator sports in these countries – football and rugby union (Ligue 1 and Top 14 in France, vs. The Premier League and Aviva Premiership Rugby in England) On the international level, we consider two "one-shot" mega events, the Olympic Games and the European Football Championship (via the 2016 edition, hosted by France), rather than recurring events such as Roland Garros or the Tour de France.

Before presenting our empirical study of these events, we outline the general concepts of CSR and its corollary, organizational social responsibility (OSR), together with the associated issue of sustainable development (SD). We also look at the current state of research into CSR/OSR and SD within the sport sector, a subject on which there is now a substantial literature. Examining both empirical and theoretical studies of CSR in sport reveals the numerous controversies and paradoxes arising from the ways in which SEOs deploy these inherently contentious concepts.

1 CSR and sport: Context and perspectives

This section looks at the adoption of CSR within the sport sector, the impact of the context in which organizations operate, and the perspectives for sport organizations to develop their CSR. After retracing the evolution of CSR from the concept's beginnings to the most recent developments, we describe the characteristics inherent to sport that have led to it being viewed as an "almost natural" vector for implicit social responsibility.

1.1 CSR: A new promise of responsible management?

CSR is a long-standing managerial concept that has been expanded greatly since it emerged. One relatively recent development of CSR originated with the premise that social responsibility should concern all types of organization, not just corporations. The result, known as organizational social responsibility (OSR), appears to provide the most suitable framework for examining social responsibility within the sport sector, which is also increasingly embracing the tenets of SD.

1.1.1 Origins of CSR and conceptual developments

CSR can trace its roots back at least as far as the early 20th century, although the term "social responsibility" was not coined until the mid-1950s, when it was applied to North American businessmen and defined as "*the obligations of businessmen to pursue those policies, to make those decisions, or to follow those lines of action which are desirable in terms of the objectives and values of our society*" (Bowen, 1953, p. 6). This seminal definition was quickly expanded to corporations, which began to take into account the notion of social responsibility through what became known as CSR. Although this acronym is generally taken to stand for corporate social responsibility, the term corporate societal responsibility has been preferred in some contexts.[1] Initial research into the concept of CSR, which continued throughout the final decades of the 20th century, was aimed at defining where it could and should be applied, often with the explicit goal of demonstrating links between socially responsible behaviour and company performance (Carroll, 1979, 1991). The emergence of stakeholder theory, which has been embraced by many studies of CSR, helped legitimize research into the relationship between CSR and performance. This theory introduced the idea that a company is not just accountable to its shareholders but to all the actors within its environment, who Freeman (1984, p. 46) called stakeholders and defined as "*any group or individual who can affect or is affected by the achievement of the organisation's objectives*". These developments led researchers in the late 1980s to explore possible links between CSR and financial performance from a functionalist perspective. By gradually making profit maximization the prime objective of CSR (Gond, 2011), this approach led to the idea that performance measures should not be solely financial, but also take into account social and environmental considerations. Methods for assessing these three components of performance, often referred to collectively as the *triple bottom line* (Elkington, 1997), have been modelled in numerous ways (Carroll, 1979, 1991; Wartick and Cochran, 1985; Wood, 1991).

Nevertheless, the failure to find concrete links between social performance and financial performance (Ulmann, 1985; Wartick and Cochran, 1985) has kept the spotlight on CSR, which is now one of the most intensively studied concepts in the management sciences (Lee, 2008). This research has led to the development of new approaches, especially since the emergence of the notion of SD, which has been a central issue on the political agenda since the 1990s, and resulted in numerous international "CSR" standards and labels, including the OECD's Guidelines for Multinational Enterprises (fifth edition in 2011); the Global Reporting Initiative's (GRI) (1997) sustainability reporting guidelines (G4 edition published in 2013); the Global Compact, formed in 2000 to pursue ten principles of SD in four focus areas; the UN's Principles for Responsible Investment, drawn up in 2005; the European Green Paper on CSR (2001); ISO standards (most notably environmental management standards: 14000/8000 and 14001/14004/14010/14012); and numerous fair trade labels.

In addition to these international incentives, national laws also impose social reporting requirements on companies, although often only on those larger than a certain size. In France, for example, social reporting requirements were first imposed on companies via article 116 of the 2001 New Economic Regulations (NRE) Act, whose provisions were expanded in 2012 by article 225 of the second Grenelle Environment Forum. The NRE Act applied only to listed companies, who have to publish reports on the actions they take to offset the social and environmental consequences of their activities, whereas the Grenelle Environment Forum applies to all companies with more than 500 employees. These laws are indicative of the tendency to impose CSR through legislation, despite the inherently voluntary nature of the concept's underlying philosophy.

1.1.2 CSR, OSR and SD: Definitions and associated controversies

Although the international organizations cited earlier (UN, OECD, etc.) have helped ensure the widespread adoption of CSR around the world, CSR takes so many different forms that it is difficult to produce a comprehensive definition of the concept. For many years, the most widely accepted definition in Europe was provided by the Commission of the European Communities (2001), according to which CSR is "*a concept whereby companies integrate social and environmental concerns in their business operations and in their interactions with their stakeholders on a voluntary basis*". As the EC's definition recognizes, the voluntary nature of CSR is an intrinsic characteristic of actions intended to demonstrate a company's social responsibility. Nevertheless, we prefer the definition drawn up for the ISO 26000 standard by more than 400 international experts over a period of five years (Capron, Quairel-Lanoizelée and Turcotte, 2011). In this non-certifiable standard, the International Standards Organisation defines social responsibility as "*the responsibility of an organization for the impacts of its decisions and activities on society and the environment through transparent and ethical behavior*" (ISO 26000, 2010). In addition to being universal, the definition included in ISO 26000 has two advantages over the Commission of the European Communities' definition. First, it extends the concept of social responsibility to organizations in general, not just companies. In fact, the new standard's objective is to encourage organizations of all sizes and all types (public bodies, associations, etc.) to restructure their management processes (R&D, purchasing, human resources, logistics, marketing, social communication, etc.)

by introducing a wide range of tools (corporate foundations, carbon balances, sustainability reports, social or non-financial performance indicators, etc.). Second, it includes the notion of SD, defined in 1987 by the World Commission on Environment and Development (Brundtland Report) as "*economic development that meets the needs of the present generation without compromising the ability of future generations to meet their own needs*".

Hence, many types of organization, including public bodies, have begun adopting a new management paradigm centred around the notions of OSR and, more generally, SD. Numerous public bodies are now being guided by the UN's Millennium Development Goals, originally published in 2000 for the period up to 2015, and then updated in 2015 as Sustainable Development Goals for the period up to 2030. While taking into account local specificities, these goals are being pursued via a range of management tools, such as national SD strategies, sustainable cities, local agenda 21s and natural environment protection standards. This paradigm has given rise to new forms of business (e.g., social businesses, Yunus, 2010) and to "bottom of the pyramid" (BOP) strategies (Prahalad, 2004; Payaud and Martinet, 2009, 2010) aimed at creating economic models suitable for the poorest communities in developing countries. It has also led some large corporations, such as Danone, to review their management methods. The "Danone Way", for example, was set up to finance initiatives based on new economic models, exemplified by the famous "Grameen-Danone" joint-venture in Bangladesh (Gond and Igalens, 2012). In addition, it has raised the issue of how a country's success is evaluated and led to the development of new indicators such as "Gross National Happiness" (Stiglitz, Sen and Fitoussi, 2009; Cohen, 2012), to complement traditional measures such as GDP. In the private sector, these "new rules of the game" have raised the prospect of (large) corporations adopting new governance and management practices and new measures of performance. This has resulted in the emergence of "true social engagement strategies" and the concept of shared value (Porter and Kramer, 2011),[2] the measurement of social performance (Gond, 2010), the issue of social control (Sautereau-Moquet, 2010) and social responsibility rating systems.

Nevertheless, even though CSR and OSR would appear to provide a pathway to a new, more responsible approach to management, the concepts remain contentious (Gond and Moon, 2011) and many commentators have expressed scepticism, if not outright criticism (e.g., Friedman, 1962, 1970), of the philosophy underlying the ways CSR/OSR and SD are deployed. An issue frequently highlighted by CSR's detractors is the disconnect between words and deeds that can be seen in some organizations' CSR strategies and practices. Consequently, although this new managerial ideology has widened the formerly narrow concept of a "Friedmanian" company, it must be viewed with caution, as some CSR/OSR initiatives may be merely a form of "greenwashing" (Friestad and Wright, 1994), that is, purely cosmetic actions intended to enhance an organization's image. Hence, even though the CSR/OSR movement has the potential to change representations of how organizations are governed, managed and evaluated, it would be naïve to think that it has profoundly changed the essence of financial capitalism (Boltanski and Chiapello, 1999).

1.2 CSR by SEOs: Context and stakes

CSR in the sport sector has been subject to intense study since the mid-2000s. Following a brief assessment of the state of play in this area, based on the most notable studies regarding each type of organization, we describe the two types of organization we focused on for our analysis of CSR by SEOs. Given the predominance of studies examining CSR and sport in Anglophone countries (mostly the USA and UK), we decided to compare approaches to CSR within professional sport in France and England.

1.2.1 State of play and definition of the types of SEO studied

The pioneering research into sport-organization CSR carried out in the mid-2000s (Babiak and Wolfe, 2006; Breitbarth and Harris, 2008; Smith and Westerbeek, 2007) paved the way for a plethora of subsequent studies and publications, including special issues of journals[3] and entire books dedicated to CSR and sustainability in sport (Paramio-Salcines, Babiak and Walters, 2013; Rodriguez, Késenne and Dietl, 2009). However, sport's ties with social responsibility go back much further than the relative novelty of this research stream might suggest (Bradish and Cronin, 2009; Godfrey, 2009). In fact, as Smith and Westerbeek (2007) noted, sport has several inherent characteristics (power to communicate, youth appeal, positive effects on health, ability to promote social interaction, ability to improve cultural understanding and integration, ability to raise awareness of environmental and sustainability issues and ability to provide immediate gratification benefits) that make it a natural vector for deploying CSR. These "natural" attributes facilitate the spread of CSR both *in* sport and *through* sport. CSR through sport concerns organizations outside the sport sector, such as sport event sponsors, which use sport for commercial ends. Although sponsors are increasingly important partners in the organization of sports events (Djaballah, Hautbois and Desbordes, 2017) and essential stakeholders in the social initiatives undertaken by sport organizations, we decided to focus on CSR in sport.

Previous studies have examined the CSR/SD practices and policies of many different types of sport organization, including international governing bodies (IOC, FIFA, UEFA, etc.), national sport federations, professional leagues and clubs, SEOs, sporting goods manufacturers and sporting goods retailers (Bayle, Chappelet, François and Maltese, 2011). In fact, the exponential increase in research into CSR and sport over the last 10 years makes it almost impossible to cite every study of CSR within each type of organization. In their recent review of research into sport organization CSR, Walzel and Robertson (2016) identified more than 700 studies published in English alone between 2006 and 2016.

For most sport organizations, the events they organize form the core of their sport offer. Of all the different types of organization listed in the previous paragraph, the two that are most obviously associated with organizing sports events are international governing bodies and national federations and professional leagues and clubs. In the case of international governing bodies, the events they supervise tend to be "one-shot" mega events, most of which are better known than their parent organization (e.g., Olympic Games vs. IOC). The competitions organized by national federations and professional leagues and clubs take place on a smaller (national) scale, but they are held more frequently. These considerations led us to concentrate our study on these two types of sports organization.

Parent and Chappelet (2015) examined the diversity of sports events, categorizing them according to their size, spatial criteria, sporting criteria, financial objectives and fame, etc. Based on these criteria, events can be situated on a continuum running from small, local competitions to major international events. All event rights holders (or owners) have had to respond to the wave of social responsibility, especially given the recent spate of sport-related scandals (doping, violence, cheating, corruption, etc.), which mean that SEOs can no longer justify their failure to implement specific social responsibility actions by falling back on the old argument of sport being naturally socially responsible. Nevertheless, we hypothesized that each event's specific characteristics will lead it to address the issues of CSR and/or SD in different ways. Hence, we decided to analyze a selection of very different SEOs and very different events. This choice enabled us to compare the way CSR is approached by major "one-shot" events (Olympic Games and European Football Championship), which are organized under the auspices of international governing bodies (IOC and UEFA, respectively) and by national events organized by national leagues (in rugby union and football). In addition, because the nature and form of a sports organization's commitment to CSR varies according to the context in which it operates (François and Bayle, 2015; François, Bayle and Gond, 2019), we wanted to study SEOs in different contexts. We addressed this issue by including in our sample two international SEOs (IOC and UEFA), which are subject to multiple cultural influences and which have to view CSR from a "globalized" perspective, and two national SEOs from countries (France and England) with different CSR cultures and contexts.

1.2.2 The importance of context to CSR: Anglophone vs. French approaches

The context in which an organization operates has a great impact on its approach to CSR.[4] This statement is easily verified by perusing the literature on CSR in sport, which is particularly abundant in the case of Anglophone cultures. Conversely, the literature pertaining to many European countries, including France, is much sparser, almost certainly due to the fact that the concept has not been embraced as widely in these countries. Nevertheless, wherever sport organization CSR has been studied, this research is a much more recent phenomenon than the implementation of CSR initiatives by SEOs, some of which have been involved in CSR for several decades.

Most studies of CSR in sport (see previous) have focused on English-speaking countries, where OSR is used strategically and often takes the form of donations to local communities. This is especially the case in the United States, where the concept of CSR is in keeping with American culture and the so-called WASP (White Anglo-Saxon Protestant) values, which encourage philanthropy by businesspeople and companies (Vogel, 1991). In this context, clubs and leagues are true vectors of CSR through their close relations with their communities (Lelore, 2011). CSR activities by these organizations include programmes involving internal human resources (players and coaches), who contribute time and money to worthy causes, generally implemented via foundations (Babiak and Wolfe, 2009; Extejt, 2004), and this has been the case for many years (Table 3.1).

Tax breaks available to sport organizations (and to donor sponsors) encourage them to carry out social initiatives within their local communities. In the United States, many such actions are enhanced or complemented by actions involving athletes, who contribute to their club's initiatives, either spontaneously or due to contractual obligations. In fact, the way sport is organized in North America, where professional sports clubs are private, commercial entities, has facilitated the development of sport organization social responsibility by making it easier to transpose social responsibility practices from the corporate world to professional sport. Nevertheless, most social responsibility initiatives remain exogenous, in other words, they are initiated either in response to external pressure (Babiak and Wolfe, 2009) or to combat negative public reactions (*ethical blowbacks*) to other aspects of an organization's operations. Hence, the CSR philosophy in the United States is essentially a case of heightened philanthropy aimed at improving the sometimes-negative image many people have of professional sport organizations.

Table 3.1 The earliest CSR initiatives by North America's four biggest professional leagues

League	*Year*	*Social Initiatives*
National Football League (NFL)	*1973*	– *Support to United Way of America (charitable organization)* – *Creation of the "NFL Charities" foundation*
National Basket-ball Association (NBA)	*1994*	– *Launch of the Read to Achieve programme (helping children from disadvantaged backgrounds to read)*
National Hockey League (NHL)	*1995*	– *Launch of the NHL Diversity programme (promote diversity and inclusion in hockey)*
Major League Baseball (MLB)	*1997*	– *Launch of a partnership with Boys and Girls Clubs of America (creation of neighbourhood championships)*

Source: adapted from Babiak (2010).

In France, the issue of CSR/OSR and its associated practices is still at an embryonic stage, possibly because professional sport has only recently emerged from its amateur roots. As a result, sport organizations, which have to fulfil public service as well as sporting roles, view social responsibility as an inherent part of their DNA. This characteristic is an intrinsic feature of French sport, whose operating model is a product of the way sport is run jointly by the private sector (which includes sport federations and, indirectly, clubs and leagues) and the public sector (represented by the ministry for sport). For example, many professional sports clubs receive public subsidies, in exchange for which they are expected to carry out public-service missions (in fields such as education and social inclusion through sport). As a result, OSR by French sport organizations remains highly exogenous, even though the private commercial sector has contributed to the development of OSR practices in recent years. Increasingly, OSR actions are deployed trilaterally, by a sport organization, the local authorities and sponsors, or bilaterally, by a sport organization and a private partner, through sports sponsorship or community sponsorship. Nevertheless, in contrast to the United States, community associations, foundations and endowment funds are not the main channels for social engagement. Hence, community associations, such as "ASM ô Solidarités" (ASM Clermont), and multi-partner corporate foundations involving clubs (PSG, OL, TFC, OM) are rare, and only two French sport federations (rugby and football) have created foundations (Fondation Albert Ferrasse and Fondation du Football, since turned into an endowment fund). Following the granting of "public utility" status in 2011, the foundation created by France's Olympic Committee (Fondation Henri Sérandour) can now claim to be French sport's leading philanthropic body.

2 The deployment of CSR by SEOs

We examined CSR from a "functionalist" or "business case" perspective in which we looked at CSR as a strategic tool. We present our analysis in two parts, beginning with the case of national sport federations and professional leagues, as represented by France's and England's top-flight rugby union and football championships, which, like most professional leagues in Europe, are subject to supervision by their national federation. We then look at the case of mega events owned by large international governing bodies, focusing on the Olympic Games, controlled by the IOC and, to a lesser extent, the UEFA Euro 2016 football championship, hosted by France.

2.1 Recurring events: A comparison of CSR practices by professional rugby union and football leagues in France and England

Leagues and clubs that organize recurring events (e.g., championships) are some of the most widely studied SEOs with respect to CSR. The analysis we present here is drawn from François, Bayle and Gond's (2019) study of the first-division professional rugby union and football championships in France and England. Table 3.2 provides general facts and figures for the four leagues. We begin by

Table 3.2 Facts and figures for the first-division rugby and football championships in France (Top 14, Ligue 1) and England (Aviva Premiership Rugby, Premier League), taken from François, Bayle, and Gond (2019)

	Top 14	*Ligue 1*	*Aviva Premiership Rugby*	*Premier League*
Body in charge of organizing the championship	Ligue Nationale de Rugby (LNR)	Ligue de Football Professionnel	Premier Rugby Limited	FA Premier League Limited
Statute of the league (year it was created)	Association under federation supervision (1998)	Association under federation supervision (1946)	Limited company (1995)	Limited company (1992)
Number of clubs involved	14	20	12	20
Global turnover in 2016	€303 million	€1,867 million	£186 million (€203 million)	£3,639 million (€3,980 million)
Main sources of finance in 2017	Partnerships (GMF, Société Générale, Orange, etc.) and TV rights (Canal+)	TV rights (Canal+, BeIn Sport) and partnerships	Partnerships (Aviva, Land Rover, etc.) & TV rights (BT Sport)	TV rights (Sky, BT Sport, BBC) and partnerships

describing the contexts in which these leagues and their constituent clubs deploy CSR, and then examine the way they implement and communicate their CSR initiatives.

2.1.1 Current context: CSR as a strategic asset

All of the leagues studied have undertaken CSR initiatives for a number of years, often in the form of social engagement with charities and/or community organizations. However, these forms of engagement have gradually been superseded by more structured and more strategic actions. In France, social engagement is a key component of the strategic plans published recently by both the Ligue Nationale de Rugby (LNR), which runs the Top 14 (T14) championship, and the Ligue de Football Professionnel (LFP), which runs the Ligue 1 (L1) championship.

Having included social engagement in its 2016 strategic plan (LNR, 2016), the LNR called upon the consultants Deloitte to help it draw up a structured approach to CSR in the form of a "social engagement strategy", which it published in 2017. Realizing the time was ripe for deploying a social strategy, the LNR created a number of programmes, which it has launched in partnership with private (SD strategy launched in 2013 by the French Rugby Federation) and public (environmental commitments by the Minister for Sport) bodies. This strategy is firmly anchored in "rugby's values" and centred around three pillars – ensure the league's internal stakeholders uphold rugby's values, build on existing social actions[5] and share values beyond the world of rugby. Programmes relating to these pillars are financed from a budget of €2.3 million, allocated for the period 2017–2021. In addition, in 2017 the LNR began examining the possibility of recruiting a dedicated CSR manager. The LFP also published a strategic plan in 2017, one of whose aims is to "*define and develop an ambitious CSR plan*" (LFP, 2017a). That same year, the LFP appointed a director of external communications for CSR and published a brochure called "Jouons la Collectif" ("Play Together"), which presents the social and community actions undertaken by the league's 20 clubs (LFP, 2017b). In fact, "Jouons la Collectif" is just the latest in a series of reports published by the LFP in order to highlight the social actions carried out by the league's clubs and demonstrate football's positive impacts (LFP, 2013, 2015).

In the UK, Aviva Premiership Rugby (APR) grouped together its national CSR programmes into two major campaigns (*Play* and *Breakthru*), which it launched in 2013 and which it deploys through its 12 clubs (Premiership Rugby, 2013a, 2013b). The *Play* campaign includes programmes aimed at increasing participation in rugby among young people and at raising standards, whereas the *Breakthru* campaign contains programmes in the fields of health, education and social advancement through rugby. APR runs these campaigns in association with strategically selected partners within the public (British Council, Department of Culture, Media and Sport, etc.) and private (Land Rover, Aviva, etc.) sectors. Local implementation of these national partnerships is ensured by the clubs' "community department" managers, who work in conjunction with the

APR's Community and CSR Director, appointed in 2012 to oversee social and community programmes.

Of the four leagues we studied, it is the Premier League's (PL) community initiatives that are the most institutionalized. The roots of this institutionalization can be traced back to the community programmes launched by successive Labour and Conservative governments in the late 1970s and 1980s, most notably the "Football in The Community" (FiTC) programme. FiTC, which was created by the Football League[6] and Professional Footballers' Association with support from the government (Mellor, 2008; Walters, 2009) in order to reconnect clubs with their local communities, resulted in many English football clubs creating their own community departments. In 2007, the PL began taking a more structured approach to CSR, launching its "Creating Chances" programme, which includes CSR initiatives in five areas: Community cohesion, education, health, participation in sport and international projects (Morgan, 2013). Steered by a dedicated community projects team, these initiatives are implemented locally by the PL's 20 clubs and financed by various bodies within English football, most notably, the PL's Charitable Fund, which allocate substantial funds to the clubs (Anagnostopulos, 2013).

2.1.2 Communication and implementation of CSR initiatives: Proof that context is more important than sector

We analyzed the communication and implementation dimensions of the four leagues' and their constituent clubs' CSR practices by assessing five indicators for each dimension. In the case of CSR communication, we assessed the media used, presence/absence of reporting, type of vocabulary used, communication about partners and orientation of the message; in the case of CSR implementation, we assessed number, type and scope of initiatives, means of delivery and partner involvement. Our analyses revealed major differences between the two countries on both dimensions of CSR.

These differences were most striking in the case of CSR communication, where they affected all five indicators. For example, English clubs use more communication channels (2.67 and 3.7 channels for APR and PL clubs, respectively) than French clubs (0.64 and 1.2 channels for T14 and L1 clubs, respectively) and CSR communication by the two French leagues and their clubs tends to be weak and non-strategic, whereas CSR communication by the two English leagues and their clubs is generally strong. In fact, because CSR is more culturally rooted and accepted in the UK than it is in France, communication has always been an integral part of CSR by English clubs and is characterized by its strategic nature, as is shown by the fact that the clubs do not hesitate to set out mission statements regarding their CSR initiatives, which they communicate via numerous channels. Furthermore, only two French football clubs (Lyon[7] and Saint Etienne), compared with a third of APR clubs and half of PL clubs, issue reports detailing their social engagement. Indeed, PL clubs are leaders in this area, as Chelsea was the first European club to publish an annual CSR report (in 2006), and Manchester United's (since 2011), Manchester City's and Tottenham's (both since 2015) CSR reports go as far as evaluating their actions' impacts.

We also found substantial differences between the two countries in terms of CSR implementation, most notably with respect to number of initiatives carried out and means of delivery. Compared with French clubs, English clubs carry out more CSR actions, many of which are bottom-up projects and local versions of national programmes. These actions are often implemented via foundations, which have become the standard channel through which English rugby and football clubs deploy CSR (all PL clubs and all APR clubs except London Irish, Northampton Saints and Wasps have set up a foundation). In contrast, only three T14 clubs and eight L1 clubs have set up a community association, endowment fund or foundation.[8] Using foundations and other similar structures allows initiatives to be implemented more strategically by giving greater exposure to associated sponsors and stakeholders.

2.2 Major "one-shot" events: The cases of the IOC and UEFA

So-called mega sports events are organized under the supervision of major sports institutions such as the IOC, FIFA and UEFA. Smaller world and continental championships are organized by other international or continental federations. The globalization of sport over the last few decades, as typified by the emergence of major new players such as Qatar, which hosted 85 international events in 2016, has been accompanied by a huge increase in the number of international competitions owned or controlled by international federations. For example, the 25 international Olympic federations organized 2,162 events in 2013, compared with just 160 in 1975.[9] The number and type of CSR and SD initiatives associated with these events is greatly dependent on both the requirements imposed by their owners and local priorities, which vary according to the host country's political, economic and cultural characteristics. The following section explores CSR within two organizations responsible for organizing one-shot mega events – the Olympic Games, controlled by the IOC, and the European Football Championship, controlled by UEFA. We begin by examining the genesis and development of CSR and SD within the IOC and then look at the way UEFA has integrated the notion of sustainability into its flagship event, focusing on its latest edition, Euro 2016, which was hosted by France.

2.2.1 Olympic social responsibility: Genesis and development

The IOC is unarguably the world's most powerful sport organization and therefore a potential leader in terms of social responsibility. In fact, the IOC has been aware of the need to convey a certain degree of Olympic social responsibility ever since its earliest years, during which Coubertin's elitist, liberal, pacifist and educational view of sport underpinned the foundation of Olympism's core values and ethics and shaped its governing body.

This initial phase of Olympic social responsibility was transformed by the "Samaranch revolution" of the 1980s, when Juan Antonio Samaranch led the IOC into the age of liberal capitalism and the market economy. As the world entered a new era, symbolized by the end of the Cold War and the break up of the Soviet Bloc, Samaranch remoulded Coubertin's original ideals to accommodate liberal economics and globalization. This period also saw the publication of the Brundtland Report (1987) and the Rio Earth Summit (1992), which catapulted SD to the top of the world's political agenda. The IOC quickly began using SD as a new argument to prove its legitimacy, adding the environment to sport and culture as one of the pillars of Olympism in 1994, creating a Sport and Environment Commission in 1995, and publishing its Agenda 21 "Sport for Sustainable Development" in 1999. The Olympic Games, especially the Winter Games as of Lillehammer 1994, expressed a desire to be ever greener and environmentally virtuous. More generally, the IOC increased its partnerships with UN agencies and began the intensive diplomacy that would finally bear fruit in 2009 when the IOC was granted observer status at the UN General Assembly. Nevertheless, a number of scandals during this period severely tarnished the reputations of the IOC and the Olympic Movement, leading to the creation of new regulatory bodies (Court of Arbitration for Sport, 1984, and World Anti-Doping Agency, 1999) and new attempts to improve the organization's governance (Chappelet, 2015).

Samaranch was succeeded as IOC president by Jacques Rogge, who oversaw the publication of two symbolic documents on "sustainability", the Olympic Movement's preferred term for SD and CSR/OSR. RIO+ 20[10] provided a list of SD actions carried out by the IOC and by Organising Committees of the Olympic Games (OCOGs), while ISO standard 20121: "*Event* sustainability *management systems* – Requirements with guidance for use" was presented as being part of London 2012's SD legacy.

SD was also the theme of a 2012 forum for international federations entitled "Increasing the positive impact of your event: Sustainable Event Management". Although this forum demonstrated the international sports movement's growing awareness of the need to produce its events as responsibly as possible, very few federations have been prepared to commit their sport to any sort of centralized social strategy, whether aimed at addressing problems within society or at promoting development through sport.

The third and most recent phase in Olympic social responsibility began with the election of Thomas Bach as IOC president in 2013, when the IOC began addressing the challenge of defining and implementing a coherent, global and integrated OSR strategy. A few large, commercial sport organizations, such as the NBA, appear to have adopted this type of approach, bringing together the league, franchises, players and partners. However, such integrated CSR strategies are very rare in the world of sport (Bayle, Chappelet, François and Maltese, 2011).

According to "The IOC Sustainability Strategy", a framework document summarizing the IOC's recent reflections on this issue, published at the end of 2016, sustainability is one of the three pillars of the Olympic Agenda 2020 (alongside credibility and youth). This document also contains two recommendations on how the Olympic Games (Box 3.1) and the Olympic Movement in general (Box 3.2) can incorporate sustainability.

Box 3.1 Recommendation 4: Include sustainability in all aspects of the Olympic Games

The IOC to take a more proactive position and leadership role with regard to sustainability and ensure that it is included in all aspects of the planning and staging of the Olympic Games.

1 Develop a sustainability strategy to enable potential and actual Olympic Games organizers to integrate and implement sustainability measures that encompass economic, social and environmental spheres in all stages of their project;
2 Assist newly elected Organizing Committees to establish the best possible governance for the integration of sustainability throughout the organization;
3 The IOC to ensure post-Games monitoring of the Games legacy with the support of the National Olympic Committee and external organizations such as the World Union of Olympic Cities (UMVO).

Box 3.2 Recommendation 5: Include sustainability within the Olympic Movement's daily operations

1 The IOC to embrace sustainability principles:

- The IOC to include sustainability in its day-to-day operations. The IOC to include sustainability in its procurement of goods and services, as well as events organization (meetings, conferences, etc.)
- The IOC to reduce its travel impact and offset its carbon emissions
- The IOC to apply the best possible sustainability standards for the consolidation of its Headquarters in Lausanne

2 The IOC to engage and assist Olympic Movement stakeholders in integrating sustainability within their own organization and operations by:

- Developing recommendations
- Providing tools, e.g., best practices and scorecards
- Providing mechanisms to ensure the exchange of information between Olympic stakeholders
- Using existing channels, such as Olympic Solidarity, to help and assist in implementing initiatives

3 To achieve the above, the IOC to cooperate with relevant expert organizations such as the United Nations Environment Programme (UNEP).

The IOC Sustainability Strategy, which centres around three areas of responsibility and five key themes (Figure 3.1), draws on both the IOC's strategic plan

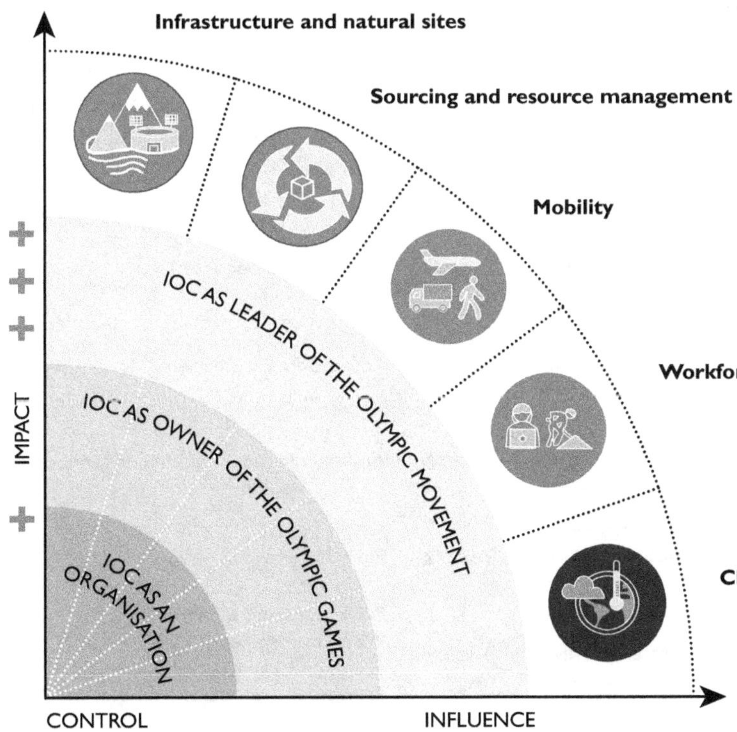

Figure 3.1 The IOC Sustainability Strategy (IOC, 2016)

and the 17 SD objectives targeted by the UN in 2015, which include eradicating poverty, combatting climate change and combatting injustice and inequality. The UN's "2030 Agenda for Sustainable Development" describes how organizations can contribute to SD and makes sport and sport institutions important partners for achieving SD objectives.[11]

2.2.2 Euro 2016: Another approach to integrating sustainability

Just like the IOC, UEFA is aware of the importance of having a coherent sustainability strategy for its flagship event. In the case of Euro 2016, this strategy was drawn up by the organizing committee and the event's internal and external stakeholders on the basis of a three-stage analysis aimed at the following:

1. Identifying the main stakeholders and their commitment to environmental, social and economic issues.
2. Setting priorities as a function of risks (probability and impact) and according to stakeholder expectations, the GRI's G4 guidelines, benchmarking, external assessments, examples of good practices, and the feasibility of corrective action plans.
3. Approving key issues and integrating them into concrete SD projects.

The resulting strategy was the subject of two "social responsibility and sustainable development" reports, published a year before (N−1) and a year after (N+1) the event and drawn up in line with the GRI's G4 guidelines and events supplement. The strategy targeted four areas that fell within UEFA's responsibility

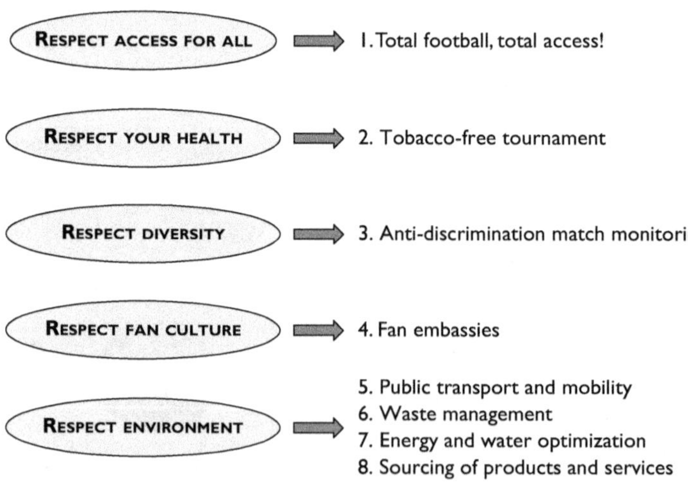

Figure 3.2 Euro 2016's eight strategic priorities for CSR/SD, taken from the Euro 2016 N+1 CSR/SD report, figure adapted from Union of European Football Association (2016)

(governance, tournament, preparations, behind the scenes) and identified eight priorities for CSR and/or SD actions (Figure 3.2). The Euro 2016 organizing committee also followed the lead of the London 2012 OCOG and applied for ISO 20121 certification. As a result, its CSR strategy, just like its quality management system, had to be designed from a continuous improvement perspective. In order to measure the strategy's success, UEFA defined eight strategic priorities containing 15 specific objectives with associated performance indicators (Table 3.3).

Table 3.3 Overview of priorities, objectives, main outcomes and performance, and lessons learned for organizers of the next edition, taken from the Euro 2016 N+1 CSR/SD report table

Priorities	*Objectives*	*Main outcomes and performance*	*Lessons learned*
Total football, total access!	• Coordinate and monitor the operational implementation of Access for All in partnership with CAFE and the stadiums • Create accessible stadiums at UEFA EURO 2016 to ensure an inclusive welcome and match experience for disabled fans	• 16,328 tickets for wheelchair users (including companions) and 6,423 tickets for easy-access seats. This accounts for about 0.9% of spectators, whereas people with such mobility problems account for about 3.8% of the population in the EU. • 50% of venues met minimum European standards for wheelchair user numbers (UEFA/CAFE standard)	• For 2020, UEFA is to consider removing rows or building platforms to improve sightlines • Access assessments should also be undertaken much earlier in the process at future final rounds, with advice given on navigation and signage ahead of the tournament
Tobacco-free tournament	• Make all stadiums tobacco-free for UEFA EURO 2016 matches (with the support of Healthy Stadia)	• The smoking of tobacco products was prohibited in all indoor and outdoor areas within the stadium perimeter, but fans did not always respect this policy	• The stadium perimeter was too ambitious; the policy should have been limited to the stadium bowl. More preventive action is also needed to facilitate communication with fans

(*Continued*)

Table 3.3 (Continued)

Priorities	*Objectives*	*Main outcomes and performance*	*Lessons learned*
			• Communication was enhanced by enthusiastic volunteers and the use of all possible channels (the media, half-time announcements, the big screen, tickets, signage, etc.). Stewards did not cooperate effectively, which needs to be improved for future events
Anti-racism and anti-discrimination	• Enforce a zero-tolerance approach, educate people and ensure that discrimination inside stadiums is reported, investigated and sanctioned	• Eight instances of racism/discrimination or misconduct were reported • Two national associations were sanctioned following incidents	• Expanding the scope of anti-discrimination measures to protect and train stewards could be a good idea
Fan embassies	• Create a fan-friendly, safe and secure environment in the host cities • Provide the best possible welcome, advice and support to fans, in cooperation with Football Supporters Europe (FSE) • Liaise between national team supporters' organizations and host cities	• 19 of the 24 teams had fan embassies, which was proportionally lower than in 2012 (when 14 of the 16 teams had fan embassies). This is because seven teams were appearing at a UEFA EURO for the first time • A fan guide app and a 24-hour helpline were made available to fans.	• Communication for UEFA EURO 2020 will be more digital • FSE to obtain recognition as the voice of the fans • Support in communicating social responsibility activities such as the no-smoking policy to be enhanced

Priorities	*Objectives*	*Main outcomes and performance*	*Lessons learned*
		• 80,000 individual fans visited fan embassies, using their services a total of 202,500 times between them	
Public transport and mobility	• Minimize the environmental impact of transport • Ensure good mobility to, between and within the host cities for spectators, visitors and residents • Encourage public transport and walking	• 150,000 additional seats in public transport in France during event • Internal public transport policy • 35,000 tonnes of CO_2 equivalent offset by UEFA and national associations	• City combi-tickets to be ensured • Shared mobility app to be improved • Offsetting of fans' travel to be included in tickets prices • Hybrid/electric vehicles in car fleet
Waste management	• Implement a 3R policy (reduce, reuse, recycle) to achieve • 50% recycling rate • Zero waste to landfill • Improved awareness among the general public	• Overall reduction in volume of waste • Recycling rate of 38% within stadiums • Creative solutions adopted in cooperation with NGOs to find second lives for items	• Dual-bin system for public areas in different cities/ countries must be coordinated well in advance • 3R policy must be set out more clearly in contracts with partners and suppliers
Energy and water optimization	• Reduce the environmental impact of energy use • Minimize the need for water	• Implementation of energy-efficient devices and technologies • Use of water-saving solutions	• Organizers required to purchase certified renewable electricity
Sourcing of products and services	• Promote responsible sourcing of products and services	• 71% of items produced in Europe; 51% of sourcing budget spent on items produced in Europe	• Stronger due diligence could have been done on CSR as regards suppliers of sensitive branded

(*Continued*)

Table 3.3 (Continued)

Priorities	*Objectives*	*Main outcomes and performance*	*Lessons learned*
	• Help buyers to consider environmental and social issues within the supply chain and encourage suppliers and licensees to follow social responsibility and sustainability guidelines	• Sourcing guide developed for buyers • Large sustainability projects in partnership with major suppliers	goods and merchandising (children's toys and textiles). • Certification should be part of the selection process for suppliers (e.g., ISO 20121)

Source: adapted from Union of European Football Association (2016)

These two case studies illustrate the increasingly proactive approaches adopted by the owners of mega sports events, whether they manage their events directly, as in the case of UEFA and the Euro football championship, or whether they oversee an outside organizing body, as in the case of the IOC and OCOGs.

2.3 CSR by SEOs: Specificities and paradoxes

Although the examples described previously show the progress made with respect to CSR and SD over the last few years, the issue remains contentious and the deployment of CSR has given rise to a number of paradoxes. This section begins by briefly summarizing the CSR practices adopted by the SEOs in our study and then describes paradoxes and contradictions within CSR practices, focusing on the issue of Olympic social responsibility and sustainability.

2.3.1 Specificities of SEO CSR by type of event

There are major differences in the way organizers of recurring events, run by leagues and clubs, and organizers of "one-shot" mega events, supervised by international governing bodies, address the issues of CSR and sustainability.

CSR relating to recurring events raises the issue of the terminology used to refer to social responsibility practices, as organizers of such events often concentrate mostly on social engagement and often overlook the other two classic dimensions (economic and environmental) of CSR and SD. In addition, our analysis shows a high degree of convergence in the types of social engagement adopted by all T14, L1, APR and PL clubs, whose actions tend to use the power of sport to address issues relating to health, education and social inclusion. On the other hand, few clubs have developed actions targeting environmental issues, although the environment is gradually rising up the CSR agendas of certain clubs, most notably L1 clubs and, to a lesser extent, PL clubs. Despite operating in very different contexts, the convergence towards implementing ever more explicit and strategic CSR actions means that similarities between the two countries in the ways clubs communicate and deploy CSR should not stop there. The most obvious sign of this convergence is the increased use of foundations and endowment funds by French clubs, which suggests that the formerly implicit and non-strategic nature of French clubs' social engagement is giving way to a more explicit way of using CSR to achieve strategic objectives.[12]

Sustainability is a much more central concern in the case of "one-shot" mega events, whose organizers have to pay particular attention to their event's environmental impact. As a result, a large amount of information about the impacts and sustainability of mega sports events has been collected by a wide variety of bodies, which may or may not be closely associated with the event (owners, organizers, consultants, public bodies), and at different times in the life of an event (before, during, after). The data collected is of many different types (strategies, measures of impacts, sustainability reports) and is generally compiled into reports that are published before and/or after major events such as the Winter Olympics (e.g., Vancouver 2010), Summer Olympics (e.g., London 2012, Rio 2016), FIFA World Cup (e.g., Rio 2014) and UEFA Euro (e.g., France 2016) (Table 3.4).

Table 3.4 Reports relating to the sustainability of sports events. Source: compiled by the authors.

Event	*Report*	*Year*
Vancouver 2010 Olympic Games	Sustainability report	2006–2007, 2007–2008, 2008–2009, 2009–2010
	Olympic Games Impact	2007, 2009, 2011, 2013
	Carbon Neutral Discussion paper	2007
London 2012 Olympic Games	Sustainability report	2012
	Olympic Games Impact	2010/2015
	Carbon Footprint Study	2010
2014 FIFA World Cup	Sustainability report	2014
UEFA EURO 2016	Social responsibility and SD	2015, 2016
Rio 2016 Olympic Games	Sustainability report	2014

2.3.2 *Paradoxes and contradictions: The case of Olympism, or how to contribute to a better world*

Despite the desire of SEOs to embrace CSR and deploy CSR initiatives within the Olympic Movement, a number of contradictions and shortfalls remain. For example, the bodies engaged to carry out impact studies prior to large events are often contracted to do so by the SEO, which raises questions about the independence and impartiality of their assessments (Gouguet and Brocard, 2014).

Thanks to massive public investment and an SD approach that is often supported and promoted by the OCOG's public partners, the Olympic Games remain the flagship vehicle for the Olympic Movement and the IOC. Nevertheless, the scope of SD actions varies greatly according to the national context (Beijing/London; Vancouver/Sochi) and Olympic Games' impacts and legacies, whether in the host country or elsewhere, remain difficult to evaluate, notwithstanding attempts to measure impacts over the longer term. Similarly, the way the IOC has structured its OSR/SD around three key themes (youth, sustainability and credibility) is open to criticism. First, the youth component of the IOC's strategy is largely borne by the Youth Olympic Games, which involves only a relatively small number of young athletes. Hence, the IOC cannot be said to have a true strategy for young people, despite obvious changes in young people's behaviours, including declining interest in the Olympic Games, in competitive sport and clubs and a tendency to do less physical exercise, leading to health problems and shorter life expectancy. Second, in terms of sustainability, the IOC's social objectives are divided into five key areas (sport for all, development through sport, women and sport, education, peace through sport), but these themes are more a declaration of intent than a structured and forceful policy. Finally, in terms of credibility, although the IOC has been attempting to address the issues of good and responsible governance since the early 2000s, it has little influence over other organizations within the Olympic Movement (national Olympic committees – NOCs, international and national federations). Thus, the widely reported governance crises that shook the Olympic system in 2015 (FIFAgate and the Russian-doping cover-up at the International Association of Athletics Federations) and 2016 (illegal sale of Olympic tickets by Patrick Hickey, an influential IOC member) are serious threats to the credibility of both the IOC as an institution and the Olympic Movement as a whole. To these scandals can be added suspicions of corruption against the former pole-vault champion and IOC member Sergei Bubka and against Frank Fredericks. These events show that the Olympic Movement is finding it difficult to truly reform its governance, despite attempts to promote the principles set out in the "Basic Universal Principles of Good Governance", introduced by the IOC in 2008, and a new governance framework drawn up by the Association of Summer Olympic International Federations (ASOIF) in 2016.

What is more, no single department within the IOC has been given overall responsibility for the organization's social strategy, which compounds the already complex task of implementation. In fact, in a classic case of "silo mentality", responsibility for the different components of the IOC's sustainability strategy (Figure 3.1) is scattered across numerous departments and commissions. Furthermore, NOCs vary greatly in terms of their autonomy and strength, with only about 20 out of 205 NOCs truly working on these issues,[13] and many international federations are poorly organized, unprofessional and uninterested in CSR and/or SD (which tends to be limited to developing sport in poorer countries and the process of attributing major events). Although the IOC's social strategy has resulted in the creation of international partnerships and global initiatives (UN, NGOs, multinationals, etc.), these partnerships are not very active around the world and can therefore be seen as mostly "cosmetic".[14] Thus, even though having a positive impact is an inherent aspect of Olympism and part of its *raison d'être*, any actions taken tend to focus uniquely on elite Olympic sport.

It could be thought that the ever-larger sums of money the IOC redistributes to NOCs and international federations would give it the power to impose OSR/SD on the Olympic Movement, but this is not the case. In fact, even in a context of reduced bids to host the Olympic Games, redistributing resources is more a way of maintaining the Olympic system's political and economic balances and of protecting an economic model based mostly on TV rights,[15] than a lever that can be used to prompt greater social responsibility by individual bodies within the system. Consequently, members of the Olympic Movement, whether NOCs, international federations or athletes, deploy OSR as they see fit. Many athletes, for example, have launched their own, personal initiatives, often in the form of charitable and community actions implemented via a foundation. Nevertheless, the Olympic symbol still has enormous power with the public, which the IOC could harness to take action on many of the world's most urgent economic, social, educational, health and environmental problems.

Conclusion

Today, SEOs are highly aware of the need to run their events in a responsible and sustainable way, and they know that if they achieve this, these events become extremely powerful tools for promoting sustainable development among their stakeholders. Nevertheless, many SEOs have insufficient resources and qualified staff to integrate a truly comprehensive CSR and/or SD approach into the organization's managerial system. Unlike large corporations, some of which have revised their production and economic models and their performance-evaluation criteria in order to incorporate CSR, many SEOs still take a partial or cosmetic approach to social responsibility.

This type of attitude to social responsibility creates substantial risks to an SEO's legitimacy, image and credibility, which can become serious enough to threaten the organization's existence. Mega events such as the Olympic Games and FIFA World Cup have made a lot of progress in terms of CSR and SD, but they remain highly dependent on the ability of a host country/city to manage sustainability and legacy issues in such a way as to justify the considerable sums invested in its event and the public subsidies it receives (as exemplified by the criticisms levelled at the 2014 Winter Olympics, 2014 Football World Cup and 2016 Summer Olympics). This is why SEOs will increasingly be obliged to show, via independent, global analyses, that their events produce positive socio-economic and environmental legacies.

Notes

1 This is notably the case in France, where CSR is sometimes referred to as "responsabilité sociétale des entreprises" rather than "responsabilité sociale des entreprises". Some French researchers consider the term "societal" to be more global than "social", a term that is often used in France to refer to the relations between employees and employers (Gond & Igalens, 2012).
2 See, for example, "Value for Nestlé" and "Value for Society".
3 See the *Journal of Sport Management*, 2009 (vol. 23, n°6) and the *Journal of Management and Organization*, 2010 (vol. 16, n°4) which include around 15 papers on the subject of CSR in sport.
4 For more on this issue, see the special issue of *European Sport Management Quarterly*, due out in 2019, on CSR in European sport. Contributors to this issue were encouraged to take a transnational comparative approach in order to reveal differences between the CSR models adopted in different countries.
5 Theme created in the light of the results of a questionnaire completed by the 12 T14 clubs and 12 Pro D2 clubs, which showed that 80% of clubs had been heavily involved in all or some of the pillars of social action (local impact, solidarity, rugby community, environment and ethics).
6 The *Football League* was created in 1888, making it Europe's oldest football competition. The "Premier League" replaced the original "first division" in 1992.
7 Because Lyon FC's holding company, OL Groupe, is a listed company, article 116 of the 2001 NRE Act and the decrees issued following the second Grenelle Environment Forum in 2012 (see Section 1of this chapter) require the club to publish a social responsibility report.
8 Three football clubs (Paris, Lyon, Marseille) have set up both an endowment fund and a foundation.
9 Source: Association of Summer International Olympic Federations (2013).
10 The document's full title was "*Sustainability through sport: implementing the Olympic movement's Agenda 21*".
11 See paragraph 37 of Agenda 2030: "*Sport is also an important enabler of sustainable development. We recognize the growing contribution of sport to the realization of development and peace in its promotion of tolerance and respect and the contributions it makes to the empowerment of women and of young people, individuals and communities as well as to health, education and social inclusion objectives*".
12 In this respect, see the numerous reports published by French leagues, such as the LFP, that now refer explicitly to the issue of CSR
13 Source: interview with a senior manager at the IOC.
14 Ibid.
15 NBC paid the record sum of $7.65 billion for the rights to televise the Olympic Games in the United States during the period 2021–2032. The American network had already obtained the rights for Sochi (2014), Rio (2016), Pyeongchang (2018) and Tokyo (2020) for $4.38 billion. After the decision to award the 2024 Summer Olympics to France and 2028 Summer Olympics to the United States (2028), the

award of the 2022 Winter Olympics to China, and FIFA's decision to award the 2018 World Cup to Russia and the 2022 World Cup to Qatar, the world's largest economic and political powers have been served for the next 10 years.

References

Anagnostopulos, C. (2013). "Getting the Tactics Right". Implementing CSR in English football, in J-L. Paramio-Salcines, K. Babiak, G. Walters (Eds.), *The Routledge handbook of sport and corporate social responsibility*. Routledge, Oxon (UK), pp. 91–104.

Babiak, K. (2010). The role and relevance of corporate social responsibility in sport: a view from the top. *Journal of Management and Organization*, 16(4), 528–549.

Babiak, K., Wolfe, R. (2006). More than just a game? Corporate social responsibility and super bowl XL. *Sport Marketing Quarterly*, 15(4), 214–222.

Babiak, K., Wolfe, R. (2009). Determinants of corporate social responsibility in professional sport: Internal and external factors. *Journal of Sport Management*, 23(6), 717–742.

Bayle, E., Chappelet, J-L., François, A., Maltese, L. (2011). *Sport et RSE. Vers un management responsable?* De Boeck Editions, Bruxelles.

Boltanski, L., Chiapello, E. (1999). *Le nouvel esprit du capitalisme*. Gallimard, Paris.

Bowen, H.R. (1953). *Social responsibilities of the businessman*. Harper & Row, New York.

Bradish, C., Cronin, J.J. (2009). Corporate social responsibility in sport. *Journal of Sport Management*, 23(6), 691–697.

Breitbarth, T., Harris, P. (2008). The role of corporate social responsibility in the football business: towards the development of a conceptual model. *European Sport Management Quarterly*, 8(2), 179–206.

Capron, M., Quairel-Lanoizelée, F., Turcotte, M-F. (2011). *ISO 26 000 : une norme "hors norme"? Vers une conception mondiale de la responsabilité sociétale*. Economica, Paris.

Carroll, A.B. (1979). A three-dimensional conceptual model of corporate performance. *Academy of Management Review*, 4(4), 497–505.

Carroll, A.B. (1991). The pyramid of corporate social responsibility: toward the moral management of organizational stakeholders. *Business Horizons*, 34(4), 39–48.

Chappelet, J-L. (2015). Autonomy and governance: necessary bedfellows in the fight against corruption in sport, in *Global Corruption Report*. Transparency International.

Cohen, D. (2012). *Homo oeconomicus. Prophète (égaré) des temps nouveaux*. Albin Michel, Paris.

Commission of the European Communities (2001). *Green paper: promoting a European framework for corporate social responsibility*. Official Publications of European Communities, Brussels.

Djaballah, M., Hautbois, C., Desbordes, M. (2017). Sponsors' CSR strategies in sport: a sensemaking approach of corporations established in France. *Sport Management Review*, 20(2), 211–225.

Elkington, J. (1997). *Cannibals with forks*. Capstone, Oxford.

Extejt, M.M. (2004). Philanthropy and professional sports teams. *International Journal of Sport Management*, 5(3), 215–228.

François, A., Bayle, E. (2015). La RSE: nouvelle composante stratégique des clubs de football professionnels européens, in M. Desbordes, N. Chanavat (Eds.), *Le marketing du football*. Economica, Paris, pp. 318–343.

François, A., Bayle, E., Gond, J.-P. (2019), A multilevel analysis of implicit and explicit CSR in French and UK professional sport. *European Sport Management Quarterly*, 19(1), 15–37.

Freeman, R.E. (1984). *Strategic management: a stakeholder approach*. Pitman, Boston.
Friedman, M. (1962). *Capitalism and freedom*. The University of Chicago Press, Chicago.
Friedman, M. (1970). The social responsibility of business is to increase its profits. *New York Times Magazine*, 13th September issue, 122–126.
Friestad, M., Wright, P. (1994). The persuasion knowledge model: how people cope with persuasion attempts. *Journal of Consumer Research*, 21(1), 1–31.
Godfrey, P.C. (2009). Corporate social responsibility in sport: an overview and key issues. *Journal of Sport Management*, 23(6), 698–716.
Gond, J-P. (2010). *Gérer la performance sociétale de l'entreprise*. Vuibert, Paris.
Gond, J-P. (2011). La responsabilité sociale de l'entreprise au-delà du fonctionnalisme: un cadre d'analyse pluraliste de l'interface entreprise – société. *Finance Contrôle Stratégie*, 14(2), 37–66.
Gond, J.-P., Igalens, J. (2012). *Manager la responsabilité sociale de l'entreprise*. Pearson, Paris.
Gond, J.-P., Moon, J. (2011). Corporate social responsibility in retrospect and prospect: exploring the life-cycle of an essentially contested concept, in J.-P. Gond, J. Moon (Eds.), *Major works in corporate social responsibility*. Routledge, Oxon, pp. 1–28.
Gouguet, J.-J., Brocard, J.-F. (2014). Grands événements sportifs: la nécessité d'une réévaluation. *Futuribles*, 401, 5–19.
International Olympic Committee (2016). IOC sustainability strategy. Executive summary. Lausanne, Switzerland.
ISO (2010). *Lignes directrices relatives à la responsabilité sociétale*. International Standardization Organization, Genève.
Lee M-D.P. (2008). A review of the theories of corporate social responsibility: its evolutionary path and the road ahead. *International Journal of Management Reviews*, 10(1), 53–73.
Lelore, E. (2011). Le club de football professionnel comme moteur de l'action socio-éducative en Europe : définition des publics et modalités d'action, in G. Robin (Ed.), *Football, Europe et régulations*. Villeneuve d'Ascq, Septentrion, pp. 133–144.
LFP (2013). *Cœur de clubs. Actions Citoyennes et Sociales des Clubs Professionnels de Football. Panorama 2013*. Publications de la Ligue de Football Professionnel, Paris.
LFP (2015). *Cœur de clubs. Actions Citoyennes et Sociales des Clubs Professionnels de Football. Panorama 2015*. Publications de la Ligue de Football Professionnel, Paris.
LFP (2017a). *Plan Stratégique de la LFP*. Publications de la Ligue de Football Professionnel, Paris.
LFP (2017b). *Jouons la Collectif ! Etat des Lieux des Actions Sociétales & Citoyennes du Football Professionnel Français*. Publications de la Ligue de Football Professionnel, Paris.
LNR (2016). *Plan Stratégique 2016–2023*. Publications de la Ligue Nationale de Rugby, Paris.
Martinet, A.-C., Payaud, M.A. (2009). Un cadre théorique intégrateur pour le management stratégique "BOP". *Revue de l'Organisation Responsable*, 4(1), 19–30.
Martinet, A.-C., Payaud, M.A. (2010). Stratégies RSE-BOP et soin des communautés humaines. Concepts et propositions génériques. *Management International*, 14(2), 31–51.
Mellor, G. (2008). The Janus-Faced sport: English football, community and the legacy of the Third Way. *Soccer & Society*, 9(3), 313–324.
Morgan, S. (2013). The Premier League. A commitment to social responsibility, in J-L. Paramio-Salcines, K. Babiak, G. Walters (Eds.), The Routledge handbook of sport and corporate social responsibility. Routledge, Oxon (UK), pp. 251–262.

Paramio-Salcines, J.L., Babiak, K., Walters, G. (2013). *Routledge Handbook of Sport and Corporate Social Responsibility*. Routledge, Oxon.

Parent, M.M., Chappelet, J-L. (2015). *Routledge Handbook of Sports Event Management*. Routledge, Oxon.

Porter, M.E., Kramer, M.R. (2011). Creating shared value. *Harvard Business Review*, 89(1/2), 62–77.

Prahalad, C.K. (2004). *4 milliards de nouveaux consommateurs*. Village Mondial, Paris.

Premiership Rugby (2013a). *Play. Creating Opportunities to Participate, Develop and Excel in Rugby*. Premiership Rugby Official Publication, Twickenham (UK).

Premiership Rugby (2013b). *Breakthru. Developing Sustainable Health, Education & Social Change Outcomes through Rugby*. Premiership Rugby Official Publication, Twickenham (UK).

Rodriguez, P., Késenne, S. Dietl, S. (2009). *Social responsibility and sustainability in sports*. Universidad de Oviedo, Oviedo.

Sautereau-Moquet, C. (2010). *Le contrôle sociétal : les cas Lafarge et Danone. De nouveaux modèles de management portés par le projet de développement durable*. Vuibert, Paris.

Smith, A.C.T., Westerbeek, H.M. (2007). Sport as a vehicle for deploying corporate social responsibility. *Journal of Corporate Citizenship*, 25, 43–54.

Stiglitz, J., Sen, A., Fitoussi, J-P. (2009). *Rapport de la commission sur la mesure des performances économiques et du progrès social*. La Documentation Française, Paris.

Ulmann, A.A. (1985). Data in search of a theory, a critical examination of the relationships among social performance, social disclosure, and economic performance of US firms. *Academy of Management Review*, 10(3), 540–557.

Vogel, D. (1991). Business Ethics: new perspectives on old problems. *California Management Review*, 33(4), 101–117.

Walters, G. (2009). Corporate social responsibility through sport. The community sports trust model as a CSR delivery agency. *Journal of Corporate Citizenship*, 35, 81–94.

Walzel, S., Robertson, J. (2016). Corporate social responsibility in professional team sport organisations. *Papier présenté à la SMANNZ Conference*, 23rd–25th November, Auckland, New Zealand.

Wartick, S.L., Cochran, P.L. (1985). The evolution of the corporate social performance model. *Academy of Management Review*, 10(4), 758–769.

Wood, D.J. (1991). Corporate social performance revisited. *Academy of Management Review*, 16(4), 691–718.

Yunus, M. (2010). *Building social business: the new kind of capitalism that serves humanity's most pressing needs*. Public Affairs, New York.

Part II

The sporting goods industry and distribution

Foreword: presentation of the four chapters of Part II

At its most basic, the ecosystem of the Sporting Goods market encompasses all individuals and all entities whose mission is to create, develop, manufacture and distribute products destined for a sports practice or that are associated with sports, under a brand that in some way is linked with this universe.

Research and development, as well as the marketing of these products, have experienced a true revolution over the last 50 years, which was stimulated as much by sociological and economic evolutions as by the changes in consumers' purchasing behaviour.

The history of sporting goods is relatively contemporary, and as is often the case, it is the result of some great human adventures, giant leaps at certain moments in time with a group of actors who made of this market what it is today: A world full of brands and technologies that are forever evolving, living and vibrating to the rhythm of demand.

Consumers have also evolved and, in a market that is in full growth, they constantly find more offers in terms of equipment and dreams. How they consume is also changing: Their purchasing behaviour and the choices they are influenced to make are impacted by global evolutions of the distribution and the economic landscape of the company sector.

The first chapter, written by Pascal Aymar, envisages a deeper analysis of the components, the reasons, and the consequences of the growth of this market. The intention is to give a deeper historic background as well as a perspective on the evolutions which have taken place within manufacturing brands and distribution, and, at the same time, to give an update on the very heavy trends which underlie these changes. At the end, this chapter offers some keys for a better understanding of the alchemy of this market, so that hypotheses can be formed on its future perspectives and concerns.

The goal of the three chapters that follow is to dive deeper into the subject that is essential to the understanding of the world of sporting goods and to shed a light from a somewhat different angle than offered by Pascal Aymar. The three core focal points being the historic background of how this market evolved and who the the current key players are, consumer understanding in terms of the evolution of sports practice and purchase choice, and, lastly, the innovation strategies within the sports industry that, as we know, are essential for brand and company developments.

The second chapter by Eugenio Di Maria, lies at the heart of the sports universe and is a key testimonial of this industry over the last 30 years. It retraces the history of the sporting goods industry and invites us to take a walk through the "park" alongside key players of the market and to discover some faces and grasp the main facts and important events that shaped the last 50 years, which will allow us to put the evolutions of this universe into perspective.

The third chapter written by Antoine Haincourt allows us to better understand the consumer sociology, relationships with brands, products and the sports universe, purchase behaviour as well as the changes that are happening, particularly those that are related to the advent of the digital world.

In the last chapter, Anna Gerke helps us to understand the innovation strategies of the key actors, the typologies that shape the different innovative approaches within the sports universe and gives us the core keys to success based on the analysis of recent history.

Chapter 4

Growth, growth drivers and the energy sources

Pascal Aymar

Introduction

Being physically active is as old as humanity itself. The large part of sports as we know it today has its roots in the 19th century. However, the history of product development intentionally designed for sports practices is far more recent, particularly when considering its modern form.

For a long time, the market focused on product equipment (to this day manufacturers are still called "suppliers"), yet, over the last 30 years, it has widely opened to products that are qualified as "softgoods", such as shoes and clothing, and "hardgoods", such as skis, rackets or balls.

At the same time, a big part of "softgoods", which was initially conceived for sport usage only, has been turned into everyday lifestyle products, that are considered simply functional and utilitarian or have a "lifestyle" connotation for those who wear them within a new universe: Sports Fashion or Sports Style, or "Casual Sports" for Anglo-Saxons.

As a result, attraction has become as important as usage itself. A lot of products that are sold never get to see anything else but urban sidewalks or waxed floorboards at parties. Consequently, their choice is based on purely aesthetic criteria rather than function.

Certain sports brands rely on their reputation and their sports heritage using it as a pretext to sometimes sell prêt-a-porter lines that have not much in common with sports.

Marketing Managers of those brands use mostly sports marketing (sponsoring/events) for their enduring sports image albeit very often their developed products have no technical characteristics of a sports product. Lacoste or Eden Park are examples as well as Le Coq Sportif, which attempted a comeback by leaning not only on the Noahs' – father and son – but also the St Etienne Greens; not to mention all the brands that only base themselves on an athlete's name, such as Blanco, or more recently Bjorn Borg or Zlatan Ibrahimovic.

In parallel to the merging phenomena of sports and lifestyle, the "real" sport continues its development and leans on brands that consumers identify as the true actors in sports.

More and more sport practices see a day that is bringing about new micro markets and regularly creating small niche companies that base themselves on a new culture or on new technologies and only cry to be developed.

Since the beginning of the 1970s, we have been witnessing a profound change in the sporting goods market which touches upon all product categories, all social classes and in all countries in the world. The monolithic sportsperson has become versatile, multi-facetted and multi-form in a context where he can keep his values and yet be modern.

This change has brought about, on the one hand, a large popularization of sports through a wide and deep penetration of different markets (who doesn't own a pair of sneakers, whatever your age?), and, on the other, a trend towards a sophistication of sport-labelled products which is still the main driver for manufacturers who need to make that difference.

Just like any buzzing market that is in high demand and has a high potential for growth, sporting goods rely on proven drivers which always grounded the development of companies whatever their sector of activity: Brands, innovation and internationalization.

- The big brands in manufacturing as well as in distribution who managed to impose themselves as leaders on this market are becoming stronger, thus creating an increasing market gap between the leaders and the followers year on year.

It is rare that big new actors arrive rapidly on the market with Under Armour being the most recent counter-example (it took nevertheless 10 years of their existence to get to be the player in the market that they are today), whereas we regularly see shooting stars rising and then rapidly falling (Fila in the 1990s, LA Gear, Umbro after its buyout by Nike, Puma most recently). We certainly don't wish this upon Under Armour, but the current trend is not in its favour.

- Innovation is omnipresent in the technical nature of materials as well as styling; whether it's for real, a promise or an illusion, this innovation makes up the essence of the brands' "storytelling" and creates the personality that they claim.
- Design, in its broader and Anglo-Saxon sense, is an element that more and more companies invest in and take into account when considering the development of brand potential as well as product range. Fashion and styling concoctions are widely applied today when developing products. It doesn't take long for new technological developments to be applied within the sports domain as it is an attractive vehicle for image and business solutions.

In short, brand and product development happens mostly in a creative and effervescent ambiance that makes this sector and its related trades particularly interesting.

- As is the case in many other market economy domains, the evolution of global demographics as well as a higher purchase power of new social classes is in close correlation with the development of the sports markets.

  Geographically, developing markets such as Asia are on the forefront of growth, yet we are already starting to see markets with an exponential growth potential such as India or the Middle East. Other markets such Brazil or Russia also show a strong developmental capacity but need to tackle their economic issues first. Wearing an international sports brand or carrying a sports product (more so than just practising a sport) is, in most of these countries, a sign of recognition for those who have managed to climb a few steps on the social ladder.

- Marketing, supply chain, distribution are other grounds to play and distinguish oneself in for the different market actors. It's not rare for "champions" to appear in one or another domain. However, if they cannot rapidly assure the core fundamentals, such as brand building and product offer, there is a great chance that all they ever be is an ephemeral flickering amongst the enduring star companies in the business sky.

At the end of the day, competition is extremely tough between manufacturing and distribution companies. Yet, they all benefit from a fertile ground that allows them to create, innovate and reinvent themselves, thus bestowing an exceptional pulling force and dynamic on this market.

Finally, the consumers are those who, in this sector more than others, are not only targets and victims of commercial strategies and those who refuse to have offers imposed, but also who are people who truly are agents of change in their own right.

Often passionate about sports and brands, and sometimes sports products, consumers interact with manufacturers by validating or contributing towards the creation of new sports, trends and changes in codes.

Like everywhere, the digital revolution gives the consumers today new means to be actors in their own environment and, in the end, it is the consumers who decide which company makes or breaks it in an extremely atomized business arena.

At the end of the day, it is highly likely that the future is brilliant for the sports economy, especially for the sporting goods domain.

Undeniably a cutting-edge industry in our current societies, this industry is just asking for new talent that is not only capable of accompanying its quantitative development but also anticipating its sociological and geographical evolutions.

In order to succeed in this industry, passion for sports is a necessary part of the profile to have. That said, it is becoming less and less sufficient to gain access to positions of responsibility.

1 A sporting goods market in full growth

The figures of the American panellist NPD, the only research company that investigates professionally and in detail the world market year on year, clearly show the remarkable growth in this sector which, over the last 10 years, increased twice as fast as the global GDP and carries its weight in the spending category of durable consumer goods.

At the same time, the developments of this market generate more and more complications: Previously established lines between the different sports are blurring, the competitive field is becoming larger, and the transformations of usages and practices are gaining in prominence, thus making it more and more difficult to read.

This growth is based essentially on four variables:

- The exponential development of clothing and footwear worn for sport but also around town
- Investment efforts of market leaders as well as their capacity to galvanize and making an already very naturally attractive market more fanciable
- The rise in demand for sporting goods by the middle classes, the "new money", in the developing markets
- The ever-rising consumer trend to focus on their health and "go green" that pushes them to awaken towards the common responsibility of our planet

1.1 The global sporting goods market

For 2016, NPD estimates global turnover of sporting goods at 389 billion € vs. 366 billion in 2015.

It is worth noting that certain observers and/or experts evaluate this figure more pessimistically as it is uncertain how much of the casual products have been taken into account in the different analysis approaches.

So there is an increase by +6% from 2015 to 2016, which represents the strongest figure in the last 10 years. Since the tough years of the economic crisis in 2007/2008 and the global economic slowdown, the global economic sports market always progressed at a rhythm between 4–6% per year.

As a point of comparison, according to the agency Bain & Co, the global luxury market, star market of the 2000s, measured 249 billion € in 2016, representing 64% of the sports market. It was stagnant compared to 2015 and its average growth by 2020 is assumed to be around 3%.

As for other base references, the yearly global automobile market comprises 1,200 billion € (sports representing thus a third of this market with products in term of unit value being obviously lower and an envisaged utility that is less marked), and the global figure for computers was at 103 billion € in 2015.

In France, the total sports market does not only include sporting products but also events, shows, services and governance and is estimated by the Ministry to be at 37 billion €.

The French sporting goods market is evaluated by different professional organizations at 12 billion €, a little under 50% of the household goods market and more than three times the size of the entire video games market in 2016 (albeit being a record year).

Another way how to measure industry dynamics is by looking at the market value of companies in the sector. For the sports industry, the market capitalization of its companies was globally valued at 19.3% in 2017. Europe particularly rewarded its companies which had an increase in capitalization of +20%, whilst the growth of the main stock exchanges (DAX CAC 40) did not exceed 12%.

When attempting to appraise the evolutions on a sport by sport basis and thus segmenting the market in that way, one quickly finds out that a big part of the products sold – even if specifically sold for sport – are transformed in usage by consumers or the fashion crowd. The examples of the Air Jordans in the United States (a clothing symbol of an entire youth generation) trail running shoes adopted by all construction workers or surferwear popularized until recent years by the urban youth (most of who never got to see a real wave before) show how difficult it is to make a clear-cut difference between its sports vs. social usage.

The reality is that one product shares at times the two usages, albeit the fact that consumers tend to buy more often two products rather than one.

We also need to be aware that the size of a sporting goods market is not necessarily in correlation with the number of people actually practising a sport or just interested in sports.

As a result, a sport like Badminton that is regularly practised by more than 200 million Chinese does not produce a bigger market than ski with its 30 million skiers worldwide, obviously not bringing the cost of the individual equipment needed for these sports into the equation as they are uncomparable.

American Football, though followed by tens of millions of people, only generates a limited amount of products be they functional or "Lifestyle".

When one does try to segment the market by sport, one realizes that the most mediatized sports are not necessarily the ones that generate the highest product sale, even if sports marketing investments into these exposed sports do create the most lucrative micro markets such as replica shirts of teams and pro-models of superstars.

As surprising as it may seem, cycling is the global number one market with nearly 15% of total sporting good sales (and we are not even taking into account toy bikes or those considered for urban transport). Despite the fact that only the Tour de France has a true worldwide broadcasting, and despite the fact that textile is still weak in the different sports practices, cycling is on top.

In second position, we find fitness/dance/gym/yoga, which generate about 40 billion €, making up just above 10% of the global market share.

These two categories have experienced the strongest growth within the last 5 years whereas other "traditional" ones are more or less stable, or regressing.

Hiking/walking/camping is in third place with 8% of market share. Whilst running, despite the formidable current infatuation with it, measures only 7%, and is on even keel with all other outdoor sports.

Table 4.1 Top 10 sports dedicated product sales global (2015–2016)

		Market Trend
1	BIKE	Sharp rise
2	FITNESS/DANSE/GYM/YOGA/...	Sharp rise
3	WALKING/HIKING	Stable
4	RUNNING	Rise
5	SWIMMING	Stable
6	FOOTBALL	Stable
7	SUMMER BOARD SPORTS (surf, paddle, ...)	Stable
8	GOLF	Drop
9	BASKETBALL	Stable
10	WINTER SPORTS	Drop

Football (or soccer), the top mediatized sports, only has a 3% market share, same as basketball. The fact is that the financial stakes for these two sports are all but in sales of dedicated products.

1.2 The four drivers of growth

1.2.1 From a niche equipment market to a mass clothing market

Apart from the United States – who has, as in many other fields, been ahead of this phenomenon – who would have thought to work in clothing or sports footwear in the 1960s?

Today, almost everyone wears sneakers, often for work, and even senior executives wear a North Face or Canada Goose jacket over their suit.

Most recent figures indicate that the "Lifestyle" share of the market, i.e., products that carry a sports brand name but are purely developed for urban use, account for more than a quarter of the total market, that is nearly 100 billion €. Essentially made up of shoes and clothing, other items such as watches or sunglasses are also part of this category and can have substantial markets.

Overall, when focusing on the nature of products sold, the estimated breakdown for 2016 regarding equipment, footwear and clothing looks like this:

- **Equipment** **39% (y/c bikes)**
- **Footwear** 27%
- **Clothing** 34%

The equipment market stays the most important one but given that it does not benefit from the "lifestyle" bonus that clothing or footwear enjoy, it is in direct correlation and fluctuates with the ups and downs of the different sports.

Ski sale is at its all time low when looking at the last 20 years, not even talking about the equipment sales of the snowboarding category, which is a market in peril. Inline skates have completely disappeared from the sports shops and sales of tennis rackets have been stagnant for years.

In contrast to that, stand-up paddle and the electric bike are experiencing a solid growth rate due to the novelty effect of these practices.

Technical connected products (GoPro, Fitbit, etc.) which have experienced an exponential rise in the years 2000 are now confronted with a lot of difficulty: On the one hand, "early adopters" are already equipped, and, on the other, it seems that regular usage of such products is disappointing to consumers. However, the trend for digital sports applications is on a steep rise.

In terms of brands, this market remains very atomized: the Japanese leader Shimano is present in cycling as well as fishing, whilst other market players that focus on equipment are a somewhat marginalized when compared to textile, footwear or non-technical accessories manufacturers.

The sports footwear market has experienced a remarkable development over the last 10 years. Of course, the global excitement for running that was reactivated by the enormous success of trail running has played an important rôle, but it is mostly thanks to the fashion phenomenon of sneakers often not even used for sports that created this uplift. It is this product category that has been rising the fastest in the last several years.

Nike is the greatest leader in this category leaving its competitors, beginning with Adidas, far behind.

Finally, the sportswear market is also progressing rapidly as it is beginning to feel the benefit from the arrival of ready-to-wear brands as well as the fashion effect, thus giving sports a more rewarding edge for young people and Millennials.

Adidas, in this sector, is a serious competitor for Nike who remains, nevertheless, the leader.

Outdoor brands such as Columbia or The North Face as well as new entrants in the Wellness domain, such as Lululemon, play their cards right and seem to have the wind in their back, and are to be reckoned with in the future.

Table 4.2 Top 10 companies by product nature, global market, equipment (2015–2016)

	Brands
1 SHIMANO (Japan)	
2 JARDEN (USA)	K2, Völkl, Dalbello, Shakespeare, . . .
3 VISTA OUTDOOR (USA)	Bushnell, Bollé, . . .
4 GIANT (Taiwan)	
5 AMERSPORTS (Finland)	Salomon, Wilson, Arc'téryx, . . .
6 FITBIT (USA)	
7 ADIDAS GROUP (Germany)	
8 GOPRO (USA)	
9 NIKE (USA)	
10 TREK (USA)	

Table 4.3 Top 10 companies by product nature, global market, footwear (2015–2016)

	Brands
1 NIKE (USA)	Nike, Converse, Jordan, Hurley
2 ADIDAS GROUP (Germany)	Adidas, Reebok
3 VF CORP (USA)	TNF, Timberland, Vans, Reef, . . .
4 NEW BALANCE (USA)	
5 SKECHERS (USA)	
6 ASICS (Japan)	
7 PUMA (Germany)	
8 FILA (Korea/Italy)	
9 ANTA (China)	
9 WOLVERINE (USA)	Merell, Saucony, Chaco, Sebago, Wolverine, . . .
10 SALOMON (Finland/France)	
10 UNDER ARMOUR (USA)	

Table 4.4 Top 10 companies by product nature, global market, clothing (2015–2016)

	Brands
1 NIKE (USA)	Nike, Converse, Jordan, Hurley
2 ADIDAS GROUP (Allemagne)	adidas, Reebok
3 VF CORP (USA)	TNF, Timberland, Vans, Reef, Nautica. . .
4 UNDER ARMOUR (USA)	
5 GILDAN (Canada)	
6 LULULEMON (USA)	
7 COLUMBIA (USA)	Columbia, Mountain Hardwear, . . .
8 HANES BRANDS (USA)	Hanes, Champion, Wonderbra, etc. . . .
9 PUMA (Germany)	
10 DESCENTE (Japan)	

1.2.2 The power and relevance of leaders

Both Adidas and Nike, respectively created and launched in 1949 and in 1972, are relatively young companies and, undeniably, market leaders in the sporting goods market.

Although global brands, and both present in almost all sports practices, they are not designing equipment, apart from balls, having previous, unsuccessful experience (Adidas in rackets and Nike in snowboards).

Nike with its just over 30 billion € in 2016 seems to be easily dominating Adidas who only counts 17 billion €. That said, only one product category (footwear) and only one country (United States) practically explains this gap between the two brands.

Nike makes almost 20 billion € with footwear alone whilst Adidas reaches an upper ceiling of around 9 billion €. In North America, Nike sales are around

15 billion € while Adidas is struggling to reach the 3 billion bar. In other product categories, notably clothing, and on other continents such as Europe and Asia, Adidas is not far off from Nike, and at times, even a touch ahead.

Nevertheless, it seems that the wind is turning. Nike recently announced for the first time in 10 years a drop in its US sales. At the same time, Adidas boasted a rise of more than 30% sales in that market, essentially thanks to footwear!

This is a historic reversal of the situation, but it remains to be seen if it is sustainable; in any case, both adversaries are hungry: Nike is committed to 50 billion $ (42 billion €) on a 5-year horizon whilst adidas envisions 22 billion € by 2022.

It's interesting to note that when considering the size of these two leaders on a global scale, they only make up about 15% of total sales worldwide. This goes to show just how atomized the market is with its thousands of small- and medium-sized enterprises, but equally suggests that Nike and Adidas have still enough space to grow organically, without having to count on their obvious financial capacity for external growth.

The situation behind these two leaders is somewhat confusing. The third place has always been a bit cursed, seeing that brands like Reebok, Puma, Fila, LA Gear, Asics etc. took it up in short successions and fell off as quickly as they mounted the podium. In recent years, Under Armour (5 billion $) seemed to be the most credible option in taking up and keeping third place. However, it appears that this American brand may also be touched by the curse of its fellow challengers as they are currently experiencing a strong decline in brand momentum as well as an important slowdown in sales, particularly in the United States, bringing up serious questions for the market.

There is also a third actor in the market in terms of turnover: The American group called VF Corp, which owns a portfolio of strong footwear as well as clothing brands: TNF (The North Face), Vans, Timberland, Napapijri, Reef, Nautica, Kipling and, more recently, Icebreaker. With a turnover of 8 billion €, VF makes about half of Adidas but its potential and know-how regarding external growth could allow it to narrow the gap with the race leader in the short term.

Puma, Asics, New Balance, Shimano, Skechers, Gildan and Amer Sports (Salomon, Atomic, Wilson, Arc'téryx etc.) are the other players whose combined sales come to around 3 billion €. Puma, New Balance, Shimano, Salomon and Arc'téryx currently enjoy good fortune. That said, in this race of the "underdogs", the weather conditions can change rapidly.

Overall, the top 20 companies in the market make up for only 1/3 of global sales, of which, unsurprisingly, 13 are American, 3 European, 3 Asian and 1 Australian.

Today, it is those 20 companies, representing about 50 brands between them, that pull the market. Even if they are not always the ones who develop new products, a breakthrough or an innovation, as we will see later on, it is they who have the marketing power and the business relevance to seduce the consumer.

Table 4.5 Top 10 companies, global market (equipment + footwear + clothing)

1	NIKE (USA)
2	ADIDAS GROUP (Germany)
3	VF CORP (USA)
4	UNDER ARMOUR (USA)
5	PUMA (Germany)
6	ASICS (Japan)
7	NEW BALANCE (USA)
8	SHIMANO (Japan)
9	SKECHERS (USA)
10	AMERSPORTS (Finland)

1.2.3 The demand for new developing markets

Sport, considered to be a leisure activity, has long been the prerogative of the developed countries.

With the exception of Japan, Asia took its time to become interested in this phenomenon, particularly due to the fact that sports practices from a performance perspective or a focus on physical effort do not come naturally to these cultures (apart from Korea), not to mention practices such as Yoga, Tai Chi etc.

South America has always been passionate about football, but the sports practice in itself had its difficulties to get off the ground.

Africa, unfortunately, does not have the means to develop the sports practice among its people, and Oceania does not have enough people to weigh on the global market despite the fact that practising levels are high.

Today, North America remains, with almost 40% of the global market, the share leader, Asia/Oceania follow with just above 30%, Europe keeps a quarter of the total share, whereas Africa and the Middle East share a meagre 5%.

However, things are changing, and North America's pedestal is being rocked.

China has become the second strongest world market in sporting goods consumption, having recently aquired more than 10% market share.

As was the case in all developing countries, it is the middle classes that are fuelling this growth by wearing a sports product by a Western brand as a sign of recognition of one's social standing. It is worth noting that in China as well as in other developing countries, big brand products (Nike, Adidas, Puma, TNF, etc.) are more expensive than in Europe, and even more so than in the United States.

1.2.4 The rise of new sport trends: Sport-health and sport-nature

Besides the organic evolution of sport, there are two sociological tangents that help carry its development:

- The rational and hedonistic quest for good health
- The ecological and environmental trend to be close to nature

Table 4.6 Top 15 premier markets for sporting good sales, global (equipment + footwear + clothing), 2015–2016

1	USA
2	CHINA
3	GERMANY
4	JAPAN
5	CANADA
6	FRANCE
7	UK
8	KOREA
9	INDIA
10	ITALY
11	BRAZIL
12	RUSSIA
13	AUSTRALIA
14	SPAIN
15	TAIWAN

SPORT-HEALTH

All signs in our societies everywhere in the world, albeit to varying degrees, show that we are strongly concerned about our health, not only about us individually but also as a community.

A we live longer and older, good health becomes synonymous with being active in old age. It is not simply about just extending life expectancy but the hope and desire to enjoy life to the full for longer.

Even younger people are a lot more preoccupied with their health these days, mainly because of their concern about their physical appearance, but also because they want to strengthen their mental health.

In addition, in developed countries, the life stage of couples setting up a home and having children has been pushed back significantly, thus giving young adults more time and freedom for their time-consuming sports practices.

A research study led by Nielsen and Les Mills in 2013 show that 76% of Millennials practise a fitness activity, which is 15% more than the adult population.

Furthermore, countries where the State bears social charges for illnesses like in France, or with populations beginning to see slides into obesity or idleness, are all concerned about taking measures to ensure individual health and reducing the cost of social security.

All these factors contribute towards the continuous development of sports, recognized by all to be a vector of good physical as well as mental health, to reach the greatest number of people.

Practising sports in order to feel good about oneself becomes a lifestyle, and fitness, health and energy are the new concepts that the media is bringing to the fore, particularly those who target women (although not exclusively).

The huge boom in running, fitness, yoga and outdoor sports clearly reflects the willingness of practitioners to do themselves good, both mentally and physically, through sports.

Measures taken by governments (such as the promotion of sports equipment design and development in China, or certain initiatives that aim to reimburse gym subscriptions in France) show how topical the subject is.

SPORT-NATURE

Everybody is aware about the fact that the younger generations, much more so than the baby-boomers, are particularly concerned and sensitive about the environment.

Sport also succumbs to this trend and so sustainability is increasingly promoted within and structures more and more the development of sport in our modern societies.

Today, the new generations are well convinced that public authorities cannot impact the big challenges that our planet is facing in isolation anymore and that it is them, personally as well as a community, who need to get fully involved, be it in conflict or complicity.

That is why products that are guaranteed ecologically responsible enjoy such a success with the young. Recent brands such as Picture Organic Clothing rely heavily on this positioning to become as successful as the pioneers, Patagonia or, more recently, Toms.

Moreover, practising sport, especially those outdoors and which are in communion with nature, is a way for young people (and at times the less young too) to campaign for the preservation of our natural environments and to make their cultural battle more meaningful.

Hence, running, which initially was an almost purely urban activity, was boosted by the arrival of trail running, a sport practised in the mountains and in communion with nature. Interesting how a bit of imagination can change previous perceptions.

Hiking has become more and more popular with families as it is a way for parents to help their children discover nature. In the same way, cycling, currently being made more accessible by power-assisted mountain bikes, allows everyone, whatever his or her physical condition, to escape to the mountains or wide, open spaces.

At last, in increasingly urban societies (in 2008 over 50% of the global population lived in cities), the search for contact and connection with nature is becoming more important: Sport brings about a reason as well as a goal, a destination and a justification to escape the city and to leave occasionally for an adventure to discover other sceneries.

It is clear that the development of outdoor sports does not solely depend on the geographic proximity of a dedicated environment. In fact, these practices are also for many the essential alternative (or the complement) to a sedentary and urban lifestyle that comes with consuming the most popular sports on TV or online, such as football and basketball.

In all, and for all these different reasons, sport is perfectly and closely linked to the new virtuous concept of "sustainability" that is becoming more and more popular.

1.3 The six sources of energy

1.3.1 The power of the brand

One of the key factors of success in the sporting goods market is undeniably brand strength.

For the consumer, sport represents a universe in which he or she cannot only let his or her imagination flow freely, but it is also a means to his or her self-actualization depending on his or her individual capacities and desires, and at the same time, it allows him or her to position him- or herself socially.

- Imagination lies at the heart when choosing what practice the consumer exercises, and not only with the young people: How many are out there and buy Patagonia whilst they imagine themselves being adventurers and ecological defenders of the planet and then only get to do one trek and, at best, two or three alpine hikes per year? How many, and not only the young, fell into Billabong's sea, sex and surf trap and others into Roxy's, yet never having seen a real wave or even touched a surfboard?

  Brands have the power to make us dream and to create emotions in us. A lot of effort is made, to varying degrees of success, to create an attractive imaginary content that reflects the new dreams of the consumer, authentic or not, in the discipline he or she embodies.

- Also, each sportsperson choses how he or she wants to distinguish and challenge him- or herself: Whether it is endurance for some or taking risks, adrenaline, adventure, strength, style figures for others – whatever the choice of sport, self-realization opportunities are endless according to one's desire and capacities.
- The social aspect of sport brands no longer needs to be proven as the previously mentioned example of the rise of Moncler into the luxury sphere shows. In Asia, and specifically China, the phenomenon is even more pronounced given that the strong population of middle managers, the "nouveaux riches", have adopted Western sports brands as a sign of status, a symbol for success.

However, the cliché of the brand being associated with a specific social group is not exclusive to developing countries: In Japan where fashion for the young is completely uninhibited and profoundly creative, "fashion victims" do not hesitate for a second to put together sport products such as Puma with luxury brands the likes of Chanel or Gucci; the Lululemon brand has experienced a spectacular growth curve with its yogawear, yet it has been adopted by all the North American Bohos; Nike's basketball trainers as well as Lacoste clothing used to be icons with Suburbia Youth in a previous era. The consumer picks up, validates and sometimes twists a brand in a such a way that he or she can choose to make it his own and which reflects best his or her personality and social affiliation.

It is interesting to note that it is becoming more and more difficult for a sports brand to get out of its original field, practice or product category, and to switch to another: The exception being the big multisport actors (Nike, Adidas, Puma). Yet even the smaller brands who have expertise in one type of product or a particular sport have a lot of difficulty in making brand extensions (brand stretching). Thus Salomon, whose roots lie in equipment, were never really as successful in clothing as they are in footwear; Oakley had to abandon its footwear project and for The North Face it was tough to develop this product category under its flagship brand (but it did succeed under Vans and Timberland); Babolat, albeit being the world leader in tennis, is painfully entering the Badminton market.

With more and more offers and an explosion of new brands on the market throughout the past 20 years, the consumer seems to group brands according to domains of expertise and seems reluctant to choose a product that is not of a reputable brand, as strong and famous as it may be. This trend is worth reflecting on by those who think they can easily switch from equipment to clothing and from clothing to footwear. The big ones understood this very well and completely retired from the equipment category as a result.

We could, in conclusion, ask the question: "Tell me what sports brands you wear, and I will tell you who you are"; this little guessing game becomes increasingly a familiar sight in the different social circles of our modern societies.

In a world that is trying to find durable benchmarks, sport brands anchor themselves in the consumers' imagination by building unique and shareable image values to identify with.

1.3.2 Consumer implication and creativity

Another particularity of the sporting goods market is that a number of practices are created by the consumer.

This was very much the case in skiing, where the "Free" practices (freestyle, freeride, freehike. . .) were initiated by young skiers who wanted to break from the traditional ski competition, but also for trail running, a new running category inspired more by consumers than brands (even if Salomon was a pioneer in this domain and contributed to its development) and wakeboard, paddle surf and even futsal.

The different sports behave like living matter and the consumer acts upon and validates the evolution of these practices and transposes his or her imagination upon them. Social networks have revolutionized the way individuals engage in sport: Every practitioner, if he or she wishes, can become a "local hero", creating his or her own way of exercising his or her sport, with his or her own fan base and his or her own communication. It's not surprising then that Adidas' latest brand platform claims the status of CREATOR via all its communication campaigns.

Federations, manufacturers and sports marketing agents are at times only "hunters" of trends that were originally inspired by the practitioners themselves, as was the case for paragliding or, currently, indoor climbing and paddle tennis.

However, there is need for caution: What may boost certain practices or sports on the one hand can kill them off on the other, and the aforementioned players have an important role to play in order to make the sport or its practices last.

The collapse of snowboarding paid the price due to the immobility and bigotry of its main stakeholders; Inline Skates disappeared because no rewarding imagery was constructed for the consumer; the current collapse of surfing references with the young is mainly caused by the greed of shareholders of companies in this sector who continuously flooded and crammed the market with ever more products; the decline of tennis, in spite of hours on television and charismatic champions, fails to attract young practitioners. All these examples show how imperative it is to continually research consumer motivation and behaviour, making sports practise more attractive and keeping consumers' curiosity stimulated. Sportspeople are fickle and this is even more the case for the younger ones: They can easily abandon climbing for paragliding, volleyball for handball, snowboarding for skiing . . . because what they want above all is to be able to see themselves in their sport and, at the same time, be known for a practise that corresponds to their values and/or is rewarding.

Sport is an activity that is generally practised in groups, yet first and foremost, it is an image builder for the individual. The choice of brands and products does not leave consumers indifferent – they deeply apply themselves, as much for achieving the desired image objective for themselves as for the group image they think they belong to or aspire to belong to, though they will never admit this.

1.3.3 The power of innovation

Although consumers are key influencers in the market, they essentially remain in their position as catalysts for ideas, pioneers who confirm trends within a community and join the early adopter rangs emitting relevant cultural codes; however, rarely do they move from the initial concept stage into a breaking innovative process.

A true game-changing innovation comes principally from manufacturers and their capacity to summon research and development investments. For a long time, this has been reserved for companies that manufacture equipment such as skis, rackets etc., whereas brands focusing on textile and footwear contented themselves with investing in style and marketing.

It was not uncommon to see companies like Salomon or Babolat investing 5% of their turnover in R&D while Nike or Adidas devoted only 1 or 2% (which in absolute value was still quite significant).

Today, the trend seems to be a decline in R&D investments among equipment manufacturers (with the exception of "wearable devices" brands such as Fitbit or GoPro) and an increase for textile and footwear makers. In fact, it appears that those markets who traditionally were in demand of regular innovation, such as winter sports, rackets sport and collective sports, with the exception of football, are the ones who suffer the most in the global arena and lack the investment means used in the past. What is happening in skiing is a big telltale sign: The main actors, albeit belonging to an affluent group, prefer to invest in other activities because the winter sports market does not guarantee them a sufficient return on their investment.

Indeed, it is paradoxical to see that, today, the global number one innovator in equipment – in terms of investment as well as generated sales of those innovative products – is Decathlon, thanks to its decision to create its own brands and its position as a major distributor in the global marketplace.

This is a shame as sport attracts, like a magnet, all innovations coming from other industries, be it from the fields of materials, mechanics, motor skills etc. Sport has borrowed in the past, and still does, from aeronautics, chemistry, automobiles etc. to find intelligent solutions for product needs that primarily aim to improve performance and utility by focusing on notions such as agility, flexibility and weight.

The one sector within the equipment category that countertrends today, and that experiences a rise in investments is the innovations of the power-assisted bikes that combine sport and mobility. We will come back to this example at a later stage.

And lastly, a sector that, after much talk about innovation, finally acts upon it is the one of connected items. Having only been put on the market in recent years, it allowed the cometal arrival of a few specialists such as Fitbit or GoPro. Unfortunately, this market is playing more and more with smoke and mirrors, having satiated the early adopter category early on and the remaining mainstream target considers them gadgets rather than helpful performance tools.

It seems, however, that footwear and textile manufacturers who up to now were very contented to just market an image rather than being concerned with possible technological developments, have started to embark on real product innovation with the primary intention to provide consumer benefits.

There are still of course textiles or technology manufacturers such as Gore-tex, Primaloft, Vibram, Michelin or Good Year who provide brands with turnkey solutions in order to add a technical nature to their products; that said, Nike, adidas, TNF, etc. are beginning to follow in Columbia's footsteps, who have already been offering new technological solutions for a long time.

One can believe that everything has already been invented in the footwear and clothing domains. Yet Hoka's trail running footwear with its oversize shock absorption sole and Odlo's first Ceramicool layers and Active Spine technology (for posture correction) show that there is still enough room for those who want to invest by innovating.

After all, innovating is above all a mindset and the result of a desire driven by the top-level management of a company: One may think that certain hardliners within the equipment category like Petzl, Elan and Salomon, whose values are intrinsically linked with consumer satisfaction, will continue to keep the innovation flame going, at least we hope so.

1.3.4 Sport's flirtation with fashion

Everyone probably realizes that the worlds of sports and fashion have more and more values and economic interests in common. Is it just an innocent flirt or is the relationship between sports and fashion already further advanced? For convenience sake, we favour the former hypothesis. Undeniably though, both universes are attracted to each other and are getting closer; at times, they are even interlaced, thus creating an unusual mix of genres for manufacturers and brands alike. The first artificial appearance happened probably about 20 years ago and seduces the consumer today.

Brands were the first to disregard their origins and extended their range by moving to the increasingly lucrative sports universe.

Let's take the example of Moncler, originally a poultry breeder from Monestier de Clermont with 1,420 inhabitants, situated in the French department of Isére (hence Moncler), who decided one day to use the feathers of his animals to make ski clothing. Since then, Moncler became, thanks to an Italian designer, one of the most beautiful success stories of luxury fashion of the past 20 years (with a turnover of 1.2 billion € and 250 million in net benefits in 2017!). Lacoste, the brand of the musketeers, has nothing to do with tennis these days even if they try to reconnect with their roots. And Puma, part of the Kering Group (Gucci, St Laurent, etc.), even if they try to progressively disengage with the brand, do not refrain themselves from playing with the synergies that the luxury and sporting goods worlds have to offer.

However, the movement is now going the other way and so today, we see ready-to-wear brands such as Sandro co-develop sneakers with Reebok and clothing with Fusalp; Nike works with brands such as Sacai and fashion designer Kim Jones; Chanel manufactures sneakers that are selling for 1,000 €; Tommy Hilfiger leans on Nadal's and Gérard Piqué's images, Mango on Zidane's, and the athletes themselves launch their own clothing lines, e.g., Bjorn Borg or, more recently, Zlatan Ibrahimovic.

This type of attraction is even more proliferated in distribution. For a long time certain sports distributors (Sport 2000, Sport Scheck, etc.) have been offering their clients fashion products, but the phenomenon of sports ranges with "Fastfashionistas" has, over the last 10 years, overrun the market at a new fashion speed.

H&M, Desigual, Zara, Uniqlo, Etam: Today, all of these big names develop sports collections which are very limited in terms of their technical aspect, but associate their original trade codes with the ones in sport design in order to create stylish products that are on the pulse of the current trends. Some go even as far as Uniqlo who signed up Djokovic to substantiate the credibility of this approach.

In terms of products, Adidas has been a forerunner in using famous designers (Stella McCartney and Yuji Yamamoto) in order to develop the two product categories fashion/sport and technical/style. Today, literally all clothing and footwear brands develop capsule ranges with famous designers or designers in the making. Open any women's magazine to see how the sports world is invested in the fashion universe and the enormous room those hybrid products creating brands take.

1.3.5 The evolution of marketing: Celebrities and communities

Whilst sponsorship of athletes and events remain the pillars of marketing for sporting goods manufacturers, classical advertising communication as it was the norm in the mid-1990s has very much declined in favour of two tools that are relatively new in the marketing tool box: Celebrity and community marketing.

Sport is, as we have seen, more and more a vector of societal image, and so it is only understandable that brands seek to lean on the leading figures in society and the media.

Actors, singers and artists are increasingly solicited to become muses of certain brands and, of course, wearing the clothes and shoes of that manufacturer is part of the package. Madonna with Adidas' three stripes on stage in the 1990s, a spectacle which is correlated with Adidas' comeback by many. Since then, stars have constantly validated and endorsed the brands they liked, especially those who paid them well for doing so. Scarlett Johannsson or, more recently, Victoria Beckham for Reebok, Rihanna for Puma, Kanye West for Adidas, Missy Elliot for Under Armour: These examples of this type of collaboration are plentiful. They pretend to be love stories ("I just love wearing that brand . . .") yet in reality, it is nothing but the most basic scheme marketing has to offer: Hiding fat contracts, some of them not falling short of those held by top athletes.

In Asia, this mode of approaching the consumer has really taken off and it is there where, without a doubt, it works best. Lacking sports references (be it athletes or practices), the consumer, for example the Chinese consumer, clings to what he or she knows in similar domains to sports, i.e., English Entertainment where the same type of media coverage can be found as in sports.

Sponsoring a star singer or a movie star can have a colossal effect on sales and there is not one major brand that does not use this marketing tool today.

The other revolution in the sports marketing domain are communities.

If there is one area where the community trend of our societies, fueled by the explosion of social networks, is perfectly adapted to, it is the one of sport. As we have seen previously, consumers project themselves socially and personally into different sports practices, and to be able to position themselves, they need to be reassured as well as nourished with information about products, brands, athletes, sports results etc.

The online and social networks facilitate the creation of communities where enthusiasts can come together and connect with other people who share the same passion and exchange. The brand's job is increasingly to penetrate these communities, not so much by monetary means or through buying media (although nothing is for free) but rather with stories, testimonials, ideas and suggestions that must be skilful, emotional and, above all, authentic. There is nothing more damaging to a brand than being rejected by a community.

"Storytelling", the capacity to tell a beautiful story and make people dream (or smile), is king, and so new professions have developed around this approach.

The viral has replaced the brutal: A small film shared 500,000 times on Facebook is more valuable than an advertising campaign that hammers on TV for a month . . . new times, new moods.

Within these two domains of celebrity and community marketing, new stars with a professional competence arise: Bloggers, trendsetters, influencers – all with a mission to relay and echo the actions led by brands. They validate and amplify, embellish and pass on to targets that they have perfectly identified and who are sensitive to these messages and how they are taken on.

In the end, attracted by celebrities wearing a certain brand and secured by the fact that the same brand has a strong bond with the communities of which the consumer is part of, he or she feels more in control of his or her choice than when he or she was subjected to simply receiving advertising messages.

And yet, this is not new, it is still just marketing.

1.3.6 A new East/West wind towards the supply chain

In the 1970s, Nike was the forerunner of the Asian sector, having decided to have its footwear produced in Vietnam. Since then, almost the entire sporting goods industry has more or less relocated all of its softgoods production (textiles, footwear, accessories)

By the end of the 2000s, 80% of sports footwear and textiles sold in the world were made in China (mainly), Vietnam (predominantly footwear), Taiwan (for bikes) and other Asian countries such as Cambodia, Thailand, the Philippines. Indonesia, Pakistan and Sri Lanka have often been an alternative for the production of basic or low added value products.

Equipment also went East, albeit not always the Far East: Eastern Europe (Romania, Bulgaria etc.) has become such a specialist for very technical products that it was difficult to have moved thousands of kilometres away from its cradle of design and practice.

All in all, Europe and the United States experienced a total loss of know-how for the former and technical products for the latter, whilst an increasingly powerful supply chain found its place based on the flow between Asia and the Western world.

The material manufacturers, the subcontractors, the organizations of standardization, etc. all those playing a part in the chain, set up base in Asia, as it was there where the business was happening.

Obviously the Chinese or Vietnamese hourly rate was the main reason for the outsourcing of production to Asia, but not the only one: Westerners quickly understood how competent China as well as other Asian nations were in producing quality items in clean, well-organized factories with conscientious staff. Of course, the idea of workers working 6 days a week in a factory, sleeping on site in bunkhouses, and returning home to their village only once every 6 months does not really correspond with the ethics of our Western society; yet, how many Chinese families have moved out of poverty because of this? Equally, let's think about to what extent this policy enabled China to shift its entire society so that, today, the country can refocus on its internal consumption.

Today, and actually for the past few years, things are significantly changing. At least six independent or interconnected phenomena are coming together to reverse this trend bringing some of the production of sporting goods back to the West.

- The first and most often mentioned by economists is the rise in Asian wages, particularly in China. The success of the Chinese economy makes it increasingly difficult for Chinese factories to find labour, even in rural areas. This phenomenon is not a recent one: China initially found a solution by creating factories in other Asian countries; nevertheless, the wage gap continues to shrink since basic pay levels are today comparable with China and Turkey.
- Secondly, Asian factories are becoming less flexible. There was a time when Western companies could afford to place their orders at Asian factories just 4 months before the departure of the merchandise, and where the production/transport lead times were short enough for distributors to place their orders in good conditions, as late as possible. The flexibility of factories was a guarantee that less well-equipped factories would also find clients and have work. Today, these factories are experiencing such large quantity of orders from Western brands and a skyrocketing domestic demand that this flexibility is impossible to maintain. Companies are being put under pressure by their distributors to commit themselves very early and without any indication on the quantity of production.
- Another reason why the Far East is becoming less attractive is the fresh competitiveness of the former Eastern block, and not only for equipment purposes. We are beginning to find technical know-how in Poland, Bulgaria, etc. that is combined with a reasonable cost for producing softgoods, lessening the cost differences with Asia and making it more attractive.
- Fourth reason: The arrival of new technologies in the footwear market, notably the "knitted" or "meshed" shoes. These new products which are mechanically industrialized give more space to machines than manpower, and, consequently, decrease labour hours to allow for production to be geographically closer to the place of consumption. Another increasingly strong market trend is the move towards the custom-made for equipment as well as

shoes and soon, textiles will shift in this direction, too (see what Solomon, Adidas, Nike are already making); this new approach can only work, today, with local sourcing.

- A fifth trend which is directly linked to the consumer is that the latter is becoming more and more sensitive to the way where and under what conditions products are being manufactured. The consumer today is more and more curious about the (hi)story of the product he or she wishes to purchase, from the choice of material, up to the conditions at work and in which country the merchandise was produced. These days companies owe their clients a supply chain that is clean, rewarding as well as transparent.
- Finally, the last criterion is related to market evolution and demand. E-commerce has considerably accelerated the consumer purchasing process (we want the product immediately and manufacturers want to be able to reproduce quickly if successful), and production/delivery lead times with Asia are increasingly problematic for an ever-more demanding client and frustrating for a manufacturer who increasingly seeks to maximize sales.

The process will take some time as the current supply chain structure is still fully rooted in Asia, but the trend is inverted with the convergence of different winds blowing back towards the West.

2 A perpetually changing distribution

We are clearly stating the obvious when writing that the distribution landscape in general as well as worldwide has completely changed over the last 50 years. However, we need to add a qualitative dimension here because each activity sector has transformed at its own pace and according to its own specifics. The sports sector is not an exception to this rule.

The distribution of sporting goods has indeed not escaped the different stages of trade evolution, but it had to adapt itself every time to the various demands of the consumer who refused that sport products are treated as if they were common mainstream products. Of course, "volume retailing" played and still plays a role in this sector, however, consumer vision linked with the resistance of certain manufacturers, notably in equipment, have without a doubt preserved this economic domain from many a diversion that mass distribution brought along for other product categories throughout the last 20 years.

To this day, and even with the arrival of the digital world, sporting goods distribution always tended to be a follower rather than cutting edge, and the relationship between the main players, manufacturers and distributors encountered hardly any war-like phases like other activity sectors, such as household appliances or tools.

This did not prevent distribution from experiencing a profound transformation that was marked by important phases which forced it to reinvent itself.

Let's look first at the successive steps of how the distribution of sporting goods has been transformed over the last half century, before we draw a picture of the current situation.

The latter will show clearly that more major changes are expected on distribution planet than in the manufacturer's galaxy. We will treat this topic at a later point when analyzing future perspectives.

2.1 The evolution of distribution throughout the last 50 years

A summary of the recent evolution of sporting goods distribution can be found hereafter in Table 4.7; it slices the recent past since the 1970s into decades.

Table 4.7 The evolution of distribution

	Distribution format	*Status*	*Shop type*	*Location*	*Consumer selling point*
1970s	SPECIALIZED	Independant	Bricks & Mortar	Town centres	Technical
	DISTRIBUTION	Affiliates			Advice
1980s	MULTISPORT CHAINS	Chain	Bricks	Shopping Centres	Offer
		Large distribution groups		Suburbs	Price
1990s	MONOBRAND SHOPS	Brands	Bricks	Town Centres	Brand Offer
		Franchise		Shopping Centres	Image
2000s	E-COMMERCE	Start-ups	Clicks	WEB	Offer
		Pure players	(web)		Price
2010s	OMNI CHANNEL	Generalists	Bricks & Clicks	WEB	Offer
		Pure players		Town Centres	Service
		Brand Internet sites			
2020s	EXPERIENTAL RETAIL	Generalists	Bricks & Clicks	WEB	Consumer Experience
		Brands		Town Centres	
		Chains		Shopping Centres	

We will see that distribution formats, status, type and geographic location of stores as well as consumer selling points have changed about every 10 years and have been marked with important turning points.

This little history, although modelled on the evolution of the French distribution in terms of dates, is also valid, give or take a few years, for the rest of the European and North American markets. Asia, which didn't have a particular distribution history, entered the scene in the 1990s, putting forward monobrand shops, before a cutting-edge Asian e-commerce that was better developed than any other one worldwide.

- In the 1970s, distribution was made up of independant distributors, most of which were set up in town centres. With a limited shop surface and product range, they were about technical advice.

  New brands as well as Nike's arrival on the market in 1972 brought a breath of fresh air and a new impetus to the sports market, and distributors wanted to take advantage of it.

  These were the glory days of brand shops and affiliates; in France, LaHutte became Intersport, Sport 2000 and a few others were fighting to get shares of the branded distributors' market. Ski was battling within its own circle, football was another fight and small retail entrepreneurs became more and more professional thanks to the support of departments who were providing a service to streamline strategy, buying and marketing.

- The 1980s were by far the most epic for the participating players and those who pushed the hardest for a change from one sporting goods distribution model to another.

  The end of the 1970s saw the advent of chain stores in Europe, a development that came about in the United States a few years before, and the 1980s were to become their growth years there.

  Big surfaces, large product collections, self-service, suburban set-ups or malls in town centres – it was this style of distribution that took over Europe in just a few years.

  Most of the time, major food distributors were the initiators and shareholders of these projects. In France alone, and in the space of a very short time, Go Sport (Genty Cathiard Group), Decathlon (Auchan), FNAC Sport (FNAC) and Sparty (Darty) appeared, as well as Disport, Spao and a few more.

  An intense distribution war in would mark those years, not only due to the very strong competition between all these names, but also because of the fierce resistance of the specialist distributors that rose against the newcomers, who were portrayed as the Antichrist.

  Manufacturers were taken hostage, and some lost out as a result of taking sides; others learnt how to navigate the unleashed ocean of competition.

- The 1990s saw the appearance of a new shop format that could not have been imagined 10 years before thanks to the rise in the power of brands (notably Nike and Adidas): The Monobrand store.

Flagship stores or opportunities with a financial partner on the outset, the attractiveness of a double margin influenced manufacturers to create their own stores that were either self-financed or franchised.

The phenomenon began its evolution in the West, but from the mid-1990s China experienced an astounding boom headed by Adidas and its leading director at the time, Sandrine Zerbib, who achieved a turnover of 1 billion € from almost nothing in just a few years.

This model, still the dominant one in China, is based on an alliance between a Chinese distributor/investor and a big brand: The distributor's role is to take on negotiations regarding store location, lease agreements and HR (recruitment and management of sales people), whilst the brand takes care of all merchandising and the marketing offer, both share the result.

The Monobrand model quickly expanded to developing countries, notably South America, but also in Europe, particularly Russia.

Interestingly, in countries where it existed, traditional distribution – be it the chain store of an affiliate, who initially looked on suspiciously seeing a form of disloyal competition set up by manufacturers (though they were beginning manufacture themselves) – realized that when a Nike or Adidas store was set up next to their multi-brand store, they sold even more of that brand!

This form of distribution became a regular feature despite the demand for substantial financial investment as well working capital and supervision.

This brought about another major change for manufacturers as they had to learn a new trade and become retailers. Many initially considered themselves experts having already worked with distributors. They quickly found out that they had to acquire a lot more know-how regarding merchandising, managing the different sales periods, shop layout etc. As the wheel continues to turn, certain brands are already in the process of developing new and even more beautiful and efficient retail concepts.

- Everybody knows that the 2000 decade marks the arrival of the digital world and e-commerce.

Initially intended for gathering information on product usage, the Internet attracts fashion product as well as sport product buyers. Those who are most attracted are the ones who want to have a bigger vision on the entire product range in order to stand out with products that cannot be found in brick and mortar distribution channels.

Often many start-ups are created based on the expertise in a particular sport or sports universe and propose, apart from a product catalogue, a sense of belonging to a community for the passionate consumers they wish to attract and whose loyalty they would like to win.

Other sites base all their communication and business model on price in order to seduce the digital newcomer who believes that this is the magic wand to buy cheaper.

Manufacturers themselves as well as retailers create their own e-commerce website but, unfortunately, they are neither fast nor strong enough to be able to take up a dominant positioning.

- By the end of the 2000s and to this day, brick and mortar distribution and e-commerce, once rivals, are beginning to realize that they can work together. E-commerce players are coming around to the fact that it is difficult to build a brand without a tangible point of sale. They have come to understand that in the field of sports, for the consumer, the process of choosing a product is an emotional one and that the opportunity to touch and see the product as well as getting personalized advice are highly appreciated by the buyer.

Studies (who were the web's biggest critics at the time) show that a handful amongst them were quite happy to get information from the web first before actually going into a shop to make the purchase.

Social shopping is evolving and allows even the most hesitant consumer to feel reassured about brands and products that he or she has identified beforehand.

The paradox about this new way of shopping that appeared with the arrival of e-commerce is that we are discovering a type of consumer that does the opposite: They go out to the shop to get the information first before ordering the product online.

In the end, we come to the realization that shopping will never be just a simple transaction: The act of sales and purchase can never be based again on just product/price. The retailer must be able to inspire the consumer differently, more profoundly, in order for him or her to effect a purchase.

The consequence: All actors, never mind what side they are on, come to the conclusion that a combination of both worlds, on- and off-line, allows for a compound of the advantages for both distribution modes. It reinforces the strengths of e-commerce – range dimension, price flexibility, a full product description – and adds to the elements which only a physical distribution channel can offer: The emotional aspect when physically holding the product and the personalized advice by a salesperson on site.

With this in mind, all e-commerce players, big or small, seek to develop their sales network: Amazon opens up stores as do the pure sports players; in China, Alibaba plans an association with 6 million small shops and hopes to convert them to becoming an extension to their e-commerce site Tmall.com.

At the same time, Intersport, Decathlon and Sport 2000 all are investing millions into their website development, not to mention manufacturers such as Adidas, Nike, Puma etc. who not only are beefing up their e-commerce but also beginning to develop ranges that cannot be found on their website. Atypical but powerful actors such as Au Vieux Camper, Globetrotter and certain board sport shops are also beginning to adapt and open up towards the digital.

- At this stage, there is little doubt that multi channel is the distribution solution that will predominate the 2020s.

  The distributors are getting creative with the application of off- and online solutions: concepts such as "click and collect", "click and try" and pop-up stores are just the beginning of new services to the consumer thanks to a clever combination of the physical and virtual world.

  Beyond these new services, we can imagine that the 2020s will be the years of "experiential retail".

  This is a different way for the consumer to adapt, try and test the products he or she wants to buy as well as live an experience with the brand, be it online or on site, and to see whether he or she is alignment with it.

  House of Vans in London is a fine example of this: Opened in 2014, it is a shop offering more than one hectare of space in which one can find a skate park, a concert hall, bars, a cinema etc.

  The consumer, free of all concerns about price or range with a multitude of ways available on how to gain information about these, and who is, by the same token, more educated and more demanding, will want to be reassured to make the right choice regarding his or her purchase on a product as well as on a brand level. The first initiatives of customization proposed by Salomon and Adidas, the experiential sports sites where one can register to practice as well as buy, the limited editions proposed by brands, the available comparisons and the exchanges within the sports communities – these are only the beginnings of a new evolution of the distribution that will again transform its landscape as it has done so regularly over these 50 last years.

2.2 The relationship between manufactures and distributors

Interestingly, manufacturers and distributors enjoy a relatively calm relationship.

Of course, there have been times of crisis, for example, when chain stores arrived on the market, when distributors decided to launch their own brands or when brands opened their own stores. However, this was nothing compared with the ruthless competition attitude between the manufacturers and distributors that exists in sectors like food, toys and household appliances.

In the sports industry, everything works in such a way as if distributors and manufacturers understood that everyone needs to earn a living so that some are able to finance innovation and brands whilst others provide consumers with the service and development they expect.

Given the highly atomized nature of both markets that also explains this situation, we anticipate that this will not last due to the acceleration of their concentrations as well as the arrival of e-commerce and DTC (direct to consumers).

2.3 The global sporting goods distribution market

As in the manufacturers' sector where two major brands, Nike and Adidas, are dominating, the offline distribution sector also observes two competing main players: Switzerland's Intersport established in 1968, the result of a fusion of different European names, and the very French Decathlon, a brilliant planet within the Nordic galaxy of Mulliez (Auchan, Leroy Merlin, Boulanger, Kiabi, etc.) which opened its first shop in France in 1976.

Following are two distribution formats that are very different from each other: Intersport, apart from owning a few flagship stores, federates essentially about 5.500 independant retailers under its name, each being affiliated with their country's central organization; whereas Decathlon is a centralized chain that is present in about 40 countries with almost 1,400 stores.

The year 2016 saw an event that despite having had little impact was nonetheless important: Intersport, historically the market leader, was caught up and overtaken by its challenger, Decathlon. The Swiss announced a turnover figure of 11 billion € including VAT for 2016 whereas the French passed the 10 billion € excluding VAT bar last year. Each represents a level of activity that is estimated to be more than double the world's # 3, the American Foot Locker.

Intersport's international structure is based in Bern/Switzerland and sets the pace within the group, develops products under its own brand, manages the framework of agreements with manufacturers and leads the alliances towards an international development. However, operational power remains within the national organizations of each country. They are the ones who deal with suppliers so that specific purchasing conditions can be proposed to their members and who develop a strong marketing policy for the promotion of the brand and the Intersport offer. The Intersport brand develops its own brands focusing on entry-level (Tecno, Mc Kinley, etc.), but the figure generated by these brands remains marginal compared to the one that is achieved with traditional manufacturers.

Intersport's two strongholds are Germany with a turnover figure of almost 2.5 billion € and a 21% market share and France, with 1.5 billion € representing 19% market share. The rest of Europe adds up to about 3 billion €, and equally, 3 billion € beyond Europe.

It is interesting to note that Intersport is absent under its own brand name in the United States (but present under another brand they own, "The Athlete's

Foot"), and, as we will find out shortly, the same scenario was true for Decathlon until recently.

Decathlon based its entire growth on the development of its own brands (today there are over 25 passion brands) and only recently extended it through international development.

After the first two decades of its existence, when Decathlon's own brands added very little technological value and when price was the only true differentiator, the native from Lille decided in the early 1990s to strongly invest in research and innovation in order to develop smart products accessible to the mainstream sport consumers.

Over 500 engineers and teams are dedicated to each passion brand who work towards the successful development of innovative products with amazing results: The tent that opens in 2 seconds, the new generation diving mask, the intelligent sleeping bag and many more.

Decathlon's own brands represent today 70% of its sales and measures over 90% in certain countries. Their economic approach is based on the fact that Decathlon sacrifices the double margin which they could claim as a manufacturer and as a distributor in favour of being able to offer often comparable products of classic manufacturing brands but at a better price than their competitors. Their know-how in terms of supply chain is another asset that allows them to be so performant.

It is worth noting that, beyond France, Decathlon comes out well ahead as the market leader in Italy and Spain.

This sports giant, albeit very French (with export not being one of the strong features of our national economy), quickly took the reins of international development. After an initial phase of just focusing on neighbouring and/or Latin countries, Decathlon started to export in a grand way to all continents with absolutely spectacular results.

Today, alongside its 300 French stores, Decathlon counts over 500 stores in Europe and more than 400 in other parts of the world, of which more than half are based in Asia. Not a month goes by without unlocking a new country: From Switzerland to Israel, across South Africa or Iran, the brand just keeps breaking into new markets.

It is also worth mentioning that Decathlon is trying to re-enter the US market quietly with a store in San Francisco, after having experienced a serious set-back in the year 2000 by buying an American chain and having had to resell it quickly. There is no doubt that the United States, the world's largest market, represents the biggest challenge for the Northern French brand for the next 10 years to come.

As for the rest, and apart from these two major players, sporting goods distribution remains atomized with powerful local or regional actors, most of whom have developed a good reputation over a long period of time, with a sound national image and in locations that are difficult to top. As every country has a particular context, manufacturers are the ones who need to adapt to this more so than

Table 4.8 Main distribution actors per country (USA/Europe), 2015–2016

	Brands
USA	Foot Locker, DICK'S, Cabela's, REI
Canada	Forzani (Intersport)
Germany	Intersport, Sport 2000
France	Decathlon, Intersport
Italy	Decathlon, Intersport
Spain	Decathlon, El Corte Inglès
Austria	Sport 2000, Intersport
Switzerland	Ochsner, Intersport
Belgium	Decathlon
UK	Sports Direct, JD Sports
Sweden	Stadium, Intersport
Norway	XXL, G Sport

distributors who face a more concentrated market. For example, with the United States, despite the fact that it has a third of the global market, neither of these two global leaders are truly present, and American distributors dominate their home market.

As we have seen earlier, in Asia and in most of Latin America (except Brazil), distribution consists of more one-brand stores that are the result of a partnership between a brand and a local actor. In China, the main acting partners for brands are Belle and Pou Sheng and work with Nike as well as with Adidas, Puma or Asics. Just this new distribution deserves a book in itself. It represents a totally different business model which will without a doubt be further developed and refined, and not only in the developing countries.

Besides traditional offline distribution (brick and mortar), there is also a growing and evolving online trade, be it on computer, tablet or phone.

At this stage of e-commerce evolution, we can reasonably consider that the sporting goods domain is neither ahead nor backwards when compared with other durable consumer goods sectors as far as the representativeness of e-commerce is concerned.

The different estimates diverge at times, but overall in 2017 the e-commerce market shared roughly account for 14% of the total value of purchases made.

In the distribution chapter, we saw how online and offline paths cross each other, but, like elsewhere, e-commerce takes on different forms and develops in all sorts of directions. Today, a plethora of new players arrive on this market with, of course, existing actors staying strong and who also want to get on the winning path.

Without being able to easily quantify everybody's share, today's online actors are

- Generalists (Amazon, Alibaba, etc.)
- Multisports (Blue Tomato, Ekosport, etc.)

Table 4.9 Top 10 sporting goods distributors (except e-commerce) worldwide 2015–2016, global (equipment + footwear + clothing)

1	DECATHLON (France)
2	INTERSPORTS (Switzerland)
3	DICK'S SPORTING GOODS (USA)
4	ACADEMY SPORTS (USA)
5	BASS PRO SHOPS (USA)
6	SPORTS DIRECT (UK)
7	CABELAS (USA)
8	BELLE (China)
9	JD SPORTS FASHION (UK)
10	REI (USA)

- Pure Players (Snowleader, etc.)
- Brand Websites (Adidas, Nike, etc.)
- Distributor Websites (Decathlon, Intersport, etc.)

With so many players on the field, online/offline duality is only the beginning. However, we can be sure that it will not only profoundly alter the landscape of the global sporting goods distribution, but also call for a reassessment of the manufacturers' trade and know-how. The game is going to get tougher and the rules of the game will surely change as well: The next 10 years will be exciting.

3 What are the future perspectives?

3.1 Are all the lights set on green?

At the risk of appearing overly optimistic, we will answer "yes".

First, from a quantitative point of view, there is no doubt that the market will continue to grow. It is even possible that the annual growth of 6% will be surpassed should the developing countries and the United States see their global economy regain a growth curve close to the one pre-crisis.

It can make us dream when we see an American spending today 300€ per year on sporting goods compared to 200€ for a Western European, 70€ for a Brazilian and only 30€ for an Asian (70€ if he or she belongs to the middle class).

Qualitatively, all previously mentioned trends (sport/health, sport/nature etc.) will continue to support practice and therefore the industry.

Sports marketing will become increasingly strong and will affect more and more non-practitioners who are nonetheless consumers of derivative products or products of partner brands.

As seen earlier, the casual sports trend will also feature prominently in sports brands, but also ready-to-wear and fashion brands will find their way into the sports universe. This can also make us dream: Will this be the end of suit and tie and moccasins for the working man, to be replaced by a piqué woven polo shirt, breathable elastic pants and footwear with adjustable cushioning?

Already today, brands like Nike, Adidas, Salomon make us spend around 200€ for a pair of sports shoes: The increase in the standard of sports products and the rise of brand status in this market are not ready to slow down. Moreover, celebrity as well as community marketing will continue to add to the dynamics and energy of the entire sports universe.

In the end, it will not be the few constraints that we will mention later that will prevent the sports market growing, and that is good news for a world that is becoming more and more virtual. Although many other sectors of our economy are facing threats, such as pollution for automobiles, less print consumption, health risks for food etc., sport remains and will remain a desired and desirable practice.

3.2 What are the opportunities for tomorrow?

3.2.1 The new El Dorados

The markets will most likely be, in our opinion, the main growth accelerators for the next 20 years.

Whether we like it or not, the country that will be contributing most to this growth is China. Having 10% of the global market share already, the Chinese market will probably hold nearly a quarter of the global pie by 2050. The rest of Asia will follow at a slower pace, depending on the development of local economies, but we can be sure that the entire continent will eventually jump on the sports wagon.

When we see what has been happening in China, we can predict that the next sports El Dorado may well be India. With 1.2 billion inhabitants, an economy in full growth, the end of the "cricket only" sports model and an opening of its borders to foreign companies, it is very likely that this market will hold significant potential in the coming years for companies, if they find a way of how to unlock it smartly, especially when keeping in mind that the Indian youth generation is larger than the Chinese one.

Furthermore, it would not be surprising to see the appearance of Indian sports brands in the coming years – along the lines of Li Ning, Anta, XTEP in China – trying to take on the bottom-end segments of the market.

Once Brazil and Russia will have digested their current crisis, they will also be important countries thanks of their size and the interest their inhabitants take in sports. The distribution which is very concentrated in Russia and very national in Brazil will certainly encounter profound changes towards a more classic development than the one the two countries have hitherto experienced.

Eastern Europe and the rest of South America will be subject to the same pace of growth as that of their respective economy in general. With an almost mechanic correlation, the richer a country becomes overall, the quicker the sports market will develop.

We can also count on slow yet steady growth in North America as well as Western and Southern Europe. To date we cannot see the reason how these markets will find an exponential growth rate, nonetheless, their wealth triggers demand, which is maintained according to the rhythm of incentives proposed by the actors in industry and distribution.

Finally, Australia and New Zealand will remain countries with a very strong sports practice rate, a strong sports product equipment ratio but with limited size of population and therefore limited consumption.

In the end, the sports sector in the BRIC countries (Brazil/Russia/India/China) will continue to grow whilst they have reached their asymptote in other economic sectors.

We will not talk about Africa here, nevertheless, we will briefly address its situation in the conclusion.

3.2.2 High technologies and new products

It would be worth writing an entire book just on technological development prospects alone and they are quite widely covered elsewhere, but, in summary, we can say that innovation in sports was up to now very focused on chemistry, mechanics, construction, materials etc., and we can expect developments in products and applications to move towards the digital, the virtual and, mainly, the custom-made.

As we have seen, consumers will become increasingly demanding and satisfaction will no longer be just based on brand and price. Expectations regarding quality and a competent offering of a holistic brand experience, its products and services are high, both in terms of technical nature as well as styling, for athletes as well as for spectators.

In terms of products, miniaturization and a higher battery power will clearly be an essential technological feature for new products and markets.

Given that the bicycle is today the main beneficiary of this technological evolution, could we not envisage that new energies take over the human capacity to push the limits of performance?

All two- or three-wheelers with a sports or urban mobility edge will generate a market explosion in the coming years.

In parallel to these wheelers, we can anticipate a step-up of accessories and textiles. A brand like Rapha has already taken up a strong positioning and we can expect others to follow suit.

As previously mentioned, customization will equally see a development in all directions; what is regarded as a luxury today and only reserved for top-level athletes will roll out effortlessly and become accessible to the mass. Distributors have an advantage in that they are already physically in contact with consumers and so have the possibility to provide them with customization that is likely to seduce them.

As far as product categories are concerned, equipment is likely to stay stagnant, footwear will continue to grow albeit to a lesser degree than the textile category, the latter being expected to bring the most innovation and added value technically and fashion-wise in the years to come.

3.2.3 The big trends in innovation

We can extrapolate the major current innovation trends in sports in order to establish an obviously simplified typology covering four big technological categories.

As we have previously pointed out, the big news for the next 10 years is that innovation will no longer be limited to products, but will extend to services, experiences and how a sport is practised. It will not only serve the sport practitioner but also his or her friends and spectators, on an individual or mass level. In addition to sport products as such, anything that touches on sports and its practice will be submitted to research and will therefore see new innovative developments.

3.2.4 The development in sport practices

Apart from cycling, a topic that that has already been widely mentioned and which appears to be the most promising market for the next 10 years, we can also expect that the wellness trend (fitness, yoga, gymnastics, Taichi, etc.) will continue to rise.

This trend will be part of a broader dimension and will go beyond just searching for purely physical and an esthetic benefit. Mindset will become more and more important in sports and practitioners will be increasingly focused on seeking to experience an inner well-being whilst practising. Anglo-Saxons, always quick to find a specialized vocabulary for new categories, have already coined this combination of physical effort and mindfulness with the barbaric term "Athleisure".

Amongst others sports that should be breezing ahead, there is one that appears to have a particularly bright future: Indoor climbing. In fact, recently, climbing gyms have been flourishing and they often come with yoga studios, a health food restaurant, a micro brewery, a music studio, etc. Everything is designed to make young people (the primary but not the only target) feel comfortable that they do not only come to climb, but also they can hook up with a community to socialize and exchange. In France, Arkose already offers a great number of such halls and has raised funds to implement an ambitious development plan. There a many other facilities of this type that have been successful in major cities like Barcelona, New York, Los Angeles, Milan, etc.

Indoor climbing is being described by some people as "the new skateboard" as both worlds hold the same value of creativity, a potential culture and the fact that they are both community-oriented practices.

Table 4.10 Trends in innovation

TYPE OF INNOVATION	*OBJECTIVE OF THAT TECHNOLOGIE*	*TARGET*	*BENEFIT OF THE INNOVATION*	*TYPES OF PRODUCTS*
1 INNOVATION IMPROVING PERFORMANCE	TECHNOLOGY FOR OPTIMIZATION	FOR ME	To be better, more performing. To be faster, stronger, more enduring, better protected	Intelligents fibres in textiles, Carbon nanotubes, Power-assisted, food supplements, . . .
2 INNOVATION MEASURING PERFORMANCE	TECHNOLOGY FOR ANALYSIS AND MEASURING	FOR MY COACH	To better understand and analyze individual or collective performance	GPS for sports people, connected items (racket, . . .) Drones . . .
3 INNOVATION RECORDING PERFORMANCE	TECHNOLOGY FOR RECORDING AND SHARING	FOR MY FRIENDS	To be able to share my experience with my community	Cameras, watches, bracelets, sharing applications . . .
4 INNOVATION ENHANCING PERFORMANCE	TECHNOLOGY FOR COMPREHENSION AND MEDIATISATION	FOR MY PUBLIC	For a more rewarding experience for the consumer, the spectator	Connected stadiums, image transposition, identification with sports people . . .

We can even go further and imagine that new footwear and clothing brands will arise to flesh out the look and culture of that practice, potentially replacing the surf universe which today fails to seduce the young generations.

To a lesser extent, it is also logical to anticipate that nature sports (hiking, mountaineering, paddle surfing, etc.) will continue to evolve as they are in alignment with the sport/nature trend.

Winter sports will remain under pressure except for hiking practices, which also fit in with the sport trends that can be practised for free without having to rely on ski lifts.

As far as team sports are concerned, football will be leading the growth thanks to China in particular and the legal or illegal betting money that will be invested in this country and Asia in general.

Running which has enjoyed exponential growth rate in the last years will very much likely plateau and may even decline somewhat, whereas for racket sports we have currently no vision on what would re-establish an uptrend.

3.2.5 The new consumer sociology

This chapter is a toast to women – it is becoming clear that women's sport practices and therefore, sports essentially practised by women will experience a major evolution in the years to come.

This will be particularly the case in Asia, the continent which will quantitatively contribute the most in terms of their sheer size of active women. Nonetheless, we can also see in the Western world, year on year, women taking a bigger piece of the total sports practitioner pie.

The signs point in the same direction: Concerns about health, developing obesity, pushing back the age of procreation, the increasing desire in women to play on the same field as men and their need to be seen as equals etc.

For a number of years now, products are being specifically developed for women that flood collections of major market stakeholders. Gone are the days where men's article were simply painted pink. Be they technical specifications or styling features, manufacturers are adapting their product to women, seducing the users and satisfying them in terms of style and usage. However, when compared with men's products, the value of women's products is capitalized to a lesser extent on performance and focuses more on comfort and practicality.

Wellness practices are evolving as we have previously seen, but the most remarkable phenomenon of recent years is the number of women taking up running. Initially a purely masculine arena, it has become a sport that is being practised by couples (and where the man is not always ahead).

A second consumer group which we will see on the rise in terms of practice and sales statistics are the seniors.

A longer life expectancy, the ability to enjoy full fitness upon retirement, continuous medical progress in anti-aging and new technologies in power assistance allow elderly people to keep on practising sports for longer and more regularly.

In terms of products, a lot of things remain to be achieved in this domain and manufacturers have not committed themselves completely to focus on the satisfaction of this target out of fear that this could age their global image.

Finally, we can expect that the market for children's sports products (mainly footwear and clothing) will experience a significant growth that will be propelled by China.

Having been limited for a long time due to the single child policy, Chinese families, where the family structure often consists of young parents and whose own parents are still alive, spend a fortune on their offspring.

The sports industry is facing the fact that in Western countries children products are as expensive as the ones for adults. As parents from Eastern countries are not prepared to pay the same price as for adult products, the sports industry is already developing its own collections that exclusively address Asian children.

3.2.6 New sport mentalities

It's safe to say that the concern for sustainable development, efforts made towards an authentic social responsibility and discourses that carry general humane messages will be the big themes of the future and will underpin the success or failure of certain brands and companies.

With increasing access to consumer information, it is no longer possible for a company to miss out on its social responsibility as its values are not only scrutinized, analyzed and dissected, but they also constitute a vital link with its customers that can either attract them or push them away.

This rising global trend will be even more at the forefront within the sports universe: Sport practitioners, and many studies confirm this, are very much ahead in terms of their ecological and societal concerns whether it is about respecting the planet or the wide disparities in our world. There is no doubt about the fact that carbon will be a topical subject for the sports economy for the next 20 years.

Another concept that is making headway is hedonism: Practioners are losing more and more interest in the quest for performance and technical progress and rather turn essentially towards "pleasure benefits" that come more from how a sport is being practised.

The notion of danger in sports is also strongly evolving.

The paradox is that the most dangerous of sports and sports practices are actually in full growth: Wingsuit, base jumping, extreme alpinism etc. are counting more and more enthusiasts, although it remains marginal. In parallel to this, all sports that are deemed violent see their legislators attempting to reduce risk and danger levels (Rugby, football, skiing, etc.).

The predictions of the 1970s cult film *Rollerball*, which foresees a sport anchored in extreme violence, is not confirmed.

3.3 How will distribution and the interface between manufacturers evolve?

This is an issue that most likely the overall sports market will deliberate the coming 10 years.

It is the result of three parallel and concomitant phenomena that we have covered previously:

- The change of global consumption patterns with, of course, the explosion of digital
- Trends in the sports industry arena where the big manufacturers weigh increasingly more
- The evolution of the distribution that remains fragmented and poorly developed internationally

To better grasp the revolution in the relationship between retailers and manufacturers, it is worth stating the recent remarks of Mark Parker, Nike's CEO. He placed a bombshell in front of all the media and specialized sports analysts who met in Portland last December by declaring that, being in a position where Nike is working with 30,000 distribution partners, the priority will from now on be the concentration of efforts, time and investments on 40 retailers, that he called the "Strategic wholesale partners". Who are they? "*Partners which are willing and able to build out unique and dedicated Nike spaces within their store environments*".

Suffice to say that this declaration made some Nike sales executives flinch; he also clearly stated that wholesale distribution in general would no longer be a priority for his company in the future.

This does not come as a surprise to those market leaders who have understood for some time now that the most important concept within their company's business strategy is DTC – direct to consumer.

For manufacturers, DTC means that all sales are directly made by them, be it through their own or franchised monobrand stores, their outlets and pop-up stores or via their websites.

Although Herbert Hainer, CEO of Adidas at the time, announced in the early 2000s that direct sales of his brand would never exceed 10% of total sales, today, Adidas is at 30%!

All top 20 manufacturers see their DTC sales grow by more than 10% a year whilst wholesale is increasingly shrivelling.

It is no wonder that all these companies today are giving DTC absolute priority as a result. Nike, known for its arrogance but also its courage, only announced it publicly.

What impact will this have for the relationship between and interaction of manufacturers and distributors?

What are the consequences for distribution itself?

It seems obvious that manufacturers are biting heavily into the distributors' part of the pie and we can expect extreme tensions between the two protagonists as we enter this new phase.

As is often the case, size and weight will decide who will want to enter the ring with the biggest on each side ganging up against the smallest. Given that Nike only works with 40 retailers worldwide, we can envisage that Foot Locker and Intersport will be amongst them.

Even if Decathlon's business approach with its own brand is different, it is likely that seeing large manufacturers expanding into distribution has triggered an acceleration for development with a view to placing themselves strategically (before eventually taking market share), not only on an international level but also in terms of number of stores.

It seems equally plausible that this trend will generate a wave that will create a concentration within the international sports distribution. Who will be at the source? Surely neither of the two leaders as they are both somewhat hindered by their respective business models. Maybe an outsider, but which one remains to be seen.

Until then, traditional distribution will withstand and fight, of course, via e-tailers who will continue to surf on the Internet wave, without question through e-commerce sites that were developed by traditional retailers with a view to shift to the omni channel, probably through more advanced experiential marketing as we have observed earlier and perhaps through a more selective choice of brands and more store space (as Mark Parker desires), for example, presented in the form of shop corners.

In any case, we can expect that the aforementioned "peace of the brave" will be broken and that the future years will be marked by a phase where big transformations concerning the functioning of the manufacturers/distributors double act will occur.

For now, the former seem to be in control of play, but we can trust the latter to defend their interests and, hopefully, be in a position to come up with new models regarding the relationship with the consumer.

Conclusion: The big stakes of the future

Boosted by current sociological trends, having recovered thanks to other strong trends such as fashion or urban mobility, self-powered by a strong innovation capacity, represented by strong and passionate companies as well as being mediatized by a world where digital makes it a place of choice, sport indeed has a bright future ahead.

Nonetheless, we can identify some major issues that the various actors will have to be vigilant about:

- The rapprochement between the worlds of fashion/ready-to-wear and sport is as we have seen one of the main drivers of this economic sector. However, it is important to be aware of the influence that this trend has on products. The arrival of "Fastfashionistas" should not make the technical aspect of sports products disappear.

- The same type of concern about price: Is the "homecoming" back to the West and the current consumerist trend not likely to send prices of sporting goods rocketing to such a level that they will become deterrent for a larger segment of consumers? It is clear that manufacturers are developing an increasingly sophisticated price segmentation. Could this be the antidote?
- The new situation that is emerging between manufacturers and distributors may provoke battles that would be harmful to the entire market.

Concerns are arising for the traditional distribution as well as American retail investors within the United States: Attracted by the expected yields at the time, they are bewildered by the bankruptcy of Sports Authority and the difficulties of other retailers.

- On another level, doping, corruption and greed are serious threats for sports as a whole. The money that goes around arouses covetousness, brings about the merchants of the temple and excites profiteers.

The image of sport is already quite chipped thanks to the mediatization of all the scandals that appear more and more often in many sectors. However, sport "bashing" must not overshadow its usual connotation for the values it conveys.

- The accessibility of sports by young people remains problematic. It is reported that, in terms of practice, the percentage of sports practitioners under 15 years of age is in decline. Is it in competition with time spent on social networks, with the money spent on mobile phones or tablets, the couch being more cozy than facing a football field in the winter?

We can laugh at today's cliché that e-sport, which, by the way, is still growing, will replace sport with youngsters, yet there is an urgent need for a public policy (cf. China) that addresses a sport incentive for the younger youth.

In a country like France it is worth noting that the educational system with its weekly 2 hours of physical education during school hours has let go of this, leaving the responsibility to promote sports practice to clubs and local authorities.

- Climate change has also become a variable when envisaging the future of certain sports.

Even if we can organize a football World Cup in Qatar and the Olympic Winter Games in Korea, global warming will inevitably encourage some sports in specific places and disfavour others. Sports that are climate

> dependant, notably winter sports, are particularly concerned: Recent studies show that as of the 2050s there will be a serious lack or no snow in Europe under 2,000 m. So what to do with low and medium altitude stations, how does their business model, currently centred on snow, need to change? And, should a plan be relaunched to build higher stations in order to not lose the winter sports clientele?

Ultimately, we can see that even if there are a few threats to sport and its industry, there is no irreversible external factor looming, and therefore nothing that appears to prevent the development of the sector, the athletes and the markets associated to it.

The employment economy in this industry should therefore continue to grow. Having an international profile, being a young multicultural and multilingual will be a prerequisite in order to evolve in this increasingly global market.

The passion for sport will also remain an essential criterion to get into this environment, but it will undoubtedly have to come with an understanding of fashion and trends among young people that was not necessarily a must until now.

Digital, the magic word, will of course inevitably be applied to the changes of the employment market in this sector, however, no doubt it will be the ability to integrate the consequences of the digital world than having digital know-how per se that will count for these new trades.

And then, of course, sales and the sales representative will forever and everywhere in all product categories remain of essence; those who have learnt the trade and proved their worth will be the clear favourites to become the main players of this industry.

Finally, we would like to finish this chapter by expressing some qualitative expectations and hopes for the future of this market, some considerations that are not necessarily of a business nature but more based on a vision for a better world, even if that may sound naïve. There are the four we would like to state:

- That all actors in this industry become aware of the social dimension that sport is taking on in our society and, therefore, that athletes and entrepreneurs also become aware of the responsibility that comes with it, to make it a clean and virtuous universe in the eyes of the actors and spectators, especially among the younger generations.
- That sport is not a political game zone and that it remains, in the public arena, focused on the concerns for collective health and for the pleasure of the people. The proven State-involved doping scandal in Russia (no doubt other countries have identical practices), State-involved manipulations to win the Olympics or world championships for their country and the sometimes unhealthy nationalist impulses linked to some athletes' results are all aspects to be banished from our universe, if we want to hold it closer to our hearts rather than our wallet.
- That we start caring about Africa, the forgotten continent and yet so in love with sport! That the plundering by recruitment of budding footballers from

this continent stop, as well as the undermining of the Kenyan Highland's ethic and dumping waste from our industries there under the pretext that they would not be able to afford other products anyway and to, finally, start giving them the means to educate their youngsters through sport.

- That the sports industry gives itself the mission of being the one that is the most advanced in terms of defending the planet, sustainability and social responsibility. If there is a sector that must prevail through the values of sport, to lead by example, it is indeed ours and we must not back off from the challenge of being the leader of the virtue that all others want to follow.

Bibliography

This bibliography does not refer to publications or specifically dated and signed analyses, but presents a list of the most reliable and relevant sources of information which we have relied on to monitor the evolution of the sporting goods industry.

The preceding chapter is, amongst other things, a result of cross referencing and putting into perspective the information gathered from these different sources.

- NPD
- GFK
- Sporting goods intelligence Europe
- Sporting goods intelligence US
- Sport Guide
- Sport Eco
- Filièresport
- Outdoor Expert
- SAZ
- Trendwatching
- Retail news Asia
- Fashionetwork
- DD & Fils
- Codezero
- Sporsora
- European Outdoor Group
- L'Union Sport et Cycle
- Ministère de la Ville, de la Jeunesse et des Sport, Pipame
- Le Monde
- Les Echos
- Le Parisien

Chapter 5

A short history of the sporting goods industry

Eugenio Di Maria

Introduction

People all over the world have been engaging in various kinds of sports since prehistoric times to keep fit, for the sake of competition, for fun or for utilitarian reasons like hunting, fishing or moving fast from one place to another – by running, horse riding or cross-country skiing. Wrestling, archery, fencing and martial arts were born early as a means of fighting and self-defence. In ancient Greece and Rome, the cult of a well-shaped body led to the construction of gymnasia where young men underwent the first lessons of physical education. Men have been exercising since then, and even before, to get ready for battle.

However, most of the tools employed in these pursuits were one-of-a-kind items, generally forged in small workshops. There was no serial production, really, even for balls, until the industrial revolution of the 19th century, which coincided more or less with the popularization of collegiate sports in the United Kingdom, Ireland and the United States.

Using animal bladders and other materials, various types of ball games have been played for centuries in all the continents, with the first organized games of golf emerging in 15th-century Scotland and with the rules for modern football established in English colleges at the start of the 19th century.

However, some of these sports were only practised by the upper classes. In any case, the shoes, the clothing and the equipment used in these activities were made by artisans or small local workshops until certain sports became more popular, engaging more people, especially with the reduction of working hours and the emergence of the middle class. Like in other sectors of mass consumption, the development of modern transportation and the advent of the media allowed the manufacturers of sports products to reach out to a greater number of customers – nationally and across national borders – creating sufficient economies of scale to industrialize manufacturing processes and to invest more in technology and marketing.

It was only at this point that a "sporting goods industry" worthy of this name took off. It would take hundreds of pages to recount its history. Barbara Smit, who has been my main collaborator for more than 15 years in our *Sporting Goods*

Intelligence Europe business newsletter and in our international sporting goods market research, wrote a whole book on Adidas and Puma, which pioneered the modern history of the sporting goods sector in the early part of the 20th century. Her book has been translated into many languages.

So, we are going to skip here the much older history of the gear that the first sportsmen wore in the gymnasia of ancient Greece and Rome to train their bodies and to compete in fabulous events like the Olympic Games, which started in Greece in 773 BC. We are going to jump directly to the 20th century, after the re-start of Olympics in 1896.

1 The Olympic and military factors

Beyond the products themselves, which were mostly mass-produced for the needs of public schools and various types of sports clubs, the start of the modern history of the sporting goods industry in all its present aspects was closely associated with the modern Olympics – notably through the sports marketing strategies pioneered by Horst Dassler, the late chief executive of Adidas, who had the genius of branding his company's products in partnership with top sports teams and well-known athletes.

The modern history of the sporting goods industry has also been driven by the growing requirements for technical shoes and clothing of the military sector and other factors. Mass production of military boots in specific sizes was reported to have started in England in the early part of the 19th century for the Napoleonic wars and in the United States in the second part of the same century in connection with the American Civil War.

After the end of World War II, many of the shoe and apparel companies that had been developing and producing highly technical products for the military sector, including Adidas itself, converted themselves to more civilian pursuits by creating a new and growing demand for sports gear by the general public, and by catering to it. For example, many of the producers of mountaineering shoes operating in the industrial cluster of Montebelluna, north of Venice, were in fact previously suppliers to certain branches of the Italian Army. Many of them used the superior anti-slip soles developed by Vibram, starting with a product that this company called "carroarmato", which is the name given to a military tank in Italian.

After the war, it was relatively natural for these and other companies all over the world, especially in Europe and the United States, to make highly technical shoes as well as clothes, tents, backpacks and sleeping bags that could be used by the general public for hiking, trekking and camping, rather than to fight in a war.

Also at this time, some individuals who loved hiking in the nature developed their own gear by using the latest fibres and technologies, and some of them created their own brands, like Osprey for backpacks, for example. This helped generalize outdoor sports that had been practised for centuries by fewer and more adventurous people, especially in mountain areas and national parks, Alaska or the Arctic. A Norwegian company, Devold, developed very sophisticated wool garments for the famous 1911 expedition of Roald Amundsen to the South Pole, and it is still in the market.

Meanwhile, the military engine continued to power the emerging sporting goods industry in different ways. Even after World War II, military overtones characterized the competition between the Communist camp of nations and the Western world during the so-called Cold War. Russia, China, East Germany and other Communist countries battled for supremacy against the United States and other countries by breeding top-level athletes for the Olympic Games and other international competitions. The selection process for the future champions raised the bar in terms of sports performance internationally, and it created a desire among a larger number of individuals to emulate them. In Communist Russia or East Germany, participation in international competitions was one way in which the athletes could cross the border and travel to the West.

2 The media engine

The modern media gave a formidable boost to sports participation. Even before the end of World War II, newspapers and the radio stimulated people to compete in popular sports like football or cycling by recounting the exploits of the champions. The advent of television in the 'fifties gave an even stronger push to general sports participation by broadcasting the Olympic Games and other international or national tournaments for specific sports such as football, rugby, cricket (in the Commonwealth states), cycling and many other spectator sports like basketball and tennis, creating new and more visible sports icons whom people could see in action. Ironically, the organizers of the competitions and the managers of the stadia initially opposed the broadcasting of the events on TV, considering it a form of unfair competition.

Anyhow, it was logical for the sports brands to be somehow associated with these broadcasts to enhance their image in the market. An increasing number of suppliers of sports gears took advantage of the sports marketing bonanza offered by all the media – not just newspapers and magazines. Tennis champions like René Lacoste and Sergio Tacchini created their own brands at this time.

More recently, another powerful and cheaper medium – the Internet, particularly with its social media – has created one more marketing platform for brand building in the sport sector, and a cheaper one to use.

3 Being fit is useful and fashionable

Meanwhile, the development of the sector acquired a new dimension without the help of spectator sports through the gradual diffusion of a new fitness consciousness as an antidote to excessive food consumption. Public and private fitness clubs began to attract members who felt it useful and appropriate to build up muscles and to slim down by exercising indoors, especially in cold countries like Russia, Norway or Sweden where it is difficult to practice sports outdoors for most of the year. Particularly in these countries, fitness clubs thrived, with some entrepreneurs creating international chains of franchised gyms.

People started to consider health and fitness clubs also as a way to socialize with like-minded people. In the United States first, and then in other countries, women started practising aerobics. The actress Jane Fonda helped to popularize cardio-vascular fitness, creating the first collective workout classic in 1982, in contrast with body building for men, who adopted cardio training later on. American brands like Reebok and LA Gear capitalized on the new fitness trend, in contrast with companies like Adidas, Puma and Converse, which were more into Olympic and team sports at the time. Nike, in turn, reacted by promoting running as a more accessible and more individual fitness activity that could be practised by anyone anywhere, and became very successful through that.

4 Going to the mountains

Cross-country skiing has been one of the oldest means of transportation. Cave drawings indicate that people were gliding on snow in China around the year 8,000 BC. In the Nordic countries and Russia, more and more people took to cross-country skiing, ski touring and telemark skiing during the fitness boom as a form of exercising in the midst of a natural environment. In warmer climates, more and more people took to swimming, hiking, fishing and camping, which have also been among the oldest sports activities, practised by people of all ages irrespective of their disposable income. With the development of long-distance transportation and mass tourism, the post-war economic boom saw a growing popularization of all kinds of outdoor sports, including the emergence of winter sports holidays involving people of all ages from all countries in fun activities for the whole family like alpine skiing.

Naturally, most of the manufacturers of alpine skis were born in and around the Alps, especially in France, Austria and northern Italy. Some of them had already started well before World War II. In Austria, the first ski manufacturers were mostly high-tech derivatives of the woodworking industry. The first cambered skis were produced by wood carvers in Telemark, Norway in 1850. An Austrian company founded in 1862 to make wheels, Kneissl, claims to have been one of the first to have been producing wooden skis on an industrial scale, starting in 1919. The technology has progressed considerably since then, culminating in the development of the first aluminium laminate skis by Howard Head in 1947 and of the first fibreglass skis by K2 in 1962, apparently based on an invention made in Montreal two years earlier. Another American company, Olin, and Elan in Slovenia put out the first carving skis in 1990.

In Italy, some of the companies that started making waterproof plastic ski boots in the 1970s were former producers of mountaineering boots who found it useful to diversify into winter products that are not labour-intensive to make. Injection-molding machines can do the job. The technology was invented by an American, Bob Lange, who produced the first vacuum-molded plastic boots in 1966.

5 Diversification doesn't always work out

Product diversification has been an engine of growth for many companies that were specializing in specific segments of the sporting goods industry. This has been especially the case among ski companies because of their excessive dependence on snow conditions.

In Austria, for example, ski producers like Fischer and Head also became manufacturers of tennis racquets. Fischer diversified further into the production of ice hockey sticks and aerospace components. Head, which also owns Tyrolia, one of the major suppliers of ski bindings, moved into scuba diving through Mares. The company's short-lived diversification into apparel and footwear in the 1980s was less successful.

Salomon, which actually started in 1947 as a metalworking shop for the manufacture of saw blades, moved into the sporting goods business by making steel edges for skis and then ski bindings, where it became a leader. It then moved on to produce ski boots under the same, strong brand name.

To diversify away from the weather-dependent winter sports business, Salomon then started to make hiking boots, where it has become a leader as the pioneer of trail running. In another major diversification move, Salomon acquired during the 1980s a big American golf brand, Taylor Made and, in the 1990s, a specialized French manufacturer of bicycle rims, Mavic.

As a leader in the category of metalwood golf clubs, Taylor Made became an appealing prey for Adidas, which bought the whole Salomon Group at a high price in 1997, but the cultural mix didn't really work out, and Adidas felt that it would be better off concentrating on sports apparel and footwear through the acquisition of Reebok, which would have given it a stronger presence in the US market. Thus, Adidas decided seven years later to keep Taylor Made and to sell the remainder of the Salomon Group's business to the Finnish Amer Sports group, which already owned another big Austrian ski company, Atomic. With the golf market turning sour, Adidas divested Taylor Made and other golf-related assets in May 2017. At around the same time, Nike stopped selling golf clubs under its own brand name.

Another French group, Rossignol, which was for a while the world's largest supplier of alpine skis, preferred to concentrate on snow sports. Like most of its Austrian competitors, it started off in 1907 as a manufacturer of wood products. It continued to focus on skis after it was taken over in 1956 by Laurent Boix-Vives, a former operator of ski lifts, who developed the brand and bought other snow sports brands like Dynastar, Lange and Look.

In 2005, Quiksilver, the leading producer of surfwear, made a bold move by convincing the elderly Boix-Vives to sell it a controlling stake in Rossignol. The move was justified by the belief that Quiksilver would allow the two groups to have a strong presence in winter and summer sports, and in mountain and water sports. It was also meant to combine their operations in the area of snowboards. Most importantly, Quiksilver's know-how would have helped Rossignol to develop a line of apparel under its brand name, which it had tried to do previously without success.

Like Adidas' acquisition of Salomon and the diversification of Adidas and Nike into golf equipment, the combination of Rossignol and Quiksilver didn't work out either for cultural and other reasons including the difficult fit between equipment and clothing. Quiksilver had to divest Rossignol three years later at a bargain price. With the financial support of Altor Equity Partners, a Swedish investment firm that previously controlled Helly Hansen and that took over its control in 2013, Rossignol is now trying again to make a strong statement in apparel, positioning itself this time in the growing premium lifestyle segment of the market.

Cultural reasons probably contributed also to the unsuccessful diversification of Italy's Benetton Group into sports during the 1990s through the acquisition of big brands like Nordica (ski boots) Prince (tennis racquets), Asolo (hiking boots) and Rollerblade (inline skates). By 2003, the former Benetton Sportsystem had been dismantled with the sale of all its assets to various parties, as the Benetton family preferred to invest their money into highways, cafeterias and other types of operations.

One of the major beneficiaries was the local Tecnica Group, which took over Nordica and Rollerblade. Controlled by the family of Giancarlo Zanatta, this other Italian group had begun operating in 1960 as a manufacturer of work boots. It launched a famous after-ski boot, the Moon Boot, in 1970. After diversifying the Tecnica brand into ski boots and outdoor boots and acquiring Nordica, it completed its portfolio of winter sports brands with the acquisition of Blizzard. Like Rossignol, Salomon and other major ski companies, the group was thus able to offer full sets of skis, boots and bindings. Zanatta's best move turned out to be its purchase of a controlling interest in Lowa, the leading German producer of outdoor shoes, in 1993. Coupled with the takeover of an Italian outdoor brand, Dolomite, it allowed the Tecnica Group to develop like Salomon a counter-seasonal business that helped it to survive the vagaries of the declining snow sports market during the last couple of decades.

During that time, the number of alpine skis sold around the world every year declined by about one-third to just over four million pairs for various reasons including the burst of the snow sports bubble in Japan, where about one million pairs were previously sold annually. Aside from the greenhouse effect, which has shortened the duration of the snow season around the world, ski retailers have been offering the possibility to simply rent the equipment. Customers have been able to use the latest models at a lower cost. The market for ski boots has fallen less precipitously, as many customers have preferred to buy well-fitting, customized models and use them when needed.

6 Varying lifecycles for certain sports

We'll talk about some other significant mergers and acquisitions later on in this chapter. We would like to point out here that Rossignol, Salomon and all other companies in the sporting goods industry have had to contend with many variable factors besides the weather, including the degree of professional management, the rate of economic progress, the growth of disposable income by the middle classes, the development of the Internet and other new technologies, the growing cost of labour in the emerging countries and – last but not least – the unpredictable cycles in the popularity of certain sports.

For example, the participation of the general public in certain types of alpine skiing and other kinds of snow, water and street sports has gone up and down dramatically, driving certain companies to develop rapidly before going under at the end of the cycle.

With their emancipation in the late 'sixties, the younger generations began to adopt alternative fun and more extreme "boardsports" (sports de glisse) like snowboarding, windsurfing, surfing and skateboarding. Without growing as fast as before, all these sports have continued to this day in various degrees except for windsurfing, which has been replaced in part by kite surfing. Not without some difficulties, category leaders like Bic Sport, Burton, Billabong and Rip Curl have survived the big waves of the boardsports market. Others have disappeared.

More recently, some young people have also been embracing a quieter water sport coming from America – stand-up paddling – or more challenging sports like indoor climbing or bouldering. Catering to their tribal instincts, they will keep waiting for something new and exciting that will set them apart.

7 Technical sportswear and footwear for the street

On the technological front, the development of technical features like the use of down feathers for quilted skiwear and cushioning for sports shoes triggered a revolution in people's everyday wear in the early 1970s coinciding with a trend toward less formal types of clothing. Since then, the border between sports and fashion, and between function and looks, has been increasingly blurred as people started wearing down-filled outerwear that was originally meant for skiing or winter hiking. In countries like Italy or Japan, brands like Ellesse and The North Face became a status symbol in streetwear during the 'seventies and the 'eighties. With the emergence of an affluent middle class, technical branded sportswear became fashionable in Russia and China a couple of decades later. In the past decade, for example, some of the wealthier Chinese people showed off with the expensive jackets of Arc'teryx, a very technical Canadian brand of outerwear that belongs to Amer Sports group.

A more modern replica of this phenomenon on a global basis has been the emergence of premium brands like Italy's Moncler and Canada Goose, two former technical brands of outerwear that are now successfully focusing on the fashion market, which can generate higher profit margins than the sporting goods retail channel.

Moncler started in the 1950s in France as a producer of sleeping bags as well as quilted cold-weather jackets for workers and skiers, but after its sale to Italian interests in 2003, it has become an expensive fashion brand that is mainly sold mainly in its own stores and in exclusive fashion boutiques and department stores.

In similar ways, the vulcanized rubber soles that were previously used in some types of sports shoes are now only used for non-technical fashion sneakers with a retro image rather than sports. Converse, which is a property of Nike since 2003, started to make basketball shoes with rubber soles back in 1917, but ran into financial difficulties in the 1970s when Adidas, Puma and other competitors introduced more technical products. It recovered in the 1980s when canvas rubber shoes regained a certain popularity but went bankrupt in the late 1990s. Under Nike's ownership, Converse still sells skate shoes, but like the skate shoes of another American brand, Vans, its styles are mostly worn as street shoes by all kinds of people, even those who have never ridden a skateboard.

Superga, an Italian footwear brand now owned by BasicNet, the parent company of Kappa, K-Way and other labels, has a similar story to tell. It started making tennis shoes with vulcanized rubber soles in the 1950s when it was owned by Pirelli, the big Italian tyre company. It added other types of athletic shoes, but it had to stop when Nike, Reebok and other major American competitors came up with more technical sports shoes with EVA soles, which have much better cushioning. BasicNet is now reviving Superga as a pure brand of vintage street sneakers that are not suitable for sports.

Many of the athletic footwear styles that were originally designed for sports performance are now worn mainly as street shoes. Adidas, Converse, Fila, Superga and others have put out recently re-engineered replicas of some of their first sports shoes, creating a new category of sport-inspired vintage items. Sneakers and athleisure – a fusion of athletic styles and fashion – have become the buzzword in the last few years, affecting also the general fashion trends.

Lately, Adidas, Nike, Puma and other brands have been launching limited-edition sneakers in collaboration with music artists and other celebrities like Kanye West or Rihanna that have sold out very quickly.

8 Team sports replicas

In the apparel sector, many items have been associated with football and other team sports for a long time without being meant to be worn for competition. In the United Kingdom, where the game of football was born, the clubs began to distinguish themselves by wearing uniform jerseys, starting with the Sheffield team in 1857. They were made by companies like Bukta from 1870 and by the Humphrey brothers from 1920.

In the 1970s, another British clothing manufacturer, Admiral, came up with the idea of selling "replica" jerseys for the fans of football teams. Umbro, a brand launched by Humphrey brothers in 1934, Adidas and others subsequently picked up the idea, paying increasingly high sponsorship fees to the best teams for the right to make and sell the players' shirts and their replicas for the general public.

The business model was quickly applied to national and local football and rugby teams all over the globe, with the major brands focusing increasingly on the best teams as well as the best players. Smaller brands like Errea and Macron in Italy, Joma in Spain and Uhlsport in Germany have been signing up contracts with less important football, rugby and handball teams.

The same phenomenon applied across the Atlantic Ocean to American football, basketball, baseball and ice hockey. Then, Umbro's relative strength in the football category led Nike to buy the English brand in 2007. Nike had already become a leader in basketball, notably through its sponsorship of a famous player, Michael Jordan, which led the Swoosh to create the famous Nike Air footwear cushioning concept. At that point of its development, Phil Knight wanted Nike to become a leader also in soccer – or global football, as it now calls it – because it is the most widely watched sport in the world. He felt he had to do this to beat Adidas, which was the leading producer of football boots and sponsor of many important football teams and players.

By that time, Umbro was the sponsor of the highly reputed Brazilian football team, Manchester United and other important "sports properties" that were subsequently transferred to the Nike brand. Incidentally, New Balance, a major brand of running shoes like Nike and Adidas, decided only recently to start doing some sports marketing and thus began to sign up a few important football teams like Liverpool to get more international visibility.

In the United States, the replica business model acquired a new dimension in the 1980s and 1990s with Champion USA and other American brands creating a whole new category of "licensed" sport-inspired casual sportswear, offering not just shirts, but also sweatshirts and other types garments bearing the insignia of sports teams affiliated with big leagues like the NBA and the NFL. It has made big strides with companies like Gildan Sportswear and Fanatics.

9 New dimensions in sports fashion

In 1998, a Canadian brand, Lululemon Athletica, innovated again by creating a new premium category of functional and fashionable athleisurewear for women, starting with its yoga pants and then with other tight-fitting types of fitness garments. It also innovated by establishing showrooms for its products that doubled up as yoga studios, and by selling its products exclusively in its own physical stores and through its own Internet websites – a vertical integration model that fashion brands like Gucci or Louis Vuitton have been following in varying degrees to maximize their profit margins.

Sports and fashion have become more intertwined lately. In the last few months, even big fashion brands like Louis Vuitton and Hermès have felt an urge to address the younger generations through allusions to action sports, the first one with skate-inspired garments designed in collaboration with Supreme, and the latter with a line of printed skateboards.

10 Increasing segmentation

The popularization of sports and the proliferation of new sports activities have been followed by an increasing segmentation of the market among the various sports categories in terms of practice, gender and price points.

This has helped many sporting goods companies to get a more distinctive brand positioning in an increasingly crowded market and to make their mark in the industry as category leaders in well-defined niches – for example Babolat in tennis, Burton in snowboarding, or Brooks, Saucony and others in running. It has also led to the birth of new stars like Hoka One One, a brand of trail running shoes launched by a former general manager of Salomon, Jean-Luc Diard, and his partners based on the new concept of a super-large sole. It is developing strongly into road running under the ownership of a big American group, Deckers Brands.

The same kind of segmentation has taken place at the retail level, with specialized sporting goods stores complementing the generalist retailers. As outdoor is the biggest segment in the wider sporting goods market, this has naturally led to the establishment of large chains of outdoor stores like Au Vieux Campeur in France or Globetrotter in Germany. A further step in this development has been the expansion of outdoor retailers like A.S. Adventure in Belgium, JD Sports Fashion in the United Kingdom or Fenix Outdoor in Sweden, which have acquired specialty outdoor retail chains in other countries. Fenix is the new owner of Globetrotter, for example.

Another way of segmenting the offer at retail has been the development of specific business models for private label offerings, like those of Decathlon, and of lowest-price propositions, like again Decathlon from France, Sports Direct from the UK and XXL from Norway.

The newest form of segmentation for the customer's journey is by channel – brick-and-mortar retailing, e-commerce or omni channel.

11 The development of the supply chain

Meanwhile, the supply chain for sports products from the design and development stage to the purchase by the end user – has developed in interesting ways in the last decades. The manufacture of many sports products, which was previously carried out by the brands at or close to their head offices, has been gradually outsourced to distant low-cost producers located far away from the markets where they are sold.

At the same time, territorial wholesale distributors have helped the brands to expand into foreign markets, while a new breed of specialized sporting goods retailers has helped the brands and their distributors to make the products available to consumers, directly or through sales agents.

The development of modern retailing has been a key factor of growth for the sporting goods sector in the last decades. Led by big retail chains like Decathlon in France or Sportmaster in Russia and by voluntary groups like Intersport or Sport 2000, the sports stores have played a key role in the development of the sporting goods sector since the 'seventies. Stimulating the market through their actual presence and their marketing activities, often organized in collaboration with the brands, they have been showcasing the vendors' products and made them available to the general public.

In some countries where multi-brand retailing was not particularly developed, like in China or India, the sports brands and their distributors took the lead in developing the market by establishing networks of mono-brand stores. With the onset of e-commerce, the direct-to-consumer distribution mode has become more common and more desirable.

12 The role of public authorities

Sport and fashion have been nourishing each other since the 1970s, with sport styles being adopted as streetwear. Meanwhile, more and more national governments and local authorities have been realizing the benefits of practising sport for the general population, the economy and the health system at different degrees, culminating in the 1990s with programs like Sport for All in the European Union. The World Health Organization has been promoting the benefits of sports for some time at the global level.

Especially in emerging economies where only a few people could afford it, public authorities pitched in with their contribution to the promotion of sports participation soon after World War II by instituting mandatory or optional sports education programs for school children and financing the construction of public sports facilities. They were doing something that only the better universities in the United Kingdom and the United States had been doing since the 19th century for the elite of the population, organizing all kinds of collegiate sports activities and competitions to make them fit for the challenges of tomorrow.

In the Nordic European countries, North America and other parts of the world, private investors began to play their part in the process in the 'eighties with the establishment of chains of fitness gyms and health clubs financed by memberships, which were originally more or less and less exclusive like the spas and gymnasia of ancient Persia, Greece and Rome. Indoor gyms have spread in relatively cold countries like Sweden or Russia, where people are prevented from practising certain outdoor sports for many months during the year. They have also spread in countries like Italy or Brazil, where the weather is often too hot to sweat it out in the open air. The Chinese government has made sport one of its five strategic priorities in its development plan for 2015 to 2020.

The most recent data indicate that the growth of sports participation and the sporting goods market, which tend to go together, have been slowing down, while remaining above the growth of the general economy and the consumption of nonfood products in general. After nearing double-digit growth rates, the global consumption of sporting goods has been rising at a rather steady annual rate of

5% for the past five years or so, according to NPD, reaching an annual level of more than $400 billion including bicycles. The growth rate increased to 6% in 2016, says NPD, thanks especially to the higher consumption of fitness-related products.

The sporting goods sector has continued to attract investors, as its average growth has remained above the rates of growth registered for the world economy. The injection of fresh capital has allowed many companies that had a credible business plan to finance useful investments for the development of new products and the growth of their own sales and profits. Many of those companies were subsequently sold to private equity investment firms or went public on the stock exchange, allowing the original investors to cash out with a nice capital gain.

Private equity investors and public offerings on the stock exchange have helped finance external growth through the acquisition of other companies in the sector, leading to the formation of highly diversified, multisport mini-conglomerates like Procter & Gamble. The two biggest conglomerates that hold a large portfolio of brands in the sporting goods sector, Amer Sports and VF Corporation, were both previously involved in other sectors, but they have ended up specializing in sporting goods.

Founded by a group of students who had graduated from the University of Helsinki, Amer started off as an importer of cigarettes and automobiles, but it eventually dropped out of these businesses to concentrate on sports through brands like Wilson, Atomic, Salomon, Mavic, Precor and Suunto.

Founded back in 1899, VF started off as a manufacture of gloves and undergarments. It changed its name to Vanity Fair in 1969 when it moved into the growing segment of denim jeans with its takeover of Lee. It followed up 20 years later with the acquisition of another jeans brand, Wrangler, entering at the same time the backpacking market with the acquisition of JanSport. It continued to invest in outdoor sports as well as action sports with its takeover of The North Face, Eastpak, Vans, Reef, Timberland, Smartwool and, most recently, Icebreaker, the leading producer of merino wool sports clothing from New Zealand. Together, these brands represent more than two-thirds of its total turnover. VF also bought other types of apparel brands like Majestic, an American producer of licenced sportswear, but subsequently divested many of them.

13 Emerging markets – the new frontier

Recently, the growth of the sports market has even been higher than that of luxury goods, which are now strongly sought after by the new middle class in China and other countries. While the athleisure market seems to have reached its peak in 2017, with the exception of strong players like Lululemon, the luxury goods market is experiencing a small rebound.

The strongest growth rates for the consumption of sports products have been recorded lately in emerging markets like China, which has become the second-largest sports market after the United States, and others where the middle class

Table 5.1 NPD's ranking of the world's major markets in terms of consumption of sporting goods in 2016

United States	*$136.6 billion*	*+7%*
China	$42.7 billion	+10%
Japan	$20.4 billion	+9%
Germany	$17.9 billion	0%
France	$13.5 billion	+3%

has been expanding rapidly and where the rate of sports participation still has to catch up with the higher standards reached in the United States and other more developed countries.

Here is NPD's ranking of the world's major markets in terms of consumption of sporting goods in 2016, including bicycles, with the increase of the market from the previous year in terms of constant currencies:

According to Sporting Goods Intelligence, the market excluding bicycles used for transportation or as toys was worth €59.7 billion in the 15 major Western European countries together in 2016, indicating an average consumption per capita of €145.09 per year. It grew by 3% in terms constant currencies.

In China, some companies that were manufacturing shoes or apparel for the Western brands decided to launch their own brands in the 1980s and the 1990s. Named after a former famous Chinese athletic champion, Li-Ning was one of the first to move in this direction, followed by other companies such as Anta Sport, China Dongxiang or 361 Degrees.

However, even the biggest Chinese sports brands have had a hard time competing in their own domestic market with much bigger and stronger international sports brands like Adidas and Nike, especially in the larger cities.

Chinese and Korean interests have reacted in part by investing in foreign sports brands. In 2008, China Dongxiang bought a Japanese brand of skiwear, Phenix. One year later, Anta acquired the rights to the Fila brand for China. At the same time, the Korean licensee of Fila, called Fila Korea, took over the rights to the Italian brand for the rest of the world with the support of Samsung. In 2016, Fila Korea also acquired the control of a big American golf company, Acushnet, which owns two important brands, Titleist for golf clubs and FootJoy for golf shoes. A big Korean sourcing group, Youngone Corporation, bought the Swiss-based Scott Sports Group in 2015.

14 Threatened by screens, sports companies react with new technologies

In most of the Western world, where sports participation rates have been more stable and where general consumption rates have slowed down, the revenues generated by the sporting goods business have been more dependent than before on the fast-changing fashion trends and the ever-more capricious weather conditions. They have also been negatively affected by the growing use of computers, tablets and smartphones at all ages and in all the countries, stealing time away from healthier sports activities.

In these conditions, the competition in the sporting goods market has become a battle for survival and market shares, with the bigger and smarter companies getting bigger, partly through acquisitions that have been often facilitated by generational changes. Innovation, good design and superior advertising have made a difference between the winners and the losers in the competitive game – at the wholesale level as well as at retail.

Technical innovation will continue to be a driver of the sports market. New products like the self-lacing and connected shoes recently launched a French start-up, Digitsole, have probably come out too early, but they show the way in which the industry is likely to evolve. Action cameras driven by drones like those of GoPro and smart sports watches, GPS-driven applications and other Internet-connected products like those of Fitbit and Garmin will certainly become more common. Wearable devices will be embedded in the fabrics of the sports garment or the sports shoe as sources of heat, as a means of tracking performance, to share experiences and for other purposes . . . and so on.

It will be interesting to see what will happen in the next few years. Anyhow, the recent resurgence of old giants like Adidas and the rapid ascent of new stars like Under Armour, a 20-year-old brand of compression garments with powerful and distinctive marketing that has diversified into shoes and connected fitness, augur well for the future of the sector. They seem to indicate that the sporting goods sector is sufficiently resilient to continue to evolve positively and dynamically.

15 The development of manufacturing and logistics

As previously indicated, sports products were made by the users themselves, craftsmen and small workshops before the industrialization of the manufacturing process. Their serial production started between the end of the 19th century and the early part of the 20th century in Europe, close to the design and product development offices of the companies operating in the sector and close to the markets they served.

Like in other fast-moving consumer goods sectors, the supply chain then moved gradually to the Far East and other low-cost sources, aside from a few interesting exceptions like the ski sector. With the growing cost of labour in China and other emerging markets, coupled with new automation technologies, the movement has recently been shifting partially in the other direction, but still limited for the most part to small runs and the production of customized items.

Like many other shoemakers that are now outsourcing the manufacture of their collections in low-cost countries, the founder of Adidas, Adolf (Adi) Dassler, started out in 1924 as a cobbler, making his own sports shoes. He made them initially in his mother's kitchen and in the home's laundry. Adolf and his old brother, Rudolf, then successfully developed, produced and sold rather sophisticated, technical shoes for sports champions in the small German village of Herzogenaurach. Their activity prospered during World War II, thanks to military contracts.

In 1947, after the war, the two brothers split and formed two separate companies on both sides of the river, Adidas and Puma, and their rivalry helped them to grow. The two companies industrialized the manufacturing process, building large factories in Germany and France. Under the management of Adi Dassler's son, Horst Dassler, Adidas also launched locally manufactured lines of apparel and accessories sold under its own brand name.

However, rising manufacturing costs in Europe and price competition from Nike and other brands that had started outsourcing their products in the Far East caused them to run into financial trouble. Bernard Tapie, who took over Adidas in 1989, two years after the death of Horst Dassler, closed many factories and moved most of the production overseas.

A similar process took place after World War II in Japan with Asics and Mizuno, which later switched like other companies to using subcontractors in China for the manufacture of shoes, clothing and accessories.

For New Balance and a few other companies that are still making or assembling their products in-house, including most ski producers, the manufacturing process consists mainly of assembling different types of components, depending on the market's demand. The more labour-intensive components are generally made in low-cost countries.

With the growth of the market and the major brands, sourcing large quantities of products from large factories in the Far East became essential at some point for the production of big series of items made at competitive prices.

The big turning point was the strategic decision made by Phil Knight, the founder of Nike, to get all its sports shoes made in Asia. The savings made at the manufacturing stage were reinvested by Nike in the development of innovative products and marketing. Knight, who had started off as an importer of Asics' shoes in the United States, founded a company initially called Blue Ribbon Sports together with Bill Bowerman in 1964, and renamed it as Nike (victory in Greek) in 1971. The two built up their brand at first around the concept of running to keep fit before associating it with basketball and other sports. It is now the biggest athletic footwear company in the world.

Gradually, many other producers of shoes, clothing, backpacks and other sports and fashion items adopted similar strategies, subcontracting the whole manufacturing process or the more labour-intensive stages. As an intermediary step, trading companies played an important role at this stage of the process. Companies like Pentland from the United Kingdom became experts in sourcing shoes and apparel from Far East producers, enduring quality control and the related logistics. Thanks to their bargaining power and their knowledge of the best factories, trading companies helped to establish a bridge between the West and the East.

For many years, Pentland and other European trading companies had a sort of monopoly on the business as they were given the exclusive right to exploit the quotas that the European Economic Community had imposed in 1994 on imports of certain shoes from China and Vietnam in order to protect European manufacturers. The import quotas were subsequently relaxed for technical athletic footwear, allowing the sports brands to establish direct connections with the manufacturers in the Far East. The quotas remained in place until 2005 for the benefit of big trading companies like Pentland in the United Kingdom, Royer in France or Cortina in Belgium, which held the quotas. The quotas were subsequently replaced for five years by anti-dumping duties on leather shoes, again with the exception of athletic footwear.

In the meantime, traders like Pentland and Royer developed other activities in the sports and fashion sectors. Royer held the French licence for Converse for many years, and it is now the licensee of Umbro in France and the distributor of New Balance in France and some other European countries. It owns many other footwear brands like Kickers, Charles Jourdan and Stephane Kelian, among many others.

Owned by the Rubin family, Pentland began as a footwear wholesaler under the name of The Liverpool Shoe Company in 1932. Before many other European companies, it started sourcing shoes in the Far East in 1964. Some of Pentland's moves have been very smart or just lucky. Under the management of Stephen Rubin, Pentland acquired a 55% stake in Reebok in 1981 for only $77,500. In 1985, Pentland listed 60% of Reebok's shares on the stock exchange in a transaction that valued the brand at $300 million. It sold its stake in Reebok in 1991 for $770 million.

Protectionism in footwear trade did not finish with the end of the European import quotas and its anti-dumping duties on shoe imports from China and Vietnam. In 2010, the world's third-largest footwear producer, Brazil, started to protect its own shoe manufacturing industry by imposing anti-dumping duties on imports of all kinds of shoes from China, including athletic footwear. Reinforced by the recent recession in the country, this allowed a local brand of sports shoes, Olympikus, to become the national leader in sports shoes in terms of volume. It forced Nike, Adidas and the Brazilian licensee of Mizuno, Alpargatas, to start making more of their shoes in Brazil.

After selling Reebok, Pentland was tempted to buy Adidas, but gave up on the deal after discovering certain anomalies in its accounts. Instead, it bought other sports brands like Speedo, Ellesse and Berghaus. It also licensed Lacoste's footwear. It later took control of one of the major British sports retailers, JD Sports Fashion, to prevent it from coming under the ownership of its main rival, Sports Direct International.

In contrast with the athletic footwear brands, which went straight to the Far East, many makers of hiking shoes and sports clothing in northern Italy began to use contract factories in Romania in the 'sixties and 'seventies instead of importing them from the Far East. Many are still getting some or all their products made in Romania and other neighbouring countries such as Bulgaria, Moldova and Ukraine.

Their trail running shoes are mostly made in Asia. On the other hand, many outdoor shoes are still made in Western Europe. Lowa gets its outdoor shoes manufactured mainly in the Czech Republic, but some of its production is still in Germany, and its biggest German competitor, Meindl, proudly boasts the fact that its shoes are made in Germany. Similarly, some Italian producers like La Sportiva, the world's largest brand of climbing shoes, market the "made in Italy" label as part of their brand value. The same can be said for Arc'teryx and Canada Goose, which pride themselves on making their clothing in Canada.

For these kinds of companies, in-house manufacturing also serves as a guarantee of good quality and as a means of protecting their technical expertise from the danger of counterfeiting and other forms of imitation. It also helps to keep inventories low and to service clients more quickly. This kind of service can be particularly useful if dealers run out of certain sizes or if they are confronted with a sudden surge in demand, which can happen if the weather is particularly cold or rainy.

In-house manufacturing remains a must for complex products like skis, which are still made in Europe. An American ski brand, K2, has had a terrible time in terms of quality control and deliveries by using a factory in China. Another US company specializing in mountain climbing equipment, Black Diamond, recently decided to repatriate the manufacturing of these products from China to its hometown of Salt Lake City, obtaining a good response from the market although the transition has not been smooth.

In the fitness equipment sector, big players like Kettler in Germany and Technogym in Italy continue to manufacture their products locally. Protected in part by anti-dumping duties on bicycles from China and Taiwan, European bike manufacturers continue to manufacture in-house, although many of the components are sourced elsewhere.

In contrast with in-house manufacturing, using subcontractors has many benefits. In addition to generally lower manpower costs, it gives a brand a certain flexibility in terms of the types of products and the choice of the manufacturing partners. In recent years, this flexibility has allowed many brands to shift the production from China, where labour wages have risen considerably, to other countries like Vietnam, Cambodia or Indonesia.

In some cases, the sports brands have followed the strategic choices of their own subcontractors. The world's largest shoe manufacturer, Yue Yuen, which is owned by Pou Chen of Taiwan, has been moving its manufacturing equipment from one country to the other in Asia to save costs and remain competitive. It has also moved some of the production to inland provinces of China, taking advantage of new infrastructures that allow it to deliver the products rapidly to the Chinese ports from where they are shipped by boat to Western markets.

The big problem with outsourcing in the Far East is that this system requires that the clients of the brands must place orders much earlier because it takes time to make big runs of many different styles and to deliver them to the various markets.

It can take 6 weeks or longer for a container to travel from Eastern China to Hamburg, Rotterdam or one of several harbours on the US Pacific Coast. The brands are forced to use expensive air freight to satisfy requests for last-minute reorders. A more recent, promising development has been the transportation of the containers to Western Europe by railroad across Siberia or Kazakhstan. Decathlon has just started to do this.

Several years ago, many Chinese producers started moving machinery to Vietnam and other less expensive Asian countries, but China has remained and will probably remain the world's largest producer of athletic footwear and apparel because of the workers' skills and the technical experience acquired by the factories in areas such as the manufacture of EVA soles. Vietnam has become the main alternative, but it will never match the capabilities of China because its population is much smaller.

The long lead times involved in mass production of sports shoes and clothing in the Far East have led many brands to take orders from their wholesale distributors and retail clients earlier. Even before becoming the biggest brand of sports shoes in the world, Nike was the first one to impose so-called futures orders from its distributors and retailers. They have to order up to 90% of the products nearly one year ahead of their delivery. The rest could be ordered from Nike's distribution centres.

Eventually, the other big brands followed a similar pattern for forward orders. While the European ski companies can still afford to take some orders at the end of February for deliveries in September or October from their European factories, with an option for reorders during the selling season, Nike, Adidas and other major brands have to start taking orders in November or December for back-to-school deliveries of most of the products. The quantities involved are much higher.

The new ordering schedule has led big brands like Adidas and Nike to pull out of big trade shows like Ispo in Munich or the former Supershow in Atlanta, where Nike used to invite key account clients from all over the world. As it was mainly catering to the big sports shoe brands, the Supershow died as a result. With its focus on European ski brands and on smaller sports brands from all over the world, Ispo has instead survived, remaining the world's biggest trade show in the sector. It has also launched satellite shows in Beijing and Shanghai for the local market, and it is offering other services all year 'round. In the United States, the only big trade show to have survived is Outdoor Retailer, which is moving from Salt Lake City to Denver, where its winter edition is going to run in January in parallel with the former SIA show for snow sports.

Looking at the future of manufacturing, it seems that a hybrid business model will be taking hold gradually in the sector, whereby the bigger runs will still be made in the Far East and small runs will increasingly be produced close to the major markets, even by the major brands. Adidas has already started to explore the use of robotics through its Speedfactory project in Germany, while Nike has been investing heavily in the development of 3D manufacturing for customized shoes. Salomon and Tecnica have also introduced customization options for hiking shoes that are already available for ski boots. At some point in the future, it seems likely that customized sports shoes will be made through 3D manufacturing in the sports stores or even in the customers' homes.

16 The development of wholesale distribution and retailing in different parts of the world

Like the manufacturing process and the related logistics, the ways in which sports products are made available to consumers have undergone a major evolution during the past few decades, with major differences from one country to another. Like with 3D manufacturing, the link between the brand and the consumer has become more direct lately at the global level, but it has taken a long time for the sporting goods industry to get there.

Before the industrialization of the sector, most suppliers of sporting goods were making them at their own local workshops and selling them directly to local consumers or to the procurement offices of the public authorities in charge of sports in their own regions or their own countries. There were very few stores that were selling the sports products of different producers to the general public.

With the development of transportation, the vendors began to expand their business geographically. In most cases, they started to venture into new territories by resorting to regional or national wholesalers who bought the products from them, stocked them and resold them to the public directly or through retailers. For the suppliers, dealing through wholesalers was essential to penetrate a market that they didn't know well enough like Japan, China or India. They also resorted to distribution partners to ensure the payment of their bills, especially in areas like Southern Italy or Southern Spain where many retailers don't always pay for the merchandise until much later, if at all.

Nike resorted to local wholesalers in these regions for a longer period than many other big brands. To help avoid problems, Nike used a wholesale distributor to cover the Russian market longer than Adidas. It still relies on distributors in small and distant markets like the Baltic states.

In some countries like Russia, going through a distributor has been necessary for most sports brands to move into the market, especially at the beginning, to cope with a complex customs clearance system. The distribution contracts signed with Russian wholesalers generally covered also the Ukraine, Kazakhstan or most or all of the former Communist countries belonging to customs-free Community of Independent States (CIS).

Regional wholesalers continue to play a very important role as intermediaries in large and populous countries like China and India. In these same countries, the brands or their wholesale partners tend to cover a large chunk of the market through huge networks of directly owned or franchised mono-brand stores in order to protect their image and reach out directly to the consumers. The development of these store networks started in the big cities and then spread to the less populated and less developed areas of the country.

In more developed economies like Japan, it has been common for sports brands to use a licensee rather than a wholesale distributor because the licensee generally has higher financial resources to finance the production of the goods and invest in market development, often adapting the product ranges to the local market. Language and differences in culture and business development models have been a hurdle for Western brands in countries like Japan, where big distributors continue to play a more important role than in the West. In China, many brands have preferred to form joint ventures with their local distribution partners.

Wholesale distributors know their national or regional markets well. They tend to have excellent contacts with the local retailers, but they take a big gross margin on the merchandise they purchase to cover their costs and the risk of not being able to resell everything that they had ordered.

In general, the sports brands have first hired a distributor or a licensee to move into a new foreign country. Eventually, they decided to set up their own sales subsidiaries in some of the bigger markets only after reaching a sufficiently high level of turnover and finding experienced managers to run them. In turn, the brands or their distributors have been covering the national markets through networks of independent agents or their own sales employees to reach out to the local retailers. At some point, the brands have begun to deal more directly with big clients like the major retail chains, treating them as "key accounts" that deserve special conditions in exchange for big orders and cooperation in merchandising and advertising.

The transition from wholesale distribution to direct sales in a particular market has been easier to accomplish for European sports brands in their expansion into other European countries. They have been able to take advantage of geographical proximity and the free movement of goods within the customs-free European Union. In the bigger markets like France, Germany, Italy, Spain or the United Kingdom, many brands have been able to cover the market directly through commission agents, setting up their own sales offices and hiring their own local sales managers or employees only after reaching a certain level of penetration.

The European economic integration has also allowed American, Japanese and Chinese brands to cover all or most of EU with a single operation, starting generally in the United Kingdom for language reasons before the establishment of the euro as a single currency. Under Armour has just begun this process as part of a major internationalization program for the brand, after consolidating its position in the US market.

As some of the European countries are just too small to be run through a single distributor or a single sales office, the vendors have been dividing the market into clusters of countries, bundling Germany together with Austria and Switzerland (the so-called DACH region), the United Kingdom with Ireland, the Netherlands with Belgium, Sweden with other Nordic countries and Denmark, or Spain with Portugal and Andorra.

Because of its big harbours, the availability of multi-lingual employees and certain tax incentives, many non-European brands have ended up setting their European headquarters in the Netherlands. That's the case for Nike, which has also been able to pay less taxes on its European profits thanks to special fiscal incentives. The brand decided to set up its huge European distribution centre in Belgium, bordering a canal that is connected with the sea. Other foreign groups like Amer Sports or Columbia Sportswear preferred to establish a European office in Switzerland for language and tax reasons.

The development of the supply chain has been slightly different in the United States, where even big companies like Adidas used different wholesale distributors for different parts of the country before setting up its own sales subsidiary there. Even for Adidas, it was too big a market to handle at the beginning on its own or through just one national distributor.

Now, Adidas, Puma, Rossignol and all the other leading sports brands have their own sales subsidiaries in the United States, which in turn work with local agents to cover the whole territory. The same office generally covers also Canada. Some foreign brands represent other complementary brands that don't compete with them in the United States to help cover their costs.

The evolution of the supply chain has been completely different in Russia, where the sporting goods market was much smaller when it opened up to Western products in the early 'nineties, after the advent of Glasnost. At that point, while most other brands tried to get in through distributors, Adidas and Reebok decided to do without a wholesale partner and set up their own sales subsidiaries early on in the process. Adidas was the only major Western brand that was well known in Russia before the end of Communism because of its tie-up with the Olympic Games. As for Reebok, it actually began sponsoring the Russian Olympic Committee.

Taking things onto their own hands, Adidas and Reebok established big networks of mono-brand stores in Russia because the sporting goods retail sector was not yet well developed at the time. They needed to properly display their products and assure customers that they were not selling counterfeits. One of Adidas' first stores in Moscow was opened in the Gum shopping mall next to Red Square.

Distributors played a key role in opening the market in Russia after Glasnost. However, they ran into big problems during the financial crisis of 1998. They could not get paid by the retailers due to the collapse of the banking system. At this point, the distributors of Kettler and Tecnica in Russia, took things into their own hands, stretching their supply chains by setting up their own retail chains, Sportmaster and Trial Sport. They are now the biggest sports retailers in the country aside from Decathlon, which came in much later.

In the more developed countries, some of the first multi-brand sports stores were actually dedicated areas in department stores like Karstadt in Germany or El Corte Inglés in Spain, which are still very important factors in their respective markets. More dedicated sports stores were generally opened in the areas where people were playing sports like golf or tennis or practising hiking, skiing, fishing and other outdoor sports activities. In remote areas like the Western part of the United States, the items were available in "general stores" that were also selling many other types of products.

In many less developed countries and regions, particularly in Eastern Europe, the better sports shoes and other types of sports gear were initially available only in supermarkets like Metro or in department stores like Tsum in Moscow. This has been changing rapidly in the last two decades or so, with supermarket chains and other retail operators developing their own specialized chains of sporting goods stores, often in association with international voluntary groups like Intersport.

For example, the biggest sporting goods retailer in Switzerland, Ochsner Sport, is owned by Deichmann, the largest chain of shoe shops in Europe, while the third-largest one after Intersport, Sport XX, is owned by the country's largest supermarket cooperative, Migros. One of the largest Austrian sports retailers, Hervis Sport, is owned by an international cooperative of supermarket operators. First founded in 1976 under a different name by Genty-Cathiard, a supermarket chain based in Grenoble, Go Sport of France is, since 1990, a property of Rallye, which also owns the Casino chain of supermarkets. The biggest Swedish sports retailer, Stadium, was taken over many years ago by the same family that owns Ikea. Kesko, a Finnish operator of supermarkets and other types of retail operations, has the Intersport licence for its country. A similar retailing group in Portugal, Sonae, which is also an operator of shopping centres, established the largest national sporting goods chain, Sport Zone, which has teamed up with JD Sports Fashion of the United Kingdom to cover the whole Iberian Peninsula.

Some of the sporting goods retailers operating in less developed countries were previously selling their products in open markets. Depending on the degree of economic development, less technical sports products, imitations of authentic products and counterfeited items could be found until recently in big open markets in the former Communist countries and other parts of the world, sold at low prices that the local people could afford. At the beginning of the new millennium, this so-called uncivilized market, where the majority of the products came from China, represented about one-quarter of the total estimated sporting market in Russia, and nearly half of the market in Ukraine. Eventually, some of the tenants of the market stalls upgraded to more exclusive closed spaces to market better merchandise, and then became regular sports retailers.

In China and some other emerging Asian markets like India, big chains of mono-brand stores have quickly become the most common form of sports retailing, even for local brands like Li Ning. Big brands like Adidas or Nike had no other way to get into the market in the absence of any big chains of sporting goods stores with the exception of Decathlon, which mostly sells its own private brands. These single-brand stores are the property of the brands themselves, especially when it comes to flagship stores in major shopping areas like Nanjing Road in Shanghai, or they are owned by big distributors and retailers like Belle International or by local franchisees.

17 Rising concentration among the vendors

There has been a certain concentration of the market at the global level around the largest brands and groups of brands, which have been gaining market share in recent years in the three main segments of sports shoes, sports apparel and sports equipment.

The market for branded athletic shoes has remained more concentrated than the other two segments, limiting new M&A activities to some extent. According to Sporting Goods Intelligence, which puts out detailed charts every year with the turnover of all the major brands in these segments for benchmarking purposes, this has been the evolution of their market shares in recent years:

Adidas and Puma have been losing market share to Nike in athletic footwear since 2011, but Adidas regained it in 2016 and Puma regained in 2017. Skechers has been making a lot of progress, especially outside the United States.

Table 5.2 Athletic footwear (US dollars)

COMPANY	*REVENUES 2016*	*GROWTH RATE*	*MARKET SHARE'*	*MS 2011*
Nike (*)	22.2 Bn	+6.9%	38.3%	36.9%
Adidas (**)	11.2 Bn	+21.3%	19.3%	21.0%
Skechers	3.56 Bn	+13.2%	6.1%	3.9%
VF Corp. (***)	3.39 Bn	+1.8%	5.8%	2.7%
New Balance	3.15 Bn	−0.3%	5.3%	4.0%
Asics	3.03 Bn	+15.6%	5.2%	5.1%
Puma	1.80 Bn	+7.6%	3.1%	5.1%

(*) including Converse
(**) including Reebok
(***) including Vans, Timberland, The North Face, Reef

Table 5.3 Athletic apparel (US dollars)

COMPANY	*REVENUES 2016*	*GROWTH RATE*	*MARKET SHARE*	*MS IN 2011*
Nike (*)	9.7 Bn	+7.1%	12.4%	10.3%
Adidas (**)	8.3 Bn	+7.3%	10.6%	11.5%
VF Corp. (***)	4.6 Bn	+2.2%	5.9%	4.3%
Under Armour	3.5 Bn	+15.4%	4.5%	1.6%
Gildan	2.6 Bn	−12.6%	3.3%	2.5%
Columbia (****)	1.9 Bn	+2.4%	2.4%	1.9%

(*) including Converse
(**) including Reebok
(***) including Vans, Timberland, The North Face, Reef
(****) including Mountain Hardwear, Prana and related accessories

Table 5.4 Sports equipment (US dollars)

COMPANY	REVENUES 2016	GROWTH RATE	MARKET SHARE	MS IN 2011
Shimano	3.5 Bn	+7.2%	5.1%	4.6%
Vista Outdoor (*)	2.5 Bn	+12.2%	3.7%	–
Newell Outdoor (**)	2.4 Bn	−11.7%	3.5%	4.6%
Fitbit	2.2 Bn	+16.7%	3.2%	–
Amer Sports (***)	1.9 Bn	+0.6%	2.8%	3.2%
Adidas (****)	1.9 Bn	+5.7%	2.7%	3.1%

(*) New group includes Camelbak, Easton, Bell and many ammunition companies
(**) Former Jarden Outdoor Solutions: K2, Pure Fishing and many other sports brands
(***) Including Atomic, Salomon, Mavic, Wilson, Precor, Suunto
(***) Including Taylor Made

Adidas, where the footwear and apparel segments are more balanced, has been constantly the leader in sports apparel until 2014, when it was overtaken by Nike. Under Armour has been the new star in this segment.

This is the least concentrated segment and the one that has undergone the biggest changes. Vista Outdoor didn't exist in 2011 and Fitbit was not a factor then. Newell Brands was born out of the merger of Newell Rubbermaid with Jarden Corp. in 2017. It has since divested K2 and other winter sports brands. Likewise, Adidas has sold Taylor Made.

18 The biggest retailers have been getting bigger, until 2015

There has also been a strong concentration of the market around the major sporting goods retailers through geographical expansion, franchising and acquisitions.

Thanks to attractive low prices and a unique vertical business model, whereby about 70% of its sales are generated by its own brands, Decathlon has become the only major multi-brand and multi-sport retailer in China, where it intends to double the number of stores to 500 within a few years. Working together with Auchan and other retail chains that belong to the same French family to occupy the same shopping malls, Decathlon has also become the largest integrated sporting goods retailer in the world, with a presence in about 30 different countries.

Decathlon's annual turnover after taxes (TTC) reached €12 billion in 2016, clearly overtaking the sales of all the independent sporting goods retailers and chains with more than 5,500 stores in some 40 countries that are affiliated with Intersport International Corporation, the largest buying and franchising group in the sector. Founded in 1968 in Paris from the merger of ten cooperatives in various countries, Intersport follows a completely different business model from that of Decathlon, which opened its first store eight years later, in 1976.

Based in Switzerland, Intersport works with licensees in various countries that provide multiple services to their retail members. They also guarantee that suppliers get paid.

Limited to a smaller national market than retailers in the United States, many European sporting goods retailers have found the benefit of expanding beyond their national borders or joining forces with others in other countries in order to obtain more bargaining power with the vendors. By internationalizing their operations in one way or another, they have been able to obtain greater economies of scale that have allowed them to order larger volumes of goods from the international brands at a discount and in return for marketing support.

Today, all the biggest sporting goods retailers in the 15 major European countries have branches abroad or are affiliated with international buying and franchising groups like Intersport International and Sport 2000 International. Decathlon has become the leader in its domestic market and in Italy, Spain and Portugal. National Intersport licensees are the leaders in Germany, Finland, Denmark and the Netherlands, and it should soon overtake Sport 2000 in Austria. Two other international sports retailers, Sports Direct and XXL, dominate the markets of the United Kingdom and Norway, respectively.

The third-largest retailer in France, the Go Sport Group, which operates under the Go Sport and Courir banners, has moved into Belgium and Poland. It has franchised its Go Sport concept in France as well as in the Middle East and other parts of the world. In 2012, Go Sport teamed up with Hervis Sport, an Austrian retailer with branches in many Eastern European countries, to form a new international purchasing cooperation, Sport Trade Marketing International (STMI). Since then, the cooperation has been enlarged to other retail chains and voluntary groups in Spain, Switzerland, Germany and Italy. Together, they operate about 1,500 shops in 27 countries.

Intersport's national licensees are cooperatives of independent retailers in most countries, including France, Germany and Spain. Others are established retailers, like Kesko in Finland or Mercator in Slovenia, that have set up a chain of directly operated or franchised sporting goods stores. Some of them have branched out in other neighbouring countries, as has been the case for the national Intersport organizations in Austria or Greece, for example. In Italy, the Intersport licence has been taken over by its largest retail member, Cisalfa Sport.

As an international buying group, Intersport has one main competitor, Sport 2000 International. It was formed in 1988 from the merger of voluntary groups in Germany, Austria, Switzerland and France, trading initially as Golden Team International. Its retail members operate some 3,800 stores in 20 countries, but in contrast with Intersport, they have no obligation to carry the Sport 2000 banner in some countries where the retail members are too individualistic and jealous about the original names on their storefronts. The biggest member of Sport 2000 International is Sports Direct, the leading sports retailer in the United Kingdom, which has been expanding to many other countries. In the last few years, Sport

2000 International as regained a foothold in several European market, thanks to less restrictive affiliation policies, and it has moved into the Middle East.

Outside Europe, Intersport is also represented in Canada, the Middle East, China and Australia. In 2012, Intersport International bought The Athlete's Foot, an international buying and franchising group with 430 athletic footwear stores in various countries. It is developing more rapidly under its new owners.

Athletic footwear specialists like France's Courir and The Athlete's Foot, which belonged to France's Rallye until 2004, competes directly with the only other truly international sporting goods retailer, Foot Locker, which operates directly more than 3,400 stores in 23 countries around the world under different banners, more than 800 of them in Europe. It has been working very closely with Nike, which still represents more than 60% of its sales in the United States, but with other brands as well.

Foot Locker was the largest US-based sports retailer until 2016, when it was overtaken by DICK'S Sporting Goods, which operates only in the United States. Like Foot Locker, DICK'S grew in part by acquiring competitors or their stores. In the biggest shake-up of the American sports retail sector since the economic recession of 2008, DICK'S bought most of the remaining big-box stores of a former big US retailer, The Sports Authority, which was liquidated. It also bought Golfsmith, one of the largest specialty retailers for golf products in the country.

Apparently, these bankruptcies and those of other big American sports retail chains were mainly caused by the strong development of e-commerce by pure players like Amazon and by the sports brands themselves. Foot Locker in the United States and Intersport in Europe are working hard to re-engineer their systems to take advantage of the Internet and to develop new omni-channel capabilities in concert with leading brands.

While American and European retailers will have to adapt quickly to the new direct-to-consumer patterns being dictated by the Internet, this will be less of a problem in big countries like China or India, where brands have been dealing directly with consumers through their mono-brand stores and where big internet retailers like the Alibaba Group have become major intermediaries between the brands and consumers. In Brazil, one of the largest sports retailers is Netshoes, which has become the world's largest pure e-tailer, servicing its domestic market and those of other Latin American countries.

Consumers look for choice, low prices and convenience, and the Internet gives them all of this. Physical stores can provide expert advice and the possibility to try out the merchandise in an exciting shopping environment, but depending on their size, they cannot stock all the products in the same space. Therefore, they are developing a hybrid online-offline model, with Internet kiosks and tablets that give customers or the sales staff access to a wider assortment in a so-called virtual extended aisle. Eventually, they will soon gain access also to the centralized inventory of a buying group or the inventories of other affiliated retailers.

Table 5.5 The largest sporting goods retailers in the galaxy

The Largest Sporting Goods Retailers In the Galaxy

Rank	*Retailer*	*Country*	*Revenues in Millions US Dollars*		*Local Currency*	*Revenues in Millions Local Currency (no Sales or VAT)*		
			2016	*2015*		*2016*	*2015*	*Change*
1	Decathlon(1)	France	$11,274	$10,100	EURO	10,192	9,100	12.0%
2	DICK'S Sporting Goods	USA	$7,922	$7,271	USD	7,922	7,271	9.0%
3	Foot Locker (2)	USA	$7,766	$7,412	USD	7,766	7,412	4.8%
4	Academy Sports	USA	$5,133	$4,513	USD	5,133	4,513	13.7%
5	Bass Pro Shops	USA	$4,580	$4,500	USD	4,580	4,500	1.8%
6	Sports Direct Intl. (2) (sport retail	UK	$3,780	$3,810	GBP	2,801	2,492	12.4%
7	only) Cabela's	USA	$3,558	$3,481	USD	3,558	3,481	2.2%
8	Belle International (sportswear only)	China	$3,395	$3,166	RMB	22,555	19,716	14.4%
9	JD Sports Fashion (3) (2)	U.K.	$3,209	$2,784	GBP	2,378	1,821	30.6%
10	Genesco	USA	$2,868	$3,022	USD	2,868	3,022	–5.1%
11	R.E.I.	USA	$2,558	$2,423	USD	2,558	2,423	5.6%
12	Canadian Tire/FGL Sports (3)	Canada	$2,514	$2,447	CAD	3,331	3,127	6.5%
13	Pou Sheng	China	$2,444	$2,300	USD	2,444	2,300	6.3%
14	Lululemon	Canada	$2,344	$2,061	USD	2,344	2,061	13.7%
15	Xebio (incl. Victoria)	Japan	$2,053	$1,830	JPY	223,353	221,391	0.9%
16	Alpen	Japan	$2,022	$1,848	JPY	220,039	223,643	–1.6%
17	Finish Line, The	USA	$1,844	$1,799	USD	1,844	1,799	2.5%
18	Sports Authority, The	USA	S1.735	$2,600	USD	1,735	2,600	–33.3%
19	L.L. Bean	USA	$1,600	$1,600	USD	1,600	1,600	0.0%
20	Fanatics	USA	$1,400	$1,265	USD	1,400	1,265	10.7%
21	Sportmaster (2)	Russia	$1.370	$1,425	RUB	91,900	86,800	5.9%
22	Gander Mountain	USA	$1,323	$1,668	USD	1,323	1,668	–20.7%

23	Super Retail Group (Sports + Leisure)	Australia	$1,117	$1,121	AUD	1,503	1,492	0.7%
24	Groupe Go Sport (4).(2)	France	$1,037	$937	EURO	937	844	11.0%
25	Big 5 Sporting Goods	USA	$1,021	$1.029	USD	1,021	1,029	–0.8%
26	Hibbett (B)	USA	$973	$943	USD	973	943	3.2%
27	XXL Sport	Norway	$930	$804	NOK	7,813	6,487	20.4%
28	Zumiez	USA	$836	$804	USD	836	804	4.0%
29	Sportsman's Warehouse	USA	$780	$707	USD	780	707	10.3%
30	Pacific Sunwear	USA	$737	$801	USD	737	801	–8.0%
31	Modell's (B)	USA	$710	$710	USD	710	710	0.0%
32	Himaraya (6)	Japan	$670	$596	JPY	72,907	72,056	1.2%
33	Dunham's (B)	USA	$639	$620	USD	639	620	3.1%
34	Stadium (2)	Sweden	$637	$605	SEK	5,453	5,100	6.9%
35	Tilly's	USA	$569	$551	USD	569	551	3.3%
36	A.S. Adventure Group	Belgium	$567	$466	EURO	513	420	22.1%
37	Hervis Sport (2)	Austria	$545	$521	EURO	493	469	5.1%
38	Grupo SBF (Centauro etc.)	Brazil	$529	$609	BRL	1,845	2,029	–9.1%
39	Gresvig (A)	Norway	$504	$525	NOK	4,237	4,237	0.0%
40	Net shoes	Brazil	$498	$452	BRL	1,740	1,506	15.5%
41	Scheels	USA	$475	$475	USD	475	475	0.0%
42	El Corte Ingles (3) (2)	Spain	$454	$432	EURO	410	389	5.4%
43	Swire Group	Hong Kong	$415	$414	HKD	3,216	3,208	0.2%
44	Ochsner (3)	Switzerland	$404	$428	CHF	406	412	–1.5%
45	Cisalfa Sport (A)	Italy	5388	$376	EURO	351	339	3.5%
46	Golfsmith	USA	$367	$494	USD	367	494	–25.7%
47	Karstadt Sport (3)	Germany	$358	$388	EURO	324	350	–7.4%
48	M it ra Adiperkasa	Indonesia	$341	$306	IDR	4,540,000	4,100,000	10.7%
49	Sierra Trading Post	USA	$330	$275	USD	330	275	20.0%
50	Sp ort-Scheck (A)	Germany	$326	$354	EURO	295	319	–7.5%
51	Sport Zone (2)	Portugal	$306	$252	EURO	277	227	22.0%
52	Vestis Retail Group (5)	USA	$300	$640	USD	300	640	–53.1%
53	Kathmandu Holdings Group (7)	New Zealand	$296	$285	NZD	426	409	4.2%
54	Vail Resorts (7)	USA	$293	$241	USD	293	241	21.6%
55	Performance Inc.	USA	$292	$275	USD	292	275	6.2%

(*Continued*)

Table 5.5 (Continued)

The Largest Sporting Goods Retailers In the Galaxy

Rank	*Retailer*	*Country*	*Revenues in Millions US Dollars*		*Local Currency*	*Revenues in Millions Local Currency (no Sales or VAT)*		
			2016	*2015*		*2016*	*2015*	*Change*
56	Sport XX	Switzerland	$287	$287	CHF	288	276	4.3%
57	Frilufts (formerly Globetrotter)	Germany	$285	$287	EURO	258	259	–0.4%
58	OpticsPlanet	USA	$261	$245	USD	261	245	6.5%
59	WSS	USA	$260	$245	USD	260	245	6.1%
60	CRC Sports	Thailand	$245	$233	THB	8,760	7,964	10.0%
61	Johshuya Co. Ltd.	Japan	$230	$207	JPY	25,000	25,000	0.0%
62	Eurosport (Sports Endeavors)	USA	$225	$225	USD	225	225	0.0%
63	Olympia Sports	USA	$217	$215	USD	217	215	0.9%
64	Worldwide Golf (8)	USA	$215	$215	USD	215	215	0.0%
65	Sheikh Shoes	USA	$175	$158	USD	175	158	10.8%
66	MC Sports	USA	$175	$350	USD	175	350	–50.0%
67	Sp ort-Master	Denmark	$160	$160	DKK	1,076	1,074	0.2%
68	Prisma	Finland	$136	$138	EURO	123	124	–0.8%
69	Monkey Sports	USA	$120	$120	USD	120	120	0.0%
70	Lifestyle Sport	Ireland	$92	$88	EURO	83	79	5.1%
71	Al-Ikhsan	Malaysia	$56	$66	MYR	249	257	–3.1%
			$98,477	$95,000		Weighted Change in Local Ciurrency		4.8%

Notes: All data Is for FY ended closest to December 31, 2016.
(1) Also in Italy, Germany, Belgium, Spain, etc.
(2) Also in other countries.
(3) Sporting goods sales only
(4) Groupe Go Sport includes Go Sport, Courir, Moviesport
(5) Includes Bob's Stores, Eastern Mtn. Sports, Sport Chalet
(6) For FY ended Aug. 31, 2016.
(7) For FY ended Jul. 31, 2016.
(8) Roger Dunn, Golf Mart, Van's, Golfer's Whse, Edwin Watts, Uinta Golf
(A) Member Intersport Buying Groip
(B) Member Nation's Best Sports Buying Group
Currency Conversions (OECD rdes)
2016 AUD1.345/$ BRL3.491/$ CAD1.325/$; CHF1.004/$; DKK6.731/$; EUR.904/$; GBP.74 1/$; HKD7.75/$; IDR13308/$ JPY108.8/$; MYR4.48/$ NOK8.400/$; NZD1.437/$; RMB6.644/$ RUB67.1; THB35.79/$
2015 AUD1.331/$; BRL3.331/$; CAD1.278/$; CHF.962/$; DKK6.725/$; EUR.901/$; GBP.654/$; HKD7.75/$; IDR13389/$ JPY121.0/$; MYR3.90/$; NOK8.064/$; NZD1.434/$; RMB6.227/$; RUB60.9; THB34.24/$

With price being a major consideration for purchasing a sports product, sporting goods retailers like Sports Direct in the United Kingdom and XXL in Norway have successfully implemented a low-price proposition for branded products in their own countries, where they have reached the leadership in a short time, growing faster than the market.

Both of them have gone public, and both of them have been internationalizing in the last few years. Announcing its intention to be represented in each country of the Eurozone, Sports Direct has been expanding mainly through acquisitions like those of Megasport in Portugal, Sportland in the Baltic countries and Sport Eybl and Sports Experts in Austria. The latter has been a relative failure, however, benefitting local competitors like Hervis and Intersport. A few months ago, Sports Direct gained a foothold in the US market by purchasing two chains of outdoor-oriented sporting goods stores that were struggling financially, Eastern Mountain Sports (EMS) and Bob's Stores, retaining only their more profitable locations.

Giving customers a lowest-price guarantee in a certain area, backed by strong marketing, XXL has been more fortunate. It has moved successfully into Sweden and Finland and is now moving into Austria, using the premises of former Eybl stores, with the goal of reaching a market share of 25% in 3 to 5 years' time. XXL has also attacked the rather difficult Danish market, starting with a web store.

It will be interesting to see what will come next. The market has been getting more concentrated at the retail stage, mirroring what has happened among the brands. The bigger integrated retail chains in the world have been generally growing faster than the global market.

The trend lasted until 2015, based on the annual global retail chart produced by Sporting Goods Intelligence, but it was not repeated in 2016, as Amazon, Zalando and the direct-to-consumer operations of the sports brands grew for the first time faster.

See Table 5.5, which doesn't include the voluntary groups like Intersport or Sport 2000 or big generalists like Walmart in the physical retail space or Amazon and Zalando on the Internet. The sales figures are before sales taxes. Some physical retailers in the United States lost a lot of ground because of the competition from the e-commerce operations of pure players and those of the sports brands themselves.

Chapter 6

New behaviour trends among consumers of sporting goods

Antoine Haincourt

> *Young people today love luxury; they are ill-mannered, despise authority. They have no respect for their elders, they chat instead of working. They no longer stand up when an adult enters the room. They are argumentative, boastful, rush to the table to devour the desserts, cross their legs and tyrannise their teachers.*

Which reactionary writer or corrupt politician made these remarks? asks Franz Olivier Giezbert in an editorial published in September 2017. He reminds us that it is none other than the great Socrates (470–379 BC) and we might almost laugh to think that "*nothing has changed from one millennium to the next*".[1]

Yet, whilst we continue to sing the same old tunes, experience the same worries as if the future of humanity is just history endlessly repeating itself, the world is changing. What is really changing today then? We live in a world of transparency and uncertainty, in a world deeply affected by economic and social crises, an increasingly urbanized world, preoccupied by environmental issues, a world where new information and communication technologies are profoundly transforming the way companies interact with their customers. It is a world where physical commerce meets the digital and disintermediated, and therefore more direct, world that allows access to products available at the far ends of the earth, where consumer communities share their opinions and recommendations in real time.

This world of today oscillates between materialism and happiness through consumption, a world in which individuals strive to satisfy their desires instantly, whereas for some, on the contrary, reducing consumption has become a new way of life.

The world of sport is also changing. The spectacle offered by major events gives sport such media importance that sportsmen and women are worshipped like rock stars. The London 2012 Olympic Games became the most publicized television event in the world. While the spectacular increases in television broadcasting rights seem to have come to an end (after 25 years of rising demand, sales of broadcasting rights of the English Premier League have stalled in 2018), the major sporting events remain an opportunity to experience great epic battles where the nicknames given to athletes attest to both a great intimacy and superhuman values, their celebration a transfiguration of accomplished acts.[2] Whilst this need to celebrate great feats is still around today and continues to be very important, the decision to practice a sport seems to be driven by new motivations: Sport is now seen as a source of harmony and self-awareness, creativity and innovation are the new core values, the quest for pleasure and autonomy have supplanted past ideals of power and victory.

This semantic shift from a physical practice, underpinned by strict rules and often reinforced by the idea of competing against others, to sport as a state of mind, reflects the profound changes that are disrupting our society.

Seen this way, how will these transformations influence the new hyper-connected consumer who has 24-hour-a-day access to information? Can we still anticipate the future expectations of the new generation of sporting goods consumers using old frames of reference? What impact will this have on the relationship between brands and consumers?

1 A rise in sports practice, but a diversity that's difficult to grasp

According to a 2010 survey (Lefèvre and Thiery, 2010), 47 million French people aged 15 to 75 reported having practised a physical activity or sport at least once during the year, i.e., 89% of those surveyed, confirming an increase of 16 points compared to 1985.[3] If this evolution attests to the massification of such activities, we can assume they would be carried out more or less regularly, more or less intensely and more or less confidently according to type, gender and age group. In 2017, physical activity was more common among young people aged 15–29 than among their elders (Cléron, Caruso Injep, 2017): 46% of them participate more than once a week, compared to 39% for those aged 30–49. Over the last 50 years, due to the dual effect of shorter working hours and longer working lives, we have gained 150,000 hours of non-working time.[4] This so-called free time has developed its own values, we are attached to it, it structures the lives of the French, and it is often used to the full. The economic crisis, because of its impact on purchasing power, has led households to make compromises in terms of their leisure spending, but it has also played an accelerating role, since leisure is a way of escaping stress.

As a consequence of the multiplicity of leisure activities that has emerged in recent years, it is the proliferation of practices that must now be noted: An individual might now practice from four to more than ten activities. Another phenomenon at work is that although the number of sports membership cards issued remains high (around 16 million memberships cards in 2016), it is not keeping pace with the increase in the number of practitioners, suggesting that people are practising sport in a freer and less supervised way. This underlying trend highlights the difficulty for sports federations of keeping up with changing expectations and practices that are increasingly breaking away from an institutional framework. In response to this growing demand for "leisure sport" many private actors have positioned themselves in the market (e.g., creation of fitness rooms, installation of five-a-side football pitches, etc.), thereby competing with the traditional services offered by sports federations.[5]

2 Motivation and action

The higher the stakes and the more ambitious the goal, the more energy an athlete will use. This mobilization is at the source of his or her motivation. Thus, the process leads to needs and objectives. The fact is that a desire to practise sporting activities has multiple motivations; sport covers a wide range of sometimes contradictory attributes and cannot therefore be defined as a homogeneous whole. Health, well-being, sociability and contact with nature seem to be the new sources of motivation for practitioners, instead of performance and victory, and as a consequence of a process of democratization of sport and individualization of sporting choices, competitive sport has given way to sport that helps to prevent burn-out.

Generally speaking, motivations for doing sport can be divided into four main categories. Those relating to characteristics such as risk, competition and performance at the rear of the pack. However, this diagnosis is dependent on the discipline practised. Thus, runners (jogging and running) more often prioritize physical sensations, commitment and physical expenditure and the improvement of their performances. They also place a higher than average emphasis on conviviality and health. Footballers, on the other hand, are more often motivated by physical aspects, as well as by competition and performance, which overall are not much cited by the majority (20% of all sports practitioners compared to 55% of footballers).

Out of more than 280 disciplines grouped by activity type, three of them clearly stand out. Walking, which covers a wide spectrum of activities, from everyday walking to trekking, is cited by two out of three people. Cited by two out of five individuals, the swimming family – from leisure bathing or diving to swimming training – comes in second place. Cycling in all its forms is not to be outdone,

Table 6.1 Motivation for practising sport in France

Motivation of participants	*% of participants*
Health, wellness	
To feel good about yourself	94
Health	90
Exercise, fitness	84
Conviviality and. . .	
Relaxation	93
Pleasure	91

Source: sport.gouv/ la pratique des activités physiques et sportives en France 2010.

with one in three people concerned. Almost one in five individuals choose gymnastics (from "wellness" to sports gymnastics, including fitness but not body building) as well as non-competitive running (jogging, running or trail running).

Cited by just over one person in ten come families of activities more usually practised on holiday, often relating to leisure practices such as skiing (downhill skiing, cross-country skiing or surfing) and bowling sports (from *pétanque* to bowling). Football, on the other hand, is practised by one in ten people. Finally, with less than 10% of the population playing racket sports, two stand out: tennis and table tennis.

2.1 Sports that are leaving stadiums behind and moving into the street show the strongest progression

While the increase in sports participation concerns almost all families of sporting activities, the two largest increases, of approximately 10 points between 2000 and 2010, relate to the two most important families – walking (excluding everyday walking from A to B) and swimming. The other notable increases stand at around +5 points. The rise of motor sports (car and motorbike, excluding everyday vehicles for transport) and dance, a family of activities not very well represented in 2000, has been noted. Among the families already well ranked in 2000 in terms of practice rates, we see the progression of cycling (excluding everyday cycling as a means of transport), running and gymnastics. With a slight increase come families of activities as diverse as skiing, football, fishing, table tennis and strength training. This evolution goes hand in hand with demassification in terms of people's needs, leading to the emergence of a new form of individualism in which each person develops his or her own way of life and asserts his or her individuality in terms of consumer habits.

3 From suffering to enjoyment, a sports evolution is underway

So, since the 'nineties, might we say that sport is to be considered more as a leisure activity increasingly linked to the notions of health, balance and well-being?

According to Gerard Mermet,[6] this concept would gradually take precedence over sport as suffering. In a hedonistic society, the decision to practice sports would be dictated primarily by the pursuit of pleasure, rather than examples set by parents or schools. Mermet also points out that many athletes also care about their appearance. This aesthetic motivation can be directed towards others, to whom one wishes to show a dynamic and seductive image. But it is more and more often narcissistic, intended to strengthen or regain self-esteem. Thus, the objective pursued seems more about a search for well-being, beauty and harmony of the body, the ingredients of social success. Whilst greater value is placed on pleasure, youth and freedom, on the other end of the scale are the values of virility and achievement, seemingly in decline.

Table 6.2 Evolution of the most popular groups of activities from 2000 to 2010

Family of activities and activities	*Rate 2000*	*Rate 2010*	*Change*
Walking	45%	57%	+12
Swimming	31%	41%	+10
Running (trail)	14%	20%	+6
Gymnastics	12%	17%	+5
Motor sports	1%	6%	+5
Cycling	27%	32%	+5
Dance	2%	7%	+5
Table tennis	5%	8%	+3
Body building	6%	8%	+2
Skiing	11%	13%	+2
Football	10%	12%	+2
Fishing	7%	9%	+2
Bowling sports	14%	13%	−1
Tennis	8%	6%	−2

Source: 2010 survey of physical and sports practice, CNDS/direction des sports, INSEP, MEOS and MJS/INSEP 2000 survey. Sample: persons residing in France (metropolitan France and overseas departments) and aged between 15 and 75 years. NB: In the groupings made for this comparison, day to day utility practices of any kind are excluded.

In 2000, 45% of those questioned said they had practised at least one activity from the walking family over the course of the past 12 months, including occasional practice and holiday periods. This figure had risen to 57% of respondents in 2010.

This theory is also supported by Gilles Lipovetsky,[7] for whom the neo-sportsperson is not obsessed by achievement: what he or she aims primarily to do is to maintain their physique, and to feel good, or at least, better. No heroic values, but a need for distraction, self-preservation, and reconciliation with oneself. For Lipovetsky, what this new world of sport reveals is none other than the social expansion of the well-being mindset.

Whilst the idea of sport as a source of pleasure and entertainment is well established today, it should not, however, hide a growing fervour for certain unusual practices that go against this ideal of well-being.

Sport is therefore being torn between two contradictory processes. For Florence Soulé-Bourneton and Sébastien Stumpp,[8] this craze reflects the key values of a "*society that exhorts the individual to possess qualities of responsiveness, autonomy and adaptability, to evaluate and optimize one's physical and cognitive resources to produce the best performance*". In an age where the individual is king, the rise of these new forms of practice are therefore credited to "*the progressive imposition in our society of an idea of competence as systematically balancing mastery of high-level performance (knowing how to do) with a range of positive attitudes (knowing how to be)*". More than one sportsperson in three will thus use a device to measure performance during sports, of which almost a quarter are smartphones. The penetration rate of connected devices is thus very high and should continue to rise in the coming years (Pipame, 2016).

4 Sporting goods consumers divide into two groups: Community-oriented vs. those concerned with manufacturing conditions

A statistical analysis made it possible to identify the drivers of purchasing motivation based on the development of standard profiles of sporting goods consumers (Pipame, 2016).

During this study, the following profiles were identified and grouped into major families:

- Community-oriented (32%)
- Ethical consumers (28%)
- Sunday participants (25%)
- Committed participants (8%)
- Performance-driven (7%)

4.1 All consumers of sporting goods can be divided into two broad categories

- The group-oriented, community dimension of their practice (desire to participate in the design of sports articles, interest in community sports practices, etc.)
- Their awareness, or not, of responsible manufacturing conditions

While **community-oriented** participants represent 32%, they are made up of a larger proportion of recent sports practitioners. More than other categories, they want to push their own limits. They also want to try out new practices, are more loyal to a particular brand and are interested in performance monitoring equipment. This profile is particularly well represented in combat sports, urban sports, running, ball sports and martial arts.

Ethically minded sports practitioners, who represent 28%, are more concerned with production conditions, from both a social and environmental point of view. They are looking for customized products that suit their body type. Being in contact with nature is one of their main motivations for practising, with little interest in competitive pursuits and a preference for "outdoor" activities – walking, swimming, snow/water sports or gymnastics. Paradoxically, their greater awareness of ethical issues is not accompanied by a higher level of expenditure, and these consumers do not have fixed ideas about particular brands.

Sunday participants, representing a quarter of the target group, are a more difficult group to understand, as they are less involved than others, practising sports in a casual way. They have no clear ideas about the brand they are going to buy and are the most sensitive to the price variable. They are represented in racket sports, ball sports, running, dancing and fitness.

Committed participants have often been practising for more than 10 years. More motivated than the average, they are ready to spend more and want to customize and test products. They are particularly well represented in equestrian sports, urban sports, combat sports, water sports and martial arts. This population has a higher proportion of

- Members of sports federations
- Divorced or separated individuals

Performance-driven participants make up 7% of sporting goods consumers, a minority group, but they are very involved. They practise their sport intensively and are very passionate about it. They tend to be over-equipped with connected technology and collect data on their activity, monitoring performance and listening to the recommendations of sports and health professionals. The average spending of individuals in this group is substantial and they tend to be more brand-loyal than other groups. Performance-driven participants are found in shooting sports, water sports, strength-related sports and athletics.

5 Y and Z, the millennial generations disrupting the world of sport

The sports industry, seeking to "create" new customers, aims to attract younger and younger followers. To do so, it must understand these new generations, whose motivations are profoundly different from those of their elders. They are aged between 18 and 34 years old in 2018, and by 2020, they will represent 40% of the world's population. More realistic than their elders, they feel ready to build their own future. These young people favour the "trial and error" approach rather than the promise of a potentially better, but distant world.

These "millennials" have grown up in a world that is more urbanized, but also more connected and mobile than ever. Whilst they might indeed be passionate about sports, they are just as passionate about video games![9]

Aware of the social and economic issues they must face up to, this generation experienced the 2008 crisis, which hit their parents particularly hard, and they are also attuned to the immense environmental challenges we face. This generation is impressive in its ability not just to survive in a world inherited from the 20th century, by speaking out – and taking control – notably through new technologies, but also by breaking norms and reinventing them.

Within this new up and coming generation, sociologists distinguish generation Y, which includes individuals born from the 1980s to the early 2000s. They are referred to as "digital natives" because they were the first to grow up with the Internet, computers and video games and they use them intuitively. They have a culture of immediacy: Pleasure is not deferred – "if there is something to do, we do it" (Monique Dagnaud). This generation, whose attention is constantly in demand, is, in both the virtual and real worlds, "here and at the same time elsewhere". Digital information is transforming their relationship with the world: While it might seem that they have shorter attention spans, they nevertheless respond more quickly than their elders to the various demands to which they are exposed and know how to perform several tasks at once.

Those born since 1995, known as Generation Z, are sometimes called "zappers". "While Generation Y grew up with the Internet, Generation Z has grown up with the rise of mobile phones and is very familiar with social media" (Olivier Houdé).

In this period of great uncertainty, we are currently experiencing, these millennials, especially those who live in the West, are in search of stability and show little optimism with regard to the economic and social situation we are now seeing. They believe, particularly in France, as in other mature economies, that the generation before them was happier than they are. Outside emerging economies, they express less confidence in the future. In general, it is social tensions and the risk of conflict that seems to fuel such doubts. Work, or more precisely, the tension that persists in the labour market, especially among the young, is one of the main fears (Millennial Deloittte Study 2017, third item cited out of 25).[10] Significantly, terrorism is a major anxiety-provoking factor (this factor is seen as twice as important as in the previous study). Paradoxically, environmental challenges are receding and are at the bottom of their list of concerns, even though, until recently, they were considered one of the major issues to be tackled. Generally speaking, millennials from mature economies are aware of policies pursued in their countries when they relate to conflict, crime, corruption and unemployment. However, they still believe that collectively they have the power to change the world and that business can play a real role in society. They are interested in others and put collaboration at the centre of the game and they like to share ideas, knowledge and skills. Technology is omnipresent in their lives, it irrigates their way of life, and allows them to communicate and express what they feel.

5.1 A new relationship with sport

These young adults have more diversified sports activities than their elders.[11] The statistics from the Sports and Fitness Industry Association (SFIA)[12] are indisputable: After two decades of uninterrupted growth, the population of runners began to decline from 2013 onwards. The reason for this decline is thought to be demographic: The millennials, who have become the largest generational group in the American population, are to blame. The latter like to vary their practice and prefer fitness and fitness sports, suggesting less interest in competition.

"*It is clear that the younger generations are no longer interested in the Olympic Games*" – Thomas Bach, President of the IOC, speaking about the London Olympic Games.[13]

A study conducted by L.E.K. consulting illustrated the widening gap between the generations. Once again in the United States, the millennials are abandoning cable TV and traditional sports for e-sports and online video game tournaments. The result has been fast in coming: ESPN, Disney's sports channel, has lost 10% of its subscribers over the last three years.

While they are turning away from traditional broadcasting channels (TV media, etc.), these new generations are also moving away from major sports events broadcasting as entertainment: The broadcasting of the Rio Olympic Games in 2016 saw a sharp rise in the average age of viewers, in line with the first television broadcast of the games in 1960. To counter this situation, the organizers of the 2018 PyeongChang Winter Olympics in South Korea are appealing to young people by introducing new disciplines that put fun and excitement at the heart of the show, including the arrival of big air snowboarding. In 2020 in Tokyo, surfing will make its first appearance, as well as skateboarding and climbing. But will this be enough to stop the disaffection of young audiences?

5.2 *Millennials are forcing us to change the way we think about sport*

This underlying trend has consequences for sporting goods manufacturing strategies. To attract these young generations, manufacturers must now provide answers, certainly digital and creative ones, that place fun and pleasure front and centre, solutions that are inspired by the worlds of video games and e-sport: "*All studies show that Americans are no longer attached to a particular sport, they like to change*" admits Tom Cove, who heads the SFIA. "*It's very characteristic of the millennials. They continue to run, but have other activities in parallel – gym, hiking, yoga. . . . They say, 'I run, but I'm not a runner'*".[14] Whilst this study is America specific, we are not dealing with an isolated phenomenon, this evolution actually suggests an underlying movement found on this side of the Atlantic too, with the French model, and European models more generally, being not so different: "The other characteristic of these digital natives is that they present many similarities across different regions of the world" (Irène Rosenfeld).

6 A sports industry that needs to reinvent itself?

These developments are not neutral: sales of running shoes, which have been decelerating for several years, stopped growing for the first time last year, while sales of classic sneakers jumped 26% (NPD). "*The top-of-the-range sneakers, designed to improve sporting performance and costing between $150 and $200, are selling less well than in the past*" (SFIA). More and more, consumers prefer cheaper versions, sold for between $60 and $90, which offer the same look as running shoes, but which will only be worn to go to the sports club or even to work.

6.1 Style as the main differentiator in a crowded market

This evolution of sport with strict codes and rules towards sport as a way of life has changed the very notion of style. This purchasing criterion is less and less thought of as a "superficial" attitude: In very crowded markets, characterized by an over-emphasis of technical aspects that are often misunderstood, aesthetic considerations simply make it easier to make a choice. Better still, in the age of personalization, it allows individuals to distinguish themselves, to be different. The choice of a pair of sneakers has little to do with technical or sporting considerations. Sneakers are city shoes that have become an external sign of relaxed style.[15]

In the case of clothing, recent empirical studies have shown that the choice of an item will very often come down to its cut. More and more, due to simple aesthetics, people look for harmony in terms of choosing tops/bottoms, so the choice of jacket will dictate the pair of trousers.

Clothing norms are becoming more flexible, as shown by the success of "athleisure", a fashion style that mixes genres, between practical, aesthetic and casual sportswear, combining beauty and comfort, like the yoga outfits that are all the rage in the United States. Silhouettes have become less formal. The major sports brands, or even ready-to-wear brands, such as Gap or J. Crew, have already expanded their offer. Uniqlo even took on the task of glamourizing the image of technical clothing: "*They made a highly theatrical arrival in France, with fanfare surrounding the launch of new products, such as the featherweight down jacket, which they sent to many influencers. Or take the Heattech range: when you think about it, it's just like something from Damart, but very well marketed*"[16] (Delphine de Canecaude).

7 Rethinking customer relations: An approval-driven system

With the rise of new technologies, the entire ecosystem of the sporting goods industry is being disrupted. The acceleration of new consumption patterns is one of the challenges facing all players in the sector. While customers remain loyal to generalist brands at a rate of around 75% (Nathalie Damery/Obsco for ISPO), the experiential dimension is at the top of the list of reasons to purchase in-store, particularly with regard to clothing and shoes. However, the role played by the Internet, and, more broadly, by all the new contact points, is becoming a worry. Sixty-four percent of consumers would thus research a product on the Internet before buying, while 37% of them practice "showrooming" – understanding and choosing a product in store and then buying it from another distributor or online. Whilst stores continue to offer dependable value, it's the service offered by sales people, the quality of advice given and the human touch in points of sale that make the difference.

7.1 Weak Internet sales for generalist distributers

While the major global brands have largely embraced the shift to e-commerce and multi-channel access, the proportion of sales made on the Internet is still low among generalist or multi-specialist distributors, who find themselves less well equipped. For Decathlon, the figure is less than 5% and for its main competitors it is lower still. However, at Decathlon, "*1 in 5 customers say they did not find the product they were looking for in store*".[17] To meet this new challenge, the company wants to make 100% of its in-store offer available on its website, compared to 90% today (François De Witte). It is developing its "click and collect" service (ordering on site, collection in store) and working to further reduce delivery times to homes or stores. The challenge is daunting when you consider that a company like Nike has set a target of 50% of its sales to be made online by 2022!

8 In the future, will community come before brand?

A study carried out in 2015 (NPD) shows that while the French market for sporting goods continues to grow, this increase is not linked to an increase in the value of products themselves, but to a change in the number of customers who buy them. The conclusion of this study might seem trivial at first sight – a simple economic consequence supposedly linked to the economic crisis that requires customers to consume, if not less, then better and with more discernment. But behind this deceptive appearance lies the new structure of the sports market, revealing a clear polarization between global brands flooding the market with products that benefit from brand premium on the one hand, and on the other, a multitude of brands with lower appeal.

8.1 Starification and cost sickness

The 2016 European Football Cup perfectly illustrates this phenomenon; even though the two main brands in the sector equipped 96% of the players, the football market is able to combine two strengths: It is both the most mediatized and the most concentrated, i.e., a huge market in which a limited number of brands compete. On the other hand, the recreational sports segment, which is much more fragmented and composed of multiple branches, is driven by several hundred players competing for a much less mediatized market.

Daniel Cohen illustrates this theory of "cost sickness"[18] established by William Baumol and William Bowen with the example of live performances, drawing a comparison with theatre actors who have experienced intense competition from much more productive industries. For Baumol, Hollywood is flooding the market with products that benefit from productivity gains that theatre performance cannot replicate and the costs of producing a play remain high. In our case, Hollywood is Nike and Adidas, who benefit from a global audience and feature global stars. On the other hand, we have niche brands whose reach is confined to a smaller market segment and who are often linked to a highly technical vision of sport.

9 The customer experience: The mantra that's shaking up the sports industry

Benefiting from a real windfall effect, it is most often these major global brands that have been able to reflect consumers' new expectations and adapt their value propositions and business models better than others.

9.1 Customization, the new norm

November 2016, Soho. It is in this district in the heart of Manhattan favoured by hipsters that Nike opens its new flagship[19] store and sets its sights on offering an extraordinary digital and immersive experience. If the immensity of the 5,000 m^2 building strikes its visitor first and foremost, it is the opportunity to customize the products to make them unique creations that marks a real break from the era of standardization. The consumer is not necessarily a great designer, but no matter, a house stylist will fly to the rescue and help to make the right choices that allow for style and performance to be combined. For those who wish to learn about the joys of running the city streets, it is a "pacer", i.e., a coach who takes you under his or her wing and the time to establish a training program that is most suitable for you. And you don't even need to be dressed in Nike to participate.

Customization has become the new norm, we've moved from adaptation, to products designed and made for us.

9.2 Time signals disruption of models

The only constant in our modern societies is change. We therefore need to constantly renew desire.

In June 2017, it was Adidas' turn to open an ephemeral structure called "the Republic of Sports" in the heart of Shanghai, in the Xitiandi district. Here, the brand is no longer selling products, but inviting each participant to redefine their own sports values.

For one month, from ten in the morning to ten in the evening, everyone was invited to come and experience basketball, yoga, football, boxing, cycling . . . even dance classes were offered, all free of charge. There were no discounts or product tests boasting the merits of this or that latest innovation. No transactions. So, what was Adidas trying to gain? To nurture the desire to live and play sports. The era of the famous USP, or Unique Selling Proposition, is over. Now it's time for the full immersive experience. Not that the principles of brand positioning are definitively disappearing, but in an era where the value of a brand or its product is first established by external forces, the principle of a position defined by the company seems less and less relevant. In the reign of total information, what these two examples illustrate is the increase in inequality between actors linked to the phenomena of digitalization and globalization. This gap, which is already widely established between the major global players in the sector, has contributed to

Figure 6.1 a–d The Republic of Sports, a 4,500 m^2 pop-up store opens in the centre of Shanghai in June 2017

Figure 6.1 a–d (Continued)

raising the level of expectations, setting new standards for the experiences offered and widely shared, while the other smaller brands have more modest international reach. Driven by the rise of e-commerce, brands have outbid each other, leading to the emergence of the phenomenon of "retailization" and setting new standards for the in-store experience. This push on two fronts not only makes the difference between global and local stars, it feeds the phenomenon, exacerbates it, relegating the smallest companies to just playing the role of cost variable.

9.3 . . . and changing values

We now live in a more heterogeneous world. For Grant Mc Cracken, over the past 20 years or so, our culture seems to have lost its centre of gravity.[20] We have entered an era characterized by a profusion of ideas, lifestyles and points of view. For McCracken, true diversity is no longer about gender, nationality or socio-professional category.

Digital technology acts as an accelerator of this "cultural dispersion" phenomenon. This profound change requires us to rethink the very foundations of commerce. We are moving from the mass market to the era of multiple micro markets. Customers are not just constantly being wooed and treated like royalty: They dictate their desires and gain a feeling of supremacy that reinforces the idea of visible individualization.

The world of yesterday was structured vertically: Ski brands such as Salomon and Rossignol have represented the values of alpine skiing for half a century – effort, order, competition, winning by 1/100th of a second, beating others. In these markets, segmentation by skill level, social class or age was relevant.

But new generations are in search of meaning and no longer subscribe to these values: The counter-culture, which has its roots in the world of more alternative practices, like surfing, now dominates on the slopes and is transmitting new values, like friendship and emotion. These consumers expect brands to speak honestly, to behave fairly.[21] They have chosen their brands – Burton, Black Crows, Zag – and in order to remain masters of the "sneaker culture", the major global brands such as Nike or Adidas avoid appearing overly dominant by increasing collaborations with artists, fashion designers and ambassadors of the constantly renewed counter-culture.

9.4 The end of production series?

The factories of the future are being given the ability to produce economically viable customized products that meet a growing demand for differentiation.

While this demand is nothing new, it has accelerated with the rise of the performance society, supported by the development of information and communication technologies. Long reserved for luxury and handcrafted products, the mass production of personalized products seemed to belong to a distant future. Yet, factories that can mass produce fully customized products already exist. Adidas inaugurated its Ansbach production plant of the future in Germany in autumn 2017. With its digital twins, and robots, the "Speedfactory" (as it's known) is designed to allow the brand to gain greater flexibility and offer its customers sneaker designs adapted to local needs. All this at a lower cost.[22]

9.5 Runners who don't all run the same way

While Londoners run before going to work or on the way home to get some exercise, which means early morning or late evening and often in the infamous British rain, their New York counterparts are used to running on asphalt, travelling longer distances and in drier weather. Travelling the world in order to better understand the diversity of their clients' practices, this information comes from the observations made by Adidas' designers. That's the goal that Adidas, based in Herzogenaurach, Germany, has set for itself: Like its great rival, Nike, they want to take the lead across the world's major capitals. From Paris to Tokyo, Los Angeles, New York, Shanghai and London, they have been listening to people, seeking to understand their habits, identifying the main differences using pressure sensors in order to feed the data into their design programs. The result: Better cushioning, especially for the middle and forefoot for New Yorkers, whilst, for safety when running in the dark, Londoners need shoes with reflective strips.

As a result of these observations, Adidas initiated the "AM4LDN" project, which stands for "Adidas made for London", in the autumn of 2017, the first edition of a series of shoes designed and produced specifically for and within each of the major chosen capitals.

9.6 Personalization in the robotics era

In this new "Speedfactory", which combines robotics and digital technology to increase flexibility, robots can be reconfigured very quickly, while the digital twin technology, developed by Siemens, allows the design and production stages to be merged and thus shortens development cycles. Soon, Adidas also plans to integrate connectivity into its products to collect usage data and integrate that into production tools.

By uniting communities of several hundred thousand enthusiasts, manufacturers and distributors alike are accumulating a unique authority to recommend and offer unrivalled product advice. Will this contextual data collected and transmitted to an algorithm make it possible to create a fully customized shoe in the future?

Conclusion

In increasingly competitive and mature markets, new consumer behaviour is one of the major challenges for manufacturers. The rise of new forms of practice, such as yoga or fitness, the rebirth of sports such as boxing in privileged urban areas, and cycling, a popular sport if ever there was one but one that has now become "swag", testifies to a profound evolution in demand. What was once just considered an activity that one did seems to have become a whole state of mind, an attitude, a new way of thinking. These modalities of practice are far removed from the historical concept of sport, traditionally associated with the values of suffering and achievement.

For new generations, this transition from "exclusive" practices to sport as a lifestyle choice has led to a new interest in so-called lifestyle brands offering more versatile products. It is no coincidence that, for some observers, the leading global brands Nike and Adidas rank highly amongst the most valued luxury and fashion brands. But these new forms of sporting practice notwithstanding, we must not forget that the competitive spirit that structures sports such as football, tennis or athletics persists, and in some cases is even becoming stronger. This cohabitation testifies to the extreme "plasticity" of sport, to its complexity.

For the consumer of sporting goods, while the performance of the products and their technical dimensions remain essential prerequisites, in some cases, aesthetics is considered to be of equal importance. New consumers are on the lookout for sources of inspiration: What matters to them is not so much the products they can buy, but the experiences they can live and share. A sign of this evolution is what consumers now expect from brands: That brands show consumers how to be better, allow them to connect with others, take part in a "big project" that has meaning, offer them platforms to express themselves and share real stories told by real people with real faces! To convince potential consumers, brands must now see themselves as more inclusive, more open and less elitist.

Paradoxically, with consumers having become less sensitive to marketing manipulation, brand development has become a hot topic. This is one of the paradoxes of the digital economy: Never before have the apparent opportunities seemed so promising, yet when companies in the sector invest massively, the returns do not seem to measure up. This "relative" decline in brand power in the decision-making process thus represents an opportunity for new entrants.

Notes

1 *Le Point*, editorial by Franz Olivier Giezbert, Sept. 2017
2 Roland Barthes, *Mythologies Seuil*, 1957
3 Mignon Patrick, "Point de repère – La pratique sportive en France: évolutions, structuration et nouvelles tendances", *Informations sociales*, 2015/1 (n° 187), pp. 10–13. URL: www.cairn.info/revue-informations-sociales-2015-1-page-10.htm
4 TNS Sofres
5 Virgile Caillet, representative of FIFAS and Gary Tribou, expert in sports markets in "Pipame – Enjeux et perspectives des industries du sport en France et à l'international" Enjeux et perspectives des industries du sport en France et à l'international, 2016 (Challenges and prospects facing sports industries in France and worldwide) URL: www.entreprises.gouv.fr/files/files/directions_services/etudes-et-statistiques/prospective/Industrie/2016-06-Pipame-Industries-sport.pdf
6 Gérard Mermet. "Francoscopie 2007". La lettre de l'économie du sport n° 880, Mars 2008

7 Gilles Lipovetsky. *Le bonheur paradoxal*. Gallimard, 2006
8 "L'ultra-trail est l'avatar d'une société de la performance", *Le Monde*, September 11, 2017
9 Médiametrie, *Média in life 2016*
10 The 2017 Deloitte Millennial survey. Apprehensive millennials: seeking stability and opportunities in an uncertain world.
11 www.lesechos.fr/21/05/2017/lesechos.fr/030346040741_comment-les-millennials-americains-ont-ringardise-la-course-a-pied.htm#ufWcAfkivrCGIWFJ.99
12 SFIA, "Sport and fitness industry association", American trade organization who educates, represents and serves the sports and fitness industry.
13 www.wsj.com/articles/how-millennials-ended-the-running-boom-1462473195
14 Etude SFIA ibid
15 www.challenges.fr/luxe/mode/comment-la-basket-est-devenue-un-signe-exterieur-de-decontraction_512968
16 http://next.liberation.fr/mode/2016/03/24/l-outdoor-est-in_1438267
17 *Les Echos*, Thurs 1February 15, 2018
18 Le monde est clos et le désir infini, Daniel Cohen, Albin Michel 2015
19 A flagship, in marketing terms, refers to a store that is emblematic of the brand, in which a company seeks to highlight its products and image as best as possible. It is also a place where the company most often seeks to provide its customers with a particular experience, most often sensory in nature.
20 Mc Cracken Grant, *Chief culture officer: How to create a living, breathing corporation*, Basic Books 2009
21 Jean Noël Kapferer, "Ré-inventer les marques" (Reinventing brands)
22 L'usine digitale (the digital factory), www.usine-digitale.fr/article/adidas-entre-dans-l-ere-de-la-personnalisation-grace-a-sa-speed-factory.N597633
Picture 6.1 to 6.4 Credit Antoine Haincourt

Bibliography

Barthes, Roland. (1957). *Mythologies*. Seuil.
Cohen, Daniel. (2015). *Le monde est clos et le désir infini*. Albin Michel.
David, C. (2010) *Edelman et Marc Singer*. HBR.
Giezbert, Franz Olivier. (September 2017). *Le Point*. Editorial.
Girard, René. (1961). *Mensonge romantique et vérité romanesque*. Grasset & Fasquelle.
Helbrunn, Benoît. (2007). *La marque*. PUF.
Lipovetsky, Gilles. (2006). *Le bonheur paradoxal*. Gallimard.
"L'ultra-trail est l'avatar d'une société de la performance". *Le Monde*, 11 September 2017
Maslow, A.H. (1954). *Motivation and personality*. Harper.
Mc Cracken, Grant. (2009). *Chief culture officer: how to create a living, breathing corporation*. Basic Books.
Mermet, Gérard. (Mars 2008). "Francoscopie 2007". La lettre de l'économie du sport n° 880.
Powel, D., Yu, J., Holyoak, Melissa Dewolf et Keith. (2017). *Online consumers choose inferior products despite evidence of their poor quality*. Stanford University.
Soman, Dilip. (2015). *"The last mile": creating social and economic value from behavioral insights*. University of Toronto Press.

Chapter 7

Innovation in the sports industry

Anna Gerke

Introduction

Sport and innovation are two intrinsically linked concepts. Athletes need innovation in order to improve continually their performance and athletes in quest for better results facilitate many innovations. Athletes include here elite athletes but also amateur athletes and leisure sport participants. However, the level and mode of involvement in innovation differs.

The concept of sport includes competitive sport, leisure sport, recreation and physical activity (Oakley and Rhys, 2008). The European Council takes an integrated approach of these categories when defining sport as "*all forms of physical activity which, through casual or organized participation, aim at expressing or improving physical fitness and mental well-being, forming social relationship or obtaining results in competition at all levels*" (Council of Europe Committee of Ministers, 2001). In all these different dimensions of sport innovation takes on different forms.

Innovation means that once something new emerges something existing disappears. This is the paradigm of "creative destruction" (Schumpeter, 1942) and "creative force" (Utterback, 1996). Innovation is a complex concept but can be broken down to the new combination of extant resources. The result of innovation are new services, products, processes, methods, markets, consumers and organizational systems and practices (Schumpeter, 1942). Bringing together the different dimensions of sport and innovation together results in the framework illustrated in Table 7.1. An example illustrates each category.

While there are few numbers available to quantify innovation in sport, new trends and developments in sports in all of the aforementioned categories are abundant. Traditional activities in the sport industry are the teaching of sports, sport infrastructure, club-organized sports, sport-related activities in cultural centres, and other sport-related activities. New tendencies relate mainly to technological evolutions that affect the sport industry. Examples are the collection and use of tremendous amounts of data during sport practice (big data); the technical equipment of sport venues to connected stadiums; connected objects for athletes at all levels; and online platforms to connect amateur athletes. Other tendencies are the emergence of new sports both indoors (e.g., CrossFit,

Table 7.1 Categories of innovation in sport and selected examples

	Competitive sport	*Leisure Sport*	*Recreation*	*Physical activity*
Service/ Product	Swimsuits introduced in Beijing Olympics 2008	New binding system for ski and snowboard boots	Home trainer to allow fitness exercises at home	Pedometer to encourage to walk in everyday life
Process/ Method	Videos taken during matches (e.g., ice hockey, football) to make better referee judgements	New sports such as Stand-up-paddle to adapt to conditions (e.g., flat water) and abilities (women, families, etc.)	Online platforms and phone apps to organize running and other sport groups	Adapted working space and hours that encourages physical activity
Market/ Consumer	Geographical extension, e.g., emerging countries like China in ocean racing	Geographical or socio-demographic extension; e.g., indoor climbing/ skiing	People that do not consider themselves to be sports people	Geographical or socio-demographic extension, for example elderly people
Organizational system/ practices	New practices in federations to attract and maintain members	New versions of traditional sport, e.g., soccer for five with adapted infrastructure	New organizational forms for sport groups, e.g., running groups	Company sport and physical activity at work facilitated by employers

Speedminton, bubble bump), and outdoors in urban and natural areas (e.g., stand-up paddle, parkour, street workout, slackline). Completely new practices like "e-sport" emerge that are considered as new sport by some, criticized by others as not fulfilling basic criteria to be classified as sport (e.g., physical activity). Sport as a vector for health and sport as medical prescription is also an increasing axis of development in the sport industry. Sport tourism is an important economic factor of the sport industry whether it is tourism for sport participation or tourism for sport spectators. All these tendencies translate into increased entrepreneurial activities. In France, for example, the increase of the number of new companies created in the sport industry was +12.7% in 2016 (Agence France Entrepreneur, 2017).

1 Innovation typologies and its applications in sports

Innovation varies in terms of the object of innovation, intensity, intention, source and time. The object of innovation corresponds to the different dimensions of innovations indicated in Table 7.1. It is about *what* is being innovated. The intensity concerns the amplitude of innovation. The intention indicates to what extent an innovation was developed by purpose or rather accidentally. Sources of innovation can be persons, organizations and inter-organizational settings. Finally, time refers to the innovation process and its different phases. The following sections develop these dimensions of innovation in more detail and within the context of sport.

1.1 Objects of innovation in sport

Innovation in sport means first and foremost technological innovation of sport equipment, gear and infrastructure. One perspective on product innovation is the marketing-driven perspective. In this perspective, innovation is part of the marketing strategy where the product as one element of the marketing mix needs to evolve constantly. Another perspective on innovation is the technology-driven perspective where innovation is triggered by technological progress rather than by marketing imperatives. Already Desbordes, Ohl and Tribou (2004) highlighted the role of innovation in the life cycle of a sport discipline since product innovation is a way to relaunch a sport that starts to decline in terms of participation (e.g., skiing as a winter sport was revived through the launch of new products like ski parabolique and snowboards). Product innovation in sport distinguishes material innovation (e.g., use of carbon fibre), new designs and functions (e.g., ski parabolique) and new technologies and systems (e.g., binding systems for snowboard boots).

Services are typically intangible, without ownership or property issues, not stockable and provided individually for each person (Kotler and Bliemel, 2001). Because of these unique properties of services, innovation of services has different drivers and dynamics than product innovation. A large part of the sport industry is based on services: Teaching sport, practising sport as leisure or competitive activity, participating in sport events as a spectator or athlete, just to name a few services-based activities in the sport industry. Most of those sport services are closely linked to tangible products (e.g., using sports gear when practising sports; wearing some merchandising products when going to watch a match in the stadium). The sport product can also be defined as combination of sport goods (i.e., tangible products) and services (Baker and Esherick, 2013). Services innovation in sport are for example new types of sport events such as fun runs (e.g., Mudday, Colour Run), extreme events (e.g., ultra-marathon), services related to sport distributed via websites or mobile phone applications (e.g., measuring individual performance, creating communities, benchmark results). Most of services innovations in sport involve also product innovation (e.g., obstacles for Mud-day, mobile phone or connected watch for applications).

Innovation in sport combining new products and services are often related to innovation of venue and practice as well. Venue, location or infrastructure refers to where a sport is practised and under what circumstances. Organizing a marathon in the mountains or at night is different from a traditional street marathon during the day. New sports such as stand-up-paddle or parkour running require innovation in terms of products and services to satisfy demands of athletes in these disciplines. Innovation of venue and innovation of practices can be defined as particular objects of innovation in the sport industry.

Another classical object of innovation, not specific to the sport industry, is processes and methods. This refers traditionally to production processes, as they exist in traditional industrial sectors such as the automobile, aviation and food industries. Since the sport industry is a services and services-goods combination-focused industry there is both traditional production process innovation (e.g., manufacturing process of surfboards through automation), but also services process innovation (e.g., innovation in terms of food and beverages delivery services in stadiums).

Innovation of organizational systems and practices are rarely specifically related to sport as long as it concerns traditional for-profit enterprises. However, innovation in the sport industry concerns not only companies in the sport business but also the public actors and non-profit organizations. Public actors are all those directly related to the state including the Ministry of Sport, sport administration departments at regional and local level, federations, leagues and local sport committees. Non-profit organizations are community sport clubs, professional clubs with a non-profit status, associations and international sport bodies (e.g., CIO). With an increasing professionalization of sport and the sport industry, the before mentioned organizations tend to innovate their internal systems, practices and processes which are traditionally bureaucratic, slow and little customer-oriented. A study on innovation in national sport organizations (i.e., federations) shows that federations perceiving competition in terms of financial and human resources are more innovative than those that do not. Involvement of paid staff in decision-making processes and positive attitudes towards change also foster innovation in federations (Winand, Vos, Zintz and Scheerder, 2013).

Innovation in terms of markets and consumers can be interpreted in various ways. One dimension of market innovation is the extension of the targeted geographical area. In terms of traditional sport equipment and apparel manufacturing, internationalization is not much of an innovation since globalization has already reached the industrial sector for a long time in terms of upstream and downstream activities (production and sales). However, market innovation concerning public and non-profit actors in the sport industry is topical. For example, sport leagues like the NBA or NFL have had a traditionally national focus. However, there have been efforts to internationalize parts of their product to target markets abroad (e.g., setting up a team or even whole league in Europe). Also big clubs like FC Barcelona or Manchester United internationalize by bringing their teams into new markets for fan tours, friendly matches and promotion of merchandising products. Finally, individual athletes that have succeeded in turning their images into brands commercialize the latter internationally (e.g., Ronaldo).

1.2 Intensity and intention of innovation in sport

When can we actually speak about innovation in sport? Does changing the colour of a new product range mean product innovation in terms of design? Does changing the itinerary of a marathon event indicate innovation? Does using social media to interact with club members represent process innovation? And is targeting women specifically with a particular product or service market innovation? In order to answer these questions, we need to understand at what point can we speak of innovation when an organization undertakes changes.

Innovation needs to be defined with regard to a point of reference or unit of adoption (Hoeber and Hoeber, 2012). There are different possible points of reference including new to the world, new to the industry, new to the company or new to the customer. An innovation can also have different levels of "newness", for example, marginal innovation includes slight modifications and amendments of existing products, services, etc. Incremental innovation includes more important changes including improvements, additions, and repositioning of products, services, brands and so on. Finally, radical innovation is what corresponds to new-to-the-world innovations, so some completely different and new products or other objects of innovation (e.g., Smartphone for product innovation, Uberization for services innovation). Radical innovations are rare in the sport industry because sport organizations and customers are rather adverse to innovation as it changes traditions and habits. Marginal and incremental innovations are common since these allow the permanent improvement of performance. An example of marginal innovation are the new product lines of board sport brands targeting specifically women. Incremental innovation is for example the continuous improvement of design for better aerodynamics of bike helmets. Radical innovation are new communities for practising sports facilitated through online platforms and mobile phone applications.

Lastly, the chapter discusses the intentionality of innovation. While some innovations are consciously pursued by a group of engineers, designers and R&D project leaders, other innovations occur accidentally by users or employees of sport organizations.

The topics of source of innovation and time of innovation are addressed more in detail in the following two sections.

2 Sources of innovation and their application in sport

This section discusses the question where does innovation come from? In other words, what and who are the sources and drivers of innovation? The answer differs depending on the different objects of innovation mentioned above. However, the general spectrum of possible sources of innovation is introduced first before discussing their application to sport and the different types of innovation in sport.

Von Hippel (1988) suggests a threefold typology of sources of innovation: The manufacturing firm itself, the supplier and the user. For this definition to hold it needs to be clear at what point an actor takes which role. For example, when is a firm a manufacturer as opposed to a supplier? In order to answer this question, von Hippel draws on the concept of functional relationship. The concept of functional relationship relates to the benefit that is derived from a new product, service or process. If firms or individuals benefit from the innovation of a given product, process or service as manufacturer, they take the role of the manufacturer. If firms or individuals benefit from the innovation as a user, they are users. Finally, if firms or individuals benefit from an innovation as supplier, they take the role of suppliers.

Von Hippel's ideas are reflected in a recent research stream and marketing paradigm called service dominant logic (SD logic). In this perspective, there are no suppliers/manufacturers and buyers but only providers and beneficiaries. Beneficiaries determine the value of a service proposition (i.e., service is defined as applied knowledge) when making use of the value proposition and in their particular context of usage (Vargo and Lusch, 2016).

In order to adapt this generic typology of sources of innovation to the specificities of the sport industry, three categories were redefined. Manufacturing firm-driven innovation was redefined as innovation driven by sport firms and organizations as driver of innovation. This includes for-profit sport product manufacturers and sport service providers, but also non-profit and public sport organizations that provide sport infrastructure, products and services. The second category is sport users to be understood as firms or individuals benefitting from sport infrastructure, products or services as users. And finally, to widen the perspective of suppliers as source of innovation, the category of inter-organizational linkages, including relationships and networks between for-profit, public and non-profit organizations, was added.

2.1 Sport firm and organization-driven innovation

The traditional source of innovation, especially in the industrial sector, is the manufacturing firm itself. The manufacturing firm invests a certain amount of resources (i.e., financial, human, material) in research and development (R&D) activities. The ratio of R&D investments/turnover is often used as an indicator to measure the level of innovation in an industry or of individuals actors. However, this indicator measures only the input, not the output of innovation. The commonly used output measure of firm-driven innovation is the number of patents. However, the relevance of these measures as only indicators has been questioned by a study run by the PricewaterhouseCoopers' business unit Strategy on the most innovative companies. The latter are rarely the ones that spend most on R&D (Viki, 2018).

In the sport industry firms have been source of innovation especially in the development of new sport equipment and apparel in the case of larger firms such as Nike, Adidas and Decathlon. Only Adidas publishes the figures necessary to measure the innovation input (0.9% R&D expenses/turnover in 2017) (Adidas Group, 2018). This figure might appear low as compared to other firms' R&D expenses, for example the two top pharmaceutical firms (i.e., Merck & Co and AstraZeneca) spent around 25% of turnover on R&D in 2017 (Strategy&, 2018). However, industry averages vary a lot and need to be taken into account when assessing firms' R&D expenditures.

In spite of quantitative figures available for R&D expenses of Nike, the firm states in its annual report 2017

> *We believe our research, design and development efforts are key factors in our success. Technical innovation in the design and manufacturing process of footwear, apparel and athletic equipment receive continued emphasis as we strive to produce products that help to enhance athletic performance, reduce injury and maximize comfort while reducing waste.*
>
> (Nike, 2018)

Innovation has also a central place in Decathlon's strategy and policy as stated on their website "L'innovation chez Decathlon" (in English: "Innovation at Decathlon" (Decathlon, 2018). Decathlon invests in innovation through an internal research centre but also decentralized innovation hubs specialized in differents sports ("universes" in Decathlon's internal language). They use both specialized R&D staff but also every individual employee as potential user and tester of new products (Gerke and Benson-Rea, 2017).

In addition to firm-driven innovation, taking the particularities of the sport industry into account, public and non-profit organizations need to be take into account in this category of innovation source as these actors are also "*producers*" of sport services and products. Public sport organizations including national, regional and communal sport administrative departments tend to have bureaucratic organizational systems and practices with little inclination for innovation and change. The same is true for national sport organizations at a different level (national, regional, departmental). Non-profit organizations rely substantially on volunteers, which limits professionalization, excellence, organizational capacity and, hence, innovation due to often insufficient resources and competencies (Hoeber and Hoeber, 2012; Newell and Swan, 1995). However, there are changing trends and exceptions to this past tradition. Those national sport organizations that have opted for a more professional functioning with paid staff and search for new revenues (e.g., sponsoring) have been more successful in the development and diffusion of innovation than those that relied on the volunteer-based model (e.g., the national governing body for football vs. the one for netball in the United Kingdom, two equally popular sports but different levels of professionalization) Newell and Swan, 1995). Results from another study show that volunteers can also be a valuable source of innovation since they are typically passionate about their sport, hence engaged, and they come from different backgrounds and therefore bring in a variety of competences and knowledge (Hoeber and Hoeber, 2012).

2.2 User-driven innovation in sport

An often-cited source of innovation is the customer who benefits of the sport products or services as a user. There are different theories how users get involved in innovation processes and the implications varies in terms of the object of innovation. Previous works focuses on user implication for sport equipment innovation (Shah, 2000). Three levels of users can be differentiated: Average user, opinion leader and the user innovator (also referred to as pioneering user, lead user, and heavy user [Gerke, 2014]). The average user might be involved in innovation through feedback loops, customer focus groups and surveys. In this case, the firm or organization still plays a leading role in soliciting the user's input. In the case of opinion users, it is slightly different as users take an active role at least in the commercialization phase of innovation as being an ambassador for sport firms and organizations. The user innovators are intrinsically driven. They engage in innovation due to inherent desires and needs to improve sport products and services provided by for-profit, public or non-profit organizations. Most studies about user innovators deal with individuals that have contributed to the technological development of sport equipment, e.g., skateboarding, snowboarding and windsurfing (Shah, 2000); kite surfing (Boutroy and Bodet, 2015; Hillairet, 2012; Tietz, Morrison, Luethje, and Herstatt, 2004); mountain biking (Lüthje, Herstatt, and von Hippel, 2005) and rodeo and freestyle-kayaking (Hyysalo, 2009). However, users can also be involved in service or process innovation. For example, users of sport products and services are often involved as volunteers in sport governing bodies at local, regional or national levels and can be drivers for process innovations. Volunteers require organizational and informational assistance to fully exploit their innovation potential for the respective non-profit sport organization (Franke and Shah, 2003). Non-profit structures are often less influenced by competitiveness and secretiveness, but they are also less structured and hence there is more space for creativity and exchange and sharing of ideas (Hoeber and Hoeber, 2012).

2.3 Innovation driven by inter-organizational linkages and open innovation

One of the specificities of the sport industry is the presence and interconnectedness of for-profit, public and non-profit sport organizations. Therefore, inter-organizational linkages including bilateral relationships and multilateral networks are sources of innovation. This category includes the suppliers as a source of innovation as indicated by Von Hippel (1988), and it includes users as long as those are organized with a collective group or organization (e.g., club). Otherwise, users are individuals and different motivations and dynamics are associated to their involvement in the innovation process as opposed to groups of users. Groups of users exchange, discuss, seek consent and provide collective opinions for several user groups (e.g., competitive, recreational, kids, women) while individuals users only speak for themselves and only take individual requirements into account. Inter-organizational linkages provide access to resources, information and some technical assistance for adoption and implementations of innovations. This is important to non-profit organizations since resources are typically scarce (Hoeber and Hoeber, 2012).

Little research has been done on inter-organizational linkages as sources of innovation in the sport industry while the body of literature of inter-organizational sources of innovation in the inter-firms context is abundant. There are numerous possible configurations of inter-organizational linkages considering the variety of actors in the sport industry: For-profit, public and non-profit organizations of varying size and sport. Just a few examples are mentioned in the following. A classical example of inter-organizational linkage for innovation is between the manufacturer as buyer and the suppliers of parts or subcontractor for services. There is often a task- or product-specific specialization that requires outsourcing of one or several step(s) of the value-adding process in the production of sport equipment and apparel. Equipment-intensive sports with specialized high unit value equipment are more concerned by this phenomenon than sports based on low unit value equipment, so-called trite sports. For example, in the sailing industry, most firms are specialized in niche businesses such as sail making, mast making or boat designing. Interactions and exchange of these specialized actors through formal or informal inter-organizational linkages is indispensable for product innovation in the sailing industry (Gerke, Dickson, Desbordes, and Gates, 2017).

Also the surfing industry is subject to innovation through inter-organizational networks as previous research shows. The most common practices are downstream information and knowledge flow, i.e., information from the manufacturer to the supplier, but also information flow and exchange from professional sport organizations to sport equipment firms. This indicates a different type of inter-organizational dyad: Sport organizations as non-profit organizations and equipment firms as for-profit organizations. There is mutual benefit as sport organizations provide input, testing and feedback in the development process and in return receives better performing equipment adapted to the athletes' requirements (Gerke, 2016).

Further inter-organizational linkages occur between amateur sport organizations, sport and territorial governing bodies, sport governing bodies (e.g., federations, leagues), sport service and consulting firms, sport media, event and communication agencies, sport venue and infrastructure management organizations and education and research institutions (Gerke, 2014). The use of multiple sources of innovation and multiple inter-organizational linkages as source of innovation makes reference to the concept of "open innovation" (Chesbrough, 2006). Open innovation can be understood as the opposite of traditional innovation through internal firm resources only. The open innovation paradigm postulates that ideas and resources external to an organization or firm should be used as much as ideas internally available (Chesbrough, 2006). Open innovation in sport involves all possible sources of innovation: the user, the focal organization's internal resources, and the linkages to various types of firms including sport product or services provider, the amateur and professional sport clubs, sport governing bodies and public sport organizations. Beyond the actors of the sport ecosystem open innovation integrates also actors from other ecosystems, for example from other industries. For example, Wemmer and Koenigstorfer (2015) investigate the phenomenon of open innovation in the context of non-profit sport clubs. They find that the commitment of the club's president and the strategic use of coopetitive environments explain the success of sport clubs in implementing innovations. They show also the role of the non-profit status and the voluntary focused resources for the innovation success.

3 The innovation process and its application in sport

Innovation is not a single event but a multievent process that follow stages in the ideal-type case (Hoeber and Hoeber, 2012). There are different approaches to decompose the innovation process. Damanpour and Schneider (2006) adopt a three-phases innovation process consisting of the stages *initiation*, *adoption decision* and *implementation*. Gerke, Dickson, Desbordes, and Gates (2017) develop a three-stages innovation process comprising the phases *ideation* (i.e., idea generation, evaluation and selection), *the invention* phase (i.e., the prototype development and testing) and the *exploitation phase* (i.e., large-scale production and commercialization). In the perspective of sustainability, the phase of *recycling/reuse* could be added. This perspective is very product-innovation oriented. While it is important to know these different phases of the innovation process, it is also important to understand that in most cases of innovation these phases do not happen in a chronological manner and some phases might be left out. In the context of innovation in sport, it is important to consider the innovation process with regards to the different types and sources of innovation in order to analyze innovation in different sectors of the sport industry. Figure 7.1 illustrates the process of innovation which is best applicable to product innovation in the sport industry.

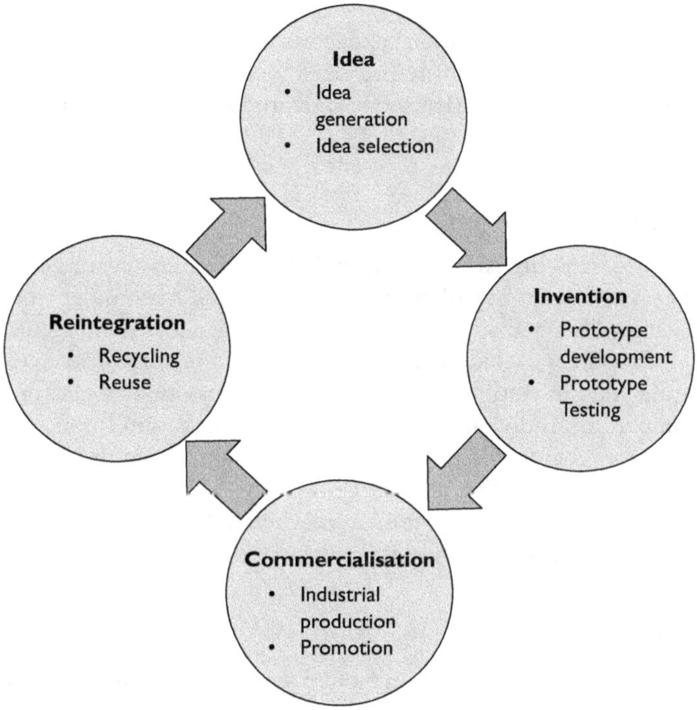

Figure 7.1 Major phases of the innovation process

Source: Adapted from Gerke (2014)

4 The success factors of innovation and its application in sport

Strategic success factors of innovation are related to characteristics of the innovation itself (e.g., the new product, service, process, organizational system or market), strategic aspects when implementing the innovation, procedural aspects in the innovation process, the fit of the marketplace with the innovation and the organizational support of the innovation (Evanschitzky, Eisend, Calantone, and Jiang, 2012). These aspects are now analyzed with regards to sport in the following paragraphs.

Products characteristics refer to the actual product advantage and whether the user actual perceives an improvement when using the new products as compared previous versions or versions from competitors. Therefore, the innovation needs to meet the users' needs and expectations. The price, meaning what the customer is willing to give up in return, needs to correspond to the users' expectations. The innovation needs to be functional and the level of sophistication and innovativeness needs to be appropriate with regards to the market and customer's expectations and capacities. A typical phenomenon in the sport industry is known as "overshooting", meaning that innovation of sport equipment goes beyond users' expectations and capacities and therefore users drop out of their previously preferred sport because they cannot cope with the technological sophistication and required budget (Thomas and Potts, 2015).

4.1 Strategy characteristics

Innovation success is linked to the overall strategy of an organization. In the case of a non-profit sport organization innovators need to consider whether the club or federation has actually the resources to implement an organization-wide innovation. Resources include financial, human and material resources. Before implementing and innovation the consideration of possible synergies and redundancies is important. Individuals concerned by an innovation through obsolesce or redundancy of previously required services, tasks, processes or products might meet innovation with hostility and hence resistance. The overall organizational culture and mentality is very important as to whether there is a general culture of creativity, openness and willingness for change or not.

4.2 Process characteristics

In addition to the question about sufficient resources available within an organization to pursue a particular innovation, another interrogation is whether there are sufficient proficiency and competences to implement and handle the innovation. This concerns, on the one hand, a certain willingness in the top management and amongst the employees or volunteers but also, on the other hand, the skill level and capacity to deal with innovation. For example, the digitalization of the payment of membership fees might create problems for older volunteer that are not used to deal with computers and software. There are other procedural issues to consider such as the coordination of innovation implementation in a large organization and the evolution of innovation processes over time.

Marketplace characteristics refer to the readiness of the market for innovation. For example, are the members of a sport organizations ready to integrate a new sport? Market characteristics refer also to the competitiveness of a market and the uncertainty in the development of a given market.

Organizational characteristics refers to the organizational structure of the innovating organizations. For example, to what degree is a sport organization centralized vs. decentralized? What is the level of formalization with an organization? How does the level of centralization facilitate or hinder innovation implementation in a sport organization? How are external relationships managed and are they impacted by innovation?

5 Sport clusters and incubators – modern hubs of sport innovation?

There is an increasing phenomenon of concentration of businesses and associated actors around sport in general or more often around one or several sport(s) in one particular geographical area. The concerned geographical area disposes usually of particular favourable conditions to practice a specific sport or several related sports (e.g., water sports). This is particularly true for outdoor sports. Another starting point for the agglomeration of sport-related businesses and associated actors in one region can be a particular sport infrastructure or venue (e.g., stadium) and/or sport club that attracts sports people, spectators and related business. This is a relatively new phenomenon, even though some of these *clusters* have their origin in long-standing history, emblematic personalities and sport affine culture. The key characteristics of these sport innovation hubs are collective actions as networks towards shared or complementary goals and collaborations in dyads or triads to achieve joint objectives (Gerke, Desbordes, and Dickson, 2015; Gerke, Dickson, Desbordes, and Gates, 2017). The following paragraphs show some illustrative examples of sport innovations hubs in the form of sport clusters and sport incubators. The purpose here is not to show an exclusive list of these initiatives but to show a few examples in more detail.

There are numerous examples of sport clusters in France that focus on outdoor sports. Most of them are based in regions that are well endowed with natural conditions favourable for various outdoor sports. The sport hub Outdoor Sport Valley (OSV) in the Rhône-Alpes region federates 430 companies and is the largest hub of sport companies in France. As the name indicates, the federating element is to be active in an outdoor sport segment, including winter and summer mountain sports, air sports, water sports and urban sports. The capital of OSV is in Annecy where this association of professionals was founded in 2009. The objective is to help the local companies to develop their economic activities by federating and representing their joint interests. The majority of members are based in the Rhône-Alpes region (75%) and are very small enterprises (68%) or small enterprises (29%). While one of OSV's missions is to contribute to the development of the existing businesses, another mission is to create an ecosystem that is favourable for the emergence of new entrepreneurial projects in the outdoor industry. Therefore, one of OSV's recent actions was to open an incubator specialized for outdoor sport-up companies. This sport incubator is now in the third year and accompanies young start-ups up to 32 months. The services provided to incubated enterprises concerns all phases of innovation from the initiation of the idea of the project through to the development of international growth. Innovation at various levels is key to the success of the companies (Outdoor Sport Valley, 2018).

A completely different audience and target group has the sport incubator based in Paris under the tribunes of the Jean Bouin rugby stadium. This incubator was started in 2015 by the Paris City Council. The name of this incubator is Le Tremplin and it is nowadays one of the largest sport business incubators with over 60 start-up enterprises incubated until today. There is a yearly intake with about 20 firms per year accepted depending on the quality of the submitted projects. The majority of the incubated firm (90%) focuses on digital applications or web-based solutions in the context of sport. Few companies have actually a tangible product as opposed to a service-based solution realized via a mobile phone application or a website. Therefore, innovation cycles are different and most of the incubated start-ups seek help with seeking seed funding and international development rather than with idea and invention phases of the innovation process.

The current complexity of these innovation eco-systems of sport are linked to the multitude of different initiatives and offers of mentoring, accompanying and incubation. The differences of these diverse propositions are often not transparent for entrepreneurs looking for support. The conditions vary a lot from monthly fees for rent and/or mentoring service up to capital share taken from the start-up. Other examples of incubator and accelerator programmes internationally are leAD, the sport accelerator in Berlin; the Sports Tech Collider in San Francisco; the Australian Sports Technology Network in Australia; the Sports Tech Hub in London and many others. More research and investigation is necessary to shed light on the structure and differences of these emerging initiatives.

Conclusions

This chapter on innovation in the sport industry recaps the key notions of innovation and interprets them in the context of the sport industry. At first, readers learn about the variety of innovation in terms of the object of innovation and in the particular context of sport, the different levels of application according to the definition of sport. Intensity and intention of innovation are important concepts to understand when studying innovation. Intention relates also to the sources and drivers of innovation. Innovation is either firm/sport organization driven, user-driven or derived from inter-organizational linkages and open innovation. The innovation process is outlined in an ideal-type process for typically product innovation, but the reader is alerted that innovation rarely takes place in a chronological and ordered manner. The question of whether an innovation is successful or not can be analyzed using a number of key success factors related to the themes: Product, strategy, process, market and organizational characteristics. Finally, the phenomenon of sport innovation hubs in the form of sport clusters and sport incubators is discussed and two examples, the Outdoor Sports Valley and the sport incubator Le Tremplin, are presented in more detail. Finally, this chapter gives some insights on what happens internationally in terms of sport innovation and entrepreneurship.

This chapter is an introductory text to innovation in the sport industry. Each of the topics treated in this chapter merits more in-depth reading in the appropriate academic journals and specialized books. This chapter provides guidance on the core concepts of innovation applied in the sport industry and is a useful reading for any sport management or marketing class that touches upon innovation in sport. It provides a useful background reading for any academic interested in doing research in innovation in the sport industry. Finally, this chapter provides practical introduction for practitioners in the sport industry to the conceptual side of innovation and helps entrepreneurs, especially in sport business, to better structure their actions towards innovation.

References

Adidas Group. (2018). Financial publications. Available online at www.adidas-group.com/en/investors/financial-reports/.

Agence France Entrepreneur. (2017). *Tendances et innovations dans l'économie du sport.* Available online at www.afecreation.fr

Baker, R.E., Esherick, C. (2013). *Fundamentals of sport management.* George Mason University, Human Kinetics, Fairfax, VA.

Boutroy, E., Bodet, G. (2015). *A socio-technical analysis of innovation in the outdoor sporting goods market: the case of the R-light shoe.* Paper presented at the European Association for Sport Management 23rd conference, Dublin.

Chesbrough, H. (2006). Open innovation: a new paradigm for understanding industrial innovation. In H. Chesbrough, W. Vanhaverbeke, J. West (Eds.), *Open innovation. researching a new paradigm.* Oxford University Press, Oxford. Available online at http://books.google.co.nz/books?hl=fr&lr=&id=lgZAyauTEKUC&oi=fnd&pg=PT2&dq=chesbrough+open+innovation&ots=7r4CDYLyhm&sig=BtkzgOdDsn3y8uTJJWQve5fbgJw&redir_esc=y#v=onepage&q=chesbrough%20open%20innovation&f=false.

Council of Europe Committee of Ministers. (2001). *Recommendation No. R (92) 13 REV of the Committee of Ministers to Member States on the revised European Sports Charter.* Available online at Strasbourg: https://wcd.coe.int/ViewDoc.jsp?id=206451.

Damanpour, F., Schneider, M. (2006). Phases of the adoption of innovation in organizations: effects of environment, organization and top managers. *British Journal of Management,* 17(3), 215–236. doi:10.1111/j.1467–8551.2006.00498.x

Decathlon. (2018). L'innovation chez Decathlon. Available online at https://conseilsport.decathlon.fr/decathlon-40-ans/linnovation-chez-decathlon-tp_8640

Desbordes, M., Ohl, F., Tribou, G. (2004). *Marketing du Sport* (3rd ed.). Economica, Paris.

Evanschitzky, H., Eisend, M., Calantone, R.J., Jiang, Y. (2012). Success factors of product innovation: an updated meta-analysis. *Journal of Product Innovation Management,* 29(S1), 21–37. doi:10.1111/j.1540–5885.2012.00964.x

Franke, N., Shah, S. (2003). How communities support innovative activities: an exploration of assistance and sharing among end-users. *Research Policy,* 32(1), 157–178. doi:https://doi.org/10.1016/S0048-7333(02)00006-9

Gerke, A. (2014). *The relationship between interorganisational behaviour and innovation within sport clusters* (Published Doctoral Dissertation), Paris-Sud University, Orsay, France.

Gerke, A. (2016). Towards a network model of innovation in sport – the case of product innovation in nautical sport clusters. *Innovation: Management, Policy & Practice,* 18(3), 207–288.

Gerke, A., Benson-Rea, M. (2017). The expansion of the sport goods industry, in U. Wagner, R.K. Storm, K. Nielsen (Eds.), *When sport meets business – capabilities, challenges, critiques.* Sage, London, pp. 11–27.

Gerke, A., Desbordes, M., Dickson, G. (2015). Towards a sport cluster model: the ocean racing cluster in Brittany. *European Sport Management Quarterly*, 5(3), 343–363. doi:10.1080/16184742.2015.1019535

Gerke, A., Dickson, G., Desbordes, M., Gates, S. (2017). The role of interorganizational citizenship behaviors in the innovation process. *Journal of Business Research*, 73, 55–64. doi:http://dx.doi.org/10.1016/j.jbusres.2016.12.005

Hillairet, D. (2012). Créativité et inventivité des utilisateurs-pionniers. Le cas de la communauté des kitesurfers. *Revue française de gestion*, 223, 91–104. doi:10.3166/RFG.223.91–104

Hoeber, L., Hoeber, O. (2012). Determinants of an innovation process: a case study of technological innovation in a community sport organization. *Journal of Sport Management*, 26, 213–223.

Hyysalo, S. (2009). User innovation and everyday practices: micro-innovation in sports industry development. *R & D Management*, 39(3), 247–258.

Kotler, P., Bliemel, F. (2001). Kapitel 15 Management von Dienstleistungen, in P. Kotler, F. Bliemel (Eds.), *Marketing-Management*, Vol. 10. Schaeffer-Poeschel, Stuttgart.

Lüthje, C., Herstatt, C., von Hippel, E. (2005). User-innovators and "local" information: the case of mountain biking. *Research Policy*, 34(6), 951–965. doi:http://dx.doi.org/10.1016/j.respol.2005.05.005

Newell, S., Swan, J. (1995). The diffusion of innovations in sport organizations: an evaluative framework. *Journal of Sport Management*, 9, 317–337.

Nike. (2018). 2017 Annual report. Available online at http://investors.nike.com/investors/news-events-and-reports/?toggle=earnings

Oakley, B., Rhys, M. (2008). *The sport and fitness sector*. Routledge, London and New York.

Outdoor Sport Valley. (2018). Le concept OSV. Available online at www.outdoorsports-valley.org/pro/presentation/projet-osv-5544-0.html

Schumpeter, J.A. (1942). *Capitalism, socialism and democracy*. Harper, New York.

Shah, S. (2000). *Sources and patterns of innovation in a consumer products field: innovations in sporting equipment*. Massachusetts Institute of Technology, Cambridge.

Strategy&. (2018). The 2017 global innovation study. Available online at www.strategyand.pwc.com/innovation1000

Thomas, S., Potts, J. (2015). Industry sustainability under technological evolution: a case study of the overshooting hypothesis in sports. *Procedia Engineering*, 112, 562–567. doi:http://dx.doi.org/10.1016/j.proeng.2015.07.246

Tietz, R., Morrison, P.D., Luethje, C., Herstatt, C. (2004). *The process of user-innovation: a case study on user innovation in a consumer good setting*. Working Paper, (29). Technische Universitaet Hamburg-Harburg, Hamburg-Harburg.

Utterback, J.M. (1996). *Mastering the dynamics of innovation*. Harvard Business School, Boston, MA.

Vargo, S.L., Lusch, R.F. (2016). Institutions and axioms: an extension and update of service-dominant logic. *Journal of the Academy of Marketing Science*, 44(1), 5–23. doi:10.1007/s11747-015-0456-3

Viki, T. (Producer). (2018, 26 March 2018). Why R&D spending is not a measure of innovation. *Leadership*. Available online at www.forbes.com/sites/tendayiviki/2016/08/21/why-rd-spending-is-not-a-measure-of-innovation/#3ef80f06c77d

von Hippel, E. (1988). *The sources of innovation*. Oxford University Press, New York.

Wemmer, F., Koenigstorfer, J. (2015). Open innovation in nonprofit sports clubs. *International Journal of Voluntary and Nonprofit Organizations*. doi:10.1007/s11266-015-9571-5

Winand, M.O., Vos, S.l., Zintz, T.O., Scheerder, J.O. (2013). Determinants of service innovation: a typology of sports federations. *International Journal of Sport Management and Marketing*, 13(1/2), 55–73.

Part III

Sport governance

Foreword: presentation of the three chapters of Part III

Sport governance is the most diverse and unknown area of sport management. As mentioned in the general introduction to our book, it is the most difficult part to place value on. However, sport governance, also called sports organization, is considered as the most important area in terms economic activity and employment. The three chapters of this third section address the most recent developments in the key areas of sport governance.

Chapter 1, written by Christopher Hautbois, aims to define the catch-all term of sport governance. It addresses the changing role of sports federation in the sport system. Especially in Europe, sports federations are at the heart of the organization of national sport for about half century. Until the 1990s, the sport system was described as stable with a uniqueness of practice, a dominancy of organized sports and a lasting and single-activity choice. Over the last two decades, major changes have taken place gradually. Sport became a complex affair with more providers suggesting six different forms of activity. Thus, there was a fragmentation of the sport market with an increasing competition between different forms of activity. Then, sport federations have to manage a new situation on the market moving from a monopoly to competition. These changes strongly influence the perspective for sport federations in marketing and development points of view. This first chapter addresses the major stakes related to these changes.

Chapter 2, written by Thierry Zintz, Mathieu Winand and Simon Gérard, offers an international perspective of the management of sport federations. Traditional managerial and governance practices revealed, time after time, their limitations, and federations were asked to implement "good" governance practices. This question arises in the context of respect for the autonomy of the sports movement within legal framework. The national framework is narrow in a globalized and digitized society and an international perspective is required. This second chapter will then review the governance of national and international federations given that it includes the main challenges with which they are confronted in terms of strategic development, the management of external threats, and positioning in the sports ecosystem

Written by Patrick Bouchet and Claude Sobry, the third chapter addresses another side of sports governance. Sport tourism is a multi-faceted phenomenon with an international dimension. This sector has been in a perpetual motion over the last 50 years to become a complex and global market. The social and economic impact of sports and intensification of active leisure activities have been boosting tourist activities in three main domains: The changes in representations of physical activity, sources of hedonism, art of living and health; the activation of the imaginary to access new tropisms and areas seen as playgrounds and/or discovery; and the multiplication and the diversification of active leisure and adventure services. The retrospective study of management and marketing of sports tourism provide a better understanding of the genesis of contemporary issues and new trends apparently emerging. This reflection is the subject of the third chapter based on international works done in journals and books.

Chapter 8

From monopoly to competition

The new strategic challenges facing public sports organizations

Christopher Hautbois

Introduction – In 2016, nearly 16 million people in France were members of a sports federation. In addition, 47 million[1] French people between the ages of 15 and 75, or 89% of the survey sample, said they had taken part in physical exercise or sport in the past 12 months (Mignon, 2015). At the European level, 40% of EU citizens say they play sport and 65% take some form of physical exercise at least once a week (European Commission, 2010). These figures confirm several things. Firstly, that physical exercise and sport, despite significant differences from one European country to another, are a widespread societal reality. Secondly, that this sporting activity extends well beyond any State framework, i.e., it is organized by schools, companies, gyms, private clubs and also local authorities. This means that non-competitive (or hobby) sports account for most of the activity, and that holidays are conducive to playing sport, to the point that it can sometimes be the main reason for going, in both summer and winter. This is called sports tourism.

This is the case in many markets, and a large number of sports providers, particularly in the public sector, face stiffer competition and have been forced to come up with a strategy, sometimes at short notice, in order to respond to varying and sometimes volatile demand. That is certainly the case for the national sporting federations, who are facing a fragmented sports market. It is also the case for local and regional authorities who in recent years have become fully fledged sports providers, particularly as part of extracurricular (after-school) or holiday activities. But, in addition to the job of running a region and providing activities for the local population, the question of how sport is run in these local areas has been marked by two recent developments: Firstly, the fact that local public bodies are now turning to sport, with the idea that it will make their region more attractive and is likely to boost the local economy (the recreational sports angle); and secondly, that these same elected representatives see the hosting and/or organization of national, or even international, sporting events as a tool for promotion, for creating a unique identity and differentiating themselves from their neighbours (the spectator sport angle).

This chapter is divided into three parts. The first outlines the concept of sports governance by proposing different key definitions. The second analyzes the profound changes that sports federations have undergone over the last 30 years, moving from being semi-public organizations to semi-private structures in some cases. The last part sheds light on how local and regional authorities have gradually moved from a purely administrative approach to sport to strategic governance.

1 Sports governance: Concepts, players and markets

As Hoye and Cuskelly (2007) and King (2017) point out, the field of sports governance is complex to analyze given the diversity of the organizations involved and the differences that exist from one country to another. Thus, sports governance generally refers to the way the sports system is managed in a given country. However, this system is the product of each country's history, culture and, sometimes, specific objectives. For example, the division of responsibility, funding and, more generally, support for sport between private and public organizations varies considerably from one nation to another. Within any given country, the difficulty of analyzing sports governance is also apparent from the variety of different stakeholders in a sports federation (*Sport National Governing Body [SNGB]*) outlined later.

The governance of a sports federation implies taking into account the (sometimes contradictory) expectations of these different stakeholders. Looking beyond the federations, however, it is the complexity of sports governance as a whole that requires a precise definition of its boundaries, key concepts, players and markets.

1.1 Definitions of key terms related to sports governance

Sports governance covers a range of different but interwoven terminologies. The literature in this field, particularly in English, provides several definitions grouped in Table 8.1.

These definitions underpin any study of sports governance.

Table 8.1 Definition of the main concepts used in the analysis of sports governance

Term	*Definition*
Sport	*All forms of physical activity which through casual or organized participation aim at improving physical fitness and mental well-being, forming social relationships or obtaining results in competition at all levels* Source: Council of Europe (1992)
	Whole range of competitive and noncompetitive active pursuits that involve skill, strategy and/or chance in which human beings engage at their own level, simply for enjoyment and training or to raise their performance to levels of publicly acclaimed excellence Source: Standeven and De Knop (1999)

Term	Definition
Tourism	*Any person visiting a country other than that in which he usually resides for a period of at least 24 hours.* Source: League of nations (1937)
	The temporary movement of people beyond their own home and work locality involving experiences unlike those of everyday life. The experience might take place as part of a holiday or as an ancillary to business travel. Source: Standeven and De Knop (1999)
Leisure	*Leisure is time free from obligations, work (paid and unpaid), and tasks required for existing (sleeping, eating). Leisure time is residual time. Leisure can also be viewed as activities that people engage in during their free time.* Source: Hurd and Anderson (2011)
Recreation	*Recreation is an activity that people engage in during their free time, that people enjoy and recognise as having socially redeeming values.* Source: Hurd and Anderson (2011)
Sports tourism	*Sport tourism includes travel away from one's primary residence to participate in a sport activity for recreation or competition, travel to observe sport at the grassroots or elite level and travel to visit a sport attraction such as sports hall of fame or water park* Source: Gibson (2006)
	All forms of active and passive involvement in sporting activity, participated in casually or in organized way for non-commercial or business/commercial reasons, that necessitate travel away from home or work locality. Source: Standeven and De Knop (1999)

1.2 Sports governance: The players

In addition to the terms used, there is also the question of who is involved in sports governance. This would be a good moment to remind ourselves of the classification of sports organizations put forward by Bayle (2007). This classification, composed of four levels ranging from the central core of sports organizations (the most integrated with the system) to the most peripheral (the least integrated), constitutes a framework covering all the types of organizations involved.

In this chapter on sports governance, we will mainly be looking at Levels 1, 3 and 4. It should also be remembered at this stage that there are three types of structure in France involved in organizing sports policy:

1 The Sports Ministry and its decentralized divisions: Regional directorates for youth, sports and social cohesion (DRJSCS), departmental directorates for social cohesion (DDCS) as well as establishments with special status, e.g., the National Mountain Sports School based in Chamonix, the National

Table 8.2 Classification of sports organizations, according to Bayle (2007)

Level 1	**Organizations at the heart of the sports sector**
	Sports federations and affiliated associations
	Professional sports leagues and clubs
Level 2	**Other sports sector organizations**
	Sports service companies
	Sports-event organizers
	Sports associations not affiliated with a sports federation
Level 3	**Sports-related organizations**
	Ministry of Education, Ministry of Sport
	Sports services offered by local and regional government
	Sports consultants, sports media, sports communication agencies
Level 4	**Organizations (unrelated to sport) using sport as management tool**
	Large companies and, more broadly, any public or private organization

School of Sailing and Water Sports located in Saint-Pierre-Quiberon, the National Riding School in Saumur, Paris-based Insep or the centres for community education and sport (CREPS). In terms of funding, the "Sports" programme (219) received €232 million in 2016 and €247 million[2] in 2017. The 2018 budget includes requests for €275.4 million in credits. The "Youth and Associations" programme (163) received €433.6 million in 2016 and €481.4 million in 2017.[3] In the 2018 budget, funding requests amount to €540.7 million, with an additional €264.3 million for sport through the National Centre for Sport Development (CNDS).

2 Sports federations and their different administrative bodies (regional leagues, departmental committees and clubs[4]) are set up as associations. Chapter III of the Act of July 16, 1984, defines their purpose as the organization of one or more sports, which they manage from hobby status through to the highest level. The memberships/licences they issue give people the right to take part in related sporting activities and the Sports Ministry can give accreditation to federations that take on a public-service role. Doing so means funds for the federations, particularly subsidies if they sign a 4-year agreement with set objectives.

Box 8.1 Approved, delegate, Olympic and non-Olympic federations

Article L.131–1 of the Sports Code states that the purpose of federations is to organize the practice of one or more sports. Article L.131–8 of the Sports Code stipulates that "accreditation" may be issued by the minister responsible for sports to federations which, in order to take on a public-service role, have adopted statutes containing certain compulsory provisions and disciplinary regulations that conform to a standard disciplinary code. The mandatory provisions of the statutes and the standard disciplinary code are defined by Council of State decree after consultation with the French National Olympic and Sports Committee. Today, 117 federations hold this accreditation, of which 92 are single-sport federations and 25 are multisport federations (some of whom organize competitions and some who do not). Accreditation gives the federations access to both financial and human resources (technical sports advisers) provided, as far as possible, by the government.

Federations approved pursuant to Article L. 131–14 of the Sports Code may also receive a delegation of authority from the Ministry for Sport. This article states that "*in each sporting discipline and for a fixed period, only one approved federation shall receive a delegation from the minister responsible for sports*". The delegation is granted for a period through to December 31 of the year in which the Summer Olympic Games are held (or by reference to the date of the Winter Olympics). The main purpose of issuing the delegation is to enable a federation to organize sporting competitions where international, national, regional or departmental titles are awarded, to select the French teams, to put forward names for the lists of top athletes, coaches, referees, judges, promising athletes and training partners. Finally, certain federations can have their accreditation withdrawn for a certain period. This was the case in 2014 with the federation for full contact and associated disciplines, and that for Thai boxing and associated disciplines.

3 The efforts made by local and regional authorities (municipalities, county councils, regional councils) in sport have continued throughout the decentralization that began in the early 1980s.[5] Today, these local and regional authorities provide essential support for public sports policy.[6] Although the scope of their intervention isn't strictly defined, there is a certain rationale behind it. Thus, support for sports-related training, regional planning and, more broadly, sporting excellence (whether through national or international events and facilities) are the common denominators in regional sports policies. The county councils encourage sport for the masses, support county- and high-level clubs, outdoor sports (through the commissions for public spaces, sites and pathways) and participate in the construction and management of sporting facilities attached to schools. The municipalities are the leading source of public sports funding in France via local policies. These include support for local sports associations, activities at the municipal sports academy, construction and management of sports facilities and support for the organization of sports events.

Generally speaking, i.e., not just in France, public-sector support for sport is justified by the concept of externality. This was introduced into economic theory by Alfred Marshall (1890) and is defined as the situation in which the behaviour of one economic agent positively or negatively affects the well-being of another without any monetary consideration. Sport can be associated with negative externalities (doping, hooliganism, damage to nature, disturbances close to the site of sports events, etc.) but it also has positive ones: Improved health, increased life expectancy, reduced absenteeism, better social integration, an improved brand image for a region, etc. Externalities pose specific problems of resource allocation and, more generally, financing. Barget and Vailleau (2008) remind us that, according to neo-classical theory, each activity receives funding based on the social utility that the goods and services produced generate for consumers. However, externalities (positive or negative) do not concern consumers but society as a whole, which therefore means that there is no commercial exchange. Thus, activity creating a positive externality will face the problem of underfunding, as all or part of the service provided is not remunerated. Conversely, activity creating a negative externality will not be offset by financial compensation. There is thus market failure, as defined by Pigou (1920). It is this market failure that makes the case for public-sector intervention. In the case of leisure sports, since no party has any interest in acting individually to encourage them (there is no financial compensation in exchange for the benefits provided by supporting the activity), it is up to the State, as guarantor of the general interest, to do so. This reasoning has been the basis for massive public support for sport in many countries for several years.

Since sport is in the general interest, the public sector is responsible for its management and financing. This initial principle is then applied at the operational level through subsidies, standards, accreditations and regulations, the scope of which varies according to periods and countries.

Thus, public authorities have traditionally been at the core of sports governance. However, the gradual commoditization of sport from the mid-1980s onwards has changed this model and, in so doing, increased the number of actors involved in the sector and, therefore, in its governance. Indeed, sports products and services began to acquire a market value during the 1990s. Private entities, notably with tourism and leisure sport links, have, therefore, positioned themselves on this growing market with a view to making money. Although the public sector (that is, the government and local authorities) continues to manage and finance the aspects of sport that are of no interest from a business point of view, it is no longer the only entity involved, but must coexist alongside these private profit-motivated companies and the non-profit associations all taking part in global sports governance.

1.3 Sports governance "markets"

The intersection of the universes and actors mentioned previously provides an overview of the entire sport system associated with global governance. This general overview is summarized in Table 8.3. Each point of intersection creates a

Table 8.3 Sectors, actors and markets involved in sports governance

Sector	*Characteristics*	*Type*	*Examples*	*Suppliers or practice methods*				
				Clubs affiliated with a national sporting federation (e.g.)	*Regional government (e.g.)*	*Self-organized sports (e.g.)*	*Private for-profit entities (e.g.)*	*Private associations (e.g.)*
Leisure (Without having to leave home)	Non-sport	Activities carried out during free time	Reading, TV, social media, cooking, outings with friends, cinema, gardening etc.	NS	(Non-sporting leisure activities provided by the town)	(Non-sporting leisure activities organized by individuals)	(Cinemas, theatres, press and other private entities offering for-profit non-sportingleisure activities)	(Non-profit associations offering non-sporting leisure activities)
	Sport	The gym or a non-adventure user experience	Tennis, basketball, football, horse riding, badminton, table tennis, judo, volleyball, athletics etc.	(Bayeux tennis club)	(Municipal sports school)	(Basketball game organized between friends)	(UrbanSoccer)	NS

(*Continued*)

Table 8.3 (Continued)

Sector	*Characteristics*	*Type*	*Examples*	*Suppliers or practice methods*				
				Clubs affiliated with a national sporting federation (e.g.)	*Regional government (e.g.)*	*Self-organized sports (e.g.)*	*Private for-profit entities (e.g.)*	*Private associations (e.g.)*
	Sport	Outdoor or adventure user experience	Sailing, running, climbing, scuba diving, rafting, cycling, golf, canoeing or kayaking, surfing, parachuting	(Coutainville sailing club)	(Classes transferred to ski or seaside centres owned by the town of Antony)	(Day trip with friends)	(FL140 parachute jump)	(Horseback trekking association in Côtes d'Armor)
Tourism (Leaving home for a period equal or superior to 24 hours prior to the activity)	Non-sport	Activities during trips or residential stays	Exploring the Cyclades in Greece, or the American West	NS	(Stays for senior citizens organized by the city of Lyon)	(Stay organized by the family themselves)	(Look Voyages)	(Neighbours forming an association to organize stays for themselves)
	Active	Outdoor or adventure user experience	Sailing, running, climbing, scuba diving, rafting, cycling, golf, canoeing or kayaking, surfing, parachuting	(Diving holiday in Madeira, organized by the Granville diving club)	(Permanent trail running circuit in La Plagne)	(Organizing a rafting weekend in Verdon with friends)	(Purchasing a trekking holiday from a specialist company such as Terre d'aventure)	(UCPA)

Semi-active	Attending a sporting event	World Cup, Olympic Games, World athletics championship	(Purchase of a ticket-transport-hotel package for Roland-Garros from a local tennis club)	(Hosting the 24 Hour of Le Mans motor race or a Euro 2016 match in Lille)	(Buying a ticket for a sports event directly, plus arranging accommodation and transport yourself)	(Purchase of a ticket-transport-hotel package from a specialist agency like Event Team)	(Purchase of a ticket-transport-hotel package from a local association)
Passive	Visiting sports facilities	Stadium, arena, museum	NS	(AS Saint-Etienne museum, visit to Emirates Stadium in London, visit to Hockey Hall of Fame in Toronto or the Sochi 2014 Olympic park)	(A family organizing its own visit to London's O2 arena)	(Purchase of a package to visit the main European football grounds from a specialist company or a professional sports club)	NS

market and compares supply and demand. The grey sections indicate the markets that will be particularly addressed in this chapter as considered to be the core of sports governance.

As we can see, looking at sports governance is a complex business because there is so much variation, with no clearly delineated limits and a greater or lesser number of participants depending on how restrictive the definition adopted is. Talking about sports governance is also complicated because of the need to talk about the whole system, not just its parts. Table 8.3 shows how intertwined the sectors and its participants are. However, for the sake of clear analysis, it was necessary to choose between a listing by sector (e.g., leisure and tourism) or by participants (e.g., federations and territories), and the second option was chosen here.

2 Sports federations: From semi-public to semi-private governance

2.1 A fragmented sports market

Until the 1990s, the sports sector, particularly in France, could be described as stable. Demand for sport had three main features:

- *Uniqueness of practice*: The majority of people wishing to take part in sport wanted to do so within the framework of a codified and regulated practice (in terms of field size, rules accepted and shared by all players with a referee responsible for enforcing them, membership of a team shown by wearing a jersey, with even a number on this jersey indicating the role to be played by each participant on the field)
- *Availability of organized practice*: For the most part, sport took place in a setting where the precise places and times of play, as well as the organization of competitions, were planned. Training was based around a specific goal (improvement of individual and team technical and physical ability in order to increase the chances of victory) and shared by all
- *A lasting and single-activity choice*: The majority of practitioners chose to play only one sport during their sporting career; the probability of seeing an individual play two different sports in parallel or successively during his or her life was, therefore, low

The nature of this demand was also reflected on the supply side: The sports club, and through it the federation with which it was affiliated, was the only provider and facilities were standardized (gymnasiums, COSEC, tennis courts, swimming pools, etc.).

From the 1990s onwards, following a sharp increase in the number of licence holders[7] and the introduction of new sports,[8] the sector has become much more fragmented. If competitive sport still accounts for part of the demand, new trends are emerging. Sport is increasingly played outside dedicated and regulated facilities. For example, the emergence of road races during this decade symbolically shows a desire on the part of athletes to get out of the stadium and no longer simply compete on the running track. In the same way, the emergence of outdoor sports shows people's desire to discover new places through sport, turning it into a way for them to benefit from an unspoilt natural setting, which thus becomes an integral part of the activity. Outdoor sports can take on the aspect of a real adventure with the development of competitions such the Raid Gauloises created in 1989 and the Raid Normand in 1993. Demand is characterized by two trends: The emergence of "sport hopping" (where several sports are played in parallel or successively over a lifetime) and the development of self-managed practice with, therefore, a decline in sport played within an organization.

These major changes have taken place gradually over several decades and have made sport a more complex affair, with both more providers and ways to take part. Starting from a principally federation-based offer in the 1980s, today there are six forms of activity:

- State-provided
- Self-organized
- Activities offered in school
- Activities offered by private entities
- Professional sport
- Activities supported by local authorities

The latter has developed mainly in France as a result of decentralization which, although it officially made no specific provision for sport *per se*, enabled villages, counties and regions to play a greater role in running the country. A lack of sports experience has not prevented these different authorities from taking over the running of this sector, considered to be important part of daily life (Bayeux, 2013). Over the years, these local authorities have, therefore, developed into fully fledged sports providers, whether for young people in the form of extracurricular or holiday activities, or for the rest of the population throughout the year.

The existence of sport in the workplace is not, strictly speaking, a new thing. The links between sport, work, employers and employees has thus been widely studied from both a historical and a sociological point of view (Arnaud, 1994; Callède, 2000; Clément, Defrance and Pociello, 1994). Some shared values (work, competition, performance, excellence) between the worlds of business and sport also led to the publication of works adopting a managerial and/or human resources perspective (Barbusse, 1997, 2002; Burlot, 1997, 2000; Fourre, 1999; Pierre, 2009, 2015). Overall, these works highlight the strong ideological and political elements of any analysis of the links between sport and work. But if this political dimension has not quite disappeared, it is the managerial aspect that seems to be predominant today. The underlying hypothesis is that the company sees sport as a way to promote the well-being of its employees, improve their performance, reduce absenteeism and, ultimately, retain its workforce. Notwithstanding the reasons for the development of sport in the workplace, the way it actually happens can vary: Provision of practice areas and equipment within the company itself, partnerships with private gyms offering perks (discounts, preferential access) for employees, games between employees organized by the company or team participation in sports competitions promoting stronger ties between employees.[9]

Today, private gyms[10] are important actors in the sports market, though it is necessary to distinguish between two types of operator. On the one hand, there are gyms offering activities derived from or inspired by a traditional sport offered by a sports federation: UrbanSoccer, Soccer Park, ZR (football), Hoops factory (basketball), Le Mur de Lyon, Blocbuster and MurMur (climbing), but there are also centres offering racket sports (padel, squash, badminton, etc.). All these allow players to choose the place, time, duration and partners for their sport. On the other, there are the fitness centres which developed massively during the 1990s. Several independent gyms and chains share the market: Lady Fitness, Lady Moving, Fitness Park, Club Moving, L'Orange bleue, Club Med Gym, etc. These gyms all have specific strategies designed to maintain or increase their market share. Recently, two leading trends have emerged: The structuring of the market around two distinct offers (low-cost fitness centres on the one hand, "premium" gyms on the other) and the constant renewal of the activities on offer (Pilates, Les Mills, Lia, step, body combat, Zumba, aqua-cycling, crossfit, etc.). With annual turnover of €2.4 billion, France ranks third in European fitness, behind the United Kingdom and Germany.[11] However, studies forecast saturation in some cities, limiting market growth. In that case, the driving force would be the creation of a denser regional network (that is, building facilities in areas where there are currently none), the offer of new services, and the constant adaptation to an ever-changing clientele and greater use of Internet and social media. That still leaves the highly risky basic assumption of these gyms' business model, that of "ghost members". These are customers who subscribe for one year but who gradually drop out after the first few weeks. The assumption is, therefore, that a gym can only break even when the customer database is bigger than the number of people it can actually accommodate, which amounts to practising a form of permanent over-booking.

Sport in schools has been around for a while. In addition to the traditional PE (physical education) courses offered at primary school and high school, based on an official curriculum set by the Education Ministry, we will also look at all sports played in school but outside lesson time. There are several different organizations for this in France: USEP for primary schools, UGSEL for private schools, UNSS for high schools, the French Federation for University Sport, or FFSU. The importance of sport in schools is generally underestimated. For example, about 1 million people in France take part in a sporting activity in high school.

Self-organized sports activities are fairly easy to define and encompass all activities initiated and managed directly by the players themselves, within more or less formal frameworks: Times, location, rules and participating players are not fixed and fluctuate throughout the year, according to the individuals or groups playing. They can be individual sports (running, cycling, hiking, swimming, tennis) or team sports (football, basketball, volleyball). The main advantage of this sort of activity is its extreme flexibility. The player is completely free to choose the time, place, duration of and partners for the activity. The other advantage is the very low cost of this type of activity once the sports equipment has been purchased. Self-organized sports saw a massive boom during the 1990s. Some of them are now experiencing a second wind, thanks to the technological advances seen since 2010. Indeed, connected sports products, social media, dedicated apps and online coaches (FizzUp, Nike Training Club, FitStar) are all new ways of encouraging self-managed sports activity, especially individual sports.

Thus, between the 1990s and 2010, there was a fragmentation of the sports market in France, as shown in Figure 8.1, which redefined the place of the national federations.

From a strategic point of view, this wider range of sports providers could be seen as an opportunity for the federations. An individual could take up a new sport at school, at work or with friends, and later wish to continue and improve his or her skills in a club affiliated to a federation. However, in practice, this transfer to the State-organized sector remains highly theoretical and is rarely observed. The different providers seem rather to be in competition with the state. Someone prepared to invest time and sometimes money in sports activity that is not organized by the State will rarely decide to add training at a club affiliated to a national

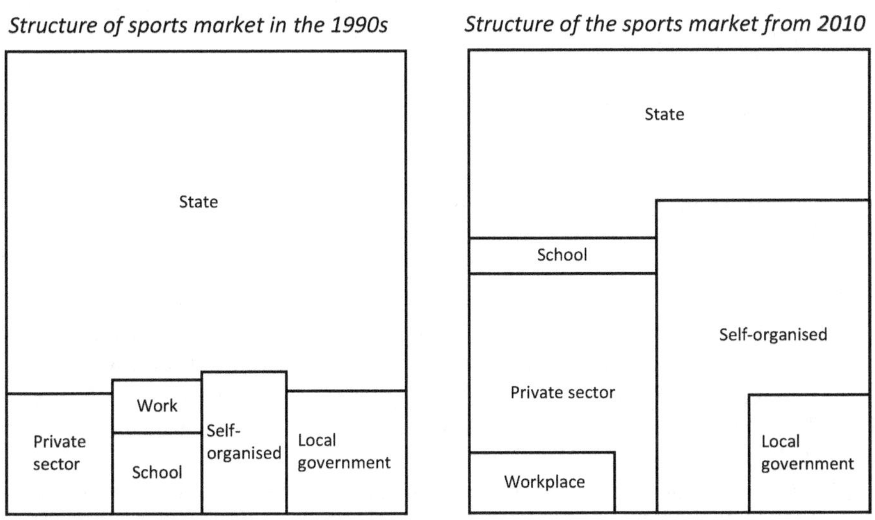

Figure 8.1 Gradual fragmentation of the French sports market between the 1990s and 2010

federation to his or her weekly schedule. This means that the federations need to rethink their development strategy and the products and services they offer without losing sight either of what makes them special or their government-defined mission, particularly the development of both top-level and mass sport. In addition, the federations also need to rethink their marketing in the light of this market fragmentation.

2.2 Greater financial autonomy and brand building: The federations' two key challenges

Since the 1990s, the subsidies paid by the French State to national sports federations in exchange for public services have been declining. This reduction means that even the small federations need to think about ways to compensate for the drop and, more generally, how to find the resources to fund their development. Even if all the federations cannot achieve financial autonomy (which, after all, is not their objective), they should nonetheless aim to reduce their dependence on public subsidies and boost capacity to generate their own revenue. This approach, which has gradually been developed since 2010, requires them to identify new sources of funding and, more broadly, build a real federation brand, capable of conveying the organization's own identity to partners (sponsors, media) as well as to members.

2.2.1 Evolution of the federations' financial model since the 1990s

Hautbois (2014) has shown that the average budget of an Olympic federation is €25.5 million[12] (around €750,000 for the minimum budget and €214 million for the maximum). If the amounts differ from one federation to another, the breakdown of the revenue is clearly identified:

- Revenue from sale of memberships/licences
- State aid
- Support from private partners
- Revenue from the sale of TV rights
- Ticket sales
- Merchandising revenue

Whether the federation is Olympic or non-Olympic, membership/licence sales represent the leading source of revenue (47%), with public subsidies in second place (26–27%), followed by partnerships (sponsors and potential TV partners) 16%. These three revenue sources alone represent on average 90% of the national sports federations' budgets.

Membership/licence sales are the sports federations' biggest source of revenue. For the French judo federation, they represented 70% (that is €19.6 million) of the total €28 million budget in 2015. For the golf federation, they accounted for 60% (or €17.36 million). For the French athletics federation, memberships represented 28% of the budget in 2015, or €8.2 million of operating income.

Revenue from the sale of memberships is comparable at the French football federation (€9 million) but it represents only 4.4% of the federation's budget, taking into account the significant revenue received by the FFF from marketing and TV rights. At the French volleyball federation, membership/licence revenue accounts for 40% (€3.2 million) of the annual budget.

For all federations, membership revenue logically depends on two factors: the number of memberships sold and their price. The total number of memberships issued by all approved sports federations was 15.9 million in 2014:[13] Little changed from 2013. Of the 15.9 million licences sold, 8.65 million were issued by Olympic single-sport federations, 2.09 million by non-Olympic single-sport federations and 5.14 million by multisport federations. We can see, therefore, that the market for licences reached a certain maturity several years ago, which means federations can no longer expect to see the number of members (and associated revenue) grow mechanically by simply increasing the size of the market. On the other hand, if the size of the market remains stable, the individual federations have evolved differently and, therefore, some saw their numbers increase between 2013 and 2014.

This was the case for the French handball federation (+3% to 515,571 members), table tennis (+4.7% to 9,111), athletics (+3.5% to 8,996) and cycling (+3% from 2009 to 2013 to 119,298). At the same time, some federations experienced a drop in the number of members: Skiing (−4.2% to 130,393), gymnastics (−2% to 298,879) and judo (−1.4% to 625,896). These figures reflect a change over one year. The change in the number of members is undoubtedly more revealing if we take into account a longer cycle, the only real indicator of a trend. In that case, the French volleyball federation lost 14% of its members between 2008 and 2014. The French golf federation went from 418,340 members in 2011 to 407,569 in 2015, a decline of 2.6% over four seasons but overall growth over 10 years was 10%. In the space of 15 years, the French basketball federation has seen a steady increase to 612,000 members in 2017 (43% increase over the period) (see Figure 8.2).

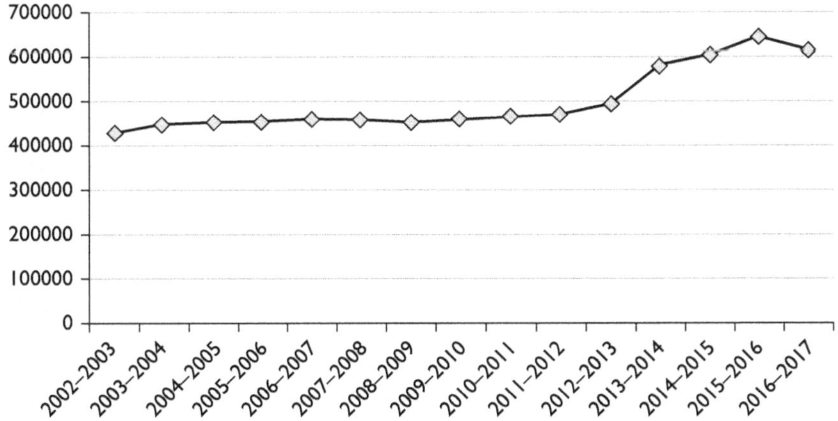

Figure 8.2 Changes in French basketball federation membership over 15 years

Table 8.4 shows the total number of members by federation in France for 2015.

The second factor affecting membership revenue is the price. Adult membership for the 2016–2017 season was €29 for the French tennis federation, €32.52 for the French badminton federation, €35 for the taekwondo federation, €36 for the horse-riding federation, €37 for the judo federation, €39.76 for membership of the ice sports federation, €53 euros for the golf federation and €86 for Junior membership of the cycling federation. Even if this rate does not correspond exactly with what the player actually pays at the beginning of the season,[14] the federations now offer sporting activities supervised by qualified instructors at very affordable prices. Making sport accessible to the greatest number is in line with the general interest mission defined by the State, meaning that the practitioner

Table 8.4 Membership of single-sport Olympic federations in France

Official French federation	*Membership*
Athletics	265,455
Rowing	43,183
Badminton	180,929
Basketball	504,187
Boxing	44,534
Canoeing-Kayaking	42,955
Cycling	118,871
Horse riding	689,043
Fencing	55,000
Football	2,018,003
Ice sports	25,917
Gymnastics	298,879
Weightlifting	53,268
Handball	515,571
Hockey	15,799
Judo-Jujitsu	567,855
Wrestling	18,747
Swimming	304,017
Modern Pentathlon	891
Skiing	130,393
Taekwondo	53,653
Tennis	1,085,399
Table tennis	202,352
Shooting	171,457
Archery	72,914
Triathlon	46,718
Sailing	272,595
Volleyball	97,837
Ice hockey	20,138
Golf	408,388
Rugby	327,818
Total	*8,652,766*

Source: French Sports Ministry

does not bear the real cost of the service. To calculate the real cost, you would have to include costs linked to the use of sports equipment (mainly financed by local authorities) as well as the value of the time spent by volunteers to supervise the activity, and even, where applicable, fees paid for the management of the clubs. This set-up reflects the core philosophy of the French sports system as it was conceived and developed historically. It is based on the positive external effects of sport that justify public support, as explained earlier. The limits of the system arise from the fact that, because of the sports federations' public-service mission, they can only very marginally manipulate the membership price to finance their development. Since the federations are not profit-making organizations, membership price positioning will always favour accessibility over increased revenue. Increases are always possible, but they must have a detailed justification and be voted on at a general assembly.[15] Consequently, the federations need to act more on the first variable (the number of members) in order to increase revenue linked to the sale of memberships. Members, therefore, are an essential lever from a strategic point of view, and the ability of a federation to recruit and retain members in an overall stagnant market has become vital. For this reason, therefore, the federations are paying increasing attention to this aspect, which will be developed in Section 2.3.

The second major revenue source for the federations is State aid, which comes in various forms: The secondment of trained sports coaches (there are a total 1,612 of them, representing aid of €112 million, according to the French Senate), subsidies paid under agreements with fixed targets, personalized grants to top athletes and high-level coaching programmes. State aid can also be indirect, e.g., legislation promoting top-level sport. This was the case of the November 27, 2015 law, aimed at protecting top-level and professional athletes and safeguarding their legal and social situation. One year after this law came into force, more than 80 companies had committed themselves to offering 176 athletes either adapted work contracts with time off for training or image and sponsorship contracts. In terms of the amount paid, the subsidies paid under the fixed target agreements are the largest after the secondment of coaches. Nevertheless, they too are declining. Thus, the overall amount earmarked for this purpose in the annual budget fell from €87 million in 2009 to €73 million in 2016 (source: French Senate).[16] The amount paid to each federation depends on the number of members, on whether or not there is a professional arm of the sport generating significant income, the number of Olympic disciplines covered by the federation and its financial situation. The result is a very uneven level of support for the different federations, ranging from 53% for rowing or canoeing to 1% for football. Although the situation varies from one federation to another, the reduction in aid (direct or indirect) is a major trend. Federations are, therefore, encouraged, sometimes by the State itself, to find their own sources of funding. And if this search for self-financing is deemed insufficient, there can be consequences. This was the case, for example, of the French ski federation, the subject of a negative report from the state auditor Cour des comptes in 2014 (see Box 8.2).

Box 8.2 "French ski federation targeted by state auditor"

State auditor Cour des comptes has gone over the finances of the French ski federation (FFS) and the National School for Mountain Sports (ENSM) with a fine-tooth comb and concluded that both depend too heavily on the State.

The FFS, which specializes in top-level skiing, is, in the eyes of the auditor, too reliant on the State which last year paid it €4.5 million, equivalent to a rate of support of 27.5%. The auditor considers this level to be high, especially given that it is not the only aid for the top-level sport. The State is also paying for 85 FFS coaches, giving the federation 5% of the total number of state-provided trainers for the country's 77 sports federations.

€7 billion in turnover

The auditor also noted that, between 2005 and 2012, the FFS received 39 grants from the National Centre for Sport Development (CNDS), for a total of €12.1 million. Grants that were used to finance activity linked to high-level sport, rather than financing equipment or facilities for the "sport for all" programme as originally intended. The auditor notes that the State's generosity does not stop there, with the Customs department offering 29 fixed-term jobs to high-level athletes during the 2012–2013 season, and the Ministry of Defence a further 28 identical contracts.

For its part, the ENSM received an annual operating grant of €7.7 million, according to the auditor. The Cour des comptes took a harsh line with the school, considering it to be very dependent on public funds. "*It forces the State to meet the extra costs and financing needs resulting from its inability to mobilise substantial resources of its own*", the report states. The overall impression is all the more damning, given that the winter sports industry is a particularly active one. Skiing business in the resorts is worth €7 billion, or 18% of French tourism revenue, and the auditor wants would like those involved to also contribute to financing the FFS.

Source: Le Figaro, November 22, 2014

The third main element in the sports federations' business model is the sale of marketing rights, generating sponsorship and partnership revenue. While studies have shown that sports sponsorship is now largely accepted by the general public,[17] questions of legitimacy may still arise when it is mentioned in connection with federations. However, the evolution of the federations' financial model requires them to be proactive in the search for private finance and to improve management of existing resources. This explains why, on average, the French Olympic federations now each have 14 partners.[18] These represent, again on average, about 15% of federation revenues, though there is a lot of variation between federations. In 2015, the French athletics federation earned €6.88 million thanks to its private partners, including €1.3 million in goods. The same year, the French football federation pocketed €84.5 million in sponsorship revenue. As for the French rugby federation, the change in the amount of private and media partnerships since 2000 is shown in Figure 8.3.

All these elements bear witness to a major change in the financial model of the sports federations since the 1990s. Today, these federations have noted the declining trend in State subsidies which, even if they are not set to disappear in the long term, will continue to shrink while public funds remain scarce. At the same time, the federations' search to find their own sources of income is becoming a priority, and this includes seeking to increase private partnerships. This new situation is reflected in many federations' development plans, as shown by the cycling federation's 2014–2017 project entitled "For a winning French cycling sector". The section about "*How financial management can help the federation*" suggests four different orientations: "*take into account the withdrawal of state funding, continue the redistribution of core resources, increase the capital and reserves of the FFC, create new resources*".

Over the last 30 years, the financial model of sports federations has, therefore, seen some major upheaval, moving from dual financing, essentially based on State aid and revenue from membership sales, to multiple financing where the quest to generate revenue has become a central issue. In a few decades, sports federations have gone from being semi-public organizations to semi-private ones, at least in terms of their financial model.

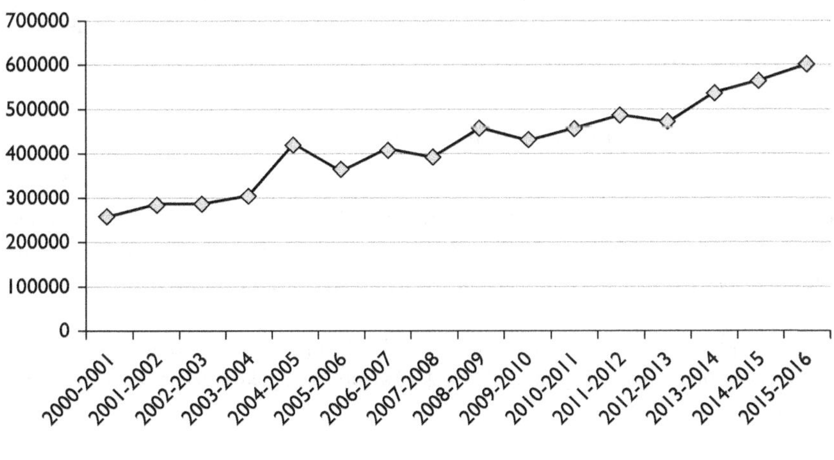

Figure 8.3 The French rugby federation's partnership and media revenue over 15 years (€'000s)

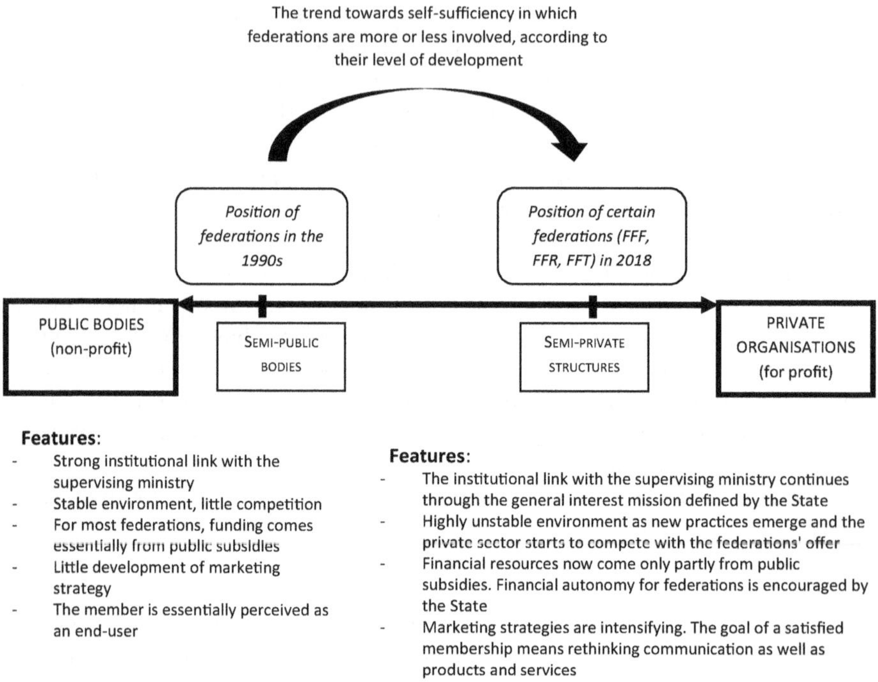

Figure 8.4 The growing self-sufficiency of national sports federations over the last 30 years

Via this process, the sports federations are aiming to be less dependent on State subsidies. It also encourages, given the increasingly competitive environment, policies with the aim of clearer differentiation vis-à-vis other sports, federation-based or otherwise, leading federations to develop their own real brands.

3.2.1 The need to build federation brands

Studies in this field (Kapferer, 1996, 2007; Keller and Lehman, 2006) distinguish between the notions of brand, brand image and brand equity. A brand makes it possible to distinguish the products offered on a market by a producer or a retailer. Article L.711–1 of the Intellectual Property Code specifies that

> *a trademark or service mark is a sign capable of graphic representation to distinguish the goods or services of a natural or legal person. The following, in particular, may constitute such a sign:*
>
> - *denominations in all forms (words, combinations of words, surnames and geographical names, pseudonyms, letters, numerals, abbreviations)*
> - *audible signs (sounds, musical phrases)*

- *figurative signs (devices, labels, seals, selvedges, reliefs, holograms, logos, synthesized images)*
- *shapes, particularly those of a product or its packaging, or those that identify a service*
- *arrangements, combinations or shades of colour.*

Brand image is the way the public perceives this brand, whether it is a person, a company, an organization, or an institution (or their products or commercial brands). Maccioni (1995) refers to a group "*of representations tending to singularise, in the public's view, awareness of a brand [. . .] which is the result of numerous investments (specifically in advertising, marketing, etc.)*".

Finally, brand equity is defined by Aaker (1997) as having five components: Brand loyalty, brand awareness, perceived quality, brand associations and other brand assets. Bayle-Tourtoulou and Dietsch (2002) add that

> *two main components underlie the value of a brand: a tangible component, directly attributable to the physical characteristics of the brand, and an intangible component, a function of both the recorded differences between subjective perceptions and objective measures of the characteristics and all other brand associations.*

Although federations are not private for-profit organizations, these days they draw up multi-year development plans that clearly include a strategic and marketing element. These notions of brand, brand image and brand equity are, therefore, a growing issue for the federations and govern their day-to-day behaviour.

However, these brand-related concepts are better understood in terms of process and strategic focus than as part of a ready-to-use "toolbox". There is, therefore, no exhaustive list of operational measures that can be applied to all federations. On the contrary, building and managing a federation brand[19] means identifying what makes up the federation's DNA, whether in terms of history, members, mindset, the way the sport is played, etc. Developing a brand means bringing together all the elements put in place by the federation that will help to promote the sport and make the public want to try, to progress and to perform: The creation or hosting of an event, using a famous sportsman to add a personal angle, a partnership with a sponsor, the brand's digital strategy, the results obtained by top players, the organization of a tour in Asia or the United States. The power of the brand is an indicator of how attractive the sport is not just to the players but also, indirectly, to advertisers, the media and, more generally, all the partners involved in its development. As part of its brand strategy, a federation must, therefore, work on its objective and tangible features, for example, the federation logo, but also on its subjective and intangible aspects, such as the values associated with the sport and the way the public sees it. In less than 10 years, nearly 15 national federations – cycling, basketball, badminton, swimming, fencing, gymnastics, canoeing, tennis, boxing, handball, ice hockey, taekwondo, sailing, volleyball – have changed their logos, showing a wish to make themselves more attractive.

In addition to the logo, federations must also work to make sure the values associated with their sport are positive ones. That was the reason the Sports and Values survey (OSV) was created in 2000 and has been regularly updated ever since. By questioning a representative sample of the French population, this survey makes it possible to know which values are over- or under-represented for a range of sports, e.g., friendliness, grace, manliness, modernity, daring, sensuality, violence, etc. However, this is only one part of the survey. Respondents also express their views on the sport in general. More specifically, their opinion may vary depending on whether they are asked about amateur, leisure, competitive or televised sport, sports within a federation or a private organization, about self-organized sport or how a sport is offered in France, Europe, abroad, etc. For a federation, working on its brand image is tantamount to working on improving the way it offers sport.

2.3 Market coverage and membership loyalty: The new cornerstones of federation development

The fragmentation of the French sports market as described previously has forced each federation to review its offer in order to better meet different demands. Broadly speaking, until the 1990s, the State-run offer focused on competitive sport, and was built around one idea: that the coaches had the knowledge to improve technical skills and physical ability as well as the individual and group skills likely to improve competition performance. The gradual evolution of demand over the following years led to a reappraisal of that offer. Setting aside the problems linked to high-level sport which remain very specific (the search for performance in competition is a priority), the medium- and long-term strategic focus of the federations in terms of "sport for all" are the following:

- *Develop sport in new areas*: The geographical distribution of a federation's members is never perfect. Some regions are still over-represented compared to others. Although football, horse riding and even athletics provide counter-examples, with members nationwide, it is not the same for other sports. We are not talking here about sports where members' location is explained mainly by factors linked to physical geography (i.e., skiing in the mountains, sailing along the coast). In basketball, for example, the federation has many members in Aquitaine (35,700 in 2017) and the Pays de la Loire (66,071) but few in Franche-Comté (5,139), Champagne-Ardenne (6,572) or Limousin (7,440). The French rowing federation has 30 clubs in Aquitaine, 39 in Brittany, 44 in Ile-de-France but only 16 in Normandy and 8 in Alsace. The most striking example is the French rugby federation whose members are traditionally based in the south of France (although more and more members living north of the Loire, particularly in the Ile-de-France region, are now joining).

- *Appeal to a wider age group*: One of the current challenges facing the sports federations is how to attract members from a wider age group. There are naturally some obstacles linked to the very nature of the activity (gymnastics is more suitable for a young public, whereas golf can be played by older people). Nevertheless, the creation of memberships aimed at a particular age category appears to be an important tool for development. In 2017, the French cycling federation created a "baby bike" membership for 2–4 year olds, priced at €15, while the handball federation has a "first steps" membership offer for 6–9 year olds.
- *Get more women to take part*: In France, men currently represent 63% of the membership of national sports federations (source: Sports Ministry, 2013). Getting more women to play your sport (or, in the case of gymnastics or riding, more men) seems, therefore, to be a source of potential growth for the federations. Indeed, some federations are making it a priority to target women, notably cycling, badminton, table tennis, etc.
- *Develop sport as a leisure activity*: Since demand for sport is no longer focused exclusively on competition, each federation is seeking to increase membership by positioning itself on the leisure pursuits market. This segment is a part of the public that would not normally join a federation but which nevertheless has important potential in view of its regular or even intensive sporting activity. This is the case, for example, for running, swimming, cycling and hiking, which have a large number of followers but few federation members. That is the reason behind the French athletics federation "I like to run" programme, while the karate federation has had some success, especially with women, by offering courses in self-defence techniques. The French basketball federation now provides an introduction to 3x3, a version of the game that did not exist previously in an institutional setting. The federations are also developing a more health-oriented approach. The French athletics federation has offered a "healthy athletics" programme since 2006, the rambling association has had a "healthy hiking" programme since 2009, the triathlon federation signed a partnership in 2014 with the ARC foundation for cancer research, and the swimming federation promotes itself as being "THE healthy sport".

Since membership appears to be one of the main drivers of federation development, they are paying more and more attention to it. In addition to member expectations, federations increasingly want to know how satisfied they are via detailed questionnaires. These studies are also sometimes aimed at former members who have left the federation. This is the case, for example, at the French gymnastics federation, which saw its membership renewal rate fall 2.37% over five years to 53.91% in 2016.[20] The study conducted by the federation in 2017 of 66,000 former members revealed several reasons for non-renewal: Lack of time due to studies or work, a house move, injury, loss of motivation but also disputes with a trainer or other member or too much mental or physical pressure.

Knowledge of these factors will influence both the content of the federation's offer and supervisor training in years to come.

The French volleyball federation faces a similar problem; despite the arrival of 39,000 new members each year, the total membership remains little changed at around 137,000. A study conducted in 2016 among former members highlighted several reasons for leaving: (1) lack of time, (2) a loss of motivation (answers were split between "lack of support during practice", "my friends have left the club" and "no longer feel I'm making progress") and (3) a desire to change from volleyball ("to take up another sport" for 2/3 of respondents, "to switch to playing sport independently" for 17%, "because of a loss of pleasure" for 15%). Here again, the federation will have to take the lessons of the study on board in order to develop its products and its relationship with members to improve satisfaction and limit non-renewal.

The environment sports federations operate in today is more complex than in the 1990s. The sports market is both more open and more fragmented, and this has affected both the business model and the medium- and long-term strategic focus. More varied programmes, detailed knowledge of what motivates members and the search for customer satisfaction have all become key issues.

3 Local and regional authorities: Switching from administrative to strategic management

Everywhere in the world, over the last 30 years or so, regional government has been gaining more autonomy. This trend is often explained by a dual process that is both economic (each territorial level of a country aspires to greater freedom to implement its development project and identify growth drivers) and legislative (especially in countries with an important tradition of centralization, the legislator has been handing over more responsibility and authority to regional bodies in recent decades). This dual process has encouraged communities to move from administrative governance based on the management of a region to strategic governance geared more towards its development. In France, Dubois (2009) has shown how the increasing powers granted to local authorities over the last 30 years highlighted the need for multi-level regional governance, particularly for town and country planning. In the sports sector, this chapter has already shown how local and regional authorities represent an essential cog in the implementation of national policy and in its financing. Dubois also underlined how the municipalities in particular are major players in this respect, coordinating what is available locally in terms of sport and providing support for local clubs. Although decentralization[21] did not originally confer any kind of authority regarding sport on local bodies, it indirectly encouraged them, by granting them greater autonomy,[22] to support the sports sector and to give themselves de facto authority. In addition to decentralization, other laws have helped to highlight the role of local authorities in sport. This is the case, for example, of the laws of July 6, 2000 and December 14, 2004, providing for the creation of a county commission for open spaces, sites and trails (CDESI), thus recognizing the success outdoor sports have had in France as an extension of the structural competence entrusted to the department in 1983 for drawing up the county plan for trails, walks and hikes (PDIPR). But more than the implementation of powers provided for by law, the closer ties between local authorities and sport have been based since the 1990s, but above all, since 2000, on strategic thinking and marketing initiatives. These reflect an increased desire to make the region a brand in its own right. That means the elected representatives act more and more as a strategist reflecting on the DNA of their brand, the assets and opportunities of their region which will provide the basis of its development. In this context, sport appears to many public decision-makers as a relevant method of differentiation. For example, the Pays-de-la-Loire region markets itself as "France's leading sports region".[23]

3.1 The role of sport in building regional brands

3.1.1 Taking a competitive environment into account when designing public development strategies

In France, the speedier transfer of power to local authorities since 2002 has helped to make them more autonomous and to strengthen regional competition. Beyond this legislative and regulatory aspect, there is growing demand for local authorities to help make the region more dynamic, maintaining or even improving wealth, employment, social cohesion and also the region's image along the way. To this end, local authorities have sought to boost the strategic aspect of their action by carrying out a SWOT-type analysis (forces/weaknesses, threats/opportunities) for their region. This automatically means competition between the local authorities, the areas involved and their State overseers. As Planque (1998, p. 23) points out, "*the introduction of the territory is also the fundamental introduction of inter-territorial competition*". This competition acts as a constraint, directly influencing the strategic choices of local decision-makers. To grow, it is not enough to merely become more dynamic or creative than in the past. Overall methods of organizing production and development must be put in place that are at least as effective as those used in other areas. Given this competitive atmosphere, each region therefore tends to position itself in relation to the others. This comparison (benchmark), all the more necessary according to the degree of competition observed, can be articulated around numerous parameters grouped into four major areas: Economic, political, socio-cultural, natural/environmental. Organized in this way, the comparison between areas can be local (vis-à-vis a neighbouring area), regional (between areas of the same region), national (between areas of the same country) or international (between areas belonging to several countries). Obviously, this kind of competition is not unique to France. On the contrary, it is a worldwide phenomenon, as shown by the annual publication of a list ranking the best performing cities.

As a result, in all these countries, local authorities are now organizing their actions in line with increasingly strategic objectives. Portal (2002, p. 231) refers to "*strategic planning as a method that seeks to introduce forms of rationality into public choices based on the definition of objectives and subjecting the determination of means to it*". Based on this, local authorities looking to come up with regional development strategy need to carry out a thorough analysis, both internally (to define the region's strengths and weaknesses) and externally (in order to include the main features of the environment in which the area is located, expressed in terms of threats and opportunities). A table can be drawn up using these four factors, before proceeding to an analysis of strategic alternatives to achieve the objective set by local decision-makers. The challenge is, therefore, to identify, build up and maintain a specific advantage, either comparative or competitive, on which to base medium- and long-term strategy. This comparative advantage encompasses all the characteristics of an organization that enable it to obtain, retain and then increase its share of a particular market: "*The only way to earn money in the medium term is to have something unique and sustainable*" (Jarrilo, 2004, p. 72). Whether in the private or public sphere, the notion of comparative advantage is the foundation of strategic management. It also requires ongoing analysis as the resources on which this advantage is based are not definitive, and so pressure from the surrounding environment can mean it is often temporary in nature. Therefore, the more specific these resources are, the greater the comparative advantage will be. This advantage will be perceived as all the more robust if attempts at imitation by competitors are unsuccessful. Certain regions, following this line of reasoning, therefore strive to build their own know-how and identity, and seek to differentiate themselves.

3.1.2 Key elements of regional brands

Studies (Kotler, Dubois, Keller and Manceau, 2006 – among others) define strategic marketing as "*a tool for choosing the field in which a company will compete (selection of a product/market pair)*". As regards promotion of a region, communication based solely on visuals (posters, leaflets, etc.) have shown their limits. Although it is still used, this type of communication is, for Cohen-Bacrie (2003), generally outdated. Nowadays, it is important to draw up a real marketing strategy likely to ensure the promotion of the community while streamlining the main elements of the communication plan. This marketing strategy may also depend on the resources of the region, its know-how, skills, the wishes of its elected officials, their interests or values.

Several parameters can be used to build up a typology of these strategies and establish a regional (sports) marketing outline. The first, and one of the most important, is the objective. Five main objectives can be defined (see Table 8.5).

As well as the objectives, there is also the question of the best medium to use. The leading one is the name of the region and, aware of its importance, several cities have changed their names in recent years, considering that the original

Table 8.5 The five main strategic objectives of regional marketing

Objective	*Description*
Awareness	Make the region known and increase the probability of it being remembered by the target public. Strategies of this type work primarily in a binary mode: Known vs. unknown. The aim is to make sure that as many people as possible (from the target audience) see the name or logo of the region (either first hand or indirectly) and remember it for as long as possible.
Image	The image corresponds more to the values with which a region wishes to be associated or claims as its own. It is, therefore, no longer simply a question of being known but of developing an image, an identity, with values that are seen as positive (by the target audience). Image strategy can either take the offensive, helping to build an identity, or be defensive, seeking to counter a current image that is either deemed negative or which no longer corresponds to the end goal.
Business and/ or tourism development	This objective is a priority for all local elected officials, who will be judged on their ability to stimulate and maintain local momentum for the creation and development of businesses, as well as the jobs linked to them. This objective also includes the desire to increase the number of tourists coming to the region to discover its most important attractions and who, just by their presence, help to boost the local economy.
Internal communication and the local community	The promotion of a region may be designed to strengthen ties with individuals or groups who are the intended targets of public policy.
Town, country planning	Changing the face of a region through new or modern infrastructure, making it easier for the population to get around day-to-day and providing offices for companies and homes for families.

one did not do it sufficient justice. The second is the logo or emblem. It must convey the region's values while showing what makes it different from others. In the United States, for example, the State of Colorado began a major undertaking in 2013, with the direct involvement of the local population, which led to a change of logo. The new one is supposed to embody the state's main features, in particular the richness and beauty of its natural setting. This leads us to the third key element of regional marketing, namely positioning. Will a given region be identified first as conducive to business development, or recognized more for its natural beauty, or its history, culture or extraordinary architectural heritage?

Within this framework, several regional marketing strategies using sport may be applied, either separately or together. Regional sports marketing was defined by Hautbois and Desbordes (2008, p. 12) as "*the use of sport to build brands and differentiate regions in terms of image, awareness, economic development or civic pride*". Two main elements will be examined here: Building a regional brand through sports tourism (participatory sports) or through sports events (spectator sports).

3.2 Using active sport tourism to boost a region's attractiveness and economic development

The global tourism market is estimated at $1,246 billion.[24] Forecasts for the period 2015–2025 show annual growth of 3.38% to reach 10.5% of global GDP at the end of the period. The sector has grown steadily over the past 30 years. In 2015, France was still the world's leading tourist destination in terms of visitors (84.5 million, +1% compared with 2014) and fourth in terms of associated revenues (€160 billion, or 7.2% of GDP).[25] Tourism accounts for 1.27 million jobs in France and, within this market, sport is an industry in its own right. The gradual emergence since the 1980s of sports tourism therefore offers, in the context of competition between different areas, prospects for differentiation and regional development. Many regions have based their development on providing sports enthusiasts with a natural setting in which to exercise. From this point of view, tourism and region become inseparable (Lozato-Giotart, 2012).

3.2.1 A very fragmented market

Sports tourism can be defined as "*the association of a stay at a destination, enhanced or determined by at least one physical and sporting activity*" (Bouchet and Lebrun, 2009, p. 168). For these authors, there are four main categories, determined by the mix of four criteria: The central or peripheral location of sports services, and whether or not they are open to tourists.

Outdoor sports today account for most of tourists' sports demands, especially when services are centrally located. Since the 1980s, the growing appeal of sport in the great outdoors, whether part of a holiday or not, has been a major trend in all Western societies. For Vigarello (1982), this trend reflects the values that encourage seeking a new relationship with oneself, with others and with nature. Since the 1980s, there have been two sides to this relationship with nature. On the one hand, nature can be wild, extreme and synonymous with adversity (Bessy

Table 8.6 Four main categories of services in sports tourism

Sports services \ *Tourist destination*	*Open to tourists*	*Closed to tourists*
Central	*Classic sports packages*	*Classic sports shops*
Peripheral	*Sports packages in outlying districts*	*Sports shops in outlying districts*

Source: Bouchet and Lebrun (2009)

and Mouton, 2004). This nature is the setting for great expeditions, cross-country rallying and various competitive challenges (the Raid Gauloises, the Marathon des Sables, the Vendée Globe race, etc.). On the other hand, there is also a tamer version of nature, designed to be as accessible as possible. It is this second version that has allowed the sports-tourism market to grow inexorably over the last 30 years.

European retail sports goods revenue in 2014 (€10.2 billion[26]) is a good illustration of this. Germany is the European leader (26% of the total turnover), followed by Ireland and the United Kingdom (13%) and France (12%). In France, Article L311–1 of the Sports Code stipulates that "*outdoor sports are practised in areas or on sites and routes which may include roads, grounds or underground areas in the public or private domain of public authorities or belonging to private owners, as well as State-owned or non-State-owned streams*". France now has 59,000 outdoor sports facilities (19% in Rhône-Alpes-Auvergne, 17% in Midi-Pyrénées-Languedoc-Roussillon[27] and 12% in Aquitaine-Limousin). That makes it, therefore, a European leader in this field, both in terms of equipment purchases and the number of outdoor sports enthusiasts (25 million, 82% of whom are tourists). This outdoor sports market, the main pillar of sports tourism, can be defined according to different typologies. First of all, by type of space:

- Mountainous
- Rural
- Maritime

Then by type of activity:

- *Aerial*: Gliding, parachuting, hang gliding
- *Land-based*: Sand yachts, orienteering, cycling/cycle tourism, hiking, mountaineering, potholing, horse riding, skiing, mountain biking, protected climbing routes
- *Water-based*: Rowing, canoeing, scuba diving, sailing, surfing, waterskiing, fishing.

Finally, and above all, outdoor sports can be defined by the players involved:

- *French outdoor sports federations* and their regional network of affiliated clubs. In 2014, France had 28,012 outdoor sports clubs and 2,483,323 outdoor sports licence-holders, including 689,043 for horse riding, 272,595 for sailing, 224,680 for hiking, 144,357 for diving, 130,393 for skiing and 126,517 for cycle tourism. However, sports tourism is only marginal here because these clubs are mainly aimed at local sportsmen and women, and so this is more the leisure sports field.
- *The regions themselves* via a tourism department, a tourist information office, or a county/regional tourism committee. The institutional role of towns,

counties and regions makes it easier to implement policies for outdoor sports if the local authority considers there is significant potential. As the body in charge of managing and developing the area, the local authority is the natural choice to coordinate all the parties involved in the outdoor sports sector. The challenge is to make it one of the region's strong points, a source of job creation and an integral part of its identity. At the county level, for example, putting the policy in place requires the creation of an open spaces, sites and trails plan (known by its French acronym of PDESI) with the help of the county commission for open spaces, sites and trails (CDESI).[28] In France, in 2015, there were 59 CDESI and 37 PDESI in existence. Loir-et-Cher, with its slogan "Sport through nature" is one example. Another can be found in Creuse, where the town of Guéret has created the outdoor sports resort of Monts-de-Guéret, grouping 26 activity sites. The resort offers courses to both local residents and tourists.

- *Micro-entreprises involved in outdoor sports services*: Either individually or family-owned, these companies are associated with a specific site where they offer one or several kinds of outdoor sports. The heads of these companies and their employees are mostly local residents who want to live and work close to nature. A lot of the companies in this sector are involved in several different activities to try and offset the seasonal nature of customer demand. France has 54,871 outdoor sports teachers: 69% of them are men and 31% women. About 71% are involved in land-based sports, 23% in water-based sports and 4% in aerial sports. Bouhaouala (2000, 2008) identified a classification system for micro-enterprises specializing in sports tourism. The author also drew attention to the "micro-mentality" (based on conceptions, values and objectives), their approach and their management methods.
- *Specialist travel agencies and tour operators*: These are mostly commercial companies offering sporting holidays. They cover a wide range of activities and international destinations and include UCPA, Terre d'Aventure and Nomade. They do not have much of a local presence, as for them, the location is simply where the sport takes place and they are only present for the duration of the stay.
- *Self-organized activities*: This has more to do with a particular type of outdoor sports rather than being a fully fledged provider. Nevertheless, self-organized activities are a major part of the sports-tourism market. The key feature here is the absence of a middle man selling the activity. It needs a local population involved in leisure sports and a more distant customer base looking for tourist and sporting activities. Self-organized activities also tend to have a knock-on effect on the local economy, notably through spending on lodging and meals.

The different providers may have different impacts and have their own strategic role to play in the region, as we can see in Figure 8.5.

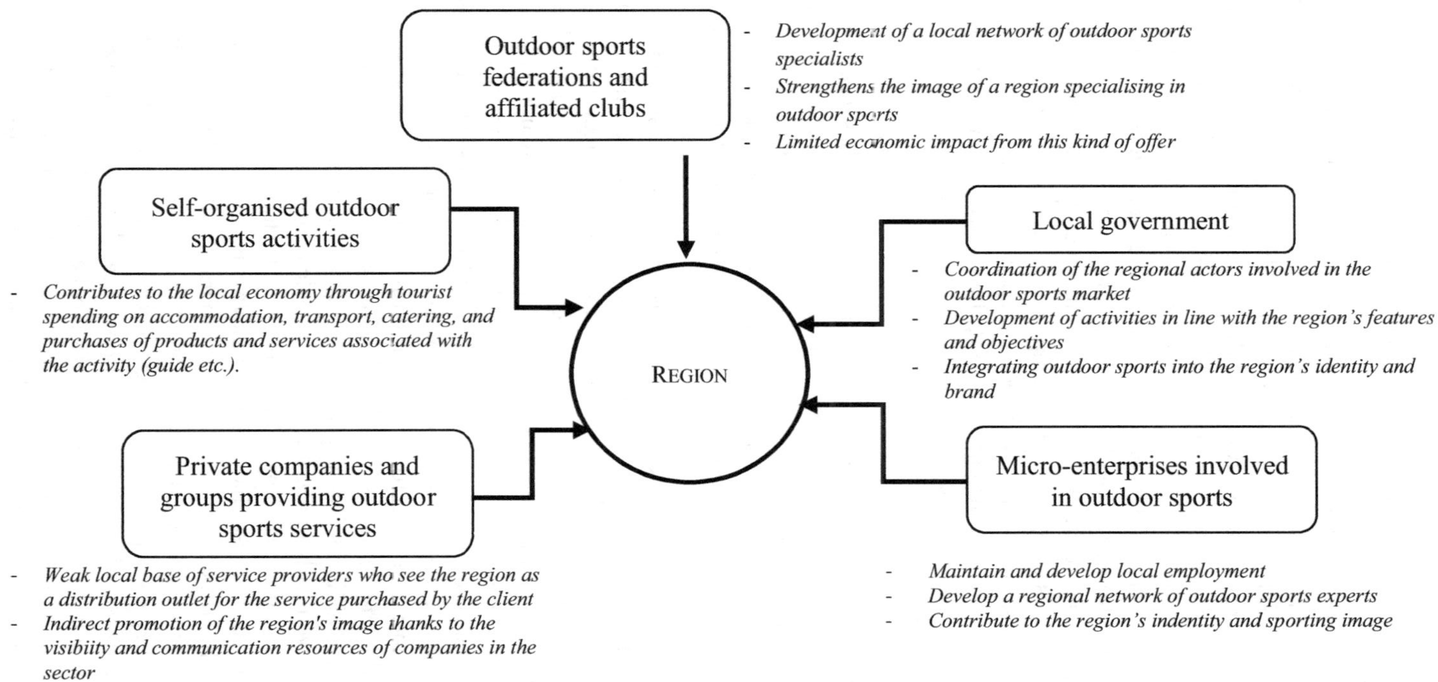

Figure 8.5 The different sports-tourism providers and their impact on the region

Many regions have used outdoor sports to build their brand image, going on to introduce proactive policies to develop and organize sports tourism. One example of this is the project tender for the nature and outdoor activity centres in the Massif Central, aimed at turning the region into a well-known tourist and sports destination. This call for projects is funded by the Massif Central Operational Programme (Feder 2014–2020) and the Massif Contract 2015–2020 which groups together the regions, the State and the counties. The aim is to develop a strategy to make the region more attractive to working people and businesses through quality tourism based on outdoor activities. Practically speaking, the goal is to diversify the clientele, boost business for sports-tourism professionals, make the Massif Central known as a sports-tourism destination and secure jobs in the sector. This is also the strategy employed by regions that depend heavily on sports tourism for their livelihood, such as mountain resorts. In a bid to strengthen their market positioning, prolong the tourist season and widen their customer base, these resorts have diversified. Morzine-Avoriaz and its Portes du Soleil resort is a good example of this. The area offers many outdoor sports during both the winter and summer seasons, ranging from skiing and mountain biking to trail running (www.morzine-avoriaz.com). In fact, the resort has recently started offering running packages (www.morzinemountainrunning.com) based around 10 or so permanent circuits. The same is true for La Plagne, which offers skiing, mountain biking, e-mountain biking, trail running etc. Diversification has thus become one of the main challenges for these regions that are already well established on the sports-tourism market.

The ski resorts are perhaps the longest established sports-tourism regions. Both France and Italy have a long and significant market presence, though smaller countries such as Switzerland, Austria and Norway are also important players.

What this chart does not show is the strong growth the skiing industry has seen in China. Although skiing there started at the end of the 1990s, it is only recently that it has really started to take off in a big way. In 2017, the country had 570 ski resorts[29] (although only 14% had five or more ski lifts) but this figure is increasing ever year.[30] Beijing's winning bid to host the 2022 Olympic Winter Games will attract new money to the sector, with a potential 1,000 resorts and 40 million skier days in the long term (compared with 17 million in 2016). China currently has about seven million skiers, equivalent to 0.5% of the population. The government aims eventually to get 300 million people taking part in winter sports.

From a strategic point of view, ski resorts currently face numerous challenges. Their ability to rise to those challenges will inevitably have an impact on whether these regions that depend so much on sports tourism will be able to develop further. According to a study carried out by Atout France in 2012, 7% of the resorts acknowledge they have problems related to access (lack of eco-friendly public transport, parking problems, lack of shuttle services, little transport available in the summer season, etc.). The same proportion believe they have problems linked to the image, communication and advertising of their resort. Around 6.7% consider their accommodation capacity and diversification to be insufficient, owing to hotel and holiday centre closures and a lack of high-end accommodation, respectively. Some 5.6% consider that their accommodation is looking outdated, and the same percentage complained about insufficient budgets and investment. More broadly, the question is this: Can these resorts remain attractive? They are having to cope with decreasing snow cover, a drop-in customer purchasing power, increased competition from other forms of tourism, the loss of local customers and a decline in foreign (at French resorts) and younger guests.

Box 8.3 Compagnie des Alpes, the world's leading ski report and leisure park operator

For 25 years, La Compagnie des Alpes (in which Caisse des Dépôts et des Consignations has a 40% stake) has been the world's number one ski resort operator. It currently manages 11 of France's largest resorts (Val d'Isère, Tignes, Les Menuires, Méribel, La Plagne, Les Arcs, Les 2 Alpes, Serre-Chevalier, Flaine, Morrillon-Saomens-Six-fer-à-Cheval), a business that generated €409.6 million of revenue in 2015–2106.

Alongside this, in 2002, the company decided to diversify, via the acquisition of Grévin&Cie, into theme and leisure parks (Parc Astérix, Futuroscope, Grévin, Walibi, etc). This branch reported revenue of €301.4 million for 2015–2016. In total, the group reported revenue of €720.2 million that financial year (+4%). It welcomed 22 million visitors at 25 sites, including 13.7 million skier days, and has 4,668 FTE employees.

Now the group's main challenge is to speed up its international growth, with one priority in particular: Gaining access to the Chinese skiing market. This means signing partnerships with local businesses to allow CDA to operate ski facilities and resorts. As part of these alliances, the group would sell a 10–15% stake to its new partners, a prospect which has aroused some concern among politicians in the Rhône-Alpes region.

3.2.2 An increasingly international client base that is proving difficult to retain

Now that sports tourism has become a global business, its customers are also becoming more international. The Americans are the biggest outdoor sports enthusiasts in volume terms. In 2016, 48.4% of the US population aged 6 and over took part in outdoor sports,[31] with 7.4% participating in winter sports, and 14.2% in water sports. This participation rate is inversely proportional to age: 61.8% of the generation born after 2000 took part in outdoor sports, falling to 57.4% for the generation born between 1980 and 1999, 51.4% for those born between 1965 and 1979 and 38% for those born between 1945 and 1964. The player profile is mostly white (70%), with an income of more than $100,000 per year (27%). The main motivations for exercising (70%) are being with friends or family (54%), being fit (51%) and being close to nature (47%).

Specifically with regard to the ski market, the United States, France, Germany and Japan lead the pack with a combined market of 11 million skiers (although the Japanese market seems to be running out of steam). The actors in this market face numerous challenges, one of which is the clear change in demand seen in recent years. The number of skier days continues to decline, along with the average daily skiing time. That means that skiing is no longer visitors' sole motivation and can even be a secondary factor. That in turn means it is necessary to come up with a range of other activities, which may or may not be sports related (e.g., the need to organize après-ski entertainment).

According to a study conducted in 2015 by the French Sports Ministry, one of the peculiarities of outdoor sports and sports tourism is the age range of the participants. You begin at an early age with your family and continue through until late in life with other seniors. For the French, the main motivation is contact with nature (61% consider this to be very important), followed by improved health (58%) and pleasure (56%). There is also a very strong correlation between the level of education and frequency of sporting activity. This also applies to income level: 27% of respondents in the highest income category do not take part in any physical activity, rising to 44% in the lowest income category.

At a local level, sports-tourism resorts conduct studies to come up with an accurate customer profile. This is the case, for example, in the Auvergne region, which carried out just such a study in 2015. It found that 80% of those taking part in outdoor sports over the summer were tourists (with six out of ten taking part in several activities) while 16% were local residents. They generally took part with their families at a site located between 20 and 40 minutes from their place of residence. They were mainly from the Rhône-Alpes and Ile-de-France regions. Their main concern was their safety during the activity. Word of mouth was their primary source of information. Overall, four out of five customers booked their activity in advance, 63% by telephone and 39% less than 2 days before. Clients were generally satisfied with their experience, the facilities and the safety conditions. The main source of dissatisfaction was the price, although 86% planned to return. More generally, Bouchet and Lebrun (2004) believe that sports tourists are looking for three different kinds of experiences: Those related to the self (the quest for performance, for thrills, and for self-discovery), those related to the surrounding space (search for adventure, discovery, authenticity) and those related to others (social interaction, assertiveness).

3.3 Sports tourism as a source of identity, promotion and pride for local residents

The various categories of sport tourism include activities that do not involve taking part in sport on holiday but instead travelling to a foreign city or country to attend sporting events. This is considered, depending on the case, as either passive sports tourism (where the consumer does not take part in the sporting activity itself) or semi-active sports tourism (where consumers are not carrying out the activity but their presence at the event site, their encouragement, their applause and their shouts are all part of the event, making them, in fact, some of the participants, hence the term "ConsumActors"). This way of using sports tourism to promote a region covers several markets: (1) The hosting and/or organization of sports events, (2) the existence of a professional sports team and (3) the presence of key sports or museum facilities, etc.

3.3.1 Sports events as a means of reaching a global audience

One-off sporting events, because they only take place over a few days or weeks, are very intense experiences. This results in a high volume of spectators and often also of media responsible for broadcasting the event. The result is that the host region gets a significant amount of exposure for what is generally considered a positive reason, because of the values and image factors associated with sports events: Joy, passion, celebration,[32] sharing, colours, cheers, etc. The international sporting event is, therefore one of the most sought-after ways as far as politicians are concerned of promoting a region. The Sportcal Institute[33] has a list of more than 30,000 events of all sizes which will be organized between now and 2026 in 200 countries and covering 150 sports. Using sports events in this way is therefore frequently and clearly a core element of regional marketing and communication strategy. So much so that it can develop into a full-blown regional specialization strategy, with the event spearheading the promotion of the region's sporting image and overall development. This approach has been the subject of many studies. Westerbeek, Turner and Ingerson (2002, p. 311) consider that "*increasingly, cities are basing their city marketing efforts around hallmark events in order to maximize the benefits to be achieved from event-driven tourism, sponsorship and media exposure*". Rein and Shields (2007), Heslop, Nadeau and O'Reilly (2013) and Herstein and Berger (2013a) all agree. We can therefore identify the following:

- *Sports events based around a city*: PyeongChang (2018 Winter Olympics), Düsseldorf (the Grand Départ of the 2017 Tour de France), Indianapolis (motor racing), etc.
- *Sports events based around a country*: Russia (2018 World Cup), Japan (2019 Rugby World Cup and 2020 Summer Olympics).

Excluding the size factor, marketing strategies using sporting events come in various different forms:

- *Sporting events organized directly by local players*: In this case, the region provides its own communications platform. This is the case, for example, of the Vendée Globe, a solo non-stop round-the-world yacht race organized by SEM Vendée, a company owned by the Vendée county council (54%), the town of Les Sables d'Olonne (20%), 28 local businesses (18%) and the Pays-de-la-Loire region (8%).

- *Sporting partnerships between different local authorities:* Another option for local government is to form partnerships with those taking part in an event. Thus, Sarthe county council is a partner, in various different ways, of the 24 Hours of Le Mans race.
- *Hosting major sporting events:* The final option is where local authorities apply to host a sporting event "owned" by an institution. This configuration is the best known since it includes most of the major world sporting events, such as the Summer and Winter Olympic Games (International Olympic Committee), the Mediterranean Games (International Committee of the Mediterranean Games), the La Francophonie Games (International Committee of the La Francophonie Games) but also the World Cup (FIFA), the European Football Championships (UEFA) and the World Athletics Championships (IAAF).

From a strategic point of view, Hautbois and Desbordes (2008) have shown that hosting a sporting event, especially an international one, is particularly useful if the aim is to increase awareness of the region, to rally local support for a major project, regional development, local economic spinoffs or to improve its image. For this reason, Russia, host country of the 2018 World Cup, decided to create a specific "signature" for the 11 cities (including St Petersburg, Sochi and Moscow) that hosted matches, blending city emblems with the competition logo. According to a FIFA statement,[34] this is "*unique and familiar imagery created in the style of the Official Look for the 2018 FIFA World Cup™ that will help the cities to show off their cultural values, architecture and natural beauty to the whole world*". The event is thus perceived here as a sounding board for regional brands. Kotler and Gertner (2002) argue that whatever type of event is used, sport is an effective vehicle for creating, influencing, strengthening or changing what people think of a given region. Westerbeek and Linley (2012) believe "*that cities that attract events in order to (re)position their image and build their brand can be likened to corporate sponsors who, for similar reasons, decide to sponsor individuals, organizations or events*". On this point, several studies (Berkowitz, Gjermano, Gomez and Schafer (2007), Preuss and Alfs (2011), Chung and Woo (2011)) have examined the impact the 2008 Olympic Games had on the image of Beijing, China and products made there. Overall, the Olympics had a positive effect on China's image but no impact on that of products made there (which continue to be perceived as lower quality goods). Gibson, Xueqing and Zhang (2008) and Chen and Funk (2010) studied the relationship between a country's image, intentions to visit and the tourist profile. In these studies, respondents had a positive perception of China and the Beijing Olympics, and this image was a good indicator of intentions to visit the country. The same is true for Westerbeek, Turner and Ingerson (2002), who believe that many people choose destinations based on large events organized there. One example that stands out of the link between sporting events, the region's perceived image and plans to visit it, is the Sydney Olympics in 2000. The Tourism Forecasting Council estimated that 1.7 million tourists visited Sydney between 1997 and 2004 as a direct result of the Olympic Games. Thus, alongside the sporting interest of an event, its main strategic advantage for the region is the ability to attract a large number of spectators and television viewers over a limited period (Table 8.7).

Table 8.7 Number of spectators and television viewers for major sporting events

Sporting Event	*Number of Spectators*	*Number of TV viewers*
Rio Olympics (2016)	7 million	2 billion
Euro 2016 (France)	2.4 million	NA
2014 World Cup (Brazil)	3.4 million	3.2 billion
Beijing Olympics (2008)	8 million	4.7 billion
2010 World Cup (South Africa)	3 million	3.2 billion
2011 Rugby World Cup (New Zealand)	600,000	NA

NA: not available

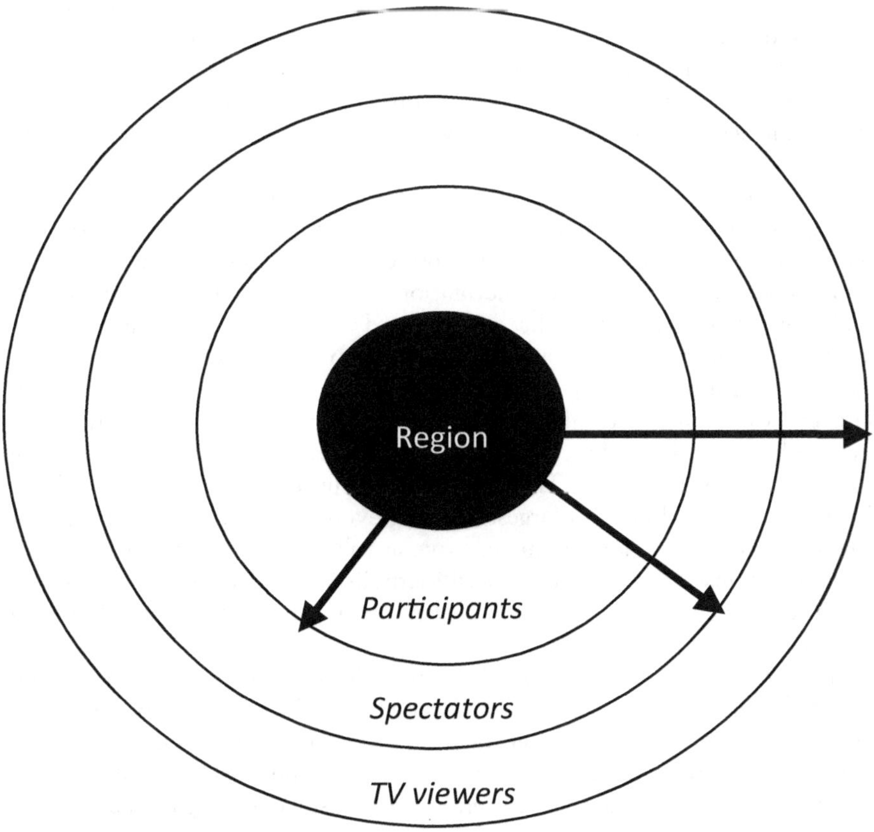

Figure 8.6 The three targets of a major sporting event as potential ambassadors for the regional brand

If the main reason for spectators to come to a region remains the event itself, it is nevertheless an opportunity to discover an unknown city or country in a positive context. These sports tourists can therefore act as ambassadors, spreading a positive word of mouth likely to trigger a virtuous circle of visits and revisits amplified by the use of social media. Media coverage of the event makes it possible to reach television viewers watching the matches but is also an opportunity for items featuring the host country or city. Even if the promotion is done via television, and therefore indirectly, the number of people reached is potentially much greater. For the region, therefore, sporting events are a way of targeting three separate groups: Spectators, television viewers and participants. This last category is in relation to races open to the general public such as marathons (70,000 participants in the New York marathon, 50,000 in Paris) or open cycling races such as the Haute Route (600 finishers for the Alpine stage in 2016) or the Etape du Tour (11,200 finishers in 2016).

There are two specific consumer types in sports tourism. The first organizes his or her own trip, including transportation, accommodation and tickets, allowing him or her to attend the competition of his or her choice. The second goes through an intermediary designing and/or marketing packages. There are, therefore, various sports-tourism agencies offering competing or exclusive offers (where the agency has received exclusive marketing rights for the package from the rights holder[35]).

According to Prebensen (2007), it is important to build up a region's image through sporting events that people either attend in person or watch on television and then talk about to their close circle. He believes that image can be influenced by three types of information: The organic image (learned from books, at school, via the media and by word of mouth), the induced image (resulting from the region's own communication and marketing efforts), and the modified-induced image (based on individual destination experience). This process applies not only to events organized in closed venues (stadiums, arenas) but also those that take place in the streets, i.e., when the sporting event comes to the public. The most striking illustration of this is the Tour de France, the world's third-largest sporting event and a textbook example of how to promote a region via media coverage for an event. The 2016 figures speak for themselves: 2,000 accredited journalists, broadcast in 190 countries, 6,300 hours of coverage, 3.4 million viewers on average on TV channels France 2 and France 3.

In addition, the use of these kinds of strategies to promote a region through sporting events must now increasingly deal with the legacy question. To be successful, the region must prove that the positive effects observed during the event will not give way to negative ones in the months and years that follow. It is, therefore, its legacy in the broadest sense that is at stake. During the 2000s, public opinion became more sensitive over the financing of major sports competitions and their sustainability over time in a difficult economic context and, more precisely, the reuse of expensive sports facilities paid for by taxpayers.

Table 8.8 Examples of packages offered by sports-tourism agencies

Agency	*Event*	*Place*	*Period*	*Price*	*Includes*
Vo2max voyage	The Two Oceans Marathon	Cape Town (South Africa)	April 12–21, 2017	€1,349	Flights and transfers 8 days/5 nights stay Hotel Accompanied by a race guide Hotel-race shuttle Support and assistance
Eventeam	2016 Olympic Games	Rio (Brazil)	August 16–23, 2016	€4,560	Flights and transfers 5 nights in double room Supports and assistance Additional charge for Olympic tickets (from €20 to €426)
Hémisphères Voyages	Formula 1 Grand Prix	Barcelona (Spain)	May 12–14, 2017	€540	Race ticket 3 days/2 nights stay 3* Hotel
Havas Voyages	6 Nations tournament (England-France)	London	February 3–5, 2017	€2,250	Eurostar/flights and transfers London guided tour 4* Hotel Full board Ticket for the match (CAT 1) Support and assistance

The way facilities used for the Olympics in Athens (2004), in Rio (2016) or at certain World Cup stadiums in South Africa (2010) and Brazil (2016) have fallen into disrepair has had a profound impact. Moreover, for Herstein and Berger (2013b), hosting a major sporting event is not enough on its own to rebuild a regional brand. Based on the Barcelona and London cases, the authors believe that a lot of money was spent for what was ultimately a limited result as far as image was concerned.

3.3.2 Professional sports clubs as co-branding partners

Cities around the world have strong relationships with at least one of their local professional sports teams. This is particularly the case in Europe where the way sports are organized means clubs are naturally and permanently attached to their region with, symbolically, its name integrated into that of the club. This is most often a city,[36] as is the case with Marseille where the famous OM is strongly associated with the city and vice versa. This is also true for Barcelona, Manchester, Munich, etc. In North America, the situation is somewhat different because professional clubs have the possibility to change city (*relocation*) or, in the case of new teams (*expansion*) within a branch, to set up where they want. So, although often clubs remain permanently in the same city and forge over time a very strong relationship with the host region, relocation is not that unusual, and the club-region relationship is not a constant in this case. However, there are many examples of very strong links between sports brands (clubs) and local brands: the Yankees and New York,[37] the Bulls and Chicago, the 49ers and San Francisco, the Lakers and Los Angeles, etc. Paradoxically, although noone would deny this relationship between professional sports clubs and their home region exists, few studies have tried to estimate or quantify its impact. Hautbois and Durand (2015), in research on the relationship between France's Ligue 1 football clubs and their home towns, suggested three types of strategy that could be implemented by local decision-makers: Proactive, dormant and follower. For the time being, the data to extend this model to other countries, championships and/or sports is lacking. However, anecdotal evidence suggests the promotion of a region, and thus potentially the creation of regional brands, can be carried out by highlighting a professional sports team or a star player. A few years ago, for example, visitors arriving at Manchester Airport were greeted by a giant photo of the Manchester United team with the slogan: "Welcome to United". In Cleveland in 2016, images of the parade celebrating the Cavaliers NBA title win were broadcast around the world and showed how close this city's links are to its basketball team and star player Lebron James, a native of neighbouring Akron.

In Barcelona, a study carried out in 2016 by Deloitte showed that FC Barcelona welcomed 2.4 million spectators during the 2014–2015 season and that the club alone accounted for 6% of local tourist activity.

3.3.3 Sports facilities and museums as showcases for the region

Stadiums and arenas, indeed all major sports facilities, have always been important symbols, bringing together spectators who have come to watch a show or performance. The sites of today's great sporting events are not that dissimilar to the Colosseum of ancient Rome. The modernization of sports venues and the transition since the 2006 World Cup to so-called fifth-generation stadiums have helped add a new dimension to these facilities, in that their managers now want to turn them into profit centres, not just cost centres (Bal and Badier, 2015; Chanavat and Desbordes, 2015). They have now taken on a life of their own and are no longer considered merely as the stage where the performance takes place. Optimization of both match-day and non-match-day revenue has become all-important. The increase in revenue on non-match days has been particularly helped by the modernity of the facilities built over the past 10 years, by the comfort they offer and above all by their design appeal, which provides them with a strong identity. These days, these grounds must be instantly recognizable, with everyone able, at least in theory, to guess the name of the home team or of the region where they are based. These changes have turned the large stadiums and arenas into places to visit in their own right. This is "sports heritage tourism" or "nostalgia sports tourism". More and more sports tourists ("passive" because they do not participate directly in any sports activity) visit these places, wanting to see the sometimes gigantic infrastructure for themselves, to (re)experience the emotion of being in a place where exceptional performances have taken place, wanting to have "behind-the-scenes" access to these performances and walk in their heroes' footsteps (or even sit in their place in the changing room). This particular market only really concerns the biggest sports facilities. These may be venues specifically associated with a club and hosting all its league matches: Emirates Stadium in London (Arsenal FC), Nou Camp in Barcelona (FC Barcelona), Barclays Center in New York (Brooklyn Nets), AT&T Stadium (formerly Cowboys Stadium) in Dallas (Dallas Cowboys), etc. However, it also covers sports venues that do not have resident clubs: Stade de France, Wembley Stadium, Twickenham, etc.

More and more grounds with a home team are now prolonging these visits by adding a club museum. These are primarily intended to glorify the image and history of a club and to show fans and tourists how unique it is using memorabilia, archive materials and films. They also aim to strengthen the visitor's attachment to this particular sports brand. Nostalgia is the driving force behind the museum offer and also the main motivation for the tourists who visit (Fairley and Gammon, 2005).

Table 8.9 Main sports venues visited worldwide

Venue Name	*City*	*Admission (per adult)*	*Duration of guided tour*
Stade de France	Saint-Denis	€15	90 minutes
Wembley Stadium	London	£20	75 minutes
Emirates Stadium	London	£20	90 minutes
Old Trafford	Manchester	£18	80 minutes
Metlife Stadium	New York	$17	90 minutes

Box 8.4 Presentation of the Liverpool Football Club museum

No visit to Anfield Stadium is complete without a visit to The Liverpool FC Story, the Club's interactive museum. Here, you'll discover over 120 years of LFC history and explore football, past and present, with the help of state-of-the-art technology and never-seen-before displays.

(. . .)

Take a tour through the Halls of Fame and see areas dedicated to stars of the past and present. See all 5 European Trophies, plus loads more silverware that LFC have won in their illustrious career. Fun for all the family with low levels exhibits and fascinating facts from LFC's official mascot, Mighty Red. Have your photo taken in the state-of-the-art photo booth – with a choice of 9 different LFC images to choose from. To enhance your experience every visitor is provided with a multimedia handset with personalized 40-minute commentary by LFC Legend, Phil Thompson, who shares his experience of starting as a fan, becoming a player, then captain, before becoming assistant manager and manager of the world's greatest football family.

It also includes player profiles, videos of your current LFC heroes in action, historic LFC moments as well as awe-inspiring moments featuring LFC's legendary 12th man – the fans. To keep the kids entertained, there're interactive games and activities including "place a penalty" where they can take a penalty at the European Cup final.

Museums can also be based around a sport, rather than a club. This is particularly the case for North America's Halls of Fame (Redmond, 1991; Snyder, 1991).

Table 8.10 Main sports venues visited worldwide

Museum Name	*City*	*Admission (per adult)*	*Created In*
Baseball Hall of Fame	Cooperstown	\$23	1939
Football Hall of Fame	Canton	\$25	1963
Basketball Hall of Fame	Springfield	\$23	1959
Hockey Hall of Fame	Toronto	\$18	1943
Nascar Hall of Fame	Charlotte	\$19.95	2010

Conclusion

As indicated in the introduction, governance is something of a catch-all term and when applied to sport, its scope is no less diverse. The aim of this section was to define clearly what is involved in sports governance. The central role of the State is one of the common denominators in the way the organizations (sports federations and local authorities) studied in these three chapters function. The main change they have faced over the last 30 years has been the state of the market in which they operate, and thus their own market positioning. If their non-market purpose has long allowed them to evolve in a non-competitive environment (even a monopolistic one in the case of the sports federations), they have evolved to become both more complex and more competitive. From the 1980s onwards, these organizations have gradually discovered the notion of competition and the need to identify strategic assets on which to base a medium- and long-term development plan.

Notes

1 Split into 22 million who take part in sport once a week and 25 million who take part less than once a week or once a week but only on holiday.
2 Split between €35.6 million to promote sport for the mass market, €164 million to develop top-level sport, €19.1 million for the use of sport as a preventative measure and protection of athletes and €28 million to promote jobs in sport.
3 Subsequently split by programme: Development of volunteer associations (€25 million), youth and education programmes (€71.4 million), civic service (€385 million).
4 The reorganization of the regions (from 22 to 13) following the NOTRe Act of August 7, 2015, required an overhaul of the federations' regional organization. Thus 19 regional leagues out of 24 had to merge with one or more others. Some leagues, like Brittany and Corsica, were not affected.
5 See Bayeux (2013) on this subject.
6 Their contribution represents about €13 billion of the €36 billion French sports market.
7 In France, for example, the number of licence holders rose from 6 million in the 1960s to 12 million at the end of the 1990s.
8 Notably what have been called "Californian" sports, such as surfing, windsurfing and hang gliding, which are based less on competition and more on fun (Loret, 1995).
9 Many sports-event organizers have caught on to this major trend and the fashion for taking part in sport with colleagues. *Run at Work*, for example, is a 6 km run for businesses in the La Défense district of Paris, followed by a social event to which all participants are invited (source: Run at Work). Other races offer the possibility to run with colleagues. This is the case of La Parisienne, which created its corporate challenge in 2004. In 2016, 665 companies took part with an average of 31 runners per team (source: La Parisienne).
10 Personal trainers can be included in this category.
11 Xerfi study (2016), Sports and fitness centres.
12 This average falls to about €16 million if we exclude the French football federation's budget (€214.2 million in 2015–2016), which artificially inflates the figure.
13 Excluding other investments. Source: French Sports Ministry, Stat-Info, n°16–04, July 2016.

14 In addition to the federation subscription, the customer also usually pays a club membership fee.
15 For example, the French judo federation voted in 2016 to increase the price of membership by €1 (for a forecast gain of €550,000) in order to retain and recruit the federal and administrative staff needed for its development. The French tennis federation's membership fee increased by €2 in 2016, mainly in connection with the expansion of the Roland-Garros stadium. Finally, a few years ago, when the Ryder Cup was only a project, the General Assembly of the French golf federation voted 83% in favour of increasing the membership fee by €3 to finance the bid and then the hosting of this event. The revenue thus obtained (€18 million) covers almost half of the total budget of the Ryder cup (€40 million).
16 For the French volleyball federation, the total State subsidy thus fell from €1,321,189 in 2012 to €1,120,900 in 2014 and has declined by 32% since 2007. Sometimes, the drop in public revenue is not linked to the State subsidy but to that of other public partners, such as other ministries and local authorities. This is the case, for example, at the French athletics federation, which saw a €1,334,000 fall in public funds between 2014 and 2015.
17 73% of the French have a high or very high opinion of sponsorship, and 79% consider it to be essential for top-level sport. (Source: "The general public's view of sponsorship", a survey carried out by Kantarsport February 21–28, 2013 on a representative sample of the French population aged 15 and over.)
18 Although this number gives an indication, it says nothing about the importance and nature (financial, material or otherwise) of their involvement with a given federation.
19 At the French basketball federation, for example, the activities of the marketing department are grouped under the heading "FFBB brand division".
20 Only 54 out of 100 members renewed their subscription in 2016.
21 These include the laws passed March 2, 1982, February 6, 1992, February 4,1995, June 25, 1999, July 12, 1999, Febebruary 27, 2002, the constitutional law of March 28, 2003, the laws of December 16, 2010, January 27, 2014 and August 7, 2015.
22 In France, public authorities benefit from a general provision stipulating that they must first carry out the duties assigned to them but that they may also finance other projects provided they are in the general interest (article L.1111–4 of the law passed on March 2, 1982).
23 Source: www.paysdelaloire.fr/politiques-regionales/sports/.
24 Source: Tourist information monitor, 2017.
25 Source: French Economy Ministry, 2017.
26 Source: EOG.
27 Renamed Occitanie, Pyrénées-Méditerranée in 2016.
28 Entity made up of representatives from local government, government services, public bodies (the National Forestry Commission), the sports sector and associations.
29 There were only 50 in 2000.
30 "Le grand bond en avant du ski en Chine" (Skiing takes a major leap forward in China), *Les Echos*, February 2, 2017.
31 Source: 2016 physical activity council report.
32 For example, the sound of vuvuzelas and the bright colours worn by the supporters are among the lasting impressions of the 2010 World Cup in South Africa.
33 Source: www.sportcal.com.
34 Source: www.fifa.com/worldcup/news/y=2016/m=3/news=2018-fifa-world-cup-russiatm-host-cities-get-their-own-unique-signatur-2769545.html
35 The IOC usually designates one agency per country to market packages for the Olympics.

36 In France, the way territories are organized means that counties or regions can also be associated with a professional sports club, sometimes even forming part of the name: Le Mans Sarthe Basket (basketball), the CA Brive-Corrèze (rugby) or the Beauvais-Oise UC (volleyball).

37 Studies have even shown that, in the past, many people mistakenly thought that the club's logo with its intertwined N and Y was that of the city.

Bibliography

Aaker, J. (1997). Dimensions of brand personality. *Journal of Marketing Research*, 34(3), 347–356.

Arnaud, A.-J. (2015). *La gouvernance, un outil de participation*. LGDJ.

Arnaud, P. (1994). *Les origines du sport ouvrier en Europe*. L'Harmattan.

Australian Sports Commission (2004). *Sport innovation and best practice: governance*. Available online at http://ausport.gov.au/ibp/governance.asp.

Bal, C., Badier, M. (2015). Les stades connectés: pilier du développement marketing des clubs de football ?, in N. Chanavat, M. Desbordes (Eds.), *Marketing du football*. Economica.

Barbusse, B. (1997). *Sport et entreprise: des apports réciproques en matière de gestion des ressources humaines*. PhD thesis from René Descartes University.

Barbusse, B. (2002). Sport et entreprise : des logiques convergentes?, *L'année sociologique*, 52(2), 391–415.

Barget, E., Vailleau, D. (2008). *Management du sport: théories et pratiques*. De Boeck.

Bayeux, P. (2013). *Le sport et les collectivités territoriales*. Ed. Pus.

Bayle, E. (2007). Essai de définition du management des organisations sportives: objet, champ, niveaux d'analyse et spécificités des pratiques managériales. *STAPS*, 1(75), 59–81.

Bayle-Tourtoulou, A.-S., Dietsch, M. (2002). Indicateur de valeur de marque et variables d'offre – Analyse empirique sur données de panel de magasins. *Recherches et Applications en Marketing*, 17(3), 7–20.

Berkowitz, P., Gjermano, G., Gomez, L., Schafer, G. (2007). Brand China: using the 2008 Olympic Games to enhance China's image. *Place Branding and Public Diplomacy*, 3, 164–178.

Bessy, O., Mouton, M. (2004). Du plein air au sport de nature, nouvelles pratiques, nouveaux enjeux, Sports de nature. Evolutions de l'offre et de la demande. *Les Cahiers Espaces*, 81, 13–29.

Bouchet, P., Lebrun, A.-M. (2004). Analyse des stratégies des prestataires de tourisme sportif et propositions de re-enchantement de l'offre, in C. Sobry (Eds.), *Le Tourisme sportif*. Septentrion.

Bouchet, P., Lebrun, A.-M. (2009). *Management du tourisme sportif, de la consommation à la commercialisation*. PUR.

Bouhaouala, M. (2000). Petites entreprises et territoire. Le cas du secteur du tourisme sportif dans le Vercors. *Montagnes Méditerranéennes*, 11, 6–12.

Bouhaouala, M. (2008). *Management de la petite entreprise des loisirs sportifs. Une approche socioéconomique*. De Boeck.

Burlot, F. (1997). *Le sport en entreprise, un outil de cohésion interne. Enjeux identitaires et mécanismes idéologiques*. PhD thesis from Paris-XI University.

Burlot, F. (2000). Le sport en entreprise: un vecteur de communication interne. *STAPS*, 53, 65–77.

Callède, J.-P. (2000). *Les politiques sportives en France. Éléments de sociologie historique*. Économica.

Chanavat, N., Desbordes, M. (2015). Le parc multifonctionnel olympique lyonnais et le grand stade, au cœur de la stratégie marketing du groupe OL, in N. Chanavat, M. Desbordes (Eds), *Marketing du football*. Economica.

Chen, N., Funk, D. (2010). Exploring destination image, experience and revisit intention: a comparison of sport and non-sport tourist perceptions. *Journal of Sport Tourism*, 15(3), 239–259.

Chung, W., Woo, C.W. (2011). The effects of hosting an international event on country image: the 2008 Summer Olympics case. *International Journal of Sports Marketing & Sponsorship*, 12(4), 281–300.

Clement, J.-P., Defrance, J., Pociello, C. (1994). *Sport et pouvoirs au XXème siècle*. PUG.

Cohen-Bacrie, B (2003). *Territoires en promotion*. Weka.

Dubois, J. (2009). *Les politiques publiques territoriales. La gouvernance multi-niveaux face aux défis de l'aménagement*. PUR

European Commission (2010). *Sport et activités physiques*. Eurobaromètre 334.

Fairley, S., Gammon, S. (2005). Something lived, something learned: nostalgia's expanding role in sport tourism. *Sport in Society*, 8(2), 182–197.

Fourre, C. (1999). *Mise en scène de la métaphore sportive dans la formation professionnelle. L'exemple des stages "outdoor" organisés pour les cadres d'entreprise*. PhD thesis from Université Paul Sabatier, Toulouse

Gibson, H., Xueqing, C.Q., Zhang, J.J. (2008). Destination image and intent to visit China and the 2008 Beijing Olympic Games. *Journal of Sport Management*, 22, 427–450.

Hautbois, C., Desbordes, M. (2008). *Sport et marketing public*. Economica.

Hautbois, C. (2014). *Le marketing des fédérations sportives*. Economica.

Hautbois, C., Durand, C. (2015). Les territoires et leurs clubs de football professionnels : comment concilier, pour le manager public, marque sportive et marque territoriale. *Politiques et Management Public*, 32(4), 347–366.

Herstein, R., Berger, R. (2013a). Hosting the Olympics: a city's make-or-break impression. *Journal of Business Strategy*, 34(5), 54–59.

Herstein, R., Berger, R. (2013b). Much more than sports: sports events as stimuli for city re-branding. *Journal of Business Strategy*, 34(2), 38–44.

Heslop, L.A., Nadeau, J., O'Reilly, R. (2013). Mega-event and country co-branding: image shifts, transfers and reputational impacts. *Corporate Reputation Review*, 16, 7–33

Honta, M. (2010). *Gouverner le sport: action publique et territoires*. PUG.

Hoye, R., Cuskelly, G. (2007). *Sport governance*. Routledge.

Hums, M.A., Maclean, J., Zintz, T. (2011). *La gouvernance au cœur des politiques des organiations sportives*. De Boeck.

Hurd, A., Anderson, D.M. (2011). *The Park and recreation professional's handbook*. Human Kinetics.

Kapferer, J.N. (1996). *Les marques: capital de l'entreprise*. Ed. d'organisation.

Kapferer, J.-N. (2007). *The new strategic brand management*. Kogan Page.

Keller, K.L., Lehmann, D.R. (2006). Brands and branding: research findings and future priorities. *Marketing Science*, 25(6), 740–760.

King, N. (2017). *Sport governance: an introduction*. Routledge.

Kotler, P., Gertner, D. (2002). Country as brand, product and beyond: a place marketing and brand management perspective. *Brand Management*, 9(4/5), 249–261.

Kotler, P., Dubois, B., Keller, K., Manceau, D. (2006), Marketing management. Pearson.

Jarrilo, J.C. (2004). *La logique stratégique*. Dunod.

Loret, A. (1995). *Génération glisse*. Autrement.

Lozato-Giotard, J.-P. (2012). *Management du tourisme, territoires, offres et stratégies*. Pearson.

Maccioni, H. (1995). *L'image de marque*. Economica.

Marshall, A. (1890). *Principes d'économie politique, livre IV*. French translation (1906). Ed. V. Giard et Brière.

Mignon, P. (2015). La pratique sportive en France: évolutions, structuration et nouvelles tendances. *Informations sociales*, 187(1), 10–13.

Pasquier, R., Simoulin, V., Weisbein, J. (2007). *La gouvernance territoriale : pratiques, discours et théories*. LGDJ

Pearce, J.A., Robinson, R.B. (2007). *Strategic management: formulation, implementation and control*. Irwin/McGraw-Hill

Pierre, J. (2009). *S'investir corps et âme en entreprise. Contribution à une sociologie de la mobilisation des cadres par le sport*. PhD thesis from Université Marc Bloch, Strasbourg.

Pierre, J. (2015). *Le sport en entreprise*. Economica.

Pigou, A. (1920). *The economics of welfare*. MacMillan and co.

Planque, B. (1998). Le développement local dans la mondialisation, in M-U Proulx (Ed.), *Territoires et développement économique*. L'Harmattan, pp. 5–23.

Portal, E. (2002). *La planification stratégique dans les collectivités territoriales françaises: analyse empirique et essai de typologie*. LGDJ.

Prebensen, N.K. (2007). Investing in an event. The case of a sledge dog race in Norway "The Finnmarkslopet". *Event Management*, 11(3), 99–108.

Preuss, H., Alfs, C. (2011). Signaling through the 2008 Beijing Olympics, using mega sport events to change the perception and image of the host. *European Sport Management Quarterly*, 11(1), 55–71.

Redmond, G. (1991). Changing styles of sports tourism: industry/consumer interactions in Canada, the USA and Europe, in M.T. Sinclair, M.J. Stabler (Eds.), *The tourism industry: an international analysis*. CAB international, pp. 107–120.

Rein, I., Shields, B. (2007). Place branding sports: Strategies for differentiating emerging, transitional, negatively viewed and newly industrialised nations. *Place Branding and Public Diplomacy*, 3(1), 73–85.

Snyder, E.E. (1991). Sociology of nostalgia: sport halls of fame and museums in America. *Sociology of Sport Journal*, 8, 228–238.

Standeven, J., de Knop, P. (1999). *Sport tourism*. Champaign.

Vailleau, D. (2008). *Management du sport: théories et pratiques*. De Boeck.

Vigarello, G. (1982). Le corps . . . entre illusions et savoirs. *Esprit*, February.

Westerbeek, H.M., Turner, P., Ingerson, L. (2002). Key success factors in bidding for hallmark sporting events. *International Marketing Review*, 19(2/3), 303–322.

Westerbeek, H.M., Linley, M. (2012). Building city brands through sport events: theoretical and empirical perspectives. *Journal of Brand Strategy*, 1(2), 193–205.

Chapter 9

The governance of sports federations

Current challenges in an international context

Thierry Zintz, Mathieu Winand and Simon Gérard

Introduction

A discussion about the current challenges facing sports federations governance in an international context is appropriate for two reasons.

The history of modern sports can be divided into two successive periods.

In 1896, from the time of the first Olympic Games of the modern era and until the last years of the 20th century, international and national sports federations developed in a monopolistic environment in which competition from alternative players was virtually non-existent in the sports market. As a result, the federations implemented managerial and governance practices which were not based on qualitative standards validated by society. In the absence of competition in the sports market, they had no reason to implement rules to ensure the quality of the services provided, the transparency of their decisions or their financial flows and were under no obligation to report extensively to other stakeholders of society. At least, this is what they believed!

At the start of the 21st century, the monetizing of sports and the increasing number of new alternative players challenged the monopolies. Traditional managerial and governance practices, confronted with new qualitative requirements from society, revealed their limitations and their excesses and the sports federations were required to implement "good" governance practices.

The second reason for investigating these challenges resides in the fact that the excesses discovered had led to violations, punishable in some instances, which justified the involvement of the public authorities, particularly the judiciary, in the governance of sports federations.

Note that the creation of the World Anti-Doping Agency in 1999 was the result of governments coming to the conclusion that the sports world could not manage the doping issue on its own. Beyond imposing disciplinary sanctions on doping athletes, the sports world was incapable of managing the criminal aspect of the activities of doping product suppliers. Today, the practices of illegal betting, match fixing and money laundering are raising the same questions about the ability of the sports world to manage these issues alone.

The question of the "good" governance of sports federations arises in the context of respect for the autonomy of the sports movement within a legal framework. The national framework is narrow in a globalized and digitized society and an international perspective is required.

This chapter will therefore first analyze the organizational systems of sports in Europe and the world.

It will then review the governance of national and international federations given that it includes the main challenges with which they are confronted in terms of strategic development, the management of external threats, and positioning in the sports ecosystem.

An analysis of the way in which the federations manage the emergence of competition from sports which are either self-organizing or supervised by private sports organizations will close out the chapter.

1 The organizational systems of sports in Europe and the world

Pieron and De Knop (2000) point out that the growing popularity of sports has justified the creation of structures to provide supervision via rules and to manage the schedules of sports events. This is how the modern sports movement was born: It grew out of the need to regulate sports to enable the organization of sports competitions, first on a national then on an international basis.

International sports competitions and the creation of universal rules for sports resulted in the need for harmonization between countries. This in turn led to the creation of supranational sports institutions such as the International Olympic Committee (IOC) and international sports federations. We should also note the development of institutions which provide an interface with public and private organizations at the continental level. The IOC, responsible for the organization of the Olympic Games as we know them today, is the emblematic representative of the world sports movement. This global sports system has created a generalized network of sports activities around the world and provides it with relatively strong supervision (Zintz and Camy 2005). In addition, world sports institutions see themselves as the guarantors of sports values, of sports rules and of sportsmanship in general. National dissemination of the rules and values is done via associations in each country, that is, the national sports federations and national Olympic committees.

International sports consist of three elements. First, the Olympic and sports movement consisting of sports organizations such as the international sports federations (IF) and the IOC. Second, the public authorities. Third, the regulatory bodies, including the Court of Arbitration for Sport (CAS) and the World Anti-Doping Agency (WADA). These organizations influence the practice of athletes at all levels.

Other organizations, indirectly tied to sports, also have a significant impact on the activities of athletes and their representative organizations. They are, on the one hand, associations of commercial companies which produce sports goods and equipment (for example, the World Federation of the Sporting Goods Industry, WFSGI, and the Federation of the European Sporting goods Industry, FESI) or sponsors (European Sponsorship Association, ESA), or advertising agencies (World Federation of Advertisers, WFA) and, on the other, the International Chamber of Commerce (ICC) and its European, national and regional counterparts, which regulate and provide information about commercial transactions.

Some key organizations of the world sports movement, as well as the sports policy of the European Union, which we consider to be an emerging stakeholder in sports at the European level, have a major impact on sports policy at the national level.

1.1 The Olympic movement

The modern international Olympic movement was born in June 1894, at the initiative of Baron Pierre de Coubertin during the Olympic Congress in Paris, and of the creation, on June 23, 1894, of the International Olympic Committee (IOC).

The IOC, headquartered in Lausanne (Switzerland), is the governing body of the Olympic movement which consists of the IOC, the international sports federations and the national Olympic committees. It also includes the organizing committees for the Olympic Games (OCOG), all of the athletes, officials, referees, judges and trainers who are governed by the Olympic Charter and, broadly speaking, the national sports federations (NSF), the sports associations and the recognized sports clubs.

The IOC is one of the oldest international non-governmental organizations (Zakus and Skinner, 2008). As soon as it was created, and with the publication of the first Olympic Charter in 1908, the IOC was already dictating the practices and principles of the global sports organization.

The economic impact of the IOC must also be highlighted. Thanks to its marketing programme (TOP Programme), revenue from television rights, the sale of seats for the Olympic Games and the commercial licences it granted, the IOC collected USD 8,046,000,000 during the 2009–2012 Olympiad (Olympic Marketing Fact File, 2016). It distributed 90% to the national Olympic committees, international federations and Olympic Games organizing committees. In the case of some national Olympic committees and of certain international federations, the IOC's contribution accounts for over 50% of resources for the Olympiad.

The IOC is one of the rare modern institutions, together with the international sports federations, to have a presence in nearly every recognized country and nation in the world.[1] The IOC, through its 206 national Olympic committees (NOC),[2] and the international sports federations, via their national sports federations, ensure the worldwide dissemination of sports and Olympic values and of ethical and good governance principles and ensure the international standardization of sports' disciplines.

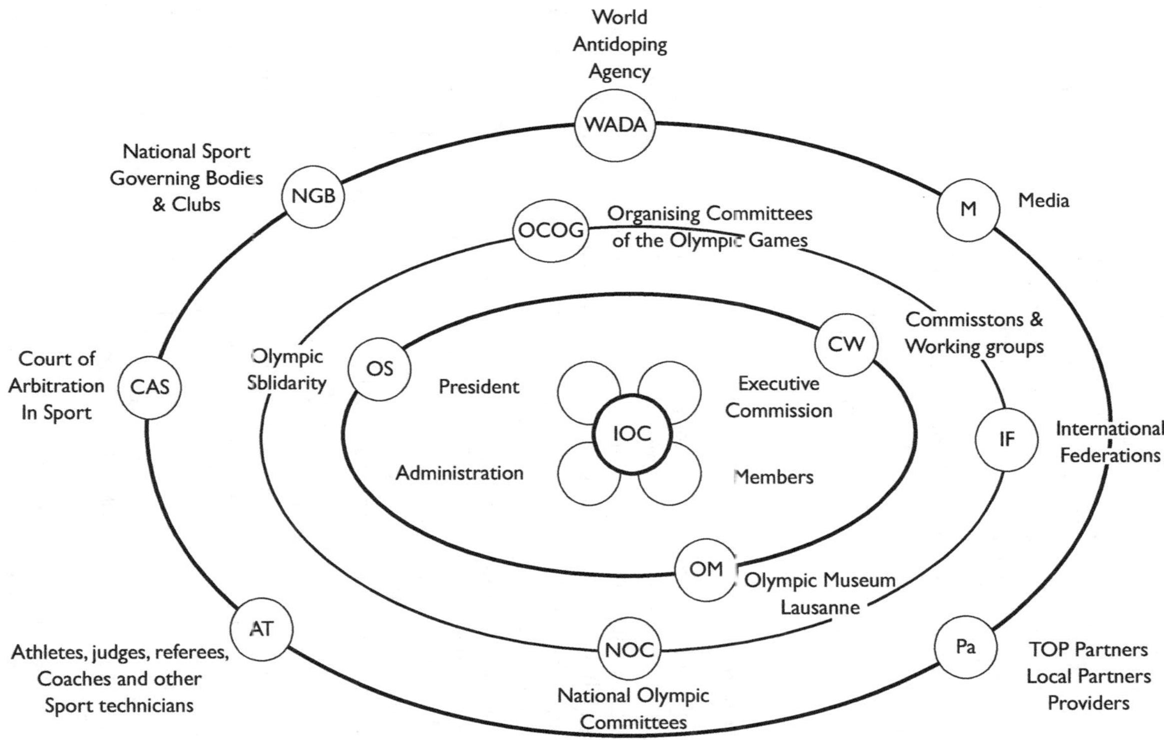

Figure 9.1 The Olympic system

Source: According to Chappelet, adapted by the authors from Robinson and Camy (2008)

The purpose of the NOCs is to disseminate the fundamental Olympic principles, contained in the Olympic Charter, in their respective countries. They oversee the preparation and selection of elite athletes for the Olympic Games and, more broadly, the development of sports for all and of high-level sports. When applicable, the NOCs also play a role in selecting a candidate city in their country to hold the Olympic Games. The 206 NOCs recognized by the IOC are all members of the Association of National Olympic Committees (ANOC). They are present on the five continents under the aegis of continental associations. On the European continent, these are the European Olympic Committees (EOC), which consist of 50 NOCs.

Note that, with respect to these Olympic organizations (IOC, EOC and NOC), similar organizations have also developed for the paralympics: The International Paralympic Committee (IPC), the European Paralympic Committee (EPC) and the National Paralympic Committees (NPCs), which are all part of the global Olympic movement.

1.2 The international sports federations

The international sports federations are part of the Olympic movement. These international non-governmental organizations ensure the integrity of the sports disciplines which they are responsible for and guarantee the legality of sports competitions. They are independent and autonomous with respect to the IOC in the administration of their sports discipline. As a result, they are responsible for the development of the rules of their sports discipline.

However, as stated earlier about the economic power of the IOC, this independence must be put in perspective. To be recognized by the IOC, their by-laws, practices and activities must conform to the Olympic Charter. In addition, international federations whose sport is on the Olympic Games programme benefit from significant financial support from the IOC, via the intermediary of Olympic Solidarity.[3] The international federations are members of a primary association which, in 2017, was renamed the Global Association of International Sport Federations (GAISF) (formerly, the General Association of International Sports Federations, GAISF, then SportAccord), but also of secondary associations based on the categorization of their sport and the type of recognition granted to them by the IOC: The Association of Summer Olympic International Federations (ASOIF), the Association of International Olympic Winter Sports Federations (AIOWF) and the Association of IOC Recognised International Sports Federations (ARISF).

The role of the international sports federations is to ensure the development of their sport at the global level and to contribute to achieving the goals set in the Olympic Charter. Therefore, their mission is to establish and update the rules of each sports discipline they are responsible for and to ensure their application by all participants with the support of their continental and national counterparts. Note that the international sports federations are also responsible for establishing criteria for admission to the events of the Olympic Games in accordance with the Olympic Charter and for submitting them for approval to the IOC. Moreover, they are also responsible for the supervision and technical management of their sport during international competitions such as the Olympic Games and the World Championships.

The national sports federations (NSF) are the national counterparts of the international sports federations. Their role is to ensure that the rules of the sports disciplines they promote in their countries are obeyed, to advertise the disciplines and to represent them and the participating athletes.[4] They provide a number of services of interest for the clubs and individual members, in exchange for a fee (Pieron and De Knop, 2000).

1.3 UNESCO and WHO

Two United Nations (UN) organizations are particularly involved in sports activities. They are the World Health Organisation (WHO), which is responsible for sports and health and the United Nations Organisation for Education, Science and Culture (UNESCO), which is responsible for sports and culture.

WHO defines health as "*a state of complete physical, mental, and social wellbeing, and not merely the absence of disease or infirmity*".[5] "Recognising the unique opportunity that exists to formulate and implement an effective strategy for substantially reducing deaths and the disease burden worldwide by improving diet and promoting physical activity, WHO adopted, in May 2004, the 'Global Strategy on Diet, Physical Activity and Health'".

Beginning in 1975, UNESCO showed an active interest in "sports for all", primarily by organizing conferences of sports ministers. In 1978, it adopted the International Charter of Physical Education and Sport which has important implications for everyone responsible for sports. It emphasizes that

> *Every human being has a fundamental right of access to physical education and sport, which are essential for the full development of his personality. The freedom to develop physical, intellectual and moral powers through physical education and sport must be guaranteed both within the educational system and in other aspects of social life.*
>
> (Article 1.)

UNESCO founded two non-governmental organizations to promote actions in favour of physical education and sports: On the one hand, the International Council of Sport Science and Physical Education (ICSSPE), which is intended to investigate for a better scientific understanding of all facets of human movement, to educate people for a better quality of life and improved health and to advocate for the benefits of an active lifestyle and the ethical values inherent in sports. And, on the other hand, the International Council for Health, Physical Education, Recreation, Sport and Dance (ICHPER), which is intended to develop and promote high standards of professional practice, research and education in these areas.

UNESCO has signed several resolutions with the IOC to promote a reduction in inequalities between the North and the South in sports. In addition, a declaration on the promotion of the Olympic Truce (a period of peace which must be complied with by the nations of the world during the Olympic Games) binds the UN and the IOC. The UN also created the Office on Sport for Development and Peace. The latter was closed in 2017 and the task of using sports as a means to promote development and peace is now an IOC responsibility, part of its strategic vision.

1.4 The regulatory bodies of international sports

Although the international and national sports organizations are the guarantors of sports rules and ensure that they are obeyed, subject to disciplinary sanctions, some disputes between sports bodies and/or athletes can require that independent organizations take a stand. These are the regulatory bodies of international sports. The institutions are, primarily, the Court of Arbitration for Sport (CAS) and the World Anti-Doping Agency (WADA). The latter intervenes via its national anti-doping organisations (NADO) and its regional offices. These organizations ensure the application of sports and related rules.

WADA is a Swiss private-law foundation created in 1999. Its goal is to promote, coordinate and monitor the fight against doping in sports in all its forms at the international level. To accomplish this, it created the World Anti-Doping Code on March 5, 2003 with the approval of the Olympic movement and the representatives of 80 countries. It took effect on January 1, 2004. The Code, which is constantly being updated, provides the regulatory framework for the fight against doping and for related education. WADA's activities are focused on a global approach to doping including monitoring compliance with the Code and the coordination of regional anti-doping organizations (or offices). It is also involved in research, education and awareness-raising for athletes. WADA encourages governments to ratify UNESCO's International Convention against Doping in Sport, which enables greater international harmonization of anti-doping legislation and rules. WADA works with its regional offices, including the European Regional Office, and the national anti-doping agencies to promote the fight against doping in their territories.

The CAS is an independent institution founded in 1984 which is responsible for deciding sports-related disputes. The disputes are strictly of a contractual or disciplinary nature (notably related to doping) and involve athletes, clubs, sports federations, the organizers of sports events, sponsors, etc. The CAS has nearly 300 arbitrators from 80 countries who specialize in sports arbitration and law.

Sports-related legal disputes have led to the development of global sports law, a *lex sportiva*, i.e., autonomous transnational rules and norms from private sports organizations such as international sports federations or the IOC which bind, via either tacit or formal contracts, those they apply to (for example, athletes, trainers and sports teams) (Siekmann and Soek, 2010). It should, however, be noted that the legal imprecision surrounding the concept of *lex sportiva* and its interpretation by legal and sports bodies has opened the door to several legal proceedings and appeals (which have received significant media coverage) by athletes who were sanctioned with heavy fines and, sometimes, with exclusion from their sport, for breaches of sports rules. Sanctions for doping are an example of this, as are the affairs related to match fixing. These affairs can also result in criminal sanctions depending on the seriousness of the accusations and the norms in effect in each country in question.

There is, therefore a specific regulatory and sanctions system in place for sports. However, the system has been challenged several times in appeals before the European civil courts by athletes and organizations who believed that they had been wronged. With the advent of the economic dimension in sports, these appeals are no longer limited to the CAS. They have moved beyond the sports world and are debated and ruled on by the European high courts (such as the Court of Justice of the European Union), based on the argument that sports has become more of an economic activity than a recreational one.

1.5 European sports policy

Although for a long time the European Union wasn't in a position to develop a legal policy specific to sports, many European policies have had an indirect impact on sports given that it is considered to be an economic activity.

The Court of Justice of the European Union (CJEU, formerly the Court of Justice of the European Communities) has been called upon to rule on several well-known affairs on last appeal including the Bosman (1995[6]), Deliège (2000[7]) and Meca-Medina (2006[8]) affairs. A number of appeals have been based on the principle of free movement of workers as it is defended by European Union authorities. This rule had been challenged by certain decisions taken within sports organizations. In each case, the CJUE confirmed that sport is governed by community law given that it is an economic activity. When this dimension does not have to be taken into account, the sports bodies are the only ones responsible for the organization of sports via the rules they implement. This application of European law to sports was deemed a "proportionate" application by the Court of Justice of the European Union.[9] The CJUE's decisions in the area of sports, particularly with respect to the Bosman affair, led the sports organizations to review their rules, but also confirmed the legitimacy of sports rules and the specificity of sports.

With the ratification of the Treaty on the Functioning of the European Union (Lisbon Treaty) in 2009, the European Union formally entrusted itself with competence for sports matters. Article 165 of the Treaty provides a legal framework for the promotion of sports at the European level and takes account of the specific nature of sport, its structures based on voluntary activity and its social and educational function.

The problems currently shaking the sports world, that is, doping and its related sanctions, the fraudulent sports betting associated with match fixing, and money laundering are condemned by the European Union. On the contrary, it supports the regulatory bodies. However, the wording of Article 165 of the Treaty is vague and leaves it wide open to interpretation.

According to the European Commission's "White Paper on Sport" (2007), the specificity of sports can be understood as meaning specific sports rules and activities (for example, limitations on the number of participants in competitions, separate competitions for men and women, the need to ensure uncertainty concerning outcomes and to preserve a competitive balance between clubs taking part in the same competitions) and specific sports organizations (autonomy and diversity of sports organizations, a pyramid structure of competitions from grassroots to elite level, solidarity mechanisms between the different levels, the organization of sport on a national basis, and the principle of a single federation per sport). These points raised and acknowledged by the European authorities are of fundamental importance for the sports movement given that they provide it with the legitimate autonomy to organize sports at different levels. This autonomy is, however, reviewed on a case-by-case basis. For example, it is restricted when the sport is an economic activity subject to EU law.

The European Union has, therefore, become an important player in international sports for all of the member countries. Nevertheless, the European Union does not intend to harmonize sports legislation and rules in member countries. Article 165 of the Lisbon Treaty explicitly excludes this scenario.

1.6 National sports systems

National sports systems are systems which operate within each country and encompass both the sports dimensions (NOC, national sports federations, sports clubs, etc.) and the legal dimensions (government, ministry of sports, etc.). They also include a cultural dimension specific to each country which reflects the way in which the general public, and particularly people working in the sports field, perceive sports and physical activity in general and each sport in particular.

The national sports bodies must respect the sports culture and national rules while conforming to the standards and rules of international sports bodies. Thus, a national sports federation must both meet the expectations of its members and internal (that is, volunteers and employees) and external (i.e., sponsors and regulatory bodies) stakeholders, comply with national regulations (legislation and ministry of sports) and with the sports rules of the NOC and of its international supervisory sports federation. However, while international standards and rules are essential for guaranteeing the international harmony of sports disciplines, they can also potentially conflict with national regulations.

All of the organizations must, therefore, act in harmony and for the benefit of sports. As stated by the IOC, athletes must be at the heart of the system. This challenge requires high-quality governance which some call "good governance".

In addition, in parallel with the growing complexity of organizing sports at the national and international levels and of its commercialization and the related interests, there is a need for greater clarity regarding the responsibilities of the organizations and individuals that organize both elite and amateur sports, guarantee sportsmanship and their values and, therefore, their governance.

In this section of the chapter, we define the governance of sports federations and the challenges it entails.

2 Governance issues

2.1 Conceptual approach

There is no single definition of good governance. Chhotray and Stoker (2009, p. 2015) attempted one, suggesting that

> *governance is about the rules of collective decision-making in settings where there are a plurality of actors or organisations and where no formal control system can dictate the terms of the relationship between these actors and organisations. (. . .) The construction of governance regimes matters to the well-being of our societies. (. . .) The processes of governance then demand to be understood analytically and empirically as a set of practices, rather than through the lens of a 'wish-list' of principles to be followed.*

Governance must, therefore, be implemented in all areas of society. It focuses on the quality of the rules, processes and practices of collective decision-making. Governance must continuously improve, given that good governance is not a state but aims to achieve effective implementation.

Good governance is increasingly becoming a central issue for sports organizations, at every level (Siekmann and Soek, 2010; Henry and Lee, 2004; Shilbury and Ferkins, 2011; German Olympic Sports Confederation, 2015). There are many possible reasons for this trend, including the pressure resulting from the need to use public funds appropriately and the responsibilities of sports organizations with respect to their sports and external stakeholders.

> *Since the middle of the 1990s, ideas have evolved at every level of society – particularly in the corporate and political worlds. Illegal acts have always been sanctioned, although some have not been emphasised as much because the societal damage they caused was not (yet) recognised.*
>
> (German Olympic Sports Confederation – DOSB, 2015, p. 3)

The DOSB (2015) also pointed out that "*rightly, the perception of what society deems to be acceptable has evolved*". Therefore, today, the simple assumption that a decision could have been unduly influenced appears to be problematic.

Invitations to dinners or to events have been targeted and friendly gifts between business partners have become atypical.

Halleux (2017, p. 4) believes that

> *some consider that the governance practices of international sports' governing bodies have not kept pace with evolutions in sport, notably the huge commercial growth of the sector and the increasing financial stakes concerned, which, as recent high-profile cases demonstrate, can create fertile ground for corrupt practices.*

In addition, events demonstrate that investing in good governance enables an organization to implement appropriate ethical behaviour, be governed effectively, be better prepared to handle risks and reach its goals more effectively (Winand, Rihoux, Qualizza, and Zintz, 2011; Zintz and Vailleau, 2008).

2.2 A stakeholder approach

As stated previously, our approach focuses on the relationships which bind European and international stakeholders to the principles of good governance in sports organizations.

The European Olympic Committees (EOC) and the Fédération Internationale de l'Automobile (FIA) organized a conference called "The Rules of the Game" in February 2001. In 2001, Jacques Rogge, who was the President of the European Olympic Committees at the time, felt that it was

> *essential to underscore that the autonomy of the Olympic Movement and of all of its parts is essential to protect its values which serve the progress of the individual and of society in general and, more specifically, the integrity of sports competitions.*

He further stated that "*participating organisations must ensure the best possible implementation of these principles which will promote increased effectiveness, better service to society and good governance*".[10]

In 2005, the Ministers Responsible for Sports of the member countries of the Council of Europe passed a "Recommendation on the principles of good governance in sport" (2005). They stated that they were

> *convinced that the successful implementation of effective good governance policies by the non-governmental organisations would help them strengthen their self-governance and their autonomy in sports matters and their relationship with the public authorities in a context of mutual respect and trust.*

The European Parliament adopted a "Resolution on the European dimension in sport" in 2012. It noted that "*good governance in sport is a condition for the autonomy and self-regulation of sports organisations, in compliance with the principles of transparency, accountability and democracy*" (p. 13).

An Expert Group on Good Governance created by the Council of the European Union as part of the EU Work Plan for Sport 2011–2014 adopted the "Principles of good governance in sport in the European Union" in 2013. It states that "*sports organisations that have not implemented good governance procedures and practices must expect to see their autonomy and self-regulation practices curtailed*" (p. 5). Given this context, an investment in good governance is an investment in successful sports (Bayle and Robinson, 2007).

2.3 Defining good governance in sports in light of the questions it raises today

A number of high-quality codes and principles of good governance, directly or indirectly related to sports, have been proposed by different players (IOC 2008, 2014, EU 2013).

However, their implementation and effectiveness in the daily management of sports organizations is not a given (Geeraert, 2015; Breitbarth, Walzel, Anagnostopoulos, Van Eekeren, 2015; Zintz and Winand, 2014).

In this respect, 2015 can be deemed an *annus horribilis* by the Fédération Internationale de Football Association (FIFA) (accused of manipulating the World Cup selection process for 2018 and 2022 for the benefit of Russia and Qatar, and accused of fraudulent financial transactions over long periods of time by high-ranking officials) and by the International Association of Athletics Federations (IAAF) (accused of hiding doping and of fraudulent financial transactions over long periods of time by high-ranking officials). These events contributed to highlighting recurrent governance issues. In addition, there was the doping scandal in Russia in which systematic government involvement now appears to be a certainty (McLaren reports, 2016 and 2017).

Note that good governance

> *refers to the ethical standards underpinning the relationships, methods and instruments of relationships within and between organisations. While there may be no best way of achieving good governance, the term is essentially normative, that is, founded on a number of common elements, such as accountability, transparency, stakeholder participation and a clear legal and ethical framework.*
>
> (Hospitality, Leisure, Sport and Tourism Network, 2007, p. 2)

Within sports organizations, good governance describes an approach which is intended to create harmony, based on ethical criteria, between the activities and the management of the federation, essential to meeting its objectives (DOSB 2015).

The DOSB (2015) suggests that organizational boundaries are permeable and that the approach taken to subjects such as transparency and integrity are learned, i.e., where is the boundary between playing hard but honestly, and dishonesty; when is a rule interpreted broadly and when has it been broken?

3 Analysis by the federations of the emergence of competition from sports which are either self-organizing or managed by private sports organizations and the capacity for innovation

Sports federations are encouraged to adapt to the expectations of their stakeholders. The increase in the number of commercial sports services providers and the popularity of non-organized sports (Vos et al., 2012) require that sports federations stand out and implement new services to meet the new expectations of their members and to attract new ones. One way to do this is to innovate (Dess and Picken, 2000; Lee, Ginn and Naylor, 2009; Tushman and O'Reilly, 1996), that is, to adopt a new idea, product or service (Damanpour, 1991).

Non-profit sports organizations such as sports federations and clubs are, in general, managed by volunteer administrators who must deal with increased competition and the changes it entails. These organizations and their members have only recently become aware of the competitive environment around them and of the need to set themselves apart with commercial offerings by developing new services (Vos et al., 2012).

They offer new types of activities (e.g., recreational sports, new sports disciplines) and services (e.g., online membership systems and services) to attract new members and ensure their loyalty.

These non-profit organizations consist of volunteers and employees who inevitably influence the way in which change and innovation are approached. Their perception of the changes resulting from innovation are important to better understanding the determinant elements of the implementation of innovation within non-profit sports organizations. Their perception and attitudes have a direct impact on the development of innovations (Damanpour, 1991). Therefore, it is valuable to analyze the way in which innovation and change are perceived by the people managing sports organizations and the impact this perception has on innovation.

Winand et al. (2013b) studied the concepts of innovation and change within sports federations by analyzing the new activities and services they implemented and the perception the main actors had of them. They attempted to identify the links between the attitudes of the actors of sports federations toward innovation, the innovation services they provided, the perception of innovations and the change they resulted in and the most important actors involved in the innovation process.

3.1 Understanding innovation

At the organizational level, innovation is generally defined as the adoption of an idea or behaviour which is new for the organization (Crossan and Apaydin, 2010; Daft, 1978; Damanpour, 1996; Damanpour and Evan, 1984; Damanpour and Schneider, 2006; Hage, 1999; Hansen and Wakonen, 1997; Van de Ven,

1986), even if it was developed by others earlier (Mohr, 1969; Rogers, 1995; Zaltman, Duncan and Holbek, 1973). Therefore, Winand, Vos, Zintz and Scheerder (2013a) consider all newly adopted activities and initiatives implemented by an organization as innovations, regardless if they were previously implemented elsewhere. In line with a number of authors (Damanpour and Schneider, 2006; Lee, Ginn and Naylor, 2009; Walker, 2008), they define innovative services (or activities) as:

> *all new services (or significant changes to services) introduced for the first time by an organisation and implemented on a regular basis by the latter to meet the expectations of the people using them, regardless if they have already been implemented by others, as long as they are new to the organisation adopting them.*
>
> (p. 33)

The authors make a distinction between innovation and change by stating that every innovation implies change whereas the inverse is not true. Damanpour and Aravind (2012) make a distinction between creativity, innovation and organizational change. Creativity leads to innovation which in turns leads to change.

From a management standpoint, the attitude of the actors toward innovation and change is considered crucial for the implementation of an innovation (Damanpour, 1991; Damanpour and Aravind, 2012; Frambach and Schillewaer, 2002).

3.2 Innovation and sports organizations

Non-profit sports organizations are recognizable by four main characteristics which influence the way in which change and the implementation of a new idea are perceived. These characteristics were highlighted by Bayle (2005): (1) Their mission is social, societal and/or sports oriented rather than profit oriented; (2) they have a mixed economy balancing private and public resources; (3) they belong to national and supranational sports systems which, among other things, establish the rules of the sports disciplines and organize international sports competition; and, (4) the status of their members is mixed, that is, they are run by volunteers and paid staff.

In the case of sports federations, "innovative services" refers to all sports and non-sports activities, initiatives or services recently adopted and for the first time, and still currently in use, to meet the expectations of members and attract new ones. These innovative services involve an organizational change in practices, structure or even culture. The organization of beach volleyball events was an innovative initiative developed by a number of volleyball federations which resulted in a change in their structure and operation. Newell and Swan (1995) made a contribution to the literature on innovation within national sports organizations (i.e., sports federations) by highlighting the role played by inter-organizational relationships. They also underscored the fact that the volunteers of non-profit sports organizations play a key role in the implementation of innovations given that most depend (entirely or partially) on them. The volunteer employees and administrators, members and supervisory bodies of non-profit sports organizations influence, facilitate or inhibit innovation. According to Newell and Swan (1995), sports federations need to innovate to acquire new resources to survive and promote their sport. However, the importance of sports traditions and stakeholders' resistance to change can prevent the implementation of an innovation (Newell and Swan, 1995; Wolfe, Wright and Smart, 2006). A significant aspect of the success of an innovation is the managerial support it receives throughout the implementation process (Caza, 2000). According to Hoeber and Hoeber (2012), who studied the implementation of a technological innovation in local sports organizations, the successful development of an innovation requires managerial support and a committed team of people, among other things.

However, it would appear that financially stable federations are not the most innovative ones, as highlighted by Winand, Vos, Zintz and Scheerder (2013a). These authors have developed a typology of sports federations based on innovation in which they show that the most innovative sports federations are those which are subject to heavy pressure to attract financial resources, operate in a highly competitive regional environment for attracting members and have employees who are involved in the management of the organization and are open to change.

3.3 The perception of innovation within community sports federations in Belgium

Winand, Vos, Zintz and Scheerder (2013a) analyzed innovation and how it is perceived by the people involved in non-profit sports organizations. They looked at sports federations in Belgium. The 144 community sports federations in Belgium have tasks and activities similar to those of the national sports federations of other countries. They are independent organizations subsidized by the public authorities, as the local sports clubs may be. They are grouped in a non-profit association and are managed autonomously, i.e., they are free to choose the volunteer administrators who manage them via a general meeting and the administrative and technical staff that work there. They provide a number of valuable services for clubs and individual members in exchange for a fee (Pieron and De Knop, 2000).

An online survey, validated beforehand, was sent to the 144 Belgian community sports federations to assess their perception of innovation and the number of innovative activities and services they had implemented recently. One key person per sports federation (i.e., president, general secretary, administrative or sports director), whose in-depth experience in the sports federation would enable them to reliably answer all of the questions, was asked to respond to the survey anonymously.

In order to assess the people and the organizations with the most influence on the innovation process, the respondents identified categories of internal (e.g., president, administrative employee, sports industry employee) and external (e.g., sports administration, sports clubs, sponsors) actors who support the implementation of new initiatives (i.e., new activities or services). The respondents also described the activities and services their sports federation had implemented for the first time over the past four years, that is, between 2006 and 2010, based on a list of general services they can offer.

In all, 101 sports federations took part in the survey, a relatively high response rate of 70%.

Winand et al. (2013b) showed that the sports federations analyzed in this study put in place new services and activities for their members and to attract new ones. These initiatives are considered to be innovations. A little over one third of the new initiatives were sports related, on average. It would therefore appear that sports federations develop a majority of indirect sports initiatives (e.g., sports equipment rentals, online recording of the results of sports events), that is, which are not sports per se but which are clearly related to sports and to the sports activities they promote. The non-sports activities are intended to provide added value to the fees paid by members. They increase the members' perceived value of the sports services at the heart of the business and missions of the federations (e.g., sports days for members, sports camps for athletes, organization of championships). This could be due to the fact that sports organizations have less freedom to develop their sport (due to the constraints of supervisory organizations) than they do related services. They therefore try to set themselves apart by promoting complementary services for which they have more room to manoeuvre.

No significant difference was found with respect to the number of innovations developed by large and small sports federations, by Olympic and non-Olympic sports organizations or by organizations which are financially dependent on, or independent of, the public authorities.

Nearly half were aware that they innovate and offer innovative services. This was a relatively high proportion, given that no broad definition of the term "innovation" was provided. The sports federations which developed multiple sports and non-sports initiatives appeared to be aware that they were innovating and that they were committing to (or had committed to) a process of change. They believed that they had changed considerably over the past 5 years, in line with the initiatives they had developed.

An important actor in the innovation process was identified in the sports federations: The sports industry employee. This person appears to be an innovation champion who supports initiatives and promotes a climate favourable to innovation. Although the president was also considered to be an important player in the innovation process by respondents, Winand, Vos, Zintz and Scheerder (2013a) did not demonstrate a link between the frequency of support received from the president and the number of innovations, contrary to the sports industry employee. The president's role is to chair the board of directors and all strategic decisions must pass through the board. Therefore, a new idea must, inevitably, receive its approval. However, it did not appear that the president was the driver of innovation, although they are a key player in the process, from study to implementation.

Note that the entire process is inevitably anchored in a context specific to each sports federation. This environment consists of external and internal factors which impact each critical step in the development of an innovation. The external factors include, among others, the environment of the federation, its sports systems (e.g., international sports federation, National Olympic Committee), the competition on the sports services market and external stakeholders (e.g., public authorities, sponsors). Internal factors include, among others, the operation and the organization of the federation, its human and financial resources, the missions assigned to it (or which it defines for itself) and its internal stakeholders.

3.4 Managerial implications

Innovation is an aspect of organizational change. The development of an attitude favourable to innovation is crucial. In addition, it would appear that it is important that the actors involved see that their organization is innovating and changing. This improves their attitude to new ideas and, therefore, to future innovations. As a result, it is important to communicate about change, that is, to provide positive information to the internal (and external) stakeholders about the changes that are taking (have taken) place in the organization. It is also important to identify an innovation champion within the organization. This champion would appear to be the sports industry employee in the sports federations. This actor impacts the organizational atmosphere. His or her implication promotes the implementation of innovations and raises the awareness of players about the need to innovate. It is therefore decisive that sports federations provide the sports industry employee with responsibility as they are the potential champion of innovation and a leader for change.

3.4.1 Limitations

This study has certain limitations, which we acknowledge. First, the perceptions and data received from each community sports federation were provided by a single person. Nevertheless, for the most part, these people had extensive experience within their federation, which enabled them to identify the new initiatives developed and to assess the change which took place during the 5 years preceding the survey. Next, the majority of the respondents were employees (vs. volunteer administrators) of their federation. This may have influenced the way they answered the survey which, however, maintained their anonymity. The perceptions collected from the federations were based on closed questions with which a degree of agreement or disagreement was required. This enabled a cross-cutting analysis to compare all of the sports federations surveyed, but it may have limited the qualifications the sports federations may have wanted to add. Lastly, the initiatives which the sports federation representatives referred to are of relative importance. Some of the initiatives may have led to a radical change in the sports federations whereas others, incremental in nature, reflected less significant change. We chose to calculate the number of initiatives developed, but a calculation detailing the degree of change resulting from the initiatives could also be of interest.

Conclusion: "Governing requires planning"

That, in any event, is what Emile de Girardin, a French politician, writer and journalist wrote in 1860. It's also the conclusion that can be drawn from the study of the governance of sports federations.

The time is gone when they existed, or believed that they existed, entirely autonomously, sure of the monopoly they had over their sport, for which they were responsible.

With the monetization of sports, our era has seen the number of stakeholders increase and the sports landscape diversify.

Governments often subsidize sports federations. They are putting conditions on their support, which are becoming increasingly demanding and include governance criteria.

The European Union and the international sports bodies are consulting with each other to ensure the relative autonomy of the sports movement, respecting its regulatory power over sports activities, but requiring that it submit to the general rules of good governance.

It is against this background that innovation appears as the adoption of new behaviour which brings change to strategies, management processes and actions in the field.

These innovations manifest themselves as new services proposed by salaried employees (innovation champions) under the responsibility of a board of directors which takes strategic decisions.

This new behaviour, these innovations, are the pillars of (good) governance which meets current challenges in an international context.

Notes

1. Although the IOC only recognises one NOC per country, some territories dependent on another country have their own NOC (for example, the American Virgin Islands and the Cayman Islands which are territories, respectively, of the United States and the United Kingdom). This is the main reason why there are currently 206 NOCs (2017) and 193 member countries of the United Nations (2016).
2. 2017 figures.
3. Olympic Solidarity is a body of the International Olympic Committee whose purpose is to provide assistance to all NCOs, particularly those with the greatest need, to enable them to develop their own organizations to promote the development of sports in their country.

4 Sport Management Committee, "Déclarations sur les principes directeurs de bonne gestion à l'attention des fédérations sportives" (document presented at the Sport Management Conference 2001).
5 World Health Organisation (WHO), Constitution of the World Health Organisation, in Key Documents, 48th edition, 2014, p. 1.
6 https://eur-lex.europa.eu/legal-content/EN/TXT/?uri=CELEX%3A61993CJ0415
7 https://eur-lex.europa.eu/legal-content/EN/TXT/?qid=1550836642000&uri=CELEX:61996CJ0051
8 https://eur-lex.europa.eu/legal-content/EN/TXT/?qid=1550836688033&uri=CELEX:62004CJ0519
9 "*The Court recognises that the specificity of sport must be taken into account in the sense that the restrictive effects of competition inherent in the organisation and proper conduct of competitive sport are not in breach of the EU competition rules, where these effects are proportionate to the legitimate genuine sporting interest pursued. In other words, the proportionality test requires that each case be assessed on its own merits according to its own particular features or characteristics. Thus, it is not possible to formulate general guidelines on the application of EU Competition Law to the sports sector*" (Commission of the European Communities, "White Paper on Sport", COM [2007] 391 final, July 11, 2007, p. 16).
10 Notes by the author taken during the conference.

References

Bayle, E. (2005). *Management des organisations sportives. Contributions à l'analyse du management des organisations hybrides*. Mémoire d'habilitation à diriger des recherches. Université Claude Bernard Lyon 1, Lyon, France.

Bayle, E., Robinson, L. (2007). A framework for understanding the performance of national governing bodies of sport. *European Sport Management Quarterly*, 7(3), 249–268.

Breitbarth, T., Walzel, S., Anagnostopoulos, C., Van Eekeren, F. (2015). Corporate social responsibility and governance in sport: oh, the things you can find, if you don't stay behind! *Corporate Governance*, 15(2), 254–273.

Caza, A. (2000). Context receptivity: innovation in an amateur sport organization. *Journal of Sport Management*, 14(3), 227–242.

Chhotray, V., Stoker, G. (2009). Governance: from theory to practice, in *Governance Theory and Practice*. Palgrave Macmillan, UK, pp. 214–247.

Council of Europe (2005). Recommendation of the Committee of Ministers to member states on the principles of good governance in sport. CM/REC (2005) 8.

Crossan, M., Apaydin, M. (2010). A multi-dimensional framework of organizational innovation: a systematic review of the literature. *Journal of Management Studies*, 47, 1154–1191.

Daft, R.L. (1978). A dual-core model of organizational innovation. *Academy of Management Journal*, 21(2), 193–210.

Damanpour, F. (1991). Organizational innovation: a meta-analysis of effects of determinants and moderators. *Academy of Management Journal*, 34(3), 555–590.

Damanpour, F. (1996). Bureaucracy and innovation revisited: effects of contingency factors, industrial sectors, and innovation characteristics. *Journal of High Technology Innovation Management*, 7(2), 149–173.

Damanpour, F., Aravind, D. (2012). Organizational structure and innovation revisited: from organic to ambidextrous structure, in M. Mumford (Ed.), *Handbook of organizational creativity*. Elsevier, London, pp. 479–509.

Damanpour, F., Evan, W.-M. (1984). Organizational innovation and performance: the problem of organizational lag. *Administrative Science Quarterly*, 29, 392–409.

Damanpour, F., Schneider, S. (2006). Phases of the adoption of innovation in organizations: effects of environment, organization, and top managers. *British Journal of Management*, 17(2), 215–236.

Dess, G.G., Picken, J.C. (2000). Changing roles: leadership in the 21st century. *Organizational Dynamics*, 28(3), 18–34.

European Parliament (2012). *Resolution of 2 February 2012 on the European dimension in sport*. 2011/2087 (INI).

European Union (EU) (2013). *Principles of good governance in sport*. Available online at http://ec.europa.eu/assets/eac/sport/library/policy_documents/xg-gg-201307-dlvrbl2-sept2013.pdf.

Frambach, R.T., Schillewaer, N. (2002). Organizational innovation adoption. A multi-level framework of determinants and opportunities for future research. *Journal of Business Research*, 55(2), 163–176.

Geeraert, A. (2015). Sports governance observer 2015 – The legitimacy crisis in international sports governance. *Play the Game*. Available online at www.playthegame.org/media/4303278/SGO_report_final_2.pdf.

German Olympic Sports Confederation (DOSB) (2015). *Good Governance in German Sports*. Available online at www.dosb.de/fileadmin/fm-dosb/downloads/dosb/GGinGermanSports_EN.pdf.

Hage, J.T. (1999). Organizational innovation and organizational change. *Annual Review of Sociology*, 25, 597–622.

Halleux, V. (2017). *Good governance in sport*. European Parliamentary Research Service.

Hansen, S.O., Wakonen, J. (1997). Innovation, a winning solution? *International Journal of Technology Management*, 13, 345–358.

Henry, I., Lee, P.C. (2004). Governance and ethics in sport, in J. Beech, S. Chadwick (Eds.), *The business of sport management*. Pearson Education, Essex, pp. 25–41.

Hoeber, L., Hoeber, O. (2012). Determinants of an innovation process: a case study of technological innovation in a community sport organization. *Journal of Sport Management*, 26(3), 213–223.

Hospitality, Leisure, Sport and Tourism Network, January (2007). *Resource guide in governance and sport*.

International Olympic Committee (IOC) (2008). *Basic universal principles of good governance of the Olympic and sports movement*. Available online at www.olympic.org/Documents/Conferences_Forums_and_Events/2008_seminar_autonomy/Basic_Universal_Principles_of_Good_Governance.pdf.

International Olympic Committee (IOC) (2014). *Olympic agenda 20+20*. Available online at www.olympic.org/Documents/Olympic_Agenda_2020/Olympic_Agenda_2020-20-20_Recommendations-ENG.pdf.

International Olympic Committee (IOC) (2016). *Olympic marketing fact file*. Available online at https://stillmed.olympic.org/media/Document%20Library/OlympicOrg/Documents/IOC-Marketing-and-Broadcasting-General-Files/Olympic-Marketing-Fact-File-2016.pdf.

Lee, R.P., Ginn, G.O., Naylor, G. (2009). The impact of network and environmental factors on service innovativeness. *Journal of Services Marketing*, 23(6), 397–406.

McLaren, R. (2016). *Independent investigation report – Parts I*. World Antidoping Agency. Available online at www.wada-ama.org/en/resources/doping-control-process/mclaren-independent-investigation-report-part-ii.

McLaren, R. (2017). Independent investigation report – Parts 2. World Antidoping Agency. Available online at www.wada-ama.org/en/resources/doping-control-process/mclaren-independent-investigation-report-part-ii.

Mohr, L.B. (1969). Determinants of innovation in organizations. *The American Political Science Review*, 63(1), 111–126.

Newell, S., Swan, J. (1995). The diffusion of innovations in sport organizations: an evaluative framework. *Journal of Sport Management*, 9(3), 317–333.

Pieron, M., De Knop, P. (2000). *Gestion et organisation du sport en Belgique*. Fondation Roi Baudouin, Brussels. Available online at www.kbs-frb.be/publication.aspx?id=177892&LangType=2060.

Robinson, L., Camy, J. (2008). *Managing Olympic sport organizations*. Human Kinetics, Champaign, IL.

Rogers, E.M. (1995). *Diffusion of innovations* (4th ed.). The Free Press, New York.

Siekmann, R., Soek, J. (2010). Models of sport governance in the European Union: the relationship between state and sport authorities. *The International Sports Law Journal*, (3–4), 93–102.

Siekmann, R., Soek, J. (2010). *Lex sportiva: what is sports law?* Asser Press.

Shilbury, D., Ferkins, L. (2011). Professionalisation, sport governance and strategic capability. *Managing Leisure*, 16, 108–127.

Tushman, M.L., O'Reilly, C.A. (1996). Ambidextrous organizations: managing evolutionary and revolutionary change. *California Management Review*, 38(4), 8–30.

Van de Ven, A.H. (1986). Central problems in the management of innovation. *Management Science*, 32, 590–607.

Vos, S., Breesch, D., Késenne, S., Lagae, W., Van Hoecke, J., Vanreusel, B., Scheerder, J. (2012). The value of human resources in non-public sports providers. The importance of volunteers in non-profit sports clubs versus professionals in for-profit fitness and health clubs. *International Journal of Sport Management and Marketing*, 11(1/2), 3–25.

Walker, R.M. (2008). An empirical evaluation of innovation types and organizational and environmental characteristics: towards a configuration approach. *Journal of Public Administration Research and Theory*, 18(4), 591–615.

Winand, M., Qualizza, D., Vos, S., Zintz, T., Scheerder, J. (2013b). Fédérations sportives innovantes: attitude, perceptions et champions de l'innovation [Innovative sport federations : attitude, perceptions and innovation champions], *Revue Interdisciplinaire sur le Management et l'Humanisme*, 6, 6–21.

Winand, M., Rihoux, B., Qualizza, D., Zintz, T. (2011). Combination of key determinants of performance in sport governing bodies. *Sport, Business and Management: An International Journal*, 1(3), 234–251.

Winand, M., Vos, S., Zintz, T., Scheerder, J. (2013a). Determinants of service innovation: a typology of sports federations. *International Journal of Sport Management and Marketing*.

Wolfe, R.A., Wright, P.M., Smart, D.L. (2006). Radical HRM innovation and competitive advantage: the Moneyball story. *Human Resource Management*, 45(1), 111–126.

Zakus, D.H., Skinner, J. (2008). Modelling organizational change in the international Olympic committee. *European Sport Management Quarterly*, 8(4), 421–442.

Zaltman, G., Duncan, R., Holbek, J. (1973). *Innovations and organizations*. Wiley, New York.

Zintz, T., Camy, J. (2005). *Manager le changement dans les fédérations sportives en Europe*. De Boeck Université, Brussels.

Zintz, T., Vailleau, D. (2008). La gouvernance des fédérations sportives. Proposition d'un cadre d'analyse et d'action. *Revue française de Gestion*, 34(187), 15–34.

Zintz, T., Winand, M. (2014). La place des fédérations sportives au sein du système sportif européen, in Christopher Hautbois (Ed), *Le Marketing des Fédérations Sportives*. Editions Economica, Paris.

Chapter 10

Sports tourism

Contemporary issues and new trends on a global market

Patrick Bouchet and Claude Sobry

Introduction

Over the past 50 years, sports tourism has been in perpetual motion to become a global structured market. From the first description of the role of sports in tourism presented by the Central Council of Physical Recreation in 1966 (Anthony, 1966), through "the advent of leisure" (Corbin, 1995) to the "triumph of sports leisure" (Rauch, 1996), decades have passed emphasizing the interest in more "active or passive" forms of sports and travel (Higham and Hinch, 2009). In the 1980s, the concept of sports tourism appeared in the literature in Europe and in the United States to define a set of practices which were both sports and tourism (Glyptis, 1982; De Knop, 1987). At the time however, the World Tourism Organization (UNWTO) did not see this form of tourism as being independent from global tourism development. It was not until 2009, in Johannesburg, that the UNWTO would set an international congress on "Tourism, Sports and Mega Events" as part of its economic interest in link with major international competitions (Armstrong, 1986; Baker and Gordon, 1976; Kolsun, 1988; Lazer, 1985; Ritchie, 1984; Williams and Zelinsky, 1970) to use the potential of the sports-tourism relation hence helping regulate a declining local and/or national economy (Beioley, Crookston and Tyrer, 1988; McDowell, Leslie and Callicot, 1988).

Meanwhile, the social and economic impact of sports and *massification* of active leisure activities have been boosting tourist activities in three main domains: (1) The changes in representations of physical activity, sources of hedonism, art of living and health, (2) the activation of the imaginary to access new tropisms and areas seen as playgrounds and/or discovery and (3) the multiplication and the diversification of active leisure and adventure services. Therefore, the reflection on this sector cannot solely be either an extension of sports or an opening of tourism to new activities dedicated to ever more curious and *activity-hungry* tourists. Sports tourism is a range of original unusual activities showing ruptures with the usual practices of tourism and sports, yet also a mix of both sports and tourism. Travelling is a direct response to specific aspirations more than an indefinite quest. By privileging the destination over the actual trip, sports tourism is instrumental in movement, saturating its meaning. In a sense, sports tourism mixes the experience of travelling and the sphere of sports activities by combining places (destination) and motor, playful and cultural activities pertaining to the world of sports. The multiplication and the diversification of discovery and travelling opportunities make the tourists less and less captive to generic representations and established tourist practices.

Sports tourism cannot therefore pretend to a legacy and tradition in the history of holidays, tourism or sports. It does remain quite an obscure product with fuzzy contours and extensible limits, constantly trying to be identified in the galaxy of local or international tourist products. In France, as in most European and American countries, the interest in sports tourism would lie in a double movement (Weed, 2006). One describes the association and growing integration of practices, of representations and of images, traditionally conveyed by sports, in tourism products while another characterizes the social amplification of sporting facts increasingly based on societal practices, escaping the sporting world and its spatiotemporal framework. By rejecting the idea of tourism as a *cannibal* concept which could be categorized according to the chosen orientations, sports tourism seems to be part of an original process of mixing practices for which benchmarks have been evolving for 50 years. Its effervescence, which is appreciated by the multiplication of fields of action, affects the understanding of what is happening. To traditional sports logic, the regional, commercial, legal, environmental, cultural and technological and security factors come into play.

On an international market oscillating between globalization and local retreat, the retrospective study of management and marketing of sports tourism will provide a better understanding of the genesis of contemporary issues and new trends apparently emerging. This reflection will be the subject of this chapter based on international works done in journals and books. Being an attractive commercial niche, competitions have strongly developed, easing the rise of highly specialized analyses, some transposed from other sectors of tourism.

For over 50 years, works and publications have turned into basic elements for one to synthesize, order hence offer fundamental knowledge to a broader audience alongside with numerous job opportunities and professional channels. It is therefore rather a question of properly highlighting and providing key concepts, approaches and tools which management sciences can offer, yet also taken from socio-economic human and social sciences. From this point of view, if one does not want to consider actors and providers of sports tourism as atypical, the fact that they develop and offer unique products and services requires carefully selecting and adapting tools and relevant methods.

Three "historical" sections structure this chapter on sports tourism. They are at the same time symptomatic of a type of scientific reflection among scholars and professionals, and of a particular mode of evolution of providers in their products: (1) the controversial dawning of sports tourism (1980–2007), (2) reflections more focused on the socio-economic valuation of destinations by sports tourism (2008–2016) in a period marked by crisis and conflicts and (3) new environmental, technological and security challenges in a context of economic recovery and global geopolitical insecurity.

1 Controversial dawning of sports-tourism sector: 1980–2007

At the end of the 1970s, sports tourism as part of the tourism sector, and a research object in its own right does not exist. It would gradually emerge in a controversial context because professionals and scientists alike took data or works from the history of holidays, tourism or sports. During the 1980–2007 era, sports tourism would be the subject of multiple observations which would, in turn, characterize the variety of its products and its uses to eventually lead to definitions striving to overcome the rooted dialectic of either sports or tourism.

1.1 First heterogeneous work on holidays

The pioneering work wondered about the characteristics of sports tourism. Participating in major sporting events such as the Olympic Games, World Championships or World Cups combined tourist services with sports services (Hall, 1992; Chalip, Green and Vander Velden, 1998; Delpy, 1996; Gibson, 1998). Another category of observation combining sports and tourism was participation in sports or leisure activities at a holiday spot (De Knop, 1987, 1990; Gibson and Yiannackis, 1992, 1994; Nogawa, Yamaguchi and Hagi, 1996). Other observations focused on the visit of cultural venues related to sports (Redmond, 1990, 1991; Gibson, Attle and Yiannakis, 1998): Museums, monuments, sports facilities or exhibitions. Among these categories of observations was a common element: The association or combination of elements coming, on the one hand, from the sphere of sports and, on the other, from services in the field of tourism. A consensus emerged on the integration of these categories of observation in what is called sports tourism.

At the time, trying to get to know sports tourism among available information at the French or the international level was twofold. In France, on the one hand, available information was limited and mostly came from studies commissioned by the French Agency for Tourism Engineering (AFIT). Other organizations belonging to the public authorities, the National Observatory of Tourism (ONT), the Department of Studies and Mountain Tourist Planning (SEATM) and the DATAR, published studies on tourism according to their specificity or to further their own work. On the other hand, the identification of sports tourism as a vector of tourism was embryonic, limited to an identification of the "structuring sports of tourism" (Origet du Cluzeau and Vicérat, 2000). Sports tourism was not an identified sector in tourism in France as it was in Canada, Australia or Mexico for example. Reports on tourism such as the 2004 INSEE holiday survey did not identify sports tourism as such yet identified sporting practices and leisure activities on holiday. These observations were linked to an established and traditional framework of interpretation which made it increasingly difficult to account for the evolution of tourist products in recent years.

The 2004 holiday survey carried out by INSEE as part of its permanent survey plan on living conditions of households (EPCV) did highlight the place of sports practices during both summer and winter holidays. In this survey, the sporting holidays were defined as stays of more than 4 days in which one or more sports activities were, occasionally or regularly, representing almost half of all holiday breaks (47%). The sporting practice could be done in the context of holidays specifically dedicated to sports then qualified as "motivated sports stays" or within the framework of "unmotivated sports stays". Most French residents favouring summer holidays, the rate of sports practices was 55% in 2004 (Stat-info 07–01–2007). The motivated summer sports stays only account for 18% of all summer holidays. The trend was more oriented towards a regular practice with more than 75% of holidaymakers daily practising a single sport (60% of holidaymakers practised a single activity) during stays in France (83%). There was no difference between the main activities practised on a daily basis and those practised during the summer holidays. The top three activities were swimming (52%), hiking (34%) and cycling (21%). The activities that followed were more technical sports such as mountain and mid-mountain sports, whitewater sports, tennis and sailing which were mainly practised during trips motivated by sports.

Although summer holidays were preferred, winter departures were increasing and accounted for 32% of all holiday breaks in 2004 (28% in 1999). The sporting activity rate was 21% for winter stays (Stat-info 06–06–2006). However, unlike summer holidays, winter holidays were very often motivated by sports (87%). Sports awareness as a vector of tourist products was gaining, yet it was not a part of a systematic reflection on the essence of sports tourism.

If the motivational studies, the analysis of the clienteles, the contribution of socio-styles and typologies were of obvious interest, one must not forget the fact that they noticed situations and interpreted evolutions more than anything else and observation tools had their limits. As a starting point of the reflection, the two official reports shared a central theme which was the state of tourism and its prospection: "Reinventing the Holidays: the New Galaxy of Tourism" (Commissariat Général au Plan and the Directorate of Tourism, 1998) and "Tourism of the 2010s: the Future of the Offer" (Origet du Cluzeau and Vicérat, 2000). In the first report, a simple observation was made on the fact that more than half of the French said that they "ha[d] done nothing special" over the holidays, with the following comment: "*this is also confirmed by the work of the French Agency of Tourism Engineering which considers that the offer dedicated to a specific type of activity concerns only 7% of the demand*" (Commissariat Général au Plan and the Directorate of Tourism, 1998).

In the second report, the aforementioned quote was mentioned twice. According to the AFIT, the truly "active" holidays – sporting or cultural – leading to thematic stays represented about 7% of the total and concerned 25% of the holidaymakers. Of course, an offer for significantly higher stays existed since the "active" holidays were more specific to the "multi-holidaymakers" (Origet du Cluzeau and Vicerat, 2000). The studies carried out by the AFIT on the physical activities supporting sports tourism gave, in each of the sports, evaluations or estimates of the number of enthusiasts around 10 million. Other sources of information did not seem to fully confirm this assessment; the Directorate of Tourism indicated in its study (2000) that 54% of those surveyed were practising a physical activity during their stay.

1.2 Progressive scientific interest in sports tourism and its definition

Since the late 1980s, there has been a growth in literature focusing on sports tourism and the number of scientific papers published under different formats (Weed, 2006) including papers commissioned by sports organizations or tourism agencies (Jackson and Glyptis, 1992; Standeven and Tomlinson, 1994), strategic visions from keynote speakers' presentations (Gibson 2002; Weed, 1999), introductory chapters (Gibson, 2003; Weed, 2005) and newspaper articles (De Knop, 1990; Gibson, 1998). However, despite the very useful overview they provided on sports-tourism research, according to Weed (2006), four main problems remained: (1) they were essentially narrative literary journals; (2) they made no distinction between different types of contributions; (3) they were written for different audiences such as policy makers, scholars, researchers and students; and (4) they did not make an evaluation of research in this area. Also, Weed (2006) suggested a classification of the studies carried out on the subject in several domains: Works centred on the concepts at the heart of the analysis of sport tourism, those focused on categorization(s) of sports tourism and those seeking to identify the relationships between sports tourism, tourism and sports. Furthermore, he highlighted that the main research in this sector was related either to the impacts of tourist sporting events, or to tourists' behavioural participation in adventure or outdoor activities and mainly in golf and skiing.

Subsequently, with the growth and maturation of sports tourism, the corpus of research tended to incorporate a range of perspectives, disciplines and methods in an attempt to move from describing what the sporting tourists, did to understanding the reasons why (Bouchet and Lebrun, 2009; Gibson, 2004; Higham and Hinch 2009; Sobry, 2004). At the same time, many books were focusing on different objects or aspects of sports tourism: Events and their impacts (Gammon and Kurtzman, 2007), activities, marketing or development (Turco, Riley and Swart, 2002; Hinch and Higham, 2001), economic, social and environmental impacts (Ritchie and Adair, 2004); stakeholders' management of destinations (Weed and Bull, 2004); globalization, mobility and regional identity (Higham and Hinch, 2009); adventurous activities (Hudson, 2003) or nautical activities (Jennings, 2007) and even the legacy of sports and tourism (Gammon and Ranshaw, 2007).

Finally, the scientific interest in sports tourism was also spread by the academic community with the acceptance of articles or special issues in peer-reviewed quality journals in the field of sports (*European Sport Management Quarterly*, *Sport in Society*, *European Journal of Sports Management*), leisure (*Leisure and Society*, *Revue Espace*) and tourism (*Journal of Vacation Marketing*, *Current Issues in Tourism*, *Tourism Review International*, *Téoros*). The creation of the *Journal of Sport*

Tourism in 1993, renamed the *Journal of Sport & Tourism* in 2006, also attested to the legitimacy and evolution of sports tourism as a basic and applied research subject. While academic awareness centred on its understanding and its organization was developing, several definitions of sports tourism appeared. Based on empirical approaches centred on repeated observations, suggestions were based on distinct categories: Practices, products or the nature of the experience. They highlighted two fundamental points of stay through sports: the pre-eminence of physical involvement in terms of investment and the type of cultural experience in relation to changes in consumption patterns and holidaymakers' behaviour. This desire to better define sports tourism continued, and in the Sport & Tourism journal alone, 31 definitions were identified between 1993 and 2014 (Van Rheenen et al, 2016).

2 Analyses even more focused on socio-economic valuation of destinations by sports tourism: 2008–2016

The growing interest in sports tourism is related to the economic impact associated and the attractiveness generated because of the values and representations it conveys mainly in terms of environment, ecology, freedom or concern for well-being. These key elements lead to debates at the heart of the reflection on local and/or national institutional communication, fair trade and relationship management. In this new context, sports tourism will then constitute an opportunity for the development and sustainability of the socio-economic activities of tourist destinations with specific characteristics and assets in relation to their heritage, gastronomic and physical offer. It is therefore considered as a producer of virtuous socio-economic effects enabling to go beyond all definitions limited by disciplinary, categorical or technical points of view until now (Bouchet and Bouhaouala, 2009).

2.1 *Socio-economic development of sports tourism in world destinations*

In 2008, according to the Organization for Economic Co-operation and Development (OECD), tourism was one of the engines of globalization and, for member countries, represented one of the most dynamic sectors (Direction du Tourism, 2008). In fact, they accounted for 70% of global tourist activity and the sector accounted for 30% of their services exports. In the same year, according to the World Travel and Tourism Council (WTTC), tourism accounted for 9.9% of the global GDP (10% in 2002), 11% of exports (11.9% in 2002) and 8.4% of global employment. In the European Union, tourism contributed 4% of the GDP (this percentage varied between 2% and 12% depending on the Member States); its indirect contribution to the GDP was much higher since tourism indirectly generated more than 10% of the European GDP and accounted for more than 12%

of total employment (Direction du Tourism, 2008). Nevertheless, in their 1982 report, experts from the World Tourism Organization (UNWTO) stated that:

> *the economic role of tourism is not limited to its effects at the international level. It is at the national level that the effects are most pronounced as tourism can be, as a productive sector, a factor of development and redistribution of economic activity.*

Tourism as an identified socio-economic sector plays a fundamental role in the French economy; in 2007, it generated consumption in the order of €117.6 billion and 894,000 salaried jobs (Direction du Tourism, 2008).

Meanwhile, holidaymakers' motives became both simple in terms of aspirations – rest, change of scenery, family or friendly gathering – and complex in terms of availability and purchasing power – holiday splitting, blurrier boundaries between work and leisure – in a context of global economic instability related to the subprime mortgage crisis. Another paradox is the increase of short stays allowing clean breaks from the daily pace with aspirations for longer stays in order to take the time to live (Touriscopie, 2007). These tourists also oscillate between last-minute purchases, according to their desires and availability, and purchases planned well in advance. However, faced with the standardization of the offer with holiday villages, urban centres, shops and leisure parks, some holidaymakers wish to become "new travelers" favouring emotions, cultural and human meetings. Others are looking for authenticity, that is to say experiencing the traditions and cultures of a country, enchantment which involves making sense, living emotions and learning about the other. This quest for authenticity is sometimes difficult to meet when traditions are lost. To solve it, some actors (countries, cities, etc.) do not hesitate to thematize certain parks such as the Puy du Fou in Vendée or Dracula in Romania, or some fake Mexican villages. "*Tourism is more of a commercial staging than a cultural experience. When the local atmosphere does not provide its share of experiences, one will recreate it artificially so that each customer is entitled to his lot of exotic clichés*" (Rifkin, 2002). This trend can be found in the likes of amusement parks such as Euro Disney or tourist resorts such as Arc 1950. The desires of the tourists are shared between rest, discovery and activities, within the same stay, with highly diversified practices during their holidays which they segment more and more over the year. As a result, if 30% of the people do not practice a particular activity, 30% choose cultural activities and 54% practice physical activity during their stay in France and abroad (Direction du Tourism, 2008). The motivations of the French being, for nine out of ten people, health, relaxation and pleasure of both sports and meeting with friends or family, providers are facing a demand for sports and recreation assets difficult to pin down. In fact, many other non-sporting activities also make it possible to satisfy such needs and one can relax and cultivate one's shape by walking in the countryside. The spectrum of physical practices being very broad, it will capture a significant part of this indecisive demand for the best use of a growing usual, and unusual, free time, a segment of particular interest in the offer including some sub-segments such as highly motivated seniors with good purchasing power.

Starting in 2008, the sports tourism sector, even if accurate and reliable data are not available, seemed to rank high in the socio-economic development of tourist destinations and was emphasized in the regional and national development policies. Sports tourism can be found in the fundamental dimensions of social organization whether on a national or a global scale on three different levels. First, at the political level, sports tourism serves as a development tool, a regional development framework and a guide for the preservation and management of natural resources. Second, at the social level, and beyond the link created between individuals, sports tourism plays a unique role in the integration of populations through employment, as well as in education for citizenship and the environment for natives and immigrants. Third, at the economic level, sports tourism is a real entrepreneurial sector, more or less seasonal depending on the regions and the activities, making it a boost in the creation of companies, jobs and activities of services.

Sports tourism being of high value, it can quickly and easily be instrumentalized by various investors such as companies, States, sports federations or even consumers. Higher the stakes, objectives and logic are, more complex and broader the resulting organization is. Sports tourism has obviously become a real source of income, activities and jobs for regions, yet also for support areas attracting customers or providing reception and/or transit areas. It is then necessary to recognize the potential which sporting leisure activities bring to the social and economic development of tourist regions on one part and, what tourism brings to the diversification of sports activities on the other part.

Thus, contrary to the vision of Kurtzman and Zauhar (2003), sports tourism appears as an economic sector in which there is a strong interaction of sports and leisure activities in tourist regions hence generating a new economic model. If its social, political and economic importance is no longer important to prove in Western and wealthy countries, since 2008, it has become a real stake of social and economic progress for the developing countries, even a real bargain in terms of foreign exchange earnings to attempt a successful reconversion of their socio-economic systems. Consequently, it should be understood that any reference to sports tourism refers more and more to the active leisure activities consumed in relation to the tourist sector or the regions, even without counting overnight stays at local or mass tourist areas (Canavan, 2013; Jeuring, 2016; Wynen, 2013). Sports tourism is therefore a real source of income and employment for both tourist regions and sending and receiving countries. Much more than just a sales pitch, as sports events might be, leisure activities are now an integral part of the holiday market. The extension observed in sports tourism both in terms of demand and supply encourages researchers from multiple fields of science such as geography, sociology, economics or management and professionals to question the structure and scope of this new socio-economic sector at a time when its main actors are trying to meet the challenges issued by globalization and the sustainable development of regions. Therefore, if one wants to apprehend sports tourism as an activity generating socio-economic value, it requires an inductive and *cross-cutting* vision, centred on its axes of development, its impacts and its modes of diversification with other tourist or leisure sub-sectors.

2.2 Extension of sports-tourism domains and offer transformation of products

Lapeyronie (2009) pointed out that, in most sources, the concept of sports tourism is analyzed differently; it is polysemic to the extent that it can be understood as movement to go practice sports, go to a sports show or even practice sports while at a resort, which is already a three-point approach. Gibson (1998) distinguished three domains:

> *active sports tourism, which refers to people who travel to take part in sports; event sports tourism, which refers to a sports event; and nostalgia sports tourism, which includes visits to sports museums, famous sports venues, and sports themed cruises.*

Pigeassou (2004) used the same items overall, yet adding activism sports tourism, that is to say travelling induced by sports movement organizations, especially federal or professional, or the setting up of sports shows or events. Hinch and Higham (2011) pointed out that pioneering work in sports tourism considers sports as being at the origin of the motivation of movement itself, which differs from Lapeyronie's approach: "*sports tourism is based on movement introducing a key variable (destination) and the processes of choice (motivation, decision)*". Pigeassou wrote (2004) adding: "*(in sports tourism) the desire to experience sports culture drives the tourist activity*". In extenso, it excludes the limitation to travelling in connection with a sports event only (Deery, Jago, Fredline, 2004), although the socio-economic activities of sports events have been strongly evolving under tourist professionals and organizers. Indeed, the global turnover of this sector was estimated at $800 billion in 2016, with an exceptional growth rate, having increased by 100 billion each year over the past 4 years.

This approach ignores stays focused on physical activities, visits to high places of sports or participation in a sports show which were not planned during a trip due to other purposes. However, for Hinch and Higham (2011) "*sport is recognized as a significant travel activity, it is a primary, a secondary or even a tertiary feature of the trip*". In his tourism classification attempt, Leiper (1990) called a tertiary attraction "*an attraction unknown by the tourists before they headed to their destination, therefore elected on other criteria, but which might become an attracting element during their stay*", what Gammon and Robinson (2003) called "tourism sport" and Sobry (2005) called "opportunity sports tourism" (Figure 10.1). The works of Bouchet and Lebrun (2009) suggested extending the domains of sports tourism as well, considering sports tourism as defined once the choice of a tourist stay has been made by a holidaymaker, in a destination largely determined by the practice of one or more physical activities, in either a natural or an artificial place, more

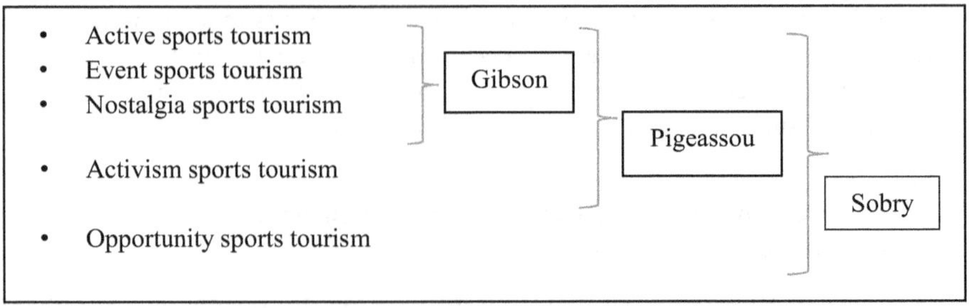

Figure 10.1 Extension of Sports-Tourism Domains

or less developed, or by the active participation in a show or a sports expedition, over several days, either embellished by one or more unexpected, accidental or contingent physical activities, or by an event or even by the presence of family or friends on the premises.

By integrating "opportunity sports tourism", the fields of application of this economic sector are growing and allowing a better understanding of how companies create jobs and participate in the animation and the valorization of a place (Bouchet and Bouhaouala, 2009) for various clienteles, whether on or off season, per day in a local tourism or during a short, medium or long stay in different types of sedentary or mobile accommodation. Given the nature, diversification and composition of the sports-tourism product considered as a set of services, the segmentation of demand by benefits then appears to be relevant to reflect the heterogeneity of holidaymakers. This form of segmentation is based on the concepts of defining attributes creating the products and, consequently, the positioning of products and brands. The role of the marketing promoter of sports tourism – associative, public and/or private – will be to identify which attributes contribute to the overall positive or negative attitude of tourists towards the destination which they value.

This conception refers to the multi-attribute model (Filser, 1994) which considered the consumer's attitude towards a product (destination) as a function of the consumer's beliefs towards the attributes of the product (destination, provider[s] and attribute[s] related to on-site available physical activities). It should be noted that the problem is further complicated due to the fact that the holidaymaker retains not only tangible characteristics of the product (economic and usage attributes), yet also intangible characteristics (physical and symbolic attributes). The questions then are many: Can a bad evaluation of the sports-tourism product on one attribute be balanced by good evaluations on other attributes? Do all attributes weigh evenly in the attitude formation process, or should they be weighed according to their relevance or target audience? The possible attributes related to the physical activities available on site can notably be the facilities, the material made available, health, relaxation and congeniality. The possible attributes of the destination can be the accommodation, catering, discovery or the change of scenery. For the provider(s), one can identify such features as pricing, trust or the degree of notoriety. In the end, from these multiple combinations, the possibilities of valorization of sports tourism turn out to be innumerable hence contradicting the operational nature of these multi-attribute models used by professionals and researchers to segment the tourist clientele and/or promote destinations.

With a pluralistic demand for dynamic and multi-activity holidays, and with the desire to be more involved in the planning of their stay as well as the inadequacy of conventional systemic models of offer and demand, new and more "experiential" approaches to sports-tourism customers are rising. Indeed, conventionally, one always tries to classify tourists according to the reason and the duration of their stays and their movements. The ancient distinction between *sunlust* – body, sports, sun – and *wanderlust* – search for the unknown and the encounter, wandering and roaming – or the opposition between hedonistic practices – sun, rest, body worship – and ascetic – active discovery, demanding physical activities – have been the basis for many segmentations of sports tourism according to eras and destinations. However, due to the multiplication of the number of destinations in a context of global hyper-competition, the search for experiences and quality/price ratio has become complementary especially at a time when the individual zaps on the paradoxes with an underlying hedonistic and emotional aim. The forms of experiment sought to represent a new segmentation tool which complements the classical variables. The holidaymakers' process of choosing (Bouchet and Lebrun, 2009) then appears as the result of a subjective evaluation, in terms of "experiential" thresholds, rather sensory and affective, and "functional" thresholds, rather rational and cognitive, between the ranges of products offered and the experiences that the tourists wish to satisfy according to their resources physical, temporal or financial. The skills and the intensity of the activities, their material and human contingencies, prioritize the agreed modes of will, of spatiotemporal and of social interaction. The most socio-demographic aspects – free time, family situation, financial level – determine or limit the possibilities of experiences, in particular in terms of types of accommodation, chosen routes or lengths of stay among others. Whatever the destination, travel, accommodation and activities chosen, once on site, the tourists can always change their stay based on opportunities offered either by providers, friends or others.

The World Tourism Organization (UNWTO, 2004) highlighted the transition from a service economy to an economy of experiences in the evolution of the tourism market. This trend was linked to the strategic interest in offering new experiences to holidaymakers, especially short stays with the aim of ensuring better satisfaction. On the one hand, one could see the implementation of strategies introducing an experiential dressing in the tourist offer for the existing providers such as hotels or theme parks, and, on the other hand, for new entrants, original positioning thanks to innovative concepts creating new experiences for customers (Anaba, Bodet, Bouchet, 2014). However, the strong development of this type of strategy raised the question of their sustainability and most of all the sustainable development of their supporting region. After the 1992 Rio Earth Summit, major environmental issues resurfaced under the influence of research dealing with global warming, endangerment of forests, among other environmental issues. According to UNWTO (2004):

> *Sustainable tourism should also maintain a high level of tourist satisfaction and ensure a meaningful experience to the tourists, raising their awareness about sustainability issues and promoting sustainable tourism practices amongst them.*

However, the holidaymakers surveyed had a hard time making the link between sustainable development and tourism, and were more sensitive to fast tourism and the quality of the experience than the protection of the natural environment (Cuvelier, 2000; Ritchie and Crouch, 2000).

3 New environmental, technological and security challenges of sports tourism in global economic recovery context and geopolitical insecurity

In terms of global tourism, sports-tourism markets are becoming more and more mature despite a change in the tropism of transmitters and receivers for a now international tourist clientele "*envious of the world*" (Urbain, 2011) and who wants to explore all regions, even as far as going to the borders of space. However, in the light of future changes, the analysis of sports tourism is complex because of its interface between the strategies of firms and market and non-market organizations on the one hand, and between holidaymakers' buying and consuming behaviour on the other hand. In fact, the current literature on the sector attests to the problem of consumer goods, *prosumer*, as factors of growth and uncertainty in an increasingly competitive and mature market. In addition, the integration of social and cultural goals into the providers' strategies and marketing mix should, concomitantly, adapt to issues related to the customers' ecological, security and technological concerns. As Jaureguiberry and Lachance (2016) pointed out, the hypermodern traveller differs from the former traveller because of one's permanent interconnection to the world and one's family through GPS, SMS, e-mail or sites, affinity or even through one's professional environment while creating a safety net in one's movements and a stop to the feeling of adventure or the cut with one's daily life. In terms of foresight, four important issues seem likely to influence the strategic actions of sports-tourism providers in the future: Branding and smart destination, the social and cultural responsibility of service providers, hyper-segmentation and hyper-connection of tourists and their co-creation and co-production of stays.

3.1 Development of brand and smart destination

With globalization and the modification of tourist tropisms (Urbain, 2011), the holiday supply market underwent significant changes forcing destinations to seriously question their attractiveness policy (Fabry 2009), preservation and/or hospitality. How much Morocco or Tunisia struggle to break the vicious circle of low-cost holidays should be proof enough that tourism in some countries in transition, such as China or Eastern-European countries, has found remunerative niches – business tourism, hydrotherapy, the Olympic Games –show that they can compete head-to-head against Western countries. In a context of economic recovery and security concerns, working towards visibility and readability of destinations has become a major challenge for all destinations (OECD, 2006) on a hyper-competitive tourism market. The challenge for a destination is to differentiate itself through a "unique" image and/or identity promoting its regional resources, heritage, gastronomy or sports (Crouch and Ritchie, 1999, 2000; Dwyer and Kim, 2003; Enright and Newton, 2004). Many studies have highlighted that the attractiveness, or non-attractiveness, of a country was built on its image in terms of global representations either political, economic, success or technological delay, cultural influence, sports or education, on representations of its tourist offer with products or services which come from it or in connection with hospitality, supposed or real, at destination. In this context, the various bodies have progressively integrated marketing and regional thinking in relation to the development of a destination brand image. *Territorial marketing* stems from four major marketing practices: Public, services, social and product (Anholt, 2007; Gayet, 2014). According to its purpose and its specificities, it comes under different names: *place branding* (Avaraham, Ketter, 2008; Kotler, Haider, and Rein, 1993), which means branding a region, *city branding* (or *city marketing*), *destination branding* in the case of tourist applications intended to increase the attractiveness of a holiday resort (Boo,Busser, and Baloglu, 2009) and more recently, the concept of *country brand* or *nation brand* which has developed a lot since the 1990s (Dinnie, 2007), although it has always been "natural" in the field of tourism and advertising communication which goes with it (Kapferer, 2011). Territorial marketing can also be associated with *made in* as well as with its meaning if not added value. There is also abundant global academic research on the effects of the country of origin (Steenkamp, 2001; Usunier and Cestre, 2007). The popularity of tourist destinations in territorial marketing and destination branding seems to be guided by a desire to differentiate oneself on holiday supply markets in order to attract more or less targeted tourists. On the sports-tourism market, one only has to observe the communication campaigns of the seaside or ski resorts as destinations, or those conducted to obtain the Summer or Winter Olympic Games.

Understanding the concepts of *smart city* and *smart destination* also seems to become a major issue for the development of tourist regions for holidaymakers and residents alike. Focusing more on digital uses would help the creation of an "intelligent" or "intelligible" ecosystem involving consumers (travellers and inhabitants), local and regional authorities, and companies mastering big data and innovative processes. This approach would promote the repositioning or strategic adaptation of tourism providers and institutions to better understand their offer towards their customers and their destination developing attractiveness while strengthening the activation of the local community. Becoming a smart tourist destination would then be a must for a region mixing human and digital aspects. Yet, beyond this approach, one must design a more intelligible tourist region focusing on the visitors' experience, particularly in its multiple forms of sports consumption or active leisure. It is therefore more than necessary to develop a demand marketing based on the experience and on the expectations of the visitors (Consumer Dominant Logic, CDL), and not only to highlight the products (Good or Service Dominant Logic) (Quan and Wang, 2004; Vargo and Lusch, 2008). Collaboration and openness of the world of technology, tourism and communities is necessary for a destination to become a more intelligible, ergonomic, human, shared and welcoming region, serving tourists and residents while benefiting all stakeholders. In these "smart" regions, the destination management organizations (DMOs) and the tourist offices involved must share relevant information, easily accessible in real time, while working with local communities, tourists and the authorities to co-create the tourist experience by wisely manipulating Wi-Fi, digital signage, QR codes and NFC technology, urban or rural facilities, connected objects hence creating a personal relationship with visitors and delivering the right information at the right time. It implies smartphones, interactive watches, connected wristbands, chatbots on instant messengers, and so on. For example, it might be wise to find ways to "animate" the destination via transportation and accommodation by already having disruptive models such as Uber, BlablaCar and OTAs on more specific geographical perimeters – parks, stations – or even more specialized customer segments – Stay22 for business travellers, Share Shed for outdoor enthusiasts. However, such development might lead to ethical risks such as the risk of dehumanizing the destination if attention is focused on the tools. In addition, legal aspects such as country legislation, anonymization of data and transparency of decision-making processes are, of course, to be considered.

3.2 Hyper-segmentation and hyper-connection of tourists

The choice of products related to sports tourism has broadened and the spectrum of tourist destinations has spread even more with individuals wanting to take pleasure, to have fun, to distinguish themselves, to show originality and even commitment through travelling. Apart from mobility obstacles related to distance, administrative formalities (visas), geopolitical factors (terrorism, political crises) and health (vaccines, epidemics), the development prospects for tourism in general and sports tourism in particular seem almost limitless with the arrival of massive new holidaymakers from emerging countries such as the BRICS. It is clear that there have been an unprecedented and heterogeneous fragmentation and growth of the clientele who has become more demanding, more connected and more difficult to target and to identify than in the era of highly seasonal and regional mass tourism (blue, white, green tourism). As a result, sports-tourism providers are forced to rely on or to develop with indicators structuring the expectations of their customers in order to optimize their offer and their turnover. Therefore, they must both understand the social and cultural fields in which holidaymakers evolve and analyze how they can experience their products through physical, spatial and social aspects and according to each context encountered in part of their stay at destination. The possibilities of stays seem therefore endless with so many activities available at a destination whether related to well-being, adventure of all kinds, sports challenges and other gatherings, mud days, raids or color-runs for humanitarian actions or charities to name a few. In addition, many requests are expressed by the clientele of sports tourism to improve their stay – sightseeing, culture and heritage, gastronomy, socializing or partying – and get an identity context in today's society giving authenticity, spicing up their lives and representing a privileged medium of expression. The term of *recreation* seems to reflect this consumption demand in which the reconstitution of the body and the mind would be at stake through an intentional, sometimes existential, project depending on the market offers and the contexts of use hoped. It is through futile or useful recreational visits that the holidaymakers would have the feeling to *rebuild*, in part, a positive identity, to *regain* self-esteem and that of others, and therefore to *retrieve* "their place" in society. It is then easier to understand the craze for selfies of all kinds and other videos shot by GoPro, made by tourists, including the youngest, in all places and at any time, to share with others the singularity of their travel experiences.

Information and communication technologies have brought the traveller into a new travel experience (Jaureguiberry and Lachance, 2016), which often results in a partial disconnection from their familiar environment. Today's traveller is therefore dragged into a "here and there at the same time", bypassing the experience of distance while raising new questions: Should one leave with a mobile phone or not? With whom will one keep contact, how often and in which situations? Why use a GPS? The possibility of being connected to the world and to one's professional or family entourage via the Internet or a mobile phone appears as what ensures the journey or erases the difficulties by reducing or minimizing the adventurous aspect. Often times in sports tourism, hazards as part of a rewarding experience during one's stay are antithetical with the need for being safe against the risks involved (illness, aggression or language barrier), sources of annoyance, loneliness or disappointment. With this ability to alternatively be connected and disconnected, the hypermodern traveller has the opportunity to solve tensions inherent in the journey, to be reachable and to reach anyone, to connect with the near and familiar world while physically far from it, hence always "here and there", an everyday adventurer, provided one takes real trips because, today, it is possible to visit the most exotic corners of the Earth without leaving one's couch and computer screen!

3.3 Co-creation and co-management of tourist stays by customers

If the tools available on the Internet allow tourism providers to have a presence and visibility, at anytime and anywhere in the world, hyper-competition is present in the tourism industry, and customers, who have become more and more demanding, do not hesitate to compare and bargain before making their decision, sometimes finding free or cheap products *via* couch surfing or housing exchange for example. Information is often consumed from smartphones, even pushed by the most influential sites such as Booking, Tripadvisor or platforms of tourist guides such as Lonely Planet or Le Routard. Social networks and their influence on tourists represent a tool which is difficult to master and which the provider must consider and integrate into one's marketing strategy, especially since the management of the presence on the Internet (SEO, description of activities, reactions to comments or implementation of a payment site) is an important part with both financial and human investments. One then witnesses a strengthening of the power of sports-tourism customers, whether in their co-creation and co-management or in their evaluation by the various professional channels via sites or personal comments. As a result, *knowledge marketing* has become a major issue optimizing customer relationships beyond Customer Relationship Management (CRM) and Knowledge Management (Curbatov, 2003). The challenge of knowledge marketing would be to *re-empower* customers to manage their own experiences and develop their own skills; tourism sports products providers could better consider the development of relational development programmes of the customers and of co-proposition of new values (services, options, projects). In this sense, it is therefore the tourists who determine the value of the products by using them and no longer (only) the providers by producing and marketing them. However, to achieve it, consumers will need to learn how to use, maintain, and adapt to these products according to specific usage situations and usage behaviours. In operational terms, this evolution might explain the emergence of organizational knowledge co-creation mechanisms in the sub-sectors of sports tourism, with a growing interest in innovation and mass-customization (or customer-made). The latter is a process of co-production whereby customers participate actively in the making of their experience of consuming products or services. According to Carù and Cova (2006), if mass-customization comes from the co-creation of the experience – the consumer is involved in the production of one's experience with the company's offer – the upward innovation is the co-creation of the offer – the consumer is involved in the definition of the products and variables of the marketing mix. Exploiting the creative potential of users is an excellent way to avoid missing new market opportunities on the one hand and qualitatively improving the endogenous capital-creativeness of companies on the other hand (Amabile, 1998). In the field of the outdoor, the examples of will of the holidaymakers attest of their participation in the development or even the maintenance of the routes or spots of practice of active leisure activities. Knowledge marketing can also be considered as an element of experiencing control by involving the customers even further in co-creation or co-management experiences with providers. It is a question here of evoking the community practices of individuals acting in co-determination processes. An example in sports spectacle tourism is related to collaborative work between fan communities and professional clubs to create more appealing media shows or museum tours dedicated to clubs.

In our contemporary societies, everyone can change one's choice of purchase or consumption as one chooses according to the places one goes and the information collected by the various professional channels or via personal sites or comments.

The influence of social networks (tools of actions/reactions) is a major stake for the visibility of the offered services; comparator systems as well as online evaluation systems (ratings, comments and sharing experiences) become essential elements in the research phase of tourist destinations. In this context, there is a growing influence of e-WOM ("word of mouth on the web") in tourism which refers to any form of positive or negative judgment, made by potential customers, current or future consumers of the service, and made available to a multitude of people or institutions via the Internet (Stieler, 2017). It takes the form of open publications in any multimedia forms (texts, videos, photos posted online) and all over the planet through the Internet. Specialized web platforms concerned with tourism such as Airbnb (apartment rentals or private homes), Booking (hotel reservations) or Tripadvisor (advice and opinion on travel, destinations, accommodation and activities) are often used to issue or consult opinions and judgments. The content, good or bad for the provider, is accessible in just a few clicks, and it is subject or not to control which is taken over and indexed by the major search engines. The tourists become players in the marketing of services, interacting with other actors and creating a multi-dimensional relationship with specific channels: Business to customer (website, newsletter, outgoing calls), customer to company (spaces of extranet type, company's Facebook page with discussion forum, incoming contact centre) and customer to customer (sites of opinion or sharing of residence, personal Facebook pages, discussion forums). Specialized platforms such as Uber, Airbnb, Blablacar, Tripadvisor and Yelp are the best known; they collect evaluations on the service providers, yet also sometimes on the customers themselves (principle of reciprocity, Bénavent, 2016). In addition, the tourists who have consumed the product ensure, through all platforms, the function of operational management control by disseminating it in the population by means of note systems and comments (Bénavent, 2016). Search or content-sharing websites, such as Google or Facebook, allow tourists to leave a review and rating on the provider's page. Thus, the product can increase in quality and kindness to the tourists who benefit by choosing a reputed service of better quality. The use of the Smartphone for mobile tourists (m-tourism) brings spontaneity, instant comment and customer relevance at any time for lived experiences.

3.4 Social and cultural responsibility of service providers

Ecological issues in sports tourism, especially outdoor sports, should become increasingly important, as the environmental sensitivity is growing among holidaymakers ever more concerned with the progressive deterioration of non-renewable resources of the environment in which the activities take place in the host regions as well as in those visited during stays. However, on the sports-tourism market, the introduction of environmental and ethical concerns should no longer be carried out in a haphazard way between stakeholders who should clearly position themselves in terms of sustainable development, respect for the environment and for the working conditions of their employees. Such an integration into a reasoned marketing policy and respectful of the future of the planet is an axis of differentiation and development that will only grow in the years to come. Moreover, at the level of service providers, some companies are now engaged in eco-design, labelling and certification procedures for practice spaces and for the materials used that is to say adventure trails at height, paintball or sailing schools (Bouchet and Hillairet, 2009). More and more *citizen* companies are also investing in the recycling of end-of-life or used products that is to say cleaning of base camps in the Himalayas or Mont Blanc, "garbage collection" operations around the area and in the depths of rivers or harbours and for involvement in nature protection missions in partnership with official organizations or NGOs with such companies as Patagonia which joins the 1% for the Planet Foundation.

Nonetheless, the legal framework governing the practice of outdoor activities in the natural environment appears relatively vague and uninviting for professionals and especially rarely adapted to the reality of their work. For example, neither the Forest Code (N.20030) applying to all French forests nor the Program for the Endorsement of Forest Certification or the Forest Stewardship Council at the international level explicitly mention rules governing the activity market companies, if not some general elements on the reception of the public, on biodiversity of the spaces and non-massive deforestation. In addition, environmental protection approaches are too often the result of uncoordinated actions with all stakeholders from the political, economic, social and environmental spheres. A good example is the failure of the implementation in France of the Center Park of Roybon in 2016. Does access to holidays necessarily have to go through the enslavement and exploitation of the riches of the support regions? This question, which should haunt tourists, does not seem to weigh heavily on their desire for pleasure, play or celebration. Thus, a societal paradox arises from the consumption of sports-tourism products: For the individual, getting rewarding experiences at all costs without worrying about the consequences; for the service provider, offering the most profitable products possible to meet this clientele, often with little concern for the damage done.

Today, in the field of leisure and sports tourism, inter-market segmentation (Catoera and Graham, 1999) seems to be essential for service providers who must adapt their approaches to local values, standards and practices. The development of Disney theme parks in the United States, Europe and now Asia, confirms this approach by emphasizing the uniqueness of each culture with its own system of values, conventions and regulations. One then joins the neologism of *glocalization* which was born in Japan by combining the words *globalization* and *localization*, the adaptation of a product to each of the places where it is sold, to each of the cultures to which it is addressed. In the field of sports tourism, there are many examples of development and adaptation to the sensitivities and needs of each local culture in certain sectors such as winter sports resorts which are stagnating beyond the issue of climate change: The number of skiers is no longer increasing and is even tending to decrease, competition is currently developing between winter sports resorts in countries historically located on the market, such as France, Austria and Switzerland. Europe and a number of Central European countries are beginning to offer quality services close to those of the leaders yet at significantly lower prices. In these conditions, local culture and folklore can serve as appealing elements for foreign clients. It is also a race for artificial snow and heavy investment on the side of former leaders to kerb the dispersion of customers, in need for loyalty. The result is a decrease in the profitability of mountain investments and the bankruptcy of some resorts. In contrast, the development of winter sports in China is impressive (three million skiers in 2011) and specific (Liu, Sobry, Li, and Liu, 2010). The Chinese government modelled on the development of sports tourism in the West and has planned the development of skiing in the country. Before the 2022 Olympic Winter Games, the target was seven million skiers in 2020 to reach 120 million 10 to 20 years later. When China won the organization of the Olympic Games in 2015, the objectives were revised upwards: 300 million skiers or about four times the number of skiers in the world today. One can easily imagine the reaction of all actors in the world of winter sports in the face of such a planned revolution. However, a pre-survey conducted early in 2017 clearly showed the limits of the Western model of winter sports in China. The Chinese do not consider a full week in a winter sports resort, are unable to name a brand of equipment, skis or clothing, and are not concerned with them because they only ski an hour or two a day and then spend their time at the restaurant with their friends (the most important thing is eating well). One can imagine the efforts that producers of goods and services for skiers will have to develop to adapt and to adapt their products to Chinese customers.

Conclusion

Fifty years after its dawning, it is possible to legitimately raise the question if sports tourism will be more creative or destructive in terms of wealth for providers, destinations, cities, regions and states. Beyond the evolutions and the stakes previously highlighted, this fundamental question prefigures the development and the organization of the actors of the sports-tourism market who participate in a deep transformation of the direction of the holidays and their finalities in a context where physical activities and sports have invaded lifestyles. In a frantic quest to maximize beneficial impacts while delivering rewarding experiences to their customers, is there not a risk for sports-tourism providers to standardize their "off-the-shelf" or "franchised" products in a *McDonaldization* process (Ritzer, 1996) to the point that destinations become theatrical parks without historical, regional, cultural or gastronomic authenticity? Or, on the contrary, in this desire to continually *re-enchant* their offer, will natives and non-natives alike acquire even more power to fight against this *commodification* of the world by participating in this experience marketing and tourism communication?

References

Amabile, T.M. (1998). *How to kill creativity*. Harvard Business Review, Boston.

Anaba, V., Bodet, G., Bouchet, P. (2014). L'écotourisme à l'épreuve du divertissement sensoriel: le cas des hébergements atypiques. *RIMHE*, 10, 58–83.

Anholt, S. (2007). *Competitive identity: the new brand management for nations, cities and regions*. Palgrave MacMillan.

Anthony, D. (1966). *Sport and tourism*. CCPR, London.

Armstrong, J. (1986). International events and popular myths, in *International events: the real tourism impact, Proceedings of the 1985 Canada Chapter Conference*, Edmonton, Travel and Tourist Research Association (Canadian Chapter), 7–37.

Avaraham, E., Ketter, H. (2008). *Media strategies for marketing places in crisis*. Butterwoth-Heinemann Ed.

Baker, M., Gordon, A. (1976). *Market for winter sport facilities in Scotland*. Scottish Tourist Board, Edinburgh.

Beioley, S., Crookston, M., Tyrer, B. (1988). London docklands: the leisure elements. *Leisure Management*, 8(2), 30–33.

Bénavent, C. (2016). *Plateformes*. Edition FYP, Paris.

Boo, S., Busser, J., Baloglu, S (2009). A model of customer-based equity and its application to multiple destinations. *Tourism Management*, 30, 219–231.

Bouchet, P., Bouhaouala, M. (2009). Tourisme sportif: un essai de définition socio-économique. *Téoros*, 28(2), 3–8.

Bouchet, P., Hillairet, D. (2009). *Les marques de sport: approches stratégique et marketing*. De Boeck, Louvain.

Bouchet, P., Lebrun, A.-M. (2009). *Management du tourisme sportif. De la consommation à la commercialisation*. PUR, Rennes.

Canavan, B. (2013). The extent and role of domestic tourism in a small island: the case of the isle of man. *Journal of Travel Research*, 52(3), 340–352

Carù, A., Cova, B. (2006). Expériences de consommation et marketing expérientiel. *Revue Française de Gestion*, 32(162), 99–113.

Catoera, P.R., Graham, J.L. (1999). *International marketing*. McGraw-Hill, Irwin.

Chalip, L., Green, C., Vander Velden, L. (1998). Sources of interest in travel to the Olympic Games. *Journal of Vacation Marketing*, 4, 7–22.

Corbin, A. (1995). *L'avènement des loisirs, 1850–1960*. Aubier, Paris.

Crouch, G., Ritchie, B. (1999). Tourism, competitiveness, and societal prosperity. *Journal of Business Research*, 44, 137–152.

Crouch, G., Ritchie, B. (2000). The competitive destination: a sustainability perspective. *Tourism Management*, 21(1), 1–7.

Curbatov, O. (2003). L'intégration du consommateur par le knowledge marketing: conception, production et consommation d'un produit personnel. *Thèse de doctorat en sciences de gestion*, Université de Nice-Sophia Antipolis.

Cuvelier, P. (2000). La fin du tourisme fordiste. *Revue Espaces*, 177, 32–37.

De Knop, P. (1987). Some thoughts on the influence of sport tourism. in *Proceedings of the international seminar and workshop on outdoor education, recreation and sport tourism*, Netenya, Wingate Institute for Physical Education and Sport, 38–45.

De Knop, P. (1990). Sport for all and active tourism. *World Leisure and Recreating*, 32, 30–36.

Deery, M., Jago, L., Fredline, L. (2004). Sport tourism or event tourism: are they one and the same? *Journal of Sport Tourism*, 9(3), 235–245.

Delpy, L. (1996). A comparison of the pre and post economic impact figures reported for the 1994 World Cup. *11th Conference of the NASSM*, Moncton, New Brunswick University.

Dinnie, K. (2007). *Nation branding: concepts, issues, practice*. Elsevier, Burlington.

Direction du tourisme (2008). *Tourisme des Français: les activités des touristes lors de leurs voyages*, Bulletin statistiques et d'études, Tourisme infos stat n° 2008–7.

Dwyer, L., Kim, C. (2003). Destination competitiveness: a model and determinants. *Current Issues in Tourism*. Available online at http://channelviewpublications.net.

Enright, M.J., Newton, J. (2004). Tourism destination competitiveness: a quantitative approach. *Tourism Management*, 25(6), 777–788.

Fabry, N. (2009). Clusters de tourisme, compétitivité des acteurs et attractivité des territoires. *Revue internationale d'intelligence économique*, 1, 55–66.

Filser, M. (1994). *Le comportement du consommateur*. Dalloz gestion, Paris.

Gammon, S., Kurtzman, J. (2007). *Sport tourism: principles and practice* (2nd ed.), Leisure Studies Association, Eastbourne, 76, pp. 111–128.

Gammon, S., Robinson, T. (2003). Sport and tourism: a conceptual framework. *Journal of Sport Tourism*, 8(1), 21–26.

Gayet, J. (2014). *Place marketing trend. Tendances et nouvelles pratiques du marketing territorial.* Editions du Panthéon, Paris.

Gibson, H.J. (1998). Sport tourism: a critical analysis of research. *Sport Management Review*, 1, 45–76.

Gibson, H.J. (2002). Sport tourism at a crossroad? Considerations for the future, in S. Gammon and J. Kurtzman (Eds.), *Sport tourism: principles and practice*. Leisure Studies Association, Eastbourne, 76, 111–128.

Gibson, H.J., Attle, S., Yiannakis, A. (1998). Segmentating the sport tourist market: a lifespan perspective. *Journal of Vacation Marketing*, 4, 52–64.

Gibson, H.J., Yiannakis, A. (1992). Some correlates of the sport lover (tourist): a life course perspective. *Conférence Annuelle de la Société Nord-Américaine de Sociologie du Sport*, Toledo.

Gibson, H.J., Yiannakis, A. (1994). Some characteristics of sports tourists: a life span perspective. *Conférence Annuelle de la Société Nord-Américaine de Sociologie du Sport*, Savannah.

Gibson, H.J. (2003). Sport tourism. In J. Parks & J. Quarterman (Eds.), *Contemporary sport management*. Human Kineticks.

Gibson, H.J. (2004). Moving beyond the "what is and who" of sport tourism to understanding "why". *Journal of Sport Tourism*, 9(3), 247–265.

Glyptis, S.A. (1982). *Sport and Tourism in Western Europe*. British Travel Education Trust, London.

Hall, C. (1992). Adventure, sport and health tourism. in C. Hall, B. Weiler (Eds.), *Special interest tourism*. Belhaven Press, Londres, 141–158.

Higham, J., Hinch, T. (2009). *Sport and tourism: globalization, mobility and identity*. Elsevier, Oxford.

Hinch, T., Higham, J. (2001). Sport tourism: a framework for research. *International Journal of Tourism Research*, 3(1), 45–58.
Hinch, T., Higham, J. (2011). *Sport tourism development* (2nd ed.), Channel View Publications, UK, Bristol.
Hudson, S. (2003). *Sport and adventure tourism*. The Haworth Press, Binghamton.
Jackson, G., Glyptis, S. (1992). *Sport and tourism: a review of the literature. Reports to the Sports Council, Recreation Management Group (Unpublished Reports)*. Loughborough University, Loughborough.
Jaureguiberry, F., Lachance, J. (2016). *Le voyageur hypermoderne. Partir dans un monde connecté*. Erès, Paris.
Jennings, G. (2007). *Water-based tourism, sport, leisure and recreation*. Elsevier, Oxford.
Jeuring, J. (2016). Discursive contradictions in regional tourism marketing strategies: the case of Fryslân, The Netherlands. *Journal of Destination Marketing & Management*, 5(2), 65–75.
Kapferer, J.N. (2011). France: pourquoi penser marque?, *Revue Française de Gestion*, 9, 13–23.
Kolsun, J. (1988). The Calgary winter Olympics visitor study. *The Operational Geographer*, 16, 15–17.
Kotler, P., Haider, D.H., Rein, I. (1993). *Marketing places: attracting investment, industry and tourism to cities, states and nations*. Free Press, New York.
Kurtzman, J., Zauhar, J. (2003). A wave in time-the Sports tourism phenomena. *Journal of Sport and Tourism*, 8(1), 35–47.
Lapeyronie, B. (2009). Retombées socio-économiques du tourisme sportif: exemples des marathons en France. *Téoros*, 37–48.
Lazer, I. (1985). The 1984 Los Angeles Olympics. *Proceedings of the Canada Travel and Tourism Association Annual Conference, International Events: The Real Tourism Impact*, Canada Travel and Tourism Association, Edmonton, pp. 137–140.
Leiper, N. (1990). Tourism attraction systems. *Annals of Tourism Research*, 17(3), 367–384.
Liu, X., Sobry, C., Li, J., Liu, J. (2010). "Joint-decentralization": some reflections on the organization structure of high-performance sports events in China. *Kinesiology*, 42(2), 132–141.
McDowell, D., Leslie, D., Callicot, R. (1988). The Birmingham Olympic Bid: selling a city. *Proceedings of the First International Conference, Planning for Tourism and Leisure*, Newtonabbey, Ulster University, 75.
Nogawa, H., Yamaguchi, Y. Hagi, Y. (1996). An empirical research study on Japanese sport tourism in sport-for-Ali events: case studies of a single-night event and a multiple-night event. *Journal of Travel Research*, 35, 46–54.
OECD (2006). *Innovation and growth in tourism*. Paris.
Origet du Cluzeau, C., Vicérat, P. (2000). *Le Tourisme des années 2010. "La mise en future de l'offre"*. La Documentation Française, Paris.
Pigeassou, C. (2004). Le tourisme sportif: une réalité sociale aux contours incertains, in C. Sobry (Ed.), *Le Tourisme Sportif*., Presses Universitaires du Septentrion, Lille, 33–66.
Quan, S., Wang, N. (2004). Towards a structural model of the tourist experience: an illustration from food experiences in tourism. *Tourism Management*, 25(3), 297–305.
Rauch, A. (1996). *Vacances en France de 1830 à nos jours*. Hachette, Paris.
Redmond, G. (1990). Points of increasing contact: sport and tourism in the modern world, in A. Tomlinson (Éd.), *Proceedings of the leisure studies Association, Second international conference, Leisure, Labour, and Lifestyles: international Comparisons*. LSA Publication, Eastbourne, pp. 158–169.

Redmond, G. (1991). Changing styles of sports tourism: industry/consumer interactions in Canada, the USA, and Europe, in M.T. Sinclair, M.J. Stabler (Éds.), *The Tourism industry: an international analysis*. CAB International, Wallingford, pp. 107–120.

Rifkin, J. (2002). *The age of access: the new culture of hypercapitalism*. Putnam, New York.

Ritchie, J.R. (1984). Assessing the impact of hallmark events: conceptual and research issues. *Journal of Travel Research*, 23(1), 2–11.

Ritchie, J.R., Adair, D. (2004). *Sport tourism: interrelationships, impacts and issues*. Channel View Publications, Clevedon.

Ritchie, J.R., Crouch, G.I. (2000). The competitive destination: sustainability perspective. *Tourism Management*, 21(1), 1–7.

Ritzer, G. (1996). *The McDonaldisation of society: an investigation into the changing character of contemporary social life*. Pine Forge Press, Thousand Oaks.

Sobry, C. (2004). *Socioéconomie du sport*. De Boeck, Bruxelles.

Sobry, C. (2005). *Tourisme sportif*. Presses Universitaires du Septentrion, Villeneuve d'Ascq.

Standeven, J., De Knop, P. (1999). *Sport tourism*. Human Kinetics, Champaign, IL.

Standeven, J., Tomlinson, A. (1994). *Sport and tourism in South East England: a preliminary assessment*. SECSR, London.

Steenkamp, J.-B. (2001). The role of national culture in international marketing research. *International Marketing Review*, 18(1), 30–44.

Stieler, M. (2017). *Creating marketing magic and innovative future marketing trends: proceedings*. Proceedings of the Academy of Marketing Science, Editions Springler.

Touriscopie (2007). *Les nouvelles avant-gardes*, 96.

Turco, D., Riley, R., Swart, K. (2002). *Sport tourism*. Fitness Information Technology, Inc., Morgantown.

UNWTO (2004). *Indicators of sustainable development for tourism destinations: a guidebook*. Madrid, Spain.

Urbain, J.D. (2011). *L'envie du monde*. Paris, Bréal.

Usunier, J.C., Cestre, G. (2007). Product ethnicity: revisiting the match between products and countries. *Journal of International Marketing*, 15(3), 32–72.

Van Rheenen, D., Cernaianu, S., Sobry, C., Wille, F. (2016). Sport tourism research in the 21st century: future prospect for an evolving epistemology, in R. Melo, C. Sobry (Eds.), *Sport tourism: new challenges in a globalized world*. Cambridge Scholars Publishing, Newcastle upon Tyne.

Vargo, S.L., Lusch, R.F. (2008). Service-Dominant Logic: continuing the evolution. *Journal of the Academy of Marketing Science*, 36(1), 1–10.

Weed, M.E. (1999). More than sports holidays: an overview of the sport-tourism link. In Scarrot, M. (Ed.), *Proceedings of the sport and recreation information group seminar, Exploring sport tourism* (pp. 3–15). SPRIG.

Weed, M.E. (2005). Sport tourism theory and method: concepts, issues & epistemologies. *European Sport Management Quaterly*, 5(3), 229–242.

Weed, M.E. (2006). Sport tourism research: a systematic review of knowledge and a meta-evaluation of methods. *Journal of Sport Tourism*, 11(1), 5–30.

Weed, M.E., Bull, C.J. (2004). *Sports Tourism: participants, policy and providers*. Butterworth-Heinemann, Oxford.

Williams, V., Zelinsky, W. (1970). On some patterns in international tourist flows. *Economic Geography*, 46, 549–567.

Wynen, J. (2013). Explaining travel distance during same-day visits. *Tourism Management*, 36, 133–140.

Conclusion

Originally, the ambition of this volume was to group together in a single resource all the elements of sports business as we know it today. With the possible exception of a few comprehensive handbooks with similar intentions, texts on sport management have most often dealt with one specific aspect (sponsorship, the economics of professional sport, governance, brands, equipment manufacturers, the role of local and regional government, sport's place in the European Union, etc.); whereas a good understanding of the global sport ecosystem and its implications for management presupposes an overall vision of all three universes. This thematic development of knowledge is perfectly understandable, as it has taken the sector nearly two decades to gradually build up a body of substantiated, detailed knowledge that is firmly anchored in the real world and which, therefore, remains far from complete. Today, we are still some way from knowing everything there is to know about sports management and this is not the time to reach any sweeping conclusions. However, with worldwide revenue of nearly €1,000 billion, this sector is undoubtedly mature enough for us to clearly identify its scope, main characteristics and major issues. Bringing together "under one roof" what today appear to be the three main aspects of sports management reflects our determination to give students, teachers and professionals a snapshot of things as they stand today. Marketing, the industry and governance are considered the three main areas of the sector today and have been dealt with in three different volumes, each coordinated by a specialist. The aim of each volume is twofold: On the one hand, to report on the emergence of the field and retrace its major phases of development, and, on the other hand, to report on the main strategic issues it is currently facing.

Part I focuses on the most visible area of sports management, that of sports marketing, widely publicized by the media. It looks at the profound changes facing the sports business. Going international, globalization, digitalization, faster communication methods, experiential marketing, co-creation of sporting events with "ConsumActors", the integration of societal issues such as sustainable development, the need for professional sport to have an exemplary image, making sponsorship investments profitable, making employees part of communication policies, and taking the need for financial fair play at European level into account are some of the immense and diverse challenges organizations have to include in their sports marketing.

The year 2019, which sees the publication of these three volumes dedicated to global sports management, is a year rich in sporting emotions with the Olympic Winter Games in PyeongChang (South Korea) and the football World Cup in Russia. These two events were highlights for sports fans around the world, but they also provided a tremendous opportunity for all those involved in sports management, whether in marketing, the industry or sports governance. Major sporting events like these are an opportunity to see the three worlds described in this book coming together on common ground. Those involved were able to use the events as growth and/or visibility opportunities for their respective activities, despite time differences that were difficult to manage. Thus, during the Winter Olympics, on the French market alone, France Télévisions, the official broadcaster of the competition, gave advertisers almost nine and a half hours of broadcast time (equivalent to 1,557 ads). On the equipment side, several brands were very visible during the Korean games. Lacoste was the French team's official equipment supplier (Odlo is a partner of the French ski federation), while the US delegation was partnered by Ralph Lauren and Nike. For all these brands, the Winter Olympics are an opportunity to showcase new products that will only be available to the consumer the next time the games come around, i.e., with a development cycle of 3 or 4 years. At the World Cup in Russia, Adidas was one of those who came out on top. In addition to being the official partner for the tournament, the "brand with three stripes" also had deals with 12 national teams, compared with 10 for Nike, its great American rival. In total, nine different equipment manufacturers supplied the 32 teams participating in the final tournament. Finally, examples of the sports governance problems outlined in Part III could be seen at both these major 2018 events. Particularly during the World Cup in Russia, sports-tourism operators were called upon to transport millions of spectators to the competition. These two events also showed how sport could be used in political strategy, whether it be for a local authority (e.g., the World Cup host cities' use of matches to boost their image) or a national one. The Winter Olympics provided the opportunity for the two Koreas to begin a sporting and diplomatic rapprochement at a time when the World Cup was at the heart of geopolitical issues between Russia and the other major world powers. These major sporting events are also good barometers of how well the three sections of the global sports business are functioning. In the run-up to the 2024 Olympics in Paris, we should also examine the outlook for this three-way union. Will the world's biggest event be an opportunity to bring these three universes closer together? Will they know how to work together in pursuit of their respective interests even better than they do today? Will these collaborations go beyond the traditional partnerships that have long been observed between a sports brand and the top-level sportsman who is its ambassador? Will sports-event organizers or professional clubs consider sponsors as true partners capable of sitting on management committees and influencing strategic decisions? Will local and regional authorities, which have gradually exited the sports-event scene in recent years, see their last large-scale involvement in this field disappear, with the widespread use in Europe and the United States of sports facilities financed 100% by the private sector? Will they be exclusively responsible for promoting sport for all? Conversely, will they return to the spotlight by organizing large-scale events from scratch with the world's best players in order to promote their region? Will sports equipment manufacturers become brands that follow trends and consumption patterns in response to consumer demand or will they be able to innovate to the point of inventing new forms of sport that may then be developed into new events, creating new demand for sport tourism? Finally, for students who would like to get involved in this sector, will the professional challenges of the future come from hyper-adaptability, i.e., the need to move, during their career, from one sector to another, making them professionals in the field (sport management) rather than only in one area (marketing, industry or sport governance)? Or will their careers require hyper-specialization, i.e., the perfect mastery of a rare skill specific to one of the three areas?

Alongside this hypothesis of closer strategic and operational links between the three universes, is the possibility of a return, once the closing ceremony of the 2024 Olympic Games is over, to a more linear approach, where the three universes continue to operate and develop without significant interaction. This process could even bring some areas closer to non-sports-related fields. One could easily see the world of sports equipment manufacturers moving closer to the principles and operating methods of mass retail, with sport no longer a central element of brand DNA. One could also imagine that bringing together a large number of spectators in a stadium, which today constitutes the traditional marker of a sporting spectacle, could no longer be considered the norm. That the emergence of the virtual, made possible by technical progress, brings professional sport closer to the entertainment industry in a broader sense, with the sporting dimension becoming secondary. We should start to see some answers to these questions in some years.

Index

Note: Page numbers in *italics* indicate a figure and page numbers in **bold** indicate a table on the corresponding page.

3D manufacturing 178

accelerator programmes 222
AC Milan (club) **26**, **27**, **28**, **29**, 69n22
Adidas 3, 35, 40–41, **41**, 57, 59, 69n16, 69n19, 125–128, **125**, **126**, **128**, 132–134, 136, 139, 142, 144–145, 147–149, 155, 161, 163–165, 167–168, 172–175, 177–178, 180–183, **182**, **183**, 201–202, 205–207, 215, 319; "Speedfactory" 178, 206
Afghanistan: Soviet invasion of 41
Africa 12, 47, 68n9, 128, 150, 158
Airbnb 311
Al-Fayed, Mohamed 64
Alibaba 66, 143, 147, 185
alpinism: extreme 154
Amazon 60, 143, 147, 185, 190
American Civil War 161
American football 8, 10, **18**, 50–51, **52**, 123, 168; *see also* NFL (National Football League)
America's Cup 40
Amundsen, Roald 162
ancient Greece 160–161, 170
ancient Persia 170
ancient Rome 160–161, 170, 266
Apple 60
archery **18**, 160, **242**
Arc'téryx **125**, 127, 166, 176
Argentina 48, 51
Arsenal FC (club) 20, **26**, **27**, 28, **28**, 54, 59, **60**, 267
Asia 37, 40, 42, 45, 56, 121, 127–128, 131, 136–139, 141, 146–147, 149, 153, 174, 176, 247, 312; -Pacific zone 2
ASICS 41, **126**, 127, **128**, 147, 174, **182**
ASO (Amaury Sport Organisation) 47
AS Roma (club) **26**, **27**, 85
Association of National Olympic Committees (ANOC) 278
Association of Summer Olympic International Federations (ASOIF) 110, 278
athleisure 151, 167–168, 171, 200
Athlete's Foot 145–146, 185
atomicity 24–25
Australia 22, 37, **39**, **45**, 47, **48**, **53**, 127, **129**, 150, 185, **187**, 222; *see also* Summer Olympics
Australian Sports Technology Network 222
Austria **45**, **147**, 163–164, 179, 181, 184, **187**, 190, 258, 313
Aviva Premiership Rugby (APR) 89, **97**, 98–100, 109; *Play* 98; *Breakthru* 98

Babolat 132–133, 169
Bach, Thomas 101, 198
badminton **17**, 123, 132, **233**, 238, 242, **242**, 247, 249
Baidu (club) 66
Bangladesh 92; "Grameen-Danone" joint-venture 92
baseball 8, 10, **18**, 50–51, **52**, **53**, 75, 80, 168; *see also* MLB (Major League Baseball)
base jumping 154
basketball 8, 10, **17**, **19**, 22–23, **23**, **52**, 55, 68n9, 71, 73, 75, 124, **124**, 131–132, 162, 167–168, 174, 202, **233**, 238–239, 241, *241*, **242**, 247–249,

266, 270n19, 271n36; *see also* NBA (National Basketball Association)
Bayern Munich (club) 12, 25, **26**, **27**, 28, **28**, **29**, 54, 59, **60**, 62, 85
Bayrou, Georges 20
Beckham, David 55, 69n19
Beckham, Victoria 136
BeIn Sport 33, 35, 68n1, **97**
Belgium 26, **29**, **45**, **48**, **54**, **147**, 169, 175, 179–180, 184, **187**, **189**, 288
Benetton 165
Big Data 81, 209, 307
Billabong 131, 166
"boardsports" (sports de glisse) 166
body building 163, 194, **195**
Borg, Bjorn 119, 135
Borussia Dortmund *see* Dortmund
Bosman ruling/judgment 26, 35, 59, 68n9, 281
"bottom of the pyramid" (BOP) strategies 92
bouldering 166
bowling 194
bowling sports 194, **195**
boxing 11, **17**, 42, 202, 206, 231, **242**, 247; kick **18**, **31**
brand: equity 246–247; image 63, 232, 246–248, 258, 307; loyalty 247; positioning 33, 169, 202
branding 76, 161, 306; city 22, 307; co- 266; country/nation 63–67, 307; destination 307; international 62; place 307; policy 50
Brazil **45**, 48, 57, 80, 121, **129**, 147–150, 168, 170, 175, 185, **187**, **263**, 265, **265**; *see also* Summer Olympics
BRIC countries (Brazil/Russia/India/China) 150, 308
Bulgaria 137–138, 176
Bundesliga 12, **52**, **54**, 60

Cambodia 137, 176
camping 123, 161, 163
Canada 10, 37, **45**, 47, 49, 51, **52**, **126**, **129**, **147**, 176, 180, 185, **186**, 297; Montreal **30**, 40, 49, 163; Toronto 40, 49, **235**, **268**; *see also* Summer Olympics; Winter Olympics
Canada Goose 124, 166, 176
canoeing **234**, 243, 247, 255
casual sports 148
casual sportswear 168, 200
Champions League 25, 27, **28**, **29**, 59, 63
Champion USA 168
Chelsea FC (club) **26**, **27**, 28–29, **28**, 54, **60**, 64, 99
Chicago Bulls 266
China 9, 38, 42, 45–48, **45**, 51, 54–55, 58, 60, 65–66, 68n5, 112–113n15, **126**, 128, **129**, 130–131, 137–138, 142–143, 147, **148**, 149–150, 153–154, 157, 162–163, 166, 170–179, **172**, 181, 183, 185, **186**, **210**, 258, 262, 307, 313; automotive market in 46; Beijing 15, **30**, 34, 42, 65, 110, 177, **210**, 258, 262, **263**; Shanghai 36, 46, 177, 181, 202, *203*, 206; single-child policy 154; *see also* Summer Olympics
classic football 2, 8, 10
Cleveland Cavaliers 266
climate change 104, 157–158, 313
Club Box 83–84
Cold War 14, 101, 161–162
Columbia Sportswear 125, **126**, 134, 180, **182**
Commission of the European Communities 91
Community of Independent States (CIS) 178
Compagnie des Alpes, La 259
"ConsumActors" 5, 261, 318
Converse **126**, 163, 167, 175, **182**
Corporate Social Responsibility (CSR) 8, 89–112, *104*, **105**, **107**, 112n1, 112n3, 112n4, 112n12; European Green Paper on 91; SEOs' deployment of 96–111; and sport 89–96
Coubertin, Baron Pierre de 100–101, 276
Council of Europe 284
Court of Arbitration for Sport (CAS) 101, 275, *277*, 280–281
"creative destruction" 50, 209
Croatia 26
cross-country skiing 160, 163, 194
CrossFit 209
Cuban, Mark 73, 86
cultural dispersion 205
Customer Relationship Management (CRM) 58, 60, 67, 76, 310
customization 144, 150, 178, 202, 310
cycling 13, **17**, **18**, 33, 42, 47–48, 123, 125, 130, 151, 162, 193–194, **195**, 202, 206, **234**, 238–239, 241–242, **242**, 245, 247, 249, 255, 264, 298

Czechoslovakia 41
Czech Republic 176

Dallas Cowboys 267
dance **18**, 72, 123, 194, **195**, 197, 202
"Danone Way" 92
Dassler, Adolf (Adi) 40, 173–174
Dassler, Horst 161, 174
Dassler, Rudolf 174
Decathlon 3, 134, 141, 144–146, **147**, 148, **148**, 156, 169, 177, 180–181, 183–184, **186**, 201, 215
de Gaulle, General Charles 14–15
Deloitte Football Money League 25, **26**, **27**, 29–30
Deng Xiaoping 65
Denmark 179, 184, **188**
DICK'S Sporting Goods 3, **147**, **148**, 185, **186**
direct to consumers (DTC) 145, 155, 170, 185, 190
diving 193, 255
Doha 42
doping 6, 94, 101, 110, 157–158, 232, 274–275, *277*, 280–282, 285; *see also* World Anti-Doping Agency (WADA)
Dortmund (club) **26**, **27**, **28**, 54, 60
draft system 11–12, 29
Drut, Guy 19

Eastern Mountain Sports (EMS) 190
East Germany 162
e-commerce 3, 139, **140**, 141–145, 147, **148**, 156, 169–170, 185, 190, 200, 205
Elliot, Missy 136
England 19–20, **29**, 30, 35, 40, **52**, 64, 89, 93–94, 96, **97**, 161, **265**; Conservative government 99; Labour government 99; London 20, 33, *35*, 50–51, 58–59, 64, 100–101, 105, 109–110, 144, 191, 198, 206, 222, **235**, 265, **265**, 267, **267**; *see also* Summer Olympics
English Football Association 19–20; FA Cup 19
ENSEP 15
ESPN 50, 199
e-sports 199
ethical blowbacks 95
Euro 2016 54, 80, 96, 100, 104–108, *104*, **105**, **109**, **235**, **263**
Europe 2, 4, 7, 9, 12–13, 19, 28–29, **30**, 34–35, 37, 40, 45, 51, 54, 64–65, 69n22, 91, 96, **107**, 123, 127–128, 137, 141–142, 145–146, **147**, 158, 161, 173–174, 176, 181, 185, 212, 225, 248, 266, 275, 295, 312–313, 320; Eastern 68n9, 137, 149, 181, 184, 307; Southern 150; Western 148, 150, 172, 176–177
European Council 209
European Economic Community 175
European Football Championship 89, 94, 100, 262
European Sponsorship Association (ESA) 276
European Union (EU) **105**, 170, 179, 276, 281–282, 285, 291, 292n9, 300, 318: Court of Justice 68n9, 281; European Parliament 284; Treaty on the Functioning of the European Union (Lisbon Treaty) 281–282
Eurosport 33, 35, **188**
e-WOM ("word of mouth on the web") 311
experiential marketing 72, 74, 156, 318
experiential retail 144

Facebook 57–58, 60–62, 80–81, 137, 311; Watch 84
fake amateurism 14, 19
fan culture *104*
fan experience 8, 71–87
Fan Relationship Management (FRM) 8, 56, 60, 75–76
Far East 137–138, 173–177
FC Barcelona (club) 12, **13**, **26**, 28, **28**, **29**, **30**, **60**, 64, 151, 213, 266–267
Fédération Internationale de l'Automobile (FIA) 3, 42–43, 284
Federation of the European Sporting goods Industry (FESI) 276
fencing **17**, 19, 160, **242**, 247
FFSA (French motorsport federation) 42
FIAT 14, 20, 40
FIFA (Fédération Internationale de Football Associations) 8, 89, 93, 100, 112–113n15, 262, 285; FIFAgate 110; *see also* World Cup
Fila 120, **126**, 127, 167, 172
Finland **125**, **126**, **128**, 184, **188**, 190
fishing 125, 163, **195**
Fitbit 125, **125**, 134, 173, 183, **183**
fitness 123, **124**, **193**, **210**, **228**
Fonda, Jane 163
football *see* American football; classic football

"Football in The Community" (FiTC) programme 99
Foot Locker 145, **147**, 156, 185, **186**
Foreman-Ali match 11
Formula 1 42–43, **44**, 45, 47, **265**; Concorde Agreements 43
Formula One Administration (FOA, formerly FOCA) 43
Formula One Management (FOM) 43–44
foundations 92, 95–96, 100, 109; Fondation Albert Ferrasse 96; Fondation du Football 96; Fondation Henri Sérandour 96
France 1, 4, 13–16, 20–22, 24, 28, **29**, **31–32**, 33–37, 45, **45**, 47, **48**, 49, 51, **52**, 54–55, 61, 63, 65, 78, 80, 89, 91, 93–94, 96, **97**, 98–100, **107**, 109, 112n1, 112–113n15, 122, **126**, 129–130, **129**, 141, 145–146, **147**, **148**, 151, 157, 163, 166, 169–170, **172**, 174–175, 179, 181, 184–185, **186–187**, **193**, **195**, 198, 200, 210, 221, 227, 229, 231–232, 236–239, 242, **242**, 248–251, 254–256, 258–260, **263**, **265**, 266, 269n7, 270n22, 271n36, 296–298, 301, 312–313; Chamonix 229; Grenelle Environment Forum 91, 112n7; INS (national sports institute) 15; Marseille 36, 54, 59, 83, 112n8, 266; Ministry of Sport (Sports Ministry) 1, 17, 212, 229–230, **230**, 260; National Assembly 15; National Centre for Sport Development (CNDS) 230, 244; New Economic Regulations (NRE) Act 91, 112n7; Paris 15–16, 43, 47, 49, 55–57, 59, 61–64, 83, 183, 206, 221–222, 230, 264, 269n9, 276, 319; school hours 16–17, 157; Senate 243; Sports Code 230–231, 255; sports federations 17, 19, **17–19**; sports subsidies 15, 17, 19, **17–19**, 22–24, **23**, 68n2, 96, 112, 230, 240, 243, 245; *see also* Summer Olympics
Francophonie Games, La 262
free market entry/exit 10, 24–25
French athletics federation 240, 245, 249, 270n16
French basketball federation 241, **241**, 249, 270n19
French cycling federation 249
French Football Federation 21, 241, 245, 269n12
French Olympic federations 245
French professional football league *see* Ligue de Football Professionnel (LFP)
French Rugby Federation 98, 245, **245**, 248
French ski federation (FFS) 243–244, 319
French volleyball federation 241, 250, 270n16

"G-14" 25
Gambardella, Emmanuel 20
generation Y 197–198
generation Z 198
geomarketing 50, 69n13
Germany 12, 16, 28, **29**, **45**, 48, **48**, 51, **52**, 54, 60, 65, 80, **125**, **126**, **128**, **129**, 145, **147**, 168–169, **172**, 174, 176, 178–180, 184, **187–189**, 206, 238, 255, 260; Berlin 11, 82, 222; Munich **30**, 177, 266; *see also* East Germany; Summer Olympics
Global Association of International Sport Federations (GAISF) 278
Global Compact 91
globalization 9, 101, 202, 212, 296, 299–300, 302, 306, 312, 318; of sport 9, 100
Global Reporting Initiative (GRI) 91, 104–105; sustainability reporting guidelines 91
Globetrotter 144, 169, **188**
glocalization 312–313
golf **17**, **31**, **124**, 160, 164–165, 172, 180, 185, **187–189**, **234**, 240–242, **242**, 249, 270n15, 299
Google 60, 311
GoPro 125, **125**, 134, 173, 309
Go Sport Group 3, 141, 181, 184, **187**, **189**
governance: definition 283–284; *see also* sports governance
Grand Prix 43–44, **44**, **45**, 64, **265**
Grand Slam 40
Greece **29**, 184, **234**; *see also* ancient Greece
Gucci 132, 135, 168
gymnastics **18**, 151, 194, **195**, 196, 241, **242**, 247, 249

hackathons 85
halls of fame **229**, **235**, 268, **268**
handball **18**, **19**, 23, **23**, **31**, 34, 84, 133, 168, 241, **242**, 247, 249

hang gliding **18**, 255, 269n8
Hanot, Gabriel 20
hardgoods 119
Hermès 168
Hervis Sport 181, 184, **187**, 190
Herzog, Maurice 15
hiking **18**, 123, **124**, 130, 153, 161, 163–166, 175, 178, 180, 199, 239, 249, 255, 298
Hitler 11
hockey *see* ice hockey
homogeneity: and pure competition 24
horse riding **17**, 160, **233**, 242, **242**, 248, 255
Hussein, Saddam 63

Ibrahimovic, Zlatan 119, 135
ice hockey 8, 10, **18**, 22, **31–32**, 49, **52**, 75, 164, 168, **210**, **235**, **242**, 247, **268**; *see also* NHL (National Hockey League)
Ikea 181
income 25, 51, 68n3, 76, 240, 243, 245, 260, 302; "match day" 25; "broadcasting" 25; "commercial" 25
incubators 221–222
India 45, 54, 121, **129**, 149–150, 170, 178, 181, 185
Indonesia 54–56, 137, 176, **187**
indoor climbing 133, 151, 166, **210**
inline skating 125, 133, 165
innovation: in sports industry 5, 56, 82, 118, 120, 127, 133–135, 145–146, 150–151, **152**, 156, 173, 192, 202, 209–223, **210**, 286–291, 310; "open" 218, 222; process 211, 216–220, *219*, 222, 286, 289; product 56, 134, 211–213, 217–218, 222; services 211–213
INSEP 14–15, 230
Instagram 57, 61, 80–81, 85
Inter Milan (club) **26**, **28**, **29**, 69n22
International Association of Athletics Federations (IAAF) 110, 262, 285
International Olympic Committee (IOC) 8, 89, 93–94, 96, 100–104, *103*, 108, 110–111, 198, 262, 270n35, 275–276, *277*, 278–280, 282, 285, 291n1, 291n3; Agenda 21 "Sport for Sustainable Development" 101, 112n10; Olympic Agenda 2020 102; Sport and Environment Commission 101; "Sustainability Strategy" 102–104, *103*, 111
International Rugby Board (IRB) 21–22, 48; as World Rugby 22
International Standards Organisation (ISO) 91, 101, 105, **108**
Internet 3, 25, 34, 56, 58, 78, **140**, 142, 156, 162, 166, 168, 173, 185, 190, 197–198, 200, 238, 309–311
Intersport 3, 141, 144–145, **147**, **148**, 156, 170, 181, 183–185, **189**, 190
Iran 60, 146
Iraq 63
Ireland 68n10, 160, 179, **188**, 255
Israel 146
Italy 12, 20, 28, **29**, **45**, 47–48, 54, **126**, 146, **147**, 163, 165–166, 168, 170, 175–176, 178–179, 184, **187**, **189**, 258; Milan 151; Rome 14, 15, **30**, 40; Serie A 12, **54**; *see also* ancient Rome; Summer Olympics

JanSport 171
Japan 38, 42, **45**, 48, **52–53**, 54, 65, 125, **125**, **126**, 128, **128**, 131, 165–166, 172, **172**, 174, 178–179, **186–188**, 260–261, 312; Nagano 42; Osaka 42; Tokyo **30**, 42, **53**, 112n15, 199, 206; *see also* Summer Olympics; Winter Olympics
jogging 193–194
Johannsson, Scarlett 136
Joshua-Klitschko match 11
Journal of Sport & Tourism 299–300
Journal of Sport Management (JSM) 39, **39**, 299
judo **18**, **233**, 240–242, **242**, 270n15
Juventus FC (club) 12, 20, 25, **26**, **28**, **29**, 40, 54, **60**, 62

K2 **125**, 163, 176, 183, **183**
karate **18**, 249
kayaking **17**, 216, **234**, **242**
Kazakhstan **48**, 177–178
Killy, Jean-Claude 19
kinesiology 36
kite surfing 166, 216
Knight, Phil 168, 174
Knysna strike 36
Kuwait 63

Lacoste 119, 132, 135, 175, 319
Lacoste, René 162

LA Gear 120, 127, 163
Latin America 2, 147, 185
leAD (Berlin) 222
Le Mans race **235**, 262
Le Tremplin (Paris) 222
LFP (Professional Football League) *see* Ligue de Football Professionnel (LFP)
lifestyle products 119, 123–124, 165, 207
Ligue de Football Professionnel (LFP) 8, 35, **54**, 78–79, 98, 112n12; Ligue 1 (L1) **23**, **52**, **54**, 60–61, 78, 89, **97**, 98, 266; "Jouons la Collectif" ("Play Together") 98
Ligue Nationale de Rugby (LNR) 22, 35, 49, 84, **97**, 98; Top 14 (T14) championship 22–23, **23**, 89, **97**, 98–100, 109, 112n5
Liverpool FC (club) **26**, **27**, **28**, **29**, 59, **60**, 168, 268
LNR (*Ligue Nationale de Rugby*/National Rugby League) 22, 49, 84, **97**, 98
logos 62–63, 247
Los Angeles Dodgers 80
Los Angeles Lakers 266
Louis, Joe 10–11
Louis-Schmeling paradox 10
Louis Vuitton 168
Lululemon Athletica 125, **126**, 132, 168, 171, **186**

Madison Square Garden 71
Madonna 136
Malaja ruling 35, 68n9
Malaysia 45, **45**, **188**
Malraux, André 14
Manchester City (club) **26**, **27**, 29, 59, **60**, 69n22, 85, 100
Manchester United (club) 25, **26**, **27**, 28, **28**, **29**, 54, **60**, 62, 68n4, 100, 168, 213, 266
martial arts 160, 196–197
Marx, Karl 40
Maslow's hierarchy of needs 9
match-day experience 71, 80–87
McDonalds 11
Mediterranean Games 262
Mexico **45**, 297; Mexico City **30**, 50; *see also* Summer Olympics
Michelin 14, 40, 134
Middle East 2, 45, 47, 121, 128, 184–185
millennials 84, 125, 129, 197–199
Mizuno 41, 174–175
MLB (Major League Baseball) 2, 8, 10, 50, **52**, 75, 85, **95**, **268**
MLS (Major League Soccer) 2, 8, 10, 85
Moldova 176
Moncler 131, 135, 166–167
monobrand stores 3, **140**, 141–142, 155
motor racing 261
motor sports 194, **195**
mountain biking 216, 255, 258
mountaineering **18**, 153, 161, 163, 255
Murdoch, Rupert 22, 48

Napoleonic wars 161
National Handball League 84
national Olympic committees (NOCs) 110–111, 275–276, *277*, 278, 282, 291n1
National Rugby League *see* Ligue Nationale de Rugby (LNR)
National School for Mountain Sports (ENSM) 244
NBA (National Basketball Association) 2, 8, 12, 33, 47, 51, **52**, 55, 60, 71, 75, 80, 82, 85–86, **95**, 101, 168, 212, 266, **268**; NBA Europe Live Tour 51
NBC 50, 112n15; Sports 50
NCAA (National Collegiate Athletic Association) 12, 40
netball 215
Netherlands, the 26, **29**, **48**, 179–180, 184; Amsterdam 82
New Balance 41, **126**, 127, **128**, 168, 174–175, **182**
New York Knicks 71, 87
New York Yankees 10, 266
New Zealand 22, 37, **39**, 150, 171, **187**, **263**
NFL (National Football League) 2, 8, 50–51, **52**, 60, 75, **95**, 168, 212; Super Bowl 50, 81
NHL (National Hockey League) 2, 8, 12, **12**, 29, 49–50, 60, 75, 80, **95**
Nielsen Sports Institute 78, 129
Nike 3, 35, 41, 56–59, 69n16, 69n19, 120, 125–128, **126**, 132–135, 137, 139, 141–142, 144–145, 147–149, 155–156, 163–165, 167–168, 172, 174–175, 177–178, 180–183, **182**, 185, 201–202, 205–207, 215, 239, 319
Nike+ Run Club (NRC) 57
North America 2, 7, 9, 38, 45, 49–50, 75, 81, 90, 95, **95**, 126, 128, 132, 141, 150, 170, 266, 268
North Face, The (TNF) 124–125, **126**, 127–128, 132, 134, 166, 171, **182**

Norway **147**, 162–163, 169, 184, **187**, 190, 258; *see also* Winter Olympics
NPD 3, 122, 171–172, **172**, 199, 201

Oceania 128
Olympic Charter 276, 278–279
Olympic Games 15–16, 30, 40, 59, 65, 80, 89, 94, 96, 100–102, *103*, **109**, 110–111, 112–113n15, 161–162, 180, 191, 198–199, 231, **235**, 262–263, **265**, 274–276, *277*, 278–280, 297, 307, 313, 320; *see also* Summer Olympics; Winter Olympics
Olympic Movement 101–103, *103*, 110–111, 276–278, 280, 284
Olympics 15–16, 33, 41, **41**, 158, 161, 270n35; *see also* Olympic Games; Summer Olympics; Winter Olympics
Olympic Truce 280
Organising Committees of the Olympic Games (OCOG) 101, 105, 108, 110, 276, *277*
organizational social responsibility (OSR) 89–92, 95–96, 101, 110–111
Organization for Economic Co-operation and Development (OECD) 91, 300; Guidelines for Multinational Enterprises 91
orienteering **18**, 255
Outdoor Sport Valley (OSV) (Rhône-Alpes) 221, 248
Owens, Jesse 11, **41**

Pacquiao-Mayweather match 11
Pakistan 137
parachuting **18**, **234**, 255
parkour 210, 212
Patagonia 130–131, 312
Pentland 174–175
perfect competition 24
pétanque **18**, **31**, 194
Peugeot Cup 14
Philippines, the 137
Pokemon Go 80
Poland 41, 47, 138, 184
Popular Front (France) 13
Portugal 26, **29**, 179, 181, 184, **187**, 190
Premier League (PL) 30, 33, 51, **52**, **54**, 89, **97**, 99–100, 109, 112n6, 191; "Creating Chances" programme 99; Charitable Fund 99
production resources: free movement of 24–25
Professional Footballers' Association 99
professionalism 14, 19–20
professional sports 2, 8, 9–11, 19–30, **23**, 40, 42, 50, **52**, 54, 93, 95–96, 217–218, **230**, **235**, 237, 261, 266, 271n36, 318, 320
PSG (Paris Saint-Germain) (club) 25, **26**, 29, 55–56, 59–64, **60**, 69n19, 74–75, 96
public finance: in French sport **23**
Puma 41, 120, **126**, 127–128, **128**, 131–132, 135–136, 144, 147, 161, 163, 167, 174, 180, 182, **182**
pure competition *see* perfect competition

Qatar 9, 29, 42, 55, 61, 63–65, 100, 112–113n15, 157, 285
QSI 61–62

racket sports 134, 153, 194, 197, 238
Rallye **31**, 181, 185
Real Madrid (club) 12, **13**, 25, **26**, 27–28, **27**, **28**, **29**, **60**, 62, 68n4
Reddit 85
Reebok 35, 41, **126**, 127, 135–136, 163–164, 167, 175, 180, **182**
Rihanna 136, 167
Rio Earth Summit 101, 306
robotics 178, 206
Rogge, Jacques 101, 284
Roland Garros 33, 35, 83, 89, **235**, 270n15
Romania **29**, 41, 137, 175–176, 301
Rossignol 35, 164–165, 180, 205
rowing **17**, 19, **242**, 243, 248, 255
rugby **18**, 19, **19**, 21–23, **23**, **31**, 33–35, 40, 48–49, 82, 89, 94, 96, **97**, 98, 100, 112n5, 154, 162, 168, 221, **242**, 245, *245*, 248, 271n36; *see also* Rugby Union
Rugby Union 19, 21, 49, 77, 89, 94, 96; Super 14 77
Rugby World Cup 21, 42, 48, 261, **263**
running 2, 40, 57, 123, **124**, 125, 130, 132, 134, 153, 160, 163–164, 168–169, 174, 176, 193–194, **195**, 196–197, 199, 202, 206, **210**, **234**, 237, 239, 249, 258
Russia 26, 42, 45, **45**, 47–48, 60, 64–65, 110, 112n15, 121, 142, 149–150, 158, 162–163, 166, 170, 178, 180–181, **186**, 261–262, 285, 319; Moscow **30**, 41–42, 180–181, 262; Sochi 110, 112n15, **235**, 262; *see also* Summer Olympics; Winter Olympics

sailing **18**, 40, 217, 230, **234**, **242**, 247–248, 255, 298, 312
salary cap 11, 30
Salomon 3, 35, **125**, **126**, 127, 132–133, 135, 144, 149, 164–165, 169, 171, 178, **183**, 205
Samaranch, Juan Antonio 101
Samsung 172
San Francisco 49ers 266
San Francisco Giants 80
SASP (*Société Anonyme Sportive Professionelle* or Professional Sports Limited Company) 20
Saucony **126**, 169
Schmeling, Max 10–11
Scotland 22, **29**, 160
scuba diving 164, **234**, 255
Serbia 26, **29**
service experience 76
SFR Sports 33, 68n1
Shanghai ranking 36
Shimano 125, **125**, 127, **128**, **183**
skateboarding 166, 199, 216
Skechers **126**, 127, **128**, 182, **182**
skiing **18**, 123–124, 132–134, 154, 163, 166, 180, 194, **195**, 205, **210**, 211, 241, **242**, 244, 248, 255, 258–260, 299, 313; *see also* cross-country skiing; waterskiing
Slovenia 163, 184
smart city 307
smart destination 306–307
Snapchat 61, 80–81
sneaker culture 205
snowboarding 124, 133, 166, 169, 199, 216
soccer *see* classic football; MLS (Major League Soccer)
social media 8, 56–59, 61–62, 80–81, 83, 86, 162, 198, 213, **233**, 238–239, 264; *see also individual social media sites*
Socrates 191
softgoods 119, 137–138
South Africa 22, 34, 42, **48**, 146, **263**, 265, **265**, 270n32
South America 12, 40, 47, 65–66, 128, 142, 149
South Korea 42, 48, 199, 319; Daegu 42; *see also* Winter Olympics
Spain **29**, 30, **45**, 47–48, **48**, 51, **52**, 54, **129**, 146, **147**, 168, 178–180, 184, **187–189**, **265**; Barcelona **30**, 151, 265–267, **265**; La Liga 12, **13**, **52**; *see also* Summer Olympics
Speedo 175
Sport 2000 3, 135, 141, 144, **147**, 170, 184–185, 190
Sport Business Journal 37
sport clusters 221–222
Sport Inbox 83–84
sport organizations: amateur 217; national 212, 215; non-profit 212, 214–218, 220, 232, 233, *246*, 286–288; professional 95, 217; public 214–215, 218, 227–273
Sport Trade Marketing International (STMI) 184
sport(s) federations 17, **17**, **18**, 41, 93, 96, 192–193, 197, 225, 227–228, 230–231, **230**, 236–250, *246*, 255, *257*, 269, 302; governance of 274–291; international 275–276, 278–280, 290; subsidies to **17**
sport: globalization of 9, 100
sport-health 128–130
sporting goods: consumers of 191–208; distribution of 139–148, **140**, **147**, **148**; history of 160–190; industry 2–3, 5, 117–224; innovation 209–224; manufacturers 1–3, 5, 34–35, 41, 45, 51, 67, 93, 119–121, 125, 133–137, 139, 141–146, 148, 153–157, 160, 163–164, 175–176, 199, 206, 214, 318–320; market 3, 117, 120, 122–123, 126, 131–132, 161, 169–170, 173, 180; retailers 2–3, 5, 35, 93, 142–143, 145, 155–157, 165, 169, 175, 177–181, 183–185, **186**, **188**, 190, 246; *see also* sports clothing; sports footwear
Sporting Goods Intelligence 172, 182, 190
sport-nature 128, 130–131
sports: collective 134; collegiate 160, 170
Sports and Fitness Industry Association (SFIA) 198–199
Sports Authority, The 157, 185, **186**
sports clothing 171, 175; *see also individual brands/manufacturers*
sports culture 75, 282, 303
Sports Direct **147**, **148**, 169, 175, 184, **186**, 190
sports economy 1, 4, 6, 121, 154
sports equipment 2, 41, 71, 130, 182, **183**, 239, 243, 289, 320
sports-event organizers (SEOs) 8, 77, 89–112, **230**, 269n9, 310, 319
sports experience 76, 237
sports footwear 124–125, 137; *see also individual brands/manufacturers*

sports governance 5, 6, 37, 225–317, **228**, **233**, 319
sports law 36, 68n11, 280
sports management 5–6, 5, 7, 9, 36–38, **38**, **39**, 42, 68n11, 72, 318–319
sports marketing 1–6, 5, 7–8, 9–68, 119, 123, 133, 136, 148, 161–162, 168, 252–253, 318–319; in 1980s Europe 30–37; birth of 9–30; books on 37–38; and celebrities 136–137; contemporary 37–67, **38**; journals 39–40; *see also* experiential marketing
sports sciences 4, 36
Sports Tech Collider (San Francisco) 222
Sports Tech Hub (London) 222
sports tourism 4, 6, 226, 227, **229**, 254–268, 295–314, *304*, 319; active *304*; event *304*; nostalgia 267, *304*; opportunity 304; packages **265**
squash **18**, 238
Sri Lanka 137
Stade de France 74–75, 83, 267, **267**
stand-up paddling 125, 166, 210, 212
Stanley Cup 12, **12**
Starbucks 11
streetwear 166, 170
strength training 194
Summer Olympics **30**, 33–34, **41**, 109, 112, 112–113n15, 261–262, 307; Athens **30**, 265; Atlanta 15, **30**, 34; Barcelona **30**; Beijing 15, **30**, 34, 42, 65, 110, **210**, 262, **263**; Berlin 11, 82; London 33, 58–59, 101, 105, 109–110, **109**, 191, 198; Los Angeles **30**; Melbourne 40; Mexico City **30**; Montreal **30**; Moscow **30**, 41–42; Munich **30**; Rio 48, 80, 109, **109**, 112–113n15, 199, **263**, 265, **265**; Rome 14–15, **30**, 40; Seoul **30**, 42; Sydney **30**, 34, 42, 262; Tokyo **30**, 42, 112–113n15, 199
surfing 133, 166, **234**
sustainability 91–93, 100–104, **103**, 108–111, **108**, **109**, 130–131, 159, 218, 264, 300, 305–306
sustainable development (SD) 45, 67, 89, 104, 111, 112n11, 154, 303, 306, 312, 318
Sweden **29**, **147**, 162, 169–170, 179, **187**, 190
swimming 13, **18**, **124**, 163, 193–194, **195**, 196, 236, 239, **242**, 247, 249, 298
Switzerland **48**, 145–146, **147**, **148**, 179–181, 184, **187–188**, 258, 276, 313

table tennis **18**, 194, **195**, **233**, 241, **242**, 249
Tacchini, Sergio 162
taekwondo **18**, 242, **242**, 247
Tai chi 128, 151
Taiwan **125**, **129**, 137, 176
Taiwan Professional League 77
team sports 153, 163, 167, 239
Telegram 60
television rights 10–11, 30, **30**, 39, 43, 49–50, 60, 276
Tencent 59, 66
tennis **18**, **31**, 40, 61, 83, 125, 132–133, 135, 162, 164–165, 167, 169, 180, 194, **195**, 207, **233**, **235**, 236, 239, 242, **242**, 247, 270n15, 298
territorial marketing 307
Thailand 137, **188**
Timberland **126**, 127, 132, 171, **182**
Titleist 172
Top 14 22–23, **23**, 89, **97**, 98
Tottenham (club) **26**, **27**, 100
Tour de France 22, 33, 89, 123, 261, 264
trail running 123, 125, 130, 132, 134, 164, 169, 176, 194, **234**, 258
transparency 24, 68n10, 191, 274, 284–285, 308
trekking 161, 193, **234**
Tripadvisor 310–311
triple bottom line 90
Turkey 138
Twickenham 50, 267
Twitter 57, 60–61, 80

Uber 213, 308, 311
UCPF 79
Ukraine 176, 178, 181
Under Armour 120, **126**, 127, **128**, 136, 173, 179, **182**, 183
Union Cycliste Internationale (UCI) 47, **48**; World Tour (ProTour) 47, **48**
Union of European Football Associations (UEFA) 8, 25–26, 28–29, 89, 93–94, 96, 100, 104–105, *104*, **105–107**, 108–109, **109**, 262; Financial Fair Play regulations 29
Unique Selling Proposition (USP) 202
United Kingdom 30, **48**, 93, 98–99, **129**, **147**, **148**, 160, 167, 169–170, 174–175,

179, 181, 184, **186**, 190, 216, 238, 255, 291n1
United Nations (UN) 91–92, 104, 279–280, 291n1; "2030 Agenda for Sustainable Development" 104; General Assembly 101; Millennium Development Goals 92; Principles for Responsible Investment 91; Sustainable Development Goals 92
United Nations Environment Programme (UNEP) 103
United Nations Organisation for Education, Science and Culture (UNESCO) 279–280; International Charter of Physical Education and Sport 279; International Convention against Doping in Sport 280
United States 9–11, 14, 24, 36, 40–42, **45**, 47–50, **48**, **52–53**, 56, 60, 65, 75, 93, 95–96, 112–113n15, 123–124, **125**, 126–128, **126**, **128**, **129**, 137, 141, 145–148, **147**, **148**, 157, 160–163, 168, 170–172, **172**, 174, 177, 180–182, 184–185, **186–188**, 190, 199–200, 247, 253, 260, 291n1, 295, 312, 320; Atlanta 15, **30**, 34, 81, 177; Boston **12**, 49; Chicago **12**, 49, 266; Dallas **44**, 73, 81, 267; Denver 85, 177; Detroit **12**, **44**, 49; Houston 55, 81; Indianapolis **44**, 261; Los Angeles **12**, **30**, 80, 151, 206, 266; New York 10, **12**, 49, 57, 71, 81, 87, 151, 206, 264, 266–267, **267**; Salt Lake City 176–177; San Francisco 80, 146, 222, 266; Santa Clara 81; *see also* Summer Olympics; Winter Olympics
USA *see* United States
USSR 14, 41

Vans **126**, 127, 132, 144, 167, 171, **182**
Vendée Globe 22, 255, 261–262
VF Corp **126**, 127, **128**, 171, **182**
Vietnam 137–138, 175–177
volleyball **18**, 23, **23**, 34, 133, **233**, 239, 241, **242**, 247, 250, 270n16, 271n36, 287

walking 13, 123, **124**, 193–196, **195**, 301
Walmart 190
waterskiing **18**, 255
WeChat 58–60
Wembley Stadium 50, 267, **267**
West, Kanye 136, 167
Wilson **125**, 127, 171, **183**
windsurfing 166, 216, 269n8
wingsuit 154
Winter Olympics 19, 33–34, **41**, 109, 231, 262, 307, 319; Beijing 42, 65, 258; Lillehammer 101; Nagano 42; PyeongChang 42, 199, 261, 319; Sochi 110, 112–113n15, **235**; Vancouver 33, 109–110, **109**
winter sports 3, **124**, 134, 153, 158, 163–165, 183, 211, 244, 258–259, 313
World Anti-Doping Agency (WADA) 101, 274–275, *277*, 280
World Athletics Championships 262
World Commission on Environment and Development (Brundtland Report) 92, 101
World Cup (football) 2, 30, 33–34, **33**, 36, 40–42, **41**, 47, 54, 57, 63, 65, 68n5, 68n10, 80, 82, 109, **109**, 111–112, 112–113n15, 157, **235**, 261–262, **263**, 265, 267, 270n32, 285, 297, 319; *see also* Rugby World Cup
World Federation of Advertisers (WFA) 276
World Federation of the Sporting Goods Industry (WFSGI) 276
World Health Organization 170, 279
World Tourism Organization (UNWTO) 295, 301, 305–306
World Travel and Tourism Council (WTTC) 300
World Union of Olympic Cities (UMVO) 102
World War II 19, 161–163, 170, 174
World Wrestling Entertainment (WWE) 84; Mixed Match Challenge 84
Wrangler 171
wrestling **18**, 19, 84, 160, **242**
WTA 83

Xi Jinping 42, 65–66
XXL **147**, 169, 184, **187**, 190

Yao Ming 51, 55
yoga 123, **124**, 128, 130, 132, 151, 168, 199–200, 202, 206
Youth Olympic Games 110
YouTube 57, 61

For Product Safety Concerns and Information please contact our EU representative GPSR@taylorandfrancis.com
Taylor & Francis Verlag GmbH, Kaufingerstraße 24, 80331 München, Germany

www.ingramcontent.com/pod-product-compliance
Lightning Source LLC
LaVergne TN
LVHW011112300926
849160LV00008B/358

9780367729004